Don't Take Your Life Personally

Ajahn Sumedho

Edited by Diana St Ruth

Buddhist Publishing Group
Totnes

Buddhist Publishing Group

PO Box 173, Totnes, Devon TQ9 9AE, UK

www.buddhistpublishing.com

www.buddhismnow.com

ISBN 978-0946672318

A catalogue record for this book is available from the British Library.

Front cover: Ajahn Sumedho tending the shrine at the 1995 Leicester Summer School.

Back cover: Ajahn Sumedho departing Beaumont Hall after the 1990 Summer School.

My first encounter with Buddhists in Britain brought me in contact with George Sharp, the late Maurice Walshe, Freda Wint and Geoffrey Beardsley, all dedicated Buddhists and Trustees of the English Sangha Trust. To these people I dedicate these pages.

Contents

Editor's Acknowledgements

I wish to thank Ros and Steve Palmer for the many hours spent in transcribing the recorded talks that form the basis of this book, and James Whelan for reading the manuscript in its final stages and offering invaluable suggestions.

Introduction

For eighteen years (1989-2006) the Buddhist Publishing Group held week-long gatherings mostly at the University of Leicester's Beaumont Hall, and these were known as 'the Leicester Summer Schools'. These events favoured no one tradition and provided a platform not only for the three main Buddhist schools but also for others besides. Ajahn Sumedho attended every Leicester Summer School from the first to the last and gave one talk a day, sometimes two. He also entered into the spirit of the event itself, calling it 'his holiday'.

After sitting every morning in a group meditation, maybe taking a quick walk in the gardens, having a noisy breakfast with the rest of us, Ajahn Sumedho would give his talk — or what he called 'offerings for reflection' — to between fifty and seventy people (depending on how many were at the Summer School that year). The final six years of these talks are what comprise this book.

Ajahn Sumedho does not try to teach Buddhism, because in truth it cannot be taught. So these talks are about learning how to see for oneself, or experience for oneself, what Buddhism really is, or what reality is. He talks about awareness, mindfulness, looking into the reality of this moment and not getting caught up in beliefs, views and opinions; and he refers continuously to his own experiences. He presents the truth of Buddhism therefore by way of a personal story which is given humorously, guilelessly and sometimes with brutal honesty. So he pretends nothing, and makes it clear that Buddhism is not about becoming the model of humanity or escaping the natural result of one's past deeds, one's kamma, but of seeing what is actually taking place now, no matter what it is. So he has put aside all pretence in his own life and suggests we do the same — as did his revered teacher, Ajahn Chah, as did the Buddha two and a half thousand years ago, and who knows how many people since — because that is what he sees as the way, the path, the route to liberation from suffering.

With great patience Ajahn Sumedho endeavours to make us see what he sees so obviously for himself, and time and again he throws us back on our own resources to wake up to the truth and wisdom within our own sphere of consciousness rather than expecting it to come from some outside source. So he does not try to persuade anyone to adopt a particular form of Buddhism or suggest that his way is the best, but merely that we look beyond culture, beyond the nature of our own personality, beyond any technique we might have adopted, and beyond all ideas of Buddhism itself, to just the reality of this moment, this very moment which cannot be defined.

His teaching, then, is not to teach anything other than to encourage people to see for themselves what is already here and now. And as one listens to him it becomes clear that whilst he gratefully and joyfully lives by the Theravadan tradition that he took up over forty years ago, and whilst he acknowledges his cultural background as an American and as a Buddhist monk and so forth, he does not identify with those things, he doesn't see himself as those things, he is free of those things, and takes his refuge in the Buddha-Dhamma-Sangha, as he calls it, or simply the awareness of each moment without being attached to the idea of self or to any idea at all, just letting whatever comes go again without holding on, without blocking that natural flow of life. 'One begins to realize', he says, 'that liberation is through letting go, through allowing life to flow, through openness and attention.'

He talks about his own challenges in life, in the monastery, the life of a monk, the sense of loyalty and responsibility which have influenced his actions — sometimes to his own discomfort — not in order to complain, but simply to say how he deals with what comes his way in terms of the reality of the moment, in terms of the dhamma. So underlying it all is the emphasis on realizing that 'liberation is now, freedom is now, *nibbāna* is now' and that it is available to us all — young or old, male or female, monastic or lay person — no matter who we are or what unfolds in our lives. He makes it clear that we are all free to live the dhamma, the truth of Buddhism, if we choose to do so, and that nothing can stop us.

Diana St Ruth

Starting from Here

Compose your minds, look inwards and become aware of
the here and now — the body, the breath, the mental state,
the mood you are in — without trying to control or judge or do
anything; just allow everything to be what it is.

For many people the attitude towards meditation is one of
always trying to change something, always trying to attain a
particular state or recreate some kind of blissful experience remembered from the past, or of hoping to reach a certain state by
practising. When we practise meditation with the idea of having
to do something, however, then even the *idea* of practice — even
the word 'meditation' — will bring up this idea that 'if I'm in a
bad mood, I should get rid of it', or 'if the mind is scattered and
I'm all over the place, I should make it one-pointed'. In other
words, we make meditation into hard work. So then there is a
great deal of failure in it because we try to control everything
through these ideas, but that is an impossibility.

Geshe Tashi[1] yesterday was saying that the idea of going off to
the cave is very attractive because there you have more control,
really. You don't have to talk to people or get caught up in confusing worldly sensory impingements. As you settle into solitude,
you experience a level of tranquillity through lack of sensory
stimulation; it is a form of sensory deprivation. That tranquillity,
however, is easily disturbed. You can't sustain it when sensory
impingements start pounding away at you again; and then you
get into, 'Let me go to my cave!' — that kind of mind; and you
begin to hate people. You see them as a threat. 'Here they come

1 Geshe Tashi Tsering of Jamyang Buddhist Centre, London.

again! They're going to disrupt my *samādhi* (concentration).' But this cannot possibly be the way to liberation. The other extreme is to think you should *not* go off to the cave and practise meditation — 'Just be natural and let everything happen!' — which is true if you can do it that way. But if you don't even know what is natural yet, it is difficult to trust yourself.

The word 'meditation' covers many mental experiences, but the goal of Buddhist meditation is to see things as they are; it is a state of awakened attention. And this is a very simple thing. It isn't complicated or difficult or something that takes years to achieve. It is so easy, in fact, that you don't even notice it. When you think in terms of having to practise meditation, you are conceiving it as something you have to attain — you have to subdue your defilements, you have to control your emotions, you have to develop virtues in order to attain some kind of ideal state of mind. You might have images of a lot of yogis sitting in remote places on mountain tops and in caves. Even a Buddha-image can convey this sense of remoteness and separation if you don't understand how to use that particular icon; and it all sounds very remote and very far from what you can expect from your life as a human being.

In developing an attitude towards formal practice or daily life practice, therefore, we very often separate the two — the 'formal' and the 'daily life'. We think of formal practice as a very controlled retreat situation where we all live by a routine, a structure; and when we leave that structured retreat, we refer to 'daily life meditation'. But that can seem hopeless, can't it? If we compare daily life with a very controlled meditation retreat, it is very different. But we can't live in that controlled structure as an ongoing experience. Geshe Tashi made this point last night when he said the real challenge is to develop attention, awakenedness, in the flow of life. This doesn't remove the option of going on retreat or diminish the value of that in any way. The point is to look at meditation as awakenedness and awareness throughout daily life in whatever way we live and in whatever conditions.

There is in that the sense of allowing things to *be* in this present moment, allowing whatever way the body is or the emotional and mental states right now to be the way they are. Just be the observer of whatever is. Right now the mood is 'this', 'I feel this'. Just be aware whether you are confused, indifferent, happy, sad, uncertain or whatever. Be that which allows things to be what they are.

For the next few minutes try to look inwards with this attitude of observing your mood, your mental quality, your emotional quality. What you find might be very precise like anger, or it might be something that is very sharp. A lot of our emotions are just nebulous, amorphous wandering things, but just put yourself in this position of the Buddha, *buddho*, the knower, this sense of awakened attention — not the judge — but simply looking and noticing what kind of mood or feeling you have right now. When you start noticing, really listening or paying attention and sustaining an awareness on just this mood or this mental state, you become aware of bodily tensions, maybe feelings of bewilderment, or maybe not quite knowing what you are supposed to be doing. But if bewilderment is there, be aware of bewilderment as a mental object. Put yourself in the position of the Buddha, the *buddho*. Your emotional state and this 'what am I supposed to be doing?' will then be seen as a mental object.

Relax into the present. If you try too hard, you put yourself into a state of tension. So it isn't a matter of making too much effort, but neither is it about not trying at all; it is rather a question of using just the right amount of attention to listen, just enough to be open to this present moment. If you force it, if you try too hard, you don't relax. Of course, if I say 'relax!' that can also mean 'lax' and you just fall asleep, so take it to mean just letting go, not having to do anything or get anything.

Awareness or paying attention is not a gaining situation; it is not something to be done in order to get anything or achieve anything; this is not a worldly state that we have to get. We are not being encouraged to *get* our *samādhi* (or concentration as we

generally interpret the word), nor is it a matter of proving anything. That generally goes with the fear that we won't be able to
do it. 'Maybe I'm one of those people that will *never* get enlightened!' is another one we all sometimes revert to. 'I don't expect
to get enlightened in this lifetime; I just don't have what it takes.'
Well, don't believe that one, either!

There are all kinds of stress reduction programmes around
these days because modern life moves too quickly for us, actually. We are propelled by high technology and all the rest of it
into stressful, fast-lane lives whether we like it or not. And this
does affect us. We get a sense of being driven and feel restless,
and tend to distract ourselves endlessly, which then creates tension and stress. When we do that to the body, however, it creates
problems for us. Relaxation is therefore something that is encouraged now in our society, just on a popular, worldly level.

I was listening to a recording recently of a woman teaching
relaxation. She said she could not use the word 'relaxation' now
because people *try* to relax, so she uses soft, gentle tones of voice
instead '. . soothing . . . soothing . . .' This is an expedient method. Words and techniques are meant to help us. They are not like
commands or things that we obsess ourselves with. Any kind of
meditation technique, or even the language that we use, is not
to be taken as a commandment to relax. 'RELAX!' in terms of
stress reduction would not help very much. What does 'relaxation' mean to you? I can't tell you that, but it is the ability to let go
of the obsessive tendencies of feeling we have to do something, it
is the ability to let go and let life be. 'I've got to get something I
don't have; I've got to get rid of the things that I shouldn't have!'
These are subconscious influences, as Geshe Tashi was saying
last night. They are underlying influences which are so deep that
we don't even notice them. That is why the word 'relax' can turn
into another thing we have to do. 'He says I have to relax! I
should be able to relax, but I can't! What's wrong with me?' This
is where 'just allowing things to be the way they are' comes in,
simply allowing tension to *be*. Even if you are stressed out at this

moment, let it be the way it is. Let whatever mental states you are in — even your compulsive tendencies, your obsessive tendencies — be what they are rather than seeing them as 'there's something wrong with me! There's something I have to get rid of!' Allow even the bad habits, the bad thoughts, tensions, pain, sadness, loneliness or whatever, to *be* at this moment, allow the sense of letting go and let life be what it is.

We seem to have problems in the Western world around guilt. This is very much a cultural tendency. In Thailand where I lived for many years, not many people seemed to have this same obsessive feeling. They knew when they had done something they shouldn't have done; they felt the same sense of shame when they told a lie and so forth, but they didn't hold to this sense of shame to the point of it becoming a kind of obsession in the way that we seem to. We feel guilty about just breathing the air or being alive, and it can go into neurotic tendencies. This is just my particular reflection on it, anyway. The Dalai Lama said that Tibetans basically like themselves; they have a sense of self- -respect. You can see this, actually. One of the things that many of us Westerners find attractive in Asian countries is the fact that people seem somehow happier there; they are more accepting of life and don't seem to look at things in such a complicated way. I certainly enjoyed living in Thailand. Somehow life there became easier for me, even though in many ways it was more difficult because I was having to learn a new culture and a new language. On an emotional level, however, I found it easier. And Ajahn Chah had an unquestionable acceptance of things as they are and of me as I was. I never felt like that in the United States. I never felt accepted or acceptable as I was; I always felt I should be better. If I were in a good place, I would think, 'Well, I could be in a better place than this.' The tendency towards guilt and negativity therefore means that one never feels good enough no matter how hard one tries.

In America you are brought up with this sense of living up to high-minded role models and ideals. You are always looking high up and comparing the realities of what you are with some ideal of what you should be. So you always come off feeling inferior. How can it be otherwise? There is no way out of that one. We are not ideals. This is not an ideal. This is the reality of flesh and blood, nerves and senses; it is all sensitivity. This is not like a Greek statue sculpted in marble and perfect in form. The Greek statue does not have to deal with nerve endings, tooth-ache, old age or anything like that. It is an ideal, an icon like the Buddha-image; it is perfect.

In the case of the Theravadan school, the *arahant* (fully en-lightened one) is the ideal. The tendency there is to take the word *'arahant'* and place it on a pedestal of idealism so that it remains remote and too high for us. We just cannot relate to it; we merely worship it from down here and maybe feel better for doing so. Looking up and worshipping an ideal can be inspiring — it can make us feel good — but then when we come back to ourselves again, to the way we are, what happens in our lives with our families, children, husbands, wives, neighbours, governments?

In community life, like at Amaravati, we are living with basi-cally good people — and it is a very nice life, a well supported life. Yet the suffering just with the personality conflicts is end-less. This person doesn't get along with that person, and that one doesn't get along with someone else. But I can't imagine that it will ever be possible to solve these problems by everyone de-veloping the same personality. Allowing things to be what they are is the attitude I have found most helpful — allowing my own mental states, the way I am on a personal level, my emotional habits, my personality in any of its aspects, good or bad. This also allows me to accept other people for what they are. It is a question of starting from here. If I can't do it here, I won't be able to do it with others. Sometimes, how we criticize others is really a reflection of how we look upon ourselves.

Ajahn Chah had this attitude about meditation being a holiday for the heart. We tend to see meditation as something we *have* to achieve — another thing we *have* to do and get — but Ajahn *holiday for the heart!*

Chah would put it in the context of a holiday. So try that, try seeing meditation in that way. This is our holiday here, isn't it? The
Summer School is a holiday, but put that word 'holiday' also into
the context of meditation. You don't have to achieve anything,
get any great insights, attain any high stages, purify yourself, get
rid of your evil thoughts, or anything at all. We are not trying to
judge thoughts in terms of their quality, for example; we are just
noting that they are 'like this'. If an evil thought comes up —
'Go and kill Ajahn Sumedho!' — just don't do it. Refrain from
acting. It is just another thought, isn't it? It is what it is and will
go away. *ever ask why it comes up so often*

Notice that we like challenges. Some people like to go to extremes, especially younger people. Young monks often want to
go to a cave, go on a fast, starve themselves, test themselves by
taking on difficult tasks that most people cannot do, because that
is part of youth. They make themselves do it. But we can't do
that kind of thing for the whole of our lives; we can't always be
thinking that meditation is some kind of striving challenge for
us. The real challenge actually lies in just being able to integrate
awareness into the most ordinary things, into the mundane realities of daily life, into the most unimpressive aspects of what we
do every day. This is being aware as a continuum. Being aware
of special situations is one thing, but to have a connected awareness — the continuum of awareness — is not so easy; it does
take patience. When you grasp the idea of continuous awareness,
you want to do it, but the realities are that you get distracted and
easily fall back into old habits, so patience is required.

One suggestion of how to maintain awareness, is to have a
sense of humility and simplicity. These things help. There is a
monk at Amaravati who tends to strive too hard, then fail, then
get depressed, then frustrated by the thought that he needs more
solitude, more isolation and a different environment. He thinks
there are too many distractions at Amaravati, too many people.
One way I have of handling this is to be grateful for the moments
I *am* mindful. If I get caught up in the life of the monastery,

pulled this way and that and am not very mindful, then suddenly — I remember! And I treasure that; I value that rather than think, 'Oh, I'm trying to be mindful but I can't do it,' and beating myself up because I vowed in the morning to be mindful the whole day, but failed. I would go into these states of, 'Oh, there I go again; I shouldn't have done that!' and nag myself, criticize myself and feel like a failure. But even if there is only one moment in the whole day when I am mindful, I can feel this 'thank you!' To me that is more helpful than beating yourself up, because that doesn't help you in any way. Meditation is not a matter of success, of being able to achieve goals and prove ourselves. Remember that.

Our emotional habits are often built around success and failure — elated by success and depressed by failure. The way to transcend that, however, is through awareness just in this present moment, this simple act of attention, this listening, openness and receptivity. Then there is a sense of relief — such a relief!

Beginning to Sense the Unborn

When you contemplate the Four Noble Truths[2] and use them as your paradigm for practice, it becomes clear that the third and fourth truths are definitely the realization of the unborn or the unconditioned *(nibbāna)*. Much of the meditation taught within Theravada Buddhism these days is *vipassanā* (insight) meditation and in this the Three Characteristics of Existence — impermanence, unsatisfactoriness, and non-self *(anicca, dukkha, anattā)* — are given tremendous emphasis. These three characteristics are common to all phenomena and they are for reflection. It isn't a question of adopting these three words and projecting them onto experience. Some people do try to do this. They hold to these particular concepts and interpret their experiences through their belief in them rather than taking the concepts and reflecting on experience. I just want to emphasize that the way is through mindfulness, intuitive attention and openness, rather than through grasping concepts, ideas, doctrines or positions.

I see many people who practise insight meditation getting stuck in continually noting the impermanence of phenomena. In that, however, the reality of cessation tends not to be realized in

---

2   Four Noble Truths: the truth of suffering *(dukkha)*, that all suffering is the result of craving or desire *(taṇhā)*, that the end of craving or desire is the end of suffering *(nirodha)*, that the path *(magga)* which is the means to the end of suffering is eightfold: right view, right thought, right speech, right action, right livelihood, right effort, right mindfulness, right concentration.

any practical way. Because of that it seems that a lot of the insight meditation centres in the West have resorted to other ways of helping people to come to the realization of cessation and the unborn, and there is a great deal of interest in Tibetan Dzogchen, Advaita Vedanta, and the teachings of Poonjaji[3]. The whole point of these teachings is the realization of the unborn or the deathless, or we could say 'ultimate reality'.

Now, when you use words to refer to something that doesn't exist, it can remain abstract. So, for us, the unborn can be just another abstraction of the mind and we wonder what it is or where it is, whether it is really true, whether there is really such a thing as the deathless. And the more we try to analyse or think about it in this way, the more we limit ourselves to the conceptual mind and the conditions of the mind that we create. At our ordination as monks in the Theravada tradition we have to say we are taking on the monastic form for the realization of *nibbāna*. But what does that mean? What does it mean to realize desirelessness, cessation, emptiness, or non-self *(virāga, nirodha, suññatā, anattā)*? These are all abstractions; they are words that point to but cannot define. Realization therefore has to come through intuition. This is what I emphasize and encourage now in the way that I teach. I see that people often don't have enough confidence or trust in their own experience of emptiness and non-self. It is so easy to fall back into the questioning mode — 'What is it?' — and want to objectify it in some way, want to pin it down or turn it into some kind of mental object that can be verified and proven, maybe scientifically.

When we use such words as 'existing' or 'not existing', they convey this sense of something coming up, existing, and then

3   H.W.L. Poonjaji who died in 1997 was a close disciple of Ramana Maharshi. He was not part of any formal tradition but became highly respected by the Advaita Vedanta and Bhakti traditions. His teachings, mostly given in Lucknow, India, were very popular among British and American *vipassanā* practitioners.

disappearing and no longer existing. Some years ago when the 'God-is-dead' fad came into being, I was just becoming a monk (bhikkhu) in Thailand. A Thai magazine, I remember, had this striking headline: 'God is dead!' That is rather a strong thing to say, and it certainly created all kinds of emotional reactions at the time. Some people didn't really care about it, but others felt it was a real attack on their basic belief and what they depended on. If God is something created, something that arises and ceases, then of course that means that God dies. The word 'God' — one of those words that we take for granted — can, however, be put into the category of the unborn, the uncreated. Even in Christian theology, Christian mysticism, the realization of God is through non-attachment, through letting go rather than through finding somebody called 'God' that comes and goes in one's life.

Generally, in Christianity, God has been given anthropomorphic qualities, so this makes it personal, makes it like a father figure, a patriarch — God the Father. And on one level that creates the sense of a personal relationship. We can all relate to the idea of a father, because that is the cultural conditioning we have had. So we assume that God is some kind of heavenly father, some powerful figure. But the reality of this moment still keeps it as some kind of abstraction of the mind. 'Where is it? Where is He?' the feminist movement asks, 'Why does God have to be a He? Why can't God be a She?' And this is a valid point. But why do we have to define God with gender at all? In Buddhism they don't have this problem because 'God', as it were, has never been anthropomorphized; it is not given any kind of human quality, or any quality whatsoever — except that of awakening to the reality of this moment.

When we emphasize the characteristics of conditioned phenomena, then, what happens? The mind goes from one thing to another, as in thought. When we get lost in thinking, one thought connects to another, and the thoughts proliferate. And if I use thought with some kind of logic, I see right now in this room, for example, that that is Robert and that is Catherine and that is Rocana; I go from one to the other. Yet the space between Catherine and Rocana is also present. But that can go completely unnoticed because the interest lies in the conditions which have qualities and that can cause some kind of emotional reaction in consciousness.

Beings that have not awakened to the unborn but are simply looking at life through the conditioned experiences they have, perceive life in a very dualistic way, always in terms of right and wrong, good and bad, male and female, black and white. These qualities become the deciding factors in their lives. There might be the logic there of 'do good and refrain from doing evil', but in terms of understanding the way things are, they are caught in the death realm, in things that exist, that arise and cease, come and go. Their lives are often fraught with suffering because they cannot keep anything as a permanent possession. When they put their faith in another person, for example, and want that person to be there for them all the time, there is always a feeling of loss when he or she goes away, even if it is just for a while and then come back again. Inevitably, also, there is the death moment and a sense of loss when what they have depended on is dead. So what does one do if one's refuge is in another person? or in an institution? or in a way of thinking? or in family life? or in a political view? or in anything which is subject to change, to birth and death?

Unawakened human beings (what we call *puthujjanas* in Pali) are forever suffering because their lives are threatened by the things that influence consciousness. They can't hold onto anything; they can't sustain anything. They may be able to sustain an illusion, of course, which is why their demands on life are sometimes just for stability, just for something they can count on — 'Don't act too strangely, don't do something eccentric, don't go funny. Keep this illusion that everything is all right and everything is going to be all right. And then in the afterlife when we die we will all go to heaven and have a Leicester Summer School up in heaven all the time!' though I think that even that could be quite boring after a few weeks.

The Buddha pointed to suffering as the first Noble Truth: 'There is *dukkha* (unsatisfactoriness).' When you go to interfaith meetings and meet people from theistic religions, you discover that a lot of them find this first Noble Truth rather depressing. They tend to see it as some kind of positioning we take on life, and think we believe that everything is unsatisfactory *(dukkha)*. If we do grasp that view (which is a misinterpretation of the first Noble Truth) then of course we will feel obliged to interpret everything in that way. And I have met people who have felt that looking at flowers is dangerous because 'after all they are just going to wilt and die! You get attached to them and then they fail you in the end.' That is a kind of perpetual wet-blanket approach to life which leads to depression. And if you keep up that kind of attitude, you are just going to feel that there is no purpose or meaning to your life. But recognize that what the Buddha was really doing was taking this most ordinary condition that we all experience and putting it into the context of a noble truth rather than regarding it as a horrible fact, as some kind of miserable statement about life or some pessimistic view.

Notice the word 'noble' in noble truth. This is a truth to be realized. We are not told to grasp or believe this truth; it isn't a belief; it isn't a dogma; it isn't a metaphysical truth; it isn't the ultimate reality. It is a very common human experience of loss, identifying with that which is unsatisfactory, with change, with the delusions we create, and the expectations and assumptions we make about our lives.

In Buddhism there are what are called 'the heavenly messengers' *(devadūtas)*, and these are old age, sickness and death. Rather than seeing these things as depressing spectres that come to us and scare us, we can see them as messengers. What does that mean in terms of our own experience of life? What *devadūtas* have we encountered? We all have, haven't we? We have all experienced loss — maybe seen our own parents getting old, getting sick and dying, maybe see ourselves getting old and are now experiencing pain and sickness — this is common to all human beings, and there is nothing wrong with it; it isn't bad. The point is to see that the conditioned realm is something to contemplate and understand rather than to make assumptions about it or try to control and bend it to our desires and will. The more we try to control the conditioned realm, the more disappointing it will become, until we finally feel despair, fear, depression and all the negative mental states that can dominate our conscious experience.

Whatever we love and cherish is inevitably subject to death. And when something we love dies, we feel grief. In noticing this — in taking up the first Noble Truth (the truth of suffering) — we are willing to learn from it instead of just feeling frightened and averse to it. If we try to get rid of suffering, deny it, push it away, run away from it, we can never really understand it; our reactions will always be some kind of resistance to any possibility of understanding. Understanding means there is a willingness to suffer. This isn't any form of masochism, but a positive sense of trust, a willingness to look at our own sense of despair, inadequacy, fear, loss, or grief, in a way that is not just thinking about it, but noticing that it is 'like this'. Then, as we examine these mental states — by understanding them, accepting them, and embracing them — we begin to see that they also cease. We begin to realize that we can't sustain them. Even though we might feel we will never get over the loss of our loved one, we can, actually. We notice that there are moments when we think of that person and feel grief, and then there are moments when we don't think of them. We may not notice those moments of not thinking of them, however, because we assume that we have this state of grief as a continuous mental state. If we are willing to trust in our own awareness of this grief, then, we will recognize that it changes. So, in accepting grief, we are no longer clinging to it; we are no longer saying it is mine or making value judgements about it. We are instead willing to feel and understand the grief, willing to be with it, willing to let it be what it is, and then what happens is — it ceases. As we then observe the cessation of grief, we can mentally note that the absence of grief is 'like this'.

In the third Noble Truth, then, there is cessation or the absence of a condition that existed but is no longer present. Now, how do we realize this? — because this is a reality. We realize it by intuitive awareness. If you think about this too much, you can't really be with it; you just get lost in your own logic, reasoning, associations, and the sense of yourself. But if you are willing to accept something for what it is — allow it to be the way it is — you look at it through wisdom and understanding rather than through some personal distortion of it. As long as you feel grief in terms of 'I am grieving and grief is mine, how can I get over this grief? What should I do about it? Life will never be the same again', you are proliferating. One of those thoughts will connect and you will be caught in perpetuating feelings of grief and projecting it onto your experience of life. You will then see the things around you through this veil, through this distortion which you adhere to.

In the second Noble Truth, the insight is to let go of the cause of suffering, which is attachment to the conditioned, the born. This attachment is the result of not understanding. It is like a habit we have and don't even know we are doing it. We are certainly not intentionally thinking, 'I'm going to hold onto this grief no matter what!' We usually try to get rid of grief, try to brush it aside or do anything to distract ourselves from it. This very desire to get rid of it, however, is attachment out of ignorance. It means we are not willing to learn from the heavenly messenger; we are merely trying to deny or resist it. So, letting go of suffering isn't a rejection out of fear, out of denial or ignorance, but is through understanding it. Letting go isn't throwing or pushing suffering away, but letting it be. You let this feeling, this emotion, *be* in the present, *be* what it is, and that takes a certain trust in your ability to bear with suffering, unpleasantness, pain, misfortune, failure, and all the disappointments of life.

Now, when we explore our conscious experience, when we look at it closely, we notice space, like the space between Rocana *spaciousness*

and Catherine, for example. This doesn't sound like anything very important, so you might say, 'Well, what is there to look at? It's just space.' But we are noting reality. When I look between these two people I can see the space between them with my eyes. It isn't that I am making it up. And if I start observing space just on a visual level, the result is a sense of spaciousness (because space doesn't have any quality to it except spaciousness). Within the space there can be blue and red, men and women, and chairs and tables, and these have certain qualities and properties to them. But all you can say about space itself — in terms of experience — is that it is spacious. This is a way of training ourselves to notice the way it is, a way of letting go of just the habitual tendency of going from one thing to the other, of admiring particular qualities or being appalled by the unpleasantness of conditions.

At this moment, therefore, we are not interested in analysing, comparing, or making anything out of conditions. We are letting them be what they are. We are opening to space and seeing that it contains us all. Space isn't just here or there, it is everywhere, it permeates everything. So by doing this we might begin to get a little more aware, a little more insight into the unborn which is here and now but which we don't notice. Space is an obvious one, of course; we can visually contemplate it. And by just taking 'space' as a word that points to the reality that exists here rather than as something to grasp, means that we are not taking a particular interest in conditions. I don't have to ask you all to leave and remove the furniture, or feel that the room is in the way, or wish for the building to be torn down — it isn't a matter of destroying or annihilating anything — it is rather that awareness begins to expand and give this sense of infinity which we might not yet have become aware of.

Before I ever meditated, I remember reading enigmatic statements like 'Eternity is now!' and thinking, 'But where is now?' Everything in my mind that was associated with now was timebound, like my personality, for example. The sense of myself as a person is a condition, and the body also is a time-bound condition. It is like this building. I can find out how old this building is, follow its history, try to understand this whole place in terms of when things were built, when the botanical gardens first appeared, how they were developed and so forth. I can take an interest in that side of things, but that is taking an interest in time-bound conditions. The flora and fauna in these gardens are certainly interesting and fascinating in themselves, but if I remain on that level, something in me will be bound to those conditions and will not see through them or beyond.

By exploring conditioned phenomena in terms of imper-manence, unsatisfactoriness and non-self *(anicca, dukkha, anat-tā)*, and by doing that in the right way rather than by just believing in the ideas of them and projecting them onto experience, I start noticing the assumption I make that people are the perceptions I have of them in my mind. On a meditation retreat in Amaravati many years ago, I asked everybody, 'Where is your mother right now?' and people responded with comments like, 'Oh, she's in Norfolk,' or wherever. But I was trying to get them to question the perception 'my mother' and to recognize that, actually, the perception 'mother' is always in the mind. You have a memory, you have a perception, you might even have an image of your mother in your mind, but those things are here and now; you have created them; they are memories that come and go accord-ing to conditions. But is that perception really your mother, or is it just what it is — a perception, a memory, a thought, an image? And when you let go of that perception, where is your mother? For me right now I don't know the answer to that. The percep-tion of my mother is that she is dead and the priest said she is in heaven. But I don't know. I do, however, *know* that I don't know, and I know that I don't *need* to know. I no longer need to hold to some view about my mother being up in heaven with the Lord as a way of making myself feel all right in this present moment. It isn't that I don't care, but I am willing to admit the limitations that I am under as a human being, as this conscious experience of being a human entity.

In the practice of meditation, then, we are beginning to awaken to the way we happen to be within the limitations of this human state. We can assume we have a common bond of humanity, a common ground in many ways, but each one of us is a unique individual entity. Different habit patterns, different cultural identities, different ways of thinking, different emotional conditions are being experienced now by everyone, and it is beyond the ability of each of us to know everything that is going on in everybody in this room, at this moment. But I can know the mental states and emotional conditions that I am witnessing at this time. And as I allow the mental state to be conscious rather than simply reacting to it or trying to control or ignore it, I begin to notice that I can't sustain that state. I begin to see that it changes very quickly, and that if I don't feed it with thinking and judging, it ceases. So, if I stop thinking and just observe, just notice, just trust in my ability to be fully attentive, awake and conscious, then it is — 'like this'.

Now, I have referred many times to my use of the 'sound of silence', a practice that I have explored over the years. I have found it a very helpful way of reflecting on experience. When I let go of everything and am just in a state of pure presence, pure being, pure awareness, I recognize this kind of vibratory background sound — or is it a vibration? In terms of perception, it seems like a sound. That is how I experience it in terms of labelling it or explaining it. And yet unlike ordinary sound, it has a continuity, a vibratory quality to it which sustains itself and is the background to all other sounds. Right now I can be fully present with this 'sound of silence' and still be talking and looking at you because it is like an embracing background; it has this sense of infinity, boundlessness, like space or consciousness. In other words, I am not caught in the manipulation of my thoughts and emotions reacting and playing with the conditions that arise in consciousness, but acknowledging and recognizing pure subjectivity. In terms of this moment, then, it is absolute subjectivity, yet non-personal. If I start claiming it in terms of 'it is mine', I am creating a person that owns it. If I don't do that, however, if I refuse to think, create, or make anything out of it, then it is what it is.

Noticing the 'sound of silence', I simultaneously notice that other sounds arise and cease within it. If I listen to the sound of a stream or a waterfall, for example, I can actually recognize the 'sound of silence' behind it. And as I tune into the 'sound of silence' and begin to rest in it more, I notice that the sound of the stream or waterfall is enhanced. Rather than cancelling out or obliterating all other sounds, the 'sound of silence' seems to enhance and support them. I can hear it in the background to music and to noisy machinery like a chainsaw or a lawnmower.

Now, wanting to claim that as some kind of attainment, comes back to this sense of 'me' being somebody who *has* something. But there is no need for claiming! The point is to trust in this ability we all have of attention to the present moment. Eternity is now. The Buddha's teaching is the teaching of awakenedness. The word 'Buddha' actually means 'awakened', and in the Thai Forest tradition they have this mantra[4] *'buddho'* which is the mantric form of 'Buddha'. The Forest ajahns — Ajahn Mun for instance — used to call it 'the one who knows'. But it isn't like a person that knows something; it is just a *knowing*, merely the reality of knowing.

It is an interesting time now in terms of this English word 'consciousness' because it is being examined most thoroughly. The tendency, however, is to regard consciousness as some kind of brain function and to define it as 'thinking'; its opposite being 'unconsciousness'. Unconsciousness is often used to mean not thinking or not being awake. In that case, unconsciousness means that consciousness no longer exists for us and is not operating in this particular form. To me, however, instead of looking at consciousness in such a limited way — as some kind of mental

---

4   Mantra: a word or sound repeated to aid concentration in meditation.

function of the brain — it is more that 'this' is the experience of consciousness, that consciousness is the natural state of being, and that these particular forms are ways of experiencing it. We have this subject-object experience. So, in terms of right now, the subject is here and you are the object; you are in consciousness. But you are not in my brain; it isn't something I can claim as any kind of creation of my own on a personal level; it is simply 'like this'. I can see *your* face but I can't see my own face. You can see my eyes but I can't see my own eyes. I can see your eyes, but you can't see your own eyes. You don't need to see your own eyes, of course, because 'seeing' is the point. And 'knowing things as they are' is the point, rather than trying to find out who it is that is knowing. That is another question. What is it that knows? Who is it that knows? What is behind all this? We want to find out. Is it God or is it ultimate truth? We want a name for it in some way because the level of conditioning that we have wants to define things, wants to hold things in forms, in perceptions. If we don't have those forms and perceptions, then we tend to dismiss, ignore, reject or even feel frightened by this experience of the unborn.

In order to appreciate the first Noble Truth (the truth of suffering), we of course have to awaken to it. The point is, we might know we are suffering because we don't get what we want, so we see the suffering through personal interpretation. We blame it on others or the world; or we get angry with God for creating us and making us suffer like this; or we just blame ourselves: 'It's my fault I'm suffering.' When we awaken to suffering, however, we don't interpret it in these ways; we merely see that it is the way it is; we begin to accept and allow things we had previously resisted, rejected and run away from. And once we begin to appreciate this, we can actually trust awakened awareness — an awakened intuitive sense of the present — as something to develop and cultivate in life. We can be aware that our own body at this moment is 'like this', sitting is 'like this', breathing is 'like this', feeling hot or cold is 'like this'. We can be aware of our mental state — whatever it is — because all things are embraced within this vast open acceptance, an awakened acceptance of this moment.

'Eternity is now' does not, however, mean that any of these conditions is eternal. Each one arises and ceases, and you quickly notice that. But if you trust the awakened state and cultivate it, you will see that that lasts beyond the length of the condition that you are experiencing. This is why I advise and encourage you to trust it.

As far as meditation is concerned, people tend to see themselves in terms of either attaining or not attaining. One thing I commonly hear is, 'I've been practising for years and I don't think I've got anywhere; I don't think I've attained anything.' In that case, the basic delusion has never been really penetrated. That 'I've not achieved anything yet' is a created thought in the present. By becoming aware that that is a created thought, however, one no longer believes such a statement or any thoughts about oneself being the reality. One begins to sense the infinite instead, the unborn, the unconditioned, the deathless in which one no longer limits oneself or binds oneself to the death-bound conditioning that one has. One begins to realize that liberation is through letting go, through allowing life to flow, through openness and attention.

Beyond the Ego

I would like us to consider the words 'awareness' and 'consciousness', because it is important to see the difference between them. The point is, we can be conscious but not aware. In fact we can be conscious and totally deluded. But the delusions that we believe in affect consciousness. So, what we are actually doing in Buddhist meditation is using wisdom *(paññā)* to inform consciousness in order to let go of the distortions or delusions that we experience.

Now, teachings like the Four Noble Truths are meant to be investigated, practised, realized and recognized by each one of us for ourselves; I cannot do it for you. And these teachings point to suffering. We talk about great hardship, famine and wars in the world, but unless those hardships affect us in the moment, our suffering might just be about feeling tired or uncomfortable from eating too much breakfast; our suffering might not be terribly important. But whatever it is, it is a noble truth. Little irritations and frustrations in the moment are noble truths — if we are willing to look at them in that way.

Words like 'mindfulness' and 'awareness' have the sense of 'wake up!' They refer to the simple act of opening, of paying attention now. You might be lost in your own personal problems, and then somebody says 'pay attention!' Then you open to the present. It is a simple act of just noticing the way it is. You start with the basis of what is here and now, just observing what the body is like right now, for example. The body is coarse, isn't it? It isn't refined like a thought or a feeling; it is an actual blood-and-guts kind of condition. It is here, it is now, and it is 'like this'.

So you notice the four postures of sitting, standing, walking and lying down. It isn't a question of achieving some ideal posture or thinking you can't get anywhere unless you assume the full lotus posture. Whatever way your posture is, just be aware of it, even if it is a bad posture. The point is to be aware, to notice.

As you pay attention to your body more and more, you will find that it adjusts itself. Trying to force your body into doing what you want it to, merely creates a lot of tension. Many people do this; they try to make the body do what it isn't ready to do or can't do, and consequently put it under a lot of stress. In meditation, however, we include the body. I used to find I didn't want to be bothered with the body — too boring! I wanted to get into refined places in my mind rather than just be with this lump, this boring thing; I wanted to go into refined blissful states. So I would put a lot of effort into concentration practices, which was really like my attempt to ignore the body. But it didn't work. The body would insist — 'Look at me!' — and would become very painful and unpleasant when ignored. So we learn to include the body in practice, and it becomes a foundation for mindfulness rather than an apparent obstruction to it.

Contemplate your body sitting right now. Just notice what it is like. Observe that sitting is 'like this'. Notice the pressure of the body on the cushion, and what comes into consciousness whilst sustaining attention on the experience of sitting. As you open the door, as it were, the body will inform you. Trying to make the body sit straight — making a determined effort to force your body into what you think is sitting straight — is a wilful act and creates a lot of stress. And even if you do manage to hold the body in a tense rigid position, you won't be able to sustain it for long. If, on the other hand, you trust more in awareness and give the body the opportunity, it will adjust itself. It knows what it needs more than you do, actually. That is because it isn't yours; it isn't really you. When you claim it, you claim something that is not really yours; so it is better to learn how to live with it. Trying to own the body or abusing it in various ways is not very considerate to it.

This sense of relaxing and opening, this kind of attention, is not 'ATTENTION!' like a military command. It is an invitation, an encouragement to sustain attention. If you feel tension in the body, let it be tension; don't try to make it go away. Trust in just allowing it to be. In that way the body will be able to do what it needs to do.

The same with physical pain. When you feel an ache or pain, accept it. Let it be painful rather than trying to get rid of it. All this pushing away, this denying, this endless rejection of conditions or experiences you don't like and don't want, is one of the causes of suffering. The attitude to encourage, then, is more like welcoming, allowing. If pain is present, allow it to be what it is.

Goenka[5] teaches an insight meditation technique which involves mentally sweeping through the body and noticing sensations. It is very good, actually. I often use it. But the method has been developed into a main technique. You start, usually, with mindfulness of the breath *(ānāpānasati)* and then you put your attention on the top of the head and become aware of any sensations you feel right up there. You can't see the top of your head, of course, but you can feel it. Then you sweep around to the back of the head, down through the face — the eyes, mouth, ears, and nose (this powerfully sensitive area of the body) — and move down to the throat, neck and shoulders, on through each arm to each hand, the trunk of the body, down through the legs, and then back up again. You notice neutral sensations like your clothes touching your skin, and this is neither pleasant nor painful, but you certainly feel it. The point is, this keeps your attention on what is present here and now, and you are doing it in a way that is fraught neither with a sense of ego nor with personal habits; you are looking at it in quite an objective way — as experience. There is the body with its pleasure, pain and neutral sensations, and there is the breath, and you are simply putting your attention on what is happening right now without judging, criticizing, or making any kind of wilful self-effort. There is no

5 S.N. Goenka, a student of Sayagyi U Ba Khin

question of trying to be the best, trying to get the perfect posture, trying to get rid of pain or trying to sit through the pain-barrier, it is just 'like this'.

Many people regard meditation either as something to accomplish, or as a way of trying to prove something. But it isn't a matter of reaching a standard of attainment or of being better than anybody else. Wanting to be successful is just supporting a sense of being a personality, an ego. Trusting oneself as a person is based on the delusion of 'I've got to prove that I can do it'. Rather than looking at it through vanity or egotism, however, look at it through an inner sense of opening, observing and noticing that which you would not ordinarily notice — just the simple act of sitting, the neutral feelings of the clothes touching the skin, the touch of one hand on the other, the upper lip touching the lower lip — just noticing things that are so ordinary you wouldn't usually give them any attention at all, you wouldn't think them important. Actually, it is through this kind of practice that we begin to understand, to develop wisdom, and to break out of old habits acquired through ignorance and not understanding the truth.

The body is here and now, the breath is here and now, the 'sound of silence' is here now, consciousness is here and now — but thought and emotion arise and cease. We are looking at things in terms of their presence and absence rather than in terms of their qualities, whether they are high, low, good or bad. This is learning to trust in intuitive attention of the present. The mind wanders because we believe in time as a reality. We are very committed to identifying with the age of the body, to the idea of the future as something we have to plan for, or the past as something to regret. We resent the unfairnesses and injustices we have been subjected to in the past, and feel guilty about the things we have done to others. In meditation we can suddenly feel incredibly guilt-ridden about something we did maybe thirty years ago, or worries can just as suddenly come into consciousness about the future.

The point is to get a feel for being present with the body and breath, especially in the beginning stages of meditation. You are just getting the sense of being in the spaciousness of the present moment without trying to solve all your problems or analyse yourself in any way. Things then naturally start coming into consciousness. On retreats people sometimes remember things they have not thought about for years, or something arises into consciousness that they have spent their lives trying to reject. But I see this as a sign of beginning to let go of that tendency to control everything. Instead of being caught in the fear and tension of controlling, you start to allow maybe what you have never allowed into consciousness before. And once you allow things into consciousness, you can let them go. But first you have to allow them, you have to allow resentment, anger, fear, guilt or anything else to become conscious.

The first Noble Truth is all about accepting or welcoming unsatisfactoriness or suffering *(dukkha)* rather than trying to resist it. You will notice then that its nature is to change and drop away. The way to liberate the mind from the subconscious fears and anxieties that we all have is simply by allowing them to be. Good psychotherapy is based on allowing things to become conscious. If life is just one long effort of denial and repression, it is misery, isn't it? To spend your whole life controlling your mind out of fear and ignorance is hell. So you begin to have the insight that there is really nothing to fear. No matter how frightened you are or how much you think you cannot stand it or cannot bear it, actually you can. The voice that says, 'Oh, I can't do it! I just can't take it!' — don't believe that. That is how one is conditioned to think, but it isn't true!

Ajahn Chah was very good at getting me to see this in myself. Sitting in a hot tropical monastery feeling totally miserable I would think, 'I can't take any more of this! — the heat, the mosquitoes, this boring lifestyle — I've had enough!' But I *could* take it, actually. I began to realize that what was going on in my mind was something not to believe, and that if I followed it, it would always limit me. If I stopped at this point, however, it would just disappear — because it didn't have a life of its own! It was just a habit.

Trust is important. There is so much fear and suspicion in our lives that we don't trust ourselves or anyone else very much. Sometimes we just live on the surface, just get by. I am not talking about trusting the ego, of course, there is no ego you can trust, mine included — but we can trust our awareness. I keep emphasizing this because it is quite important. I cannot make you do it, of course, but I can encourage you. The point is, if you don't trust awareness enough, you are always going to be thrown into doubt and self-disparagement. When I trust, it is in this attention. I trust in the ability to listen. The voice that says, 'I can't stand it!' — I don't trust that! But I trust my ability to listen to it and know it for what it is. When some kind of condition or emotion comes up, or when there isn't anything at all, it is — 'like this'. Trust that! Trust just knowing whatever is. If there is nothing, then nothing is 'like this'.

A lot of our experience is of confusion, doubt and uncertainty, but we don't like these kinds of feelings, do we? We prefer clarity and certainty. There is a lot of resistance to confusion and doubt. But trust in your ability to know that confusion. Sometimes life is just confusing. We can't really expect it to be always perfectly well arranged on the level of conditioned experience. We might like to have everything completely efficient where nothing confuses us, where we know what time it is and when to do this and when to do that, a neat package of certainty like in Switzerland. The Swiss are masters at organizing life, aren't they? But they are not necessarily a joyful people, and there is also a lot of confusion there. When we depend on having everything certain and clear, we resist confusion and can get very angry when things don't work properly. It is like wanting India to have the certainty of, say, Britain. You see Westerners freaking out when they go to India, just blowing up because they can't take the uncertainty or confusion that usually revolves around life there.

If we begin to notice confusion as confusion and uncertainty as uncertainty, there is a clarity in that. The clarity is in the knowing of it as it is, rather than in trying to straighten out the conditioned world so that it never upsets or confuses us. There is no point in asking for the impossible, demanding something that can never really be. The conditioned world is changing according to conditions and we don't really have that much control over it. Clarity comes through our awareness of this fact rather than through trying to organize and bend the conditioned world *?* to fit an image that makes us feel all right and gives us a sense of security.   *controversial monastic*

The point is, the ego is a mental object. So, when you give the ego your power, you are empowering something that doesn't have any wisdom. Your experience of life will then always be distorted through that, and you will suffer endlessly as a result. The Buddha's teaching is about getting beyond the ego (not trying to annihilate it, though!) and getting to the pure subject, the absolute subject, the *buddho*, the Buddha, awareness, just simple attention, listening, opening. You cannot get beyond this centre, this still point in which you have perspective on the turning world around you. If you are out on the wheel, you are caught on the dizzying momentum of going round in circles. We call it 'saṁsāra' — 'saṁsāra-vaṭṭa' means 'going round in circles' — endless cycles, not really going anywhere but round. That is why when you do things from ignorance, you find yourself coming back and repeating the same things over and over again. You are out on the perimeter, moving round with it. Getting to the very centre, the still point, on the other hand, is by the simple act of attention. You don't have to spend years learning how to do this; it is not a skill that is too refined or too remote for any of you; it is just learning to recognize and trust it. From this still point you can observe the things that are revolving; you see changing conditions for what they are without being taken over by them, by that which you previously identified with. And you see that your personality or self-view is conditioned.

Pay attention right now and say your name to yourself — 'I

am . . . (and use your own name).' Listen to yourself repeat 'I am (Ajahn Sumedho), I am (Ajahn Sumedho).' That is listening to your ability to think and create yourself as a person, as a name. And when you stop thinking 'I am (Ajahn Sumedho)', there is awareness, isn't there? It is pure subjectivity, absolute subjectivity; it is attentive, conscious. But what happened to Ajahn Sumedho? Now, at first you may not quite realize the profundity of this technique, but as you explore it, you will see the difference between pure subjectivity and those moments when you create yourself as a subject, as a person.

When I get into the 'Ajahn Sumedho' perspective, it is a matter of 'I can't stand any more of this!' and going into liking, disliking and all the habits of this personality. But if I trust in the awareness of it, then it is non-personal. I can be aware of this personality if it grumbles or complains or whatever, and no longer feel an impulse to believe in it, empower it, or follow it any more. The way my personality has developed over the years causes me a lot of suffering, so if I depend on that to give me happiness, I won't have any!

The point to notice is the difference between becoming a personality that is the subject of your experience, or being the absolute subject (your awareness). Now, this is an intuitive sense. My experience is to trust the absolute subject. The personality is not something that I trust or believe in any more. It takes a willingness to investigate this, however. It is not a matter of coming from a rejection of the personality, but of knowing its limitation and no longer operating from personal reactions. This is something to experiment with.

Clinging to the personality belief is a fetter which always restrains one from seeing the path, from stream-entry[6]. It is therefore important to explore what the personality belief *(sakkāya-*

---

6   Stream-Entry *(sotāpanna)*: one who, after the disappearance of the three fetters (personality belief, sceptical doubt, attachment to rules and rituals) has entered the stream to *nibbāna*, is no more subject to rebirth in lower worlds, and is firmly established, destined to full enlightenment.

diṭṭhi) is. If you believe yourself to be this physical body and this person with these memories, you will operate from that. Your emotional reactions and habits will all be yours, and that is what you will be endlessly influenced by. Getting to the still point, on the other hand, getting to the absolute subject beyond the personality, is where you begin to listen to your personality and not judge it, not make nasty statements about it or try to change it — 'I would like to have a better personality!' — but rather get to know it as a mental object, as something that comes and goes. We do tend to assume that we are this personality all the time. In terms of direct experience, however, we see it more as just a convention.

When I talk about personality belief, I am referring to the thing we create, that which we believe ourselves to be as a person. We all have our obsessions, identities, peculiarities and so on; we carry them with us and identify with them. Now, it isn't a matter of dismissing or denying these, but of putting them into perspective. If we want to know what we really are — it is this pure subject. On a personal level, we create separation through becoming obsessed with 'my view', 'what I think of you', 'what you need', and so on. The way we talk to one another and even the way we think about ourselves can be very aggressive.

The monks and nuns at Amaravati have become very interested in non-violent communication. We call it 'right speech'. It is learning to be free from blaming. In America, we tend to put people up against the wall: 'Okay, what do you think? I want an answer *right now!*' In Asia they are very good at the face-saving technique where things are said in an indirect way to give people some space. At least that is considerate, better I think than, 'I can tell you what's wrong with you! I can tell you what you need to do!' People telling each other what they think of them can be cruel and arrogant: 'I know what *you* need!' I asked?

Instead of operating from this kind of thing, we can develop a willingness to listen both to others and to ourselves. We can listen to our own personality even if it is being nasty and horrible. We don't have to agree with it! If we are in a terrible mood just grumbling, complaining and blaming, we can learn to listen in an accepting way and see what happens. Instead of being the critic or controller, we can be more compassionate, more accepting, we can be that pure presence and live in this world without fear and without creating conflict and personal problems with others.

isn't this
desire for
"personality"
change

a lot is use of words

Buddha Knows Dhamma

I went to Thailand to become a monk in 1966 when the Forest tradition was already becoming highly regarded there. Prior to decent roads and railways in Thailand, not many people knew about the *dhutanga* monks[7], these Forest monks. Now they are the most famous. Even Ajahn Maha Boowa got his picture in the *Guardian* newspaper recently and has become a sort of celebrated international figure. Over the years there has been a lot of disillusionment with the traditional town and city monasteries in Thailand and scandals have been reported about them in Thai newspapers. So, it is the Forest tradition that is now revered. Even the King has gravitated towards it, and whatever the King does everybody else also tends to do.

Now, in the Thai Forest tradition practices are given around the word *'buddho'* (Buddha, the awakened). It is used as a kind of mantra. Instead of wandering in thought and getting caught up in conceptual proliferations, one can use this two syllable word *'bud-dho'.* Luang Por Chah[8] used it, and so did Ajahn Maha Boowa, Ajahn Mun and all these celebrated Thai Forest ajahns. They base their practice on the discipline (Vinaya) and mindfulness around daily life, and then the *'buddho'* can be used as a mantra. If one repeats this mantra over and over again, the tendency for the mind to wander diminishes and after a while just these two syllables *bud-dho* sustain themselves. One can get to

---

7 *Dhutanga bhikkhus:* monks who practise special observances.

8 Luang Por Chah and Ajahn Chah are the same person. 'Luang Por' in Thai means 'revered father' (a title of respect for an elder monk) and 'Ajahn' in Thai means 'teacher'.

the point then of even dropping those two syllables, and there remains a sense of emptiness and tranquillity which is the result of the cessation of the proliferating, thinking mind. So this *buddho* can be used as a kind of inner chant and tranquillizing technique.

I found that its real value, however, was in reminding me of the inner *buddho*, this sense of awakened attention, this taking refuge in the Buddha, this *Buddhaṁ saraṇaṁ gacchāmi* (I take refuge in the Buddha) as we say. Putting this into the awareness, the development of attention to life, has great significance. You begin to see the power of the word 'Buddha' itself as the awakened, that which is awake, aware. Buddha can remain in our minds as a kind of historical figure, or we can talk about Buddha as some kind of force in the universe. Alternatively, we can speculate about it. In terms of insight meditation practice, however, we do not speculate about anything, we do not try to figure out whether there actually was a Buddha or question whether his life is historically accurate. Can we prove that the Buddha actually walked on seven lotuses when he was born? Are we going to say we won't believe it until we have actual historical proof? But that is ridiculous! That is just concerning ourselves with things that aren't really important and can only be guessed at. Either believe or don't believe, but don't make a problem about it. *Buddho*, then, is something we internalize.

When we say *Buddhaṁ saraṇaṁ gacchāmi* (the traditional Theravada formula in Pali for taking refuge in the Buddha) it can be undertaken as a kind of ceremony, or it can become perfunctory — people just saying it parrot-fashion not realizing the significance of it as a sense of refuge. In meditation, however, we are dealing with the forces of nature, and a lot of them are pretty terrifying and dark, so if we don't feel a sense of safety within ourselves, we could become very frightened by things that arise in consciousness. They can be threatening on a personal level. But in this sense of refuge, we transcend the personal habits we have. The point is, we need a mirror in order to see our own personality as just a series of reflections rather than as a reality. So '*buddho*' is like that mirror. You can also call it 'mindfulness', 'awakenedness' or 'awareness'.

I have used *buddho* for years in my own practice, and have found it very helpful. If your mind is very active — thinking, proliferating — you can keep it busy with something like *buddho* rather than worrying about whether the sky is going to fall in on you or what is going to happen next year. *Mala* beads[9] can also be used whilst using the *buddho, buddho, buddho,* just keeping up this refrain and keeping the mind busy in a way that is not just following and reinforcing negative habits of worry, fear and anxiety about yourself, the future, or the past. If you are going to think, just think '*buddho*'. As I say, you can use it with *mala* beads which work very well with this, or you can use it with the breath — inhaling '*bu*', exhaling '*ddho*'. This keeps your attention; your mind doesn't wander; you are just thinking this two-syllable word, just deliberately thinking in a way that does not convey proliferation. *Buddho* is independent, so doesn't lead you into thoughts about something else.

Now, being the *buddho*, being Buddha, is the really important one. How does that strike you? 'Ajahn Sumedho thinks he's the Buddha!' But if I think I am the Buddha, that is not *being* Buddha, is it? That is my personality thinking some deluded thought. Being Buddha is not a personality thing; it is not a personal attainment but an immanent act of attention. However, if I *be* Buddha, as it were, that reflects the 'Ajahn Sumedho', this sense of 'me' being this person that wants to be or doesn't want to be, or whatever.

I have different names now. When you get into the monastic system, you get all kinds of names. My mother named me 'Robert'. In my generation in the States, however, two-syllable names were too much to expect, so it ended up as 'Bob' all the time, and I never liked the sound of that — 'Bob'! So I was glad to change it. 'Sumedho', I think, is a little more dignified. But in Thailand

9   Similar to a rosary.

when you get to my age you get these venerable monikers as well, like 'Luang Por' which means something like 'revered father', and things like this. But these are just conventions that have come into the system; they are not meant to be things that hold you on a personal level. The real refuge of course is in the awareness.

Buddho, then, is 'Buddha knows dhamma[10]'. This is the paradigm of consciousness where there is the subject and the object. When I talk about the absolute subject, this is the *buddho* (you can put it in that way). You can also call it 'refuge in the Buddha' or *'being* Buddha'. It is just the tension of the moment where you rest in this point of stillness and silence, and you can't get beyond this point. You can go out to the turning wheel, but if you stay in the still point — T.S. Eliot's 'the still point of the turning world' is a good image — that is being Buddha. Now, this is just for contemplation, for beginning to see how to use traditional words to actually help us to awaken and be attentive, rather than leaving them as exotic terms that we adopt as part of our vocabulary. See them as useful ways of reminding yourself to be in this state of attention, this awareness.

The relationship of Buddha to dhamma, then, is 'that which is awake knows the dhamma'. So the dhamma is the truth of the way it is. That word 'dhamma' is all about our experience in the present; it is all dhamma. Conditions are dhammas — they arise and cease. And the *amatadhamma* (the deathless or the unborn) is the reality that we begin to recognize in this position of *buddho,* of *being* Buddha.

Sometimes we say, 'Well, that's life! That's the way it is!' in a kind of negative, complaining way with a sense of resignation to unfairness or injustice or whatever. We say, 'Well, what can you do?' But that is not Buddha knowing dhamma. In the sense of Buddha knowing dhamma 'the way it is' has no judgement in it; it isn't a question of comparing the way it is with the ideals of what we would like or what should be; it is simply 'like this'.

10 *Dhamma* (Pali); *dharma* (Skt.): the reality, the way it is.

And there is a sense of sustaining this *buddho*, this attention. I find also that by just resting in the 'sound of silence' (this kind of resonating vibration) the thinking mind stops — and yet there is a sense of being in this pure presence, this state of *being* Buddha that is quite natural and sustainable. This is not a cultivated, unnatural state. Luang Por Chah used to call it 'our real home'. It is where we can rest, where we can be, and it is natural, so we don't have to make it, hold it, or keep depending on conditions to allow it to exist. When we begin to recognize this, we realize that it is 'the way it is' all the time whether conditions are pleasant or horrible. This is the refuge.

Learning to trust in this refuge allows us to integrate into the life that we have with all its distractions, problems, difficulties, pleasures and pains. Once we really get a feeling and an understanding of this reality, we can go wherever we want and always be in this state of awareness — because it isn't destroyed by the conditions that we are experiencing. This, however, takes real surrender and faith.

The word 'surrender' often gives the impression of one giving up, of a kind of negative, unconditional surrender. It may be better to use the word 'relaxation' if the word 'surrender' is too much for us. What I am pointing to is this letting go, just this trusting in something we can't objectively hold up or let others know about. We can know it intuitively, of course, and we can begin to trust it rather than just trusting in the personality which endlessly doubts and gets caught in feeling intimidated by what others say, or by all the other experiences we have.

As a Buddhist monk, I am in the centre of a worldwide Buddhist movement, so I get all these things coming at me — different attitudes, views, opinions and challenges. If I didn't have this strength within, it would be pretty difficult sometimes; one can feel like a ping-pong ball just being battered from one end of the table to the other by so many strong views and opinions. The Buddhist world is chock-a-block full of them, and then there are the New Age groups, the interfaith groups, the scientists, and so on. The encouragement I give, however, is to learn to recognize intuitive wisdom. It isn't *that* difficult, it isn't so refined and special that it is beyond any of us, it isn't something we will miss if we are not absolutely at our peak. We begin to realize, in fact, that intuitive wisdom is so ordinary that we just might not notice it! — like the space in the room, or the fish in the water that says 'I'm looking for water' whilst being surrounded by it. We are surrounded. The *buddho* is everywhere. It isn't some special, refined type of *samādhi*, some concentrated state that we get as a result of living in a cave for ten years; it is accessible all the time — because it is here and now. And the here-and-now can hold anything — war or peace, health or sickness, a blossoming life or a life that is falling apart — whatever. None of these things is a problem, really, for this sense of refuge. The problem is not with the conditioned realm, but with how we understand it.

The Buddha-Dhamma-Sangha[11] brings us into the reality of our own human limitation. It is not just in terms of Buddha-dhamma (the Buddha's teaching), but also in terms of our humanity (the sangha, or community), in being men and women with interests and the determination to practise. Sangha is not something personal; it isn't a question of taking it as some kind of personal quality; it always has this sense of the group — 'the Church' in Christianity and 'the Sangha' in Buddhism. We are not operating on an individual level of 'I'm Ajahn Sumedho. I'm going to do my practice independently. I don't need *you*; I can do it myself. I don't need those monks and nuns and all those people; I'm going to prove that I can do it and get it together all on my own!' There is no sense of humility in that. That is the ego which is determined to sustain itself as an independent condition. 'Sangha', then, has this sense of the group, of all of us taking refuge in that which is good, in our humanity which refrains from doing evil and does good in terms of morality *(sīla)* or gen-

---

11 Buddha-Dhamma-Sangha: the Enlightened One, the teaching or truth, and the community or monastic community.

erosity *(dāna)*. We don't just think of ourselves. The encourage-ment always is to help, to share, to be generous. And there is the commitment to practise, the intention to give up selfish, personal preferences for the welfare of the Sangha. So the Sangha works as a refuge in the world of living, breathing, humanity. But then it gets misinterpreted, it gets idealized or relegated to meaning only arahants or only highly attained beings, or only monks. You hear people say that in order to take refuge in the Sangha you have to become a monk or a nun. Somebody told me he couldn't be a Buddhist because he didn't want to shave his head. But you can be a Buddhist and *keep* your hair!

As I have said before, the 'sound of silence' to me, is this still point. We can see a point as one little dot, aim for it, and ex-clude everything else in the process; or we can see the point as something that includes everything — as in the case of intuitive awareness *(satisampajañña)*. When we are into the more con-ditioned aspects of our personality, we see a point, concentrate on it, and have to suppress and separate off all that is outside of that point. The other way of looking at it, is to see the point as that which includes. To me this is what 'right concentration' in the Eightfold Path[12] really means. It is not shutting the world out, it is not absorbing just into this very refined little point in order to get right concentration *(sammāsamādhi)*, it is the point that includes everything. Everything belongs, and that means every-thing good as well as bad. So when I rest in this silence, in this stillness, it is like a point — but it includes everything. I don't have to close my eyes, turn round and look away, or even stop talking, in order to be in this still point, because it includes even my talking right now. My talking like this is not interfering with this still point. The 'still point' or the 'sound of silence' has this sense of expansiveness; it has no boundary and just seems to permeate everywhere.

At first you might think of the 'sound of silence' as some kind

---

12 Eightfold Path: right view, right thought, right speech, right action, right livelihood, right effort, right mindfulness, right concentration.

of buzz in the ear. Some people when they hear it, don't like it because they identify it as tinnitus or something annoying. The word 'buzz' itself isn't a particularly nice word, is it? When we talk about buzzes, it usually refers to unpleasant sounds. If we call it a hum, that would be better, because what you call it helps you accept it. If you call it 'tinnitus' you are just going to hate it. But if you call it 'the primordial sound', or the 'cosmic hum', or 'Krishna's flute' it's more interesting. It seems to be that which is before everything, because if you recognize it and stay with it for a while, you begin to find that you stop thinking. And when you stop thinking, you stop re-creating your emotional habits, you stop busily protecting and controlling.

Thought proliferates, so when you think, you just go from one thought to another. You might manage to stop yourself thinking, but then it starts up again and you get angry with yourself for thinking too much when you don't want to! So you might ask yourself, 'How can I stop the thinking? I'm such an obsessive thinker, I just think too much. How can I stop it?' But if you are going to think, do it deliberately. Don't just wander in thought, but deliberately think *'buddho'*, say. Then you will cease being averse to your thinking mind, you will cease *trying* to stop thinking and will just accept it; you will just rest in the silence. Then you will have this sense of emptiness. The 'sound of silence' can seem like a buzz in the ear, maybe, but as you trust it more, you realize that it is expansive, that it has no boundary, that it is everywhere and permeates everything. This is how I experience it. Even calling it 'sound' can be misleading, because then one thinks of the perception one has of sound. It is more like something behind the sounds of everything, if you notice — it underlies, is the background, is 'the one point that includes' and so includes all sounds.

In the Forest tradition putting on and taking off the robes is regarded as one of the practices. You have this complicated robe to wear, and you are told when you first ordain: 'The monk should be mindful when putting on his robe and when taking off his robe . . .' this is the ideal. We might not be used to being mindful around dressing and undressing — at least I wasn't; it wasn't something I was particularly interested in and probably thought about anything but what I was doing at the time. Putting on the robe, then, is given as a practice. Actually, a lot of monks would love us to wear trousers instead, and part of me wouldn't mind that at all. But in another way, I feel somehow that after wearing this thing for so long, it would be a shame to give it up. Also, it is a way of accepting something that is not all that convenient, a bit of a trouble, and it has taught me a lot. The mind proliferates, complains and judges, but from this still point you see how you can really make yourself unhappy about things that aren't all that important. The way I see it, if this is the way they do it, then do it this way. Don't make it into a problem. Resting in this stillness allows the sense of putting on the robe without getting lost in the wandering mind or getting caught in the perfunctory habit of rushing in and putting it on as quickly as possible. These are ways of slowing down and giving more attention to the details of ordinary life. The same with washing the dishes or taking a bath. These things can be meditations in the 'sound of silence'.

I used to like washing the dishes at Amaravati after the morning porridge because it's cold in the winter on that hill! You can go into the scullery where there are these nice windows. The sun shines in and there are these deep stainless steel sinks which hold lots of hot water and nice suds. Then washing the dishes in the silence, I found, even sensually pleasant. When I was a child my parents used to make my sister and me wash the dishes after dinner. Because of that I developed an aversion to washing dishes. So my immediate personal reaction to doing it was, 'Oh no, washing dishes!' Of course, being the most senior monk at Amaravati, I can get out of jobs like that quite easily; it isn't as though they ask me to do it. But what I am saying is that the perception of washing dishes can be a negative one — 'They have to be washed; let's get them out of the way so we can go to the temple and practise!' My personality thinks like that: 'You've got to wash the dishes! You've got to be responsible! You can't just leave all these dirty dishes around. They've got to be washed — that's sensible — so I'll wash them. I'll get them done as quickly as possible so that I can get to my practice — because practice is in the temple; it isn't in the scullery!' So one can change from that perception to this sense of expansion, to the silence and still-ness that contains everything. Then the 'one point that includes' allows the scullery to be a place of practice. When one abides in this stillness, one can find a sort of pleasure even in doing some-thing as ordinary as washing dishes. And as something one has to do every day, it is not really that unpleasant. This is learning to integrate the awareness.

If you have the idea that you just have to be mindful without this sense of including whatever arises, you are always going to be failing at it. Then you will get discouraged and think, 'I can't practise in daily life; I can only really practise on retreat where I don't have to wash the dishes or cook or talk to people. Then I can really practise. That's where it's at! In the office, in the supermarket, in the kitchen, at home with the kids screaming — I can't do it!' That is seeing practice just in terms of being able to concentrate, in terms of not being aggravated by harsh impinge-ment or a lot of activity. But that is like sensory deprivation, the kind of concentration you get by cutting off sensory contact to whatever is happening where you are. Your refuge, however, is in the still point, not in some idea that things are in your way. If I have the idea that I can only be mindful in a very controlled meditation retreat, then I am already primed to seeing every-thing else in life as an obstruction. So I am being too narrow. I am idealizing mindfulness and making it into something only possible when conditions are a particular way.

Years ago when I was a novice monk *(sāmaṇera)*, I fell into a heap on the floor of my *kuṭī* and started crying, 'I can't do it! It's too much! I can never do this!' And yet, while I was sobbing in a heap of anguish, there was something watching it all. It was like a programme going on but I was not that programme; it was as though it wasn't me any more, but it was happening and there was something knowing it was happening which wasn't a heap of anguish. And it was all very clear. If any of you had seen me at that time you would have thought, 'Oh, Ajahn Sumedho is really having a bad time. He's having a breakdown. I've never seen him so upset.' That is why I say you can't judge these things, because if you had judged it from how it appeared, you would not have understood it.

Many of you I am sure have found yourselves going off emotionally, yet with something at the back of you knowing it isn't that way. Emotions are conditioned into us, aren't they? That is why we can have very immature emotions even when we are quite old. It is embarrassing to have childish emotions when you are a dignified sixty-seven year old bloke like I am, especially when you are supposed to be some kind of 'wise master of meditation.' But I don't despair about it because it doesn't mean anything, really. The teaching on Dependent Origination (paṭicca-samuppāda) or what they also call in Pali 'idappaccayatā' is that when certain conditions arise, there are certain results. So, conditions arise for emotions, and emotions follow. That is why, if you are in the buddho (this awareness), you have more of a perspective on what is happening, even though on a mature, intellectual, judgemental level, what has arisen might seem silly or foolish. There is a kind of superego that likes to knock you down and tell you how silly you are. But don't believe that either! That is another habit we have. Alternatively, we can trust in the buddho and see that this emotional thing — no matter how foolish or silly it might appear — belongs at this moment. It is what is included in the point that includes, so it belongs; it is not something that should not be. As you relate to things like that, you can actually let them go. If you see them on a personal level, you are still holding to them in some way, and are not allowing them to go.

One monk recently went to see his family, and during his visit had these amazing emotional swings. The conditions were there for feelings that had not previously been resolved. Even though he is in his thirties, being at home brought up this sense of 'little boy' and 'mother and father' and all this kind of thing. If the conditions are present — no matter how old you are — this is how you feel. We might be annoyed or angry with our parents because we think they are making us feel like this, but they are not; it is just that the conditions are there. As we begin to understand it, we can at least work from this point. We don't have that much control, of course, over what our parents do. If I shout, 'YOU ALWAYS TREAT ME LIKE A CHILD!' they will just feel guilty and maybe try to act how they think I want them to. And then it goes back again to this other thing. It isn't a matter of making it into a problem, however, but of recognizing how our emotional nature can be stuck in patterns that we acquire when we are children.

When we grow up, we try to take on the role of the adult, but underlying that there might be emotional habits that have never been accepted and understood, and these can come out in breakdowns and so forth. And when people get old they very often go through all sorts of things. My father went through a whole range of temper tantrums which stemmed from all the little things he had never resolved in his life — at ninety! It is sad to see, isn't it? But realize you are going to have to face this at some time in your own life. So I want to encourage you to see that meditation includes this; it is not that we are just seeking a blissful state. In certain situations we can revert to the most childish reactions. As we acknowledge this, however, and trust more in our awareness, then as these things come up — and we don't have to make them happen, they will just happen in our lives — we can trust in being the *buddho*, the knower, rather than the personality that is having a tantrum!

Welcoming Everything

Notice that having breakfast and talking stimulates and stirs up the mind. So now is the opportunity to observe this. Just notice it without trying to do anything about it. Witness this sense of having eaten breakfast and having talked to people, and the result is 'like this'. You are noticing the way it is. It is not a matter of approving or disapproving of anything, but of just noticing this awakened state where there is awareness. And it is intelligent; it knows the way it is. There are no comments about it in terms of how it should or should not be; it is just noticing that *this* is the way it is. So there is this attitude of welcoming rather than of being caught up in a habit pattern of trying to control or get rid of, or trying to attain some particular mental state.

People sometimes want to recreate blissful *samādhi* experiences they remember having had on past retreats. They try to make them happen again by attempting to suppress thought or control things. The point is, awareness includes everything, so it isn't a matter of thinking you shouldn't desire anything, that you should just sit there and not have any desires; that would be coming from an ideal again, an ideal of how things should be. So, in awareness, we are not operating from comparing the reality of this moment with an ideal, but rather of accepting and welcoming the way it is — even if we don't like the way it is. It isn't a matter of liking, but of learning to welcome even what we don't like and don't want.

Years ago I developed a welcoming practice. This is because I am someone who finds welcoming — particularly in the case of certain mental states — very difficult. There are states I don't

like and habitually reject. I have this sense of just pushing them
away, just doing this to life, kind of pushing them away. This
was my — what would you call it? — approach to life? Anyway, my approach was to not let it approach. So then this sense
of welcoming occurred to me as a way of remembering not to
reject mental states. It wasn't that I had intended to reject them
when they came; it was just force of habit. So then the intention
was to welcome even what I didn't like or didn't want — those
unpleasant mental states, those difficult situations.

In the Theravada tradition we have this word *'mettā'* (loving-kindness), and *mettā* is about welcoming everything. There
is nothing divisive or critical in *mettā*. When you develop *mettā*,
therefore, it is towards everything in the universe. You have *mettā* for the devils, the demons, the angels, the enemy, the friends,
the mosquitos, flies, germs, birds, the precious little kittens and
the beloved doggies — everything. There is no preference. It is
not a question of saying, 'I want 90% of *mettā* to go to *this* person and about 1.1% to go to the demons'. You are not being picky
about it. It is welcoming conditioned phenomena totally — the
whole range from heaven to hell, from the best to the worst.

So what is the effect on your mind when you start developing
this attitude of loving-kindness *(mettā)*? It counterbalances your
critical tendencies, doesn't it? Your critical mind excludes things
— 'This is better than that. This is how it should be, not that.
This person I approve of, but this one I don't. There shouldn't be
these evil people. There shouldn't be criminals. There shouldn't
be paedophiles. There shouldn't be this, there should only be
that.' You can get caught up in personal preferences and weighing one thing against the other. But *mettā* is not critical and it is
not idealistic, it is not generating a loving quality towards everything in the sense of liking or approving of it. Liking depends on
conditions having to be such that you like them. *Mettā* is more
like unconditional love. It is this welcoming, a kind of generosity, an uncritical acceptance of the whole range of phenomena in
whatever form it takes.

As many of you know, we develop *mettā* beginning with ourselves. The formula we use is something like: 'May I abide in wellbeing.' So the first part of the practice is always directed towards yourself, just learning to accept yourself for what you are. That means welcoming and accepting everything about yourself — your dark side, your good side, your bright side, your stupid side, your evil side, whatever — learning to accept uncritically even the things you really don't like about yourself. And this I found most difficult. My critical faculties are not all that rampant when turned outward, but they tend to go into a tirade when turned inward. I am much more critical of myself than of anyone else.

So, 'May I abide in wellbeing' is a reminder of wishing well to this being here, this condition, this human body, this person with its habits and emotions, whatever they are. Rather than endlessly thinking you have to get rid of things because you shouldn't be this way, you shouldn't feel like this, there is a sense of welcoming even something very unpleasant. So *mettā* allows all things because they belong. Everything belongs in this moment because it is here, it is like this. If I come along and say 'this shouldn't be here' that is my personal sense of not wanting something. The reality of the moment, however, is that because it is here, it belongs.

One thing I found when living in Asia was this sense of belonging — even though I am an obvious foreigner — and this used to baffle me. I have lived in India, Malaysia and Thailand. And in all those countries I have felt at home; I always felt as though I belonged. Yet, in many ways, I didn't. There I was, a big white man living in a Forest monastery with all these small Thai monks. I looked out of place, an anachronism, a foreigner in terms of appearance. On the emotional level, however, I always felt at home, and began to recognize that the one thing many of us like about the Asians is that they have this sense of everything belonging — lepers, mad people, the beautiful, the ugly, the rich, the poor, the high caste, the low, whoever. The Asians seem to have this total acceptance of it all, that anyone has just as much right to be there as anyone else, that because you are there, you belong.

Mettā, then, is this sense of being at home, of allowing, of accepting and being patient with what you don't like and don't want, of allowing what you find irritating, disgusting and revolting, whatever. It is a question of learning not to get lost in reactions, but rather to be patient and accepting, to welcome even the dark side of your experience. That takes patience, doesn't it? For me at least it does, because emotionally I am conditioned to trying to push things away, trying to get rid of them. Patient acceptance is also about welcoming the good side, but in a way that does not demand it. When happiness is present, welcome it, allow it to arise. But also allow it to cease. To be able to do this takes attentiveness, takes this *buddho*, this still point, this sense of pure presence which includes all that *is* right now.

I was talking to someone this morning about grief. This, of course, is an emotion we all experience. In the West, however, we don't seem to know how to deal with it, often looking on it as an indulgence, a kind of 'making a lot out of nothing'. We can think we are being quite rational by dismissing feelings of grief. I see this in other people and I can also see it in myself. Before I ever practised meditation my tendency was to dismiss grief whenever it came up in my life. I felt it was more noble to say, 'Oh, just get on with life! Don't make a scene.' That seemed more noble than just sitting around crying and weeping and making everybody feel terrible — 'Just get on with life!' That of course is an ideal and might seem noble, but at the same time it isn't respecting what one is feeling; it is merely trying to push one's feelings aside. So, in awareness we are willing to grieve, not in terms of indulging in grief — it isn't a matter of holding onto it, wallowing in it and feeling sorry for ourselves — but of being willing to allow the emotion to become conscious, to respect it because it is a natural emotional experience.

The Buddha pointed to unsatisfactoriness *(dukkha)* as the first

Noble Truth, and in that context he referred to old age, sickness, death, grief, sorrow, despair and anguish. Grief, then, is the first Noble Truth. So it is a question of welcoming it because it is a noble truth and not some kind of personal weakness. Put it into that context of understanding. And understanding the first Noble Truth (dukkha) is one of the insights. If your reaction to grief is always rejecting and pushing it away, you have no way of understanding it. This loving-kindness, then, is a way of welcoming. Grief is something to welcome rather than to reject or ignore.

From this still point whenever you feel a sense of loss or separation from the loved, it is more like noting — it is 'like this', it feels 'like this'. What does it feel like here in the body itself? Do you feel it in the lower part of the body, or in the heart, maybe? I notice — and this is my own experience — that as I open to people in the present, I actually feel as though the doors that have been closed here in the heart are opening. I used to think I didn't have a heart. People kept talking about 'heartfelt feelings', and I would think, 'I don't think I have any.' I was such an up-in-the-head type of person that I was never really very aware of what I was feeling. So I put forth effort to be aware on the level of the heart. But there was a strong resistance to it. My rational mind would think, 'Sounds pretty soppy to me . . !' I didn't want to identify myself with these heartfelt feelings. The tendency to think that such things sound emotional and weak is a criticism, though, isn't it? But when I contemplate it, I find this sense of the doors opening. And when I am in this still point and with somebody directly I find it very real. With this group here there is a sense of a heart relationship. I can feel a sense of openness in this area of the heart, and it is an intuitive feeling. I don't think you could measure it with scientific instruments, but this is the best I can do to describe the experience. I also notice, when I go into a critical mode of reactivity, that it seems as though the doors close again. Then I am back in the old pattern of not feeling anything.

When you are caught in thinking, you don't really feel very

much, because thinking has no sensitivity. That is why people who think all the time are often very insensitive. They live in a rational world that is quite beautiful in its own way, but there is no feeling in it. Opening to sensitivity is not a matter of trying to tell yourself to be sensitive; it is rather recognizing that the realm you are living in is 'like this'. And this is not an ideal realm; it is not the perfect place; it is not how things *should* be according to the ideals of what is the best, what is fair or just or perfect. In this realm things change. So fairness is not always going to be what you experience. The atrocities, the serial killers, the wars, the unfairness and the tyrannies, as well as the justice, fairness and goodness — they all belong in this realm. And no matter how much you try to make life into a Garden of Eden, you embrace along with it the forces of your own destruction and the destruction of the garden itself — because that is the way it is. It is not that there is anything wrong.

What are we supposed to learn from this? Ask yourself. I mean, this is obviously something to learn from, isn't it? If it is my fault, then maybe I should do something about it — go to a shaman to exorcize the snakes in my mind, maybe. The idea that it is my fault is one way of looking at it. But it isn't. The Buddha pointed to the dhamma which includes everything; it is all-inclusive. I find that just by contemplating life in this way I am suddenly more interested in it. It no longer seems like an endless struggle with everything. When operating on a personal level — from how things *should* be — it seems that life is always a struggle, and I can never win the battle. As much as I try to control things, try to make them good and make myself what I think I should be, there is always this other side that has to be rejected and denied. It inevitably keeps pounding in my consciousness, demanding attention, taking it all very personally, and then the sense of uselessness and hopelessness, and even, 'Maybe I shouldn't be here! Maybe I don't belong here!'

In terms of taking refuge in the dhamma, then, there is this sense of awakening, the *buddho*, noticing the way it is. The Thais have an acceptance of life that Americans don't have. Luang Por Chah was never idealistic in terms of monks being perfect, being always kind and unselfish. In fact, he would find our weaknesses and mistakes and the way we took ourselves seriously, very amusing. Then he would get us to look at the absurdity of our expectations, the absurdity of trying to make ourselves into something we could never be. This, I think, was one of Luang Por Chah's greatest gifts.

Awareness, then, is just noticing the way it is — the way your body is for one thing, and the way your mental state is — so it is embracing, welcoming, noticing, but not critically. So being aware is being alert, awake, and intelligent; it is an alive sense of being, yet it is not passive or a negative acceptance of life through any kind of resignation to fate. You might have denied and rejected things in the past, but in awareness you include and open to them. Awareness includes even feeling that 'it shouldn't be like this' — it also includes that! There is nothing you can think or say or do that doesn't belong at this moment. No matter how complicated your thought process might be, it belongs; no matter what state your body is in or your emotional state — whether you feel successful and happy or depressed and a failure — it all belongs.

Then there is a sense of, 'Oh, what a relief! I don't have to endlessly try to purify myself or try to make myself better. I can actually rest a bit — maybe relax and trust — what a relief!' But then we think, 'What will I do if I don't have to do anything?' If we grasp this idea of 'not having to do anything', that also becomes absurd. So 'not having to do anything' is a reflective statement rather than an ideal you hold to. If you attach to 'Now I don't have to do anything', that becomes an ideal again.

The point is to try to use language for reflection rather than for taking a position on anything. This sense of 'I've got to get something I don't have.' What is that? Be the observer of it. 'I'm not good enough the way I am; I've got to make myself better; I've got to do something to improve myself.' What is that like when you observe it as a mental state? To me it is an incredible pushiness all the time, a sense of always being goaded on. And as long as I don't recognize it and don't see it in terms of dhamma, it affects everything I do; it is a kind of underlying influence of how I experience life. This constant sense that I have to get something I don't have, that I'm incomplete, imperfect, not good enough, and that I've got to become enlightened, is *bhavataṇhā* in the second Noble Truth. This is the desire to become, so it is the cause of suffering.

When we grasp this desire to become *(bhavataṇhā)*, we experience unsatisfactoriness *(dukkha)*. *Vibhavataṇhā* is where you have the feeling that you have to get rid of something. You have to get rid of greed because you are too greedy, and you have to get rid of anger because good people are not angry, and you have to get rid of jealousy because it is disgusting to be jealous, and you have to conquer your fears because a brave person is fearless, you have to get rid of . . . whatever. It is all *vibhavataṇhā* — 'I'm not good enough the way I am. I'm greedy. I get angry. I get jealous and frightened. And I've got to get rid of these emotions.' Just notice this attachment to what seems very good.

In a logical sense we should purify the mind; we should free ourselves from these passions. These are imperatives in the holy life — having to purify and free ourselves from the lower realms, the passions, the selfishness. It isn't that that is wrong, but just notice the attachment to the idea that 'I've got to get rid of this; it's my problem and I'll never be enlightened as long as I have this anger'. This is what the Buddha was constantly pointing to, this attachment *(upādāna)*, which is coming from the sense of 'I am this person; I am this body; these are my problems and they are blocking me from enlightenment; I've got to get rid of them'. The whole thing is based on the delusion of 'I am this person'.

So *buddho* transcends the personal, the personality belief *(sakkāyadiṭṭhi)*; it embraces everything and therefore embraces your personality rather than judges it. This is when we talk about 'the absolute subject' rather than 'the personal subject'. When we attach to a personality, we *become* a personality and interpret experience through the distortions of our personal habits. And as long as that illusion is not seen through, not realized and accepted, we are always going to be frightened. If we are the human body and if we are the person, we can be physically harmed and emotionally humiliated. We all experience these things in many ways. Bodies are vulnerable states, and emotionally we can be damaged just by what somebody might say to us or how they look at us. On a personal level, therefore, being harmed in some way is an ever-present possibility. This is taking things personally and makes the situation that we are living in rather fraught.

Learning to see this in terms of dhamma, then, in terms of this *buddho* or this still point, gives us the perspective on the way things are. This is developing wisdom rather than just reinforcing personal views of everything, because wisdom is a universal; it is not personal; it is not 'I am wise'. We cannot claim wisdom as some kind of personal attribute, but it certainly operates when we let go of identifying with the personality and the body. If we do claim it on a personal level, if we do start interpreting it in terms of 'I am an attained person, I am an arahant' or anything like that, then we call it 'spiritual defilement', the impurities that come through insight practices. That is why there are very strict rules about this in the bhikkhu-discipline.

There are four disrobing rules, and one of them is if a bhikkhu claims high states that are not true just to delude or exploit others. Even if I have no bad intention and start saying that I am an arahant as a result of a particular experience, that is also an offence I have to confess. I have had experiences through heavy concentration where I *have* felt I was enlightened, 'Oh, I'm enlightened now!' But really it is better not to say anything. Ajahn Chah would say, 'Well, just keep quiet and practise a little more, and then it'll go away.'

Even in Thailand there are people constantly looking for arahants — 'Who is an arahant? Who is a stream-enterer?' There is a strong desire to achieve and attain, and to know what other people's attainments are. So, as soon as they hear that somebody is enlightened, they run off to them. One monk I remember years ago claimed he was enlightened (this was one of Ajahn Chah's disciples) and a whole lot of monks suddenly left Ajahn Chah for him. Ajahn Chah wasn't claiming anything, so they left him because they wanted to be with an enlightened master — but they were disappointed!

The point is, most of us prefer to put our trust in those who say they are enlightened. You get these people who are very confident, these gurus that appear and say, 'I am the Messiah!' or 'I am the Maitreya Buddha of this era!' and people flock to them. Some of these 'gurus' are so confident, in fact, that their confidence has a kind of sparkle to it. When you are really positive, you have a kind of radiant quality about you. The cults that you hear about seem to have the craziest teachings, and the leaders are the most obvious con artists, some of them totally convinced of their own enlightenment. And that kind of confidence is very powerful. So, when we don't trust ourselves, we easily give ourselves over to people we think know what they are doing.

The essence of the Buddha's teaching, however, is awakenedness. The Buddha was saying 'wake up!' not 'I am the Buddha and you must believe in me.' His teaching is an invitation and an encouragement to awaken. That means *you* wake up rather than depending on *me* waking up. This, to me, is very meaningful. In the beginning I felt a lack of something. I didn't feel good enough. I felt I was a defiled person, a weak person and couldn't trust myself, and I wanted to find somebody I could trust. This of course in the end led me to Ajahn Chah. But his emphasis was always on waking *me* up rather than encouraging me to bind myself to *him*. He could see what I was doing and kept pointing it out. I would ask him, 'You know, Ajahn Chah, I've been practising for many years, am I a stream-enterer now?' And he would say, 'How do you expect me to know?' He would throw me back on myself. 'If *you* don't know, why do you think *I* would know?'

And whenever I tried to lean on him in that way, he would —
in a gentle way, I never felt he was pushing me away — try to
awaken me to what I was doing, to my longing to depend on
other people because I thought they were wise and I was not.
Actually, he was very effective in getting me to see what I was
doing.

I also had this fear of taking responsibility for being wise. My
personality would say, 'Don't think *you* will ever be wise!' My
personality has this tyrant, so it says, 'You can't trust yourself.
You're a mess! Do you think *you* are ever going to be wise?'
and it would go on like that. Then I began to see that this inner
tyrant was a habit. It wasn't alive; it was a dead thing and would
say the same thing no matter what. No matter how good I was, I
could never be good enough. No matter how strict I was with the
Vinaya, I could never be strict enough. People would say, 'Oh,
Ajahn Sumedho, that was a really good talk you gave,' and the
inner tyrant would go, 'No it wasn't!' So, no matter how much
the world came forth and said, 'You're *really* good, you're *really*
wise, you're *really* the best,' the inner tyrant would say, 'You're
not!'

By recognizing that this inner tyrant was a habit, I realized
that though it seemed alive, it wasn't; it was just something reactive. I then began to see it as something not to believe, something
that didn't have any wisdom, something that was dead; it was
nothing; it was just that when this button was pushed it went:
'You're not good enough!' and when it was pushed again: 'You're
not good enough!' pushed again: 'You're not good enough!' And
that is all it could say. So don't believe that kind of thing! Don't
give it any ground in your consciousness.

'I am not good enough the way I am and need to practise in
order to become enlightened' is a sense of 'I', 'me as a person
who has got to do something now in order to become something
in the future'. And by contemplating such things, one realizes
it is all based on delusion. For one thing, eternity is *now*. When
you contemplate the present moment, the future is the unknown,

isn't it? What is tomorrow right now? It is what you don't know. You can speculate, guess, and so forth, but this is all taking place now. The past is what you remember, so you remember yesterday or ten years ago, but that is a memory arising in the present. And 'I am this person' is an assumption, isn't it? When you observe your personality, it changes according to conditions. So, your personality changes according to the conditions you are in. Whether you are with friends or enemies, with your parents or with your husband or wife, with your colleagues, alone, in the monastery, or at the Summer School, your personality changes accordingly — because that is the way it is; it adapts itself to the particular conditions present. Yet one has this assumption that 'I am this person all the time'. What we are actually doing, of course, is creating assumptions and never questioning them, never looking into what we are doing.

Awakened awareness allows us to see this. When we rest in this *buddho* or this pure state of being, this listening, this attention, we begin to see how changeable and ephemeral the personality is, and how it depends on conditions for it to be happy or sad, ebullient, depressed, bored, or fulfilled, or for it to feel accepted or rejected. But awareness transcends these personality conditions; it is a constant factor — as distinct from the personality which is ephemeral — and we begin to see that we cannot trust our personality as our identity because it is not what we are, even though it says so and seems so. We therefore break out of its limitations through awareness — not by rejecting the personality, not by trying to *not* have a personality (which would be impossible anyway) — but by ceasing to be committed to the personality as 'myself'.

We limit ourselves all the time by committing ourselves to the personality; we bind ourselves, often, to very unpleasant limitations that we habitually get caught in. Once we see that, we can free ourselves, we can let go. Our real identity then is in the awareness and in this attitude of welcoming, of *mettā*. By trusting awareness, we can learn from it, and find that we can accept and welcome even the most horrible things, the things we are most frightened of. Once we trust in this practice, we find that we have space even for what we most dread. Then that fear and dread drops away . . .

Don't be Afraid of Trusting Yourself

I 'm on a sabbatical leave this year, which is quite a nice change. After being involved in teaching retreats and giving talks for thirty years or more, I asked for some time off — and now I am wondering if I ever want to go back to teaching again. Actually, 'sharing knowledge' is a more accurate way of thinking about what I do, because I don't particularly like the idea of being a teacher and holding to that position. That would be like establishing the sense of 'I'm the teacher and you're the student', and that for some people is never questioned, so one can easily get stuck into roles like that.

With the practice of awareness we get behind the conventions that we are conditioned by. As John Peacock[13] was saying last night, our interpretation of Buddhism is conditioned by our cultural way of perceiving things; the interpretation of the words and even the English translations that we choose are influenced by our own conditioned mind. A Christian missionary will interpret Buddhism one way and a psychologist or lawyer, say, will interpret it another. So recognize that awareness is the ability you have to get to 'ground zero', to the point *before* you were conditioned, to 'the face before you were born', to the deathless before you were ever caught into a cultural or social conditioning process.

What is pure awareness? Where is it? When most of us first

---

13 Lecturer in Buddhist Studies, Bristol University, and Director of Sharpham Centre for Contemporary Enquiry, Devon.

start meditating we come from a place of ignorance. I started with the thought, 'I am a confused person and need to practise meditation in order to become enlightened.' That was how I saw myself when I started meditating years ago; I saw myself in this critical way — 'I shouldn't be the way I am; I've got to be better than this by doing something that will make me better in the future.' In some ways, on a conventional level, this was true. It wasn't that it was a totally false perception, but it *was* a perception. If we grasp such perceptions, they will influence how we experience what teachers say, how we read scriptures, and how we treat the religious conventions and techniques we use.

In Thailand I noticed that Westerners who ordain into the Thai system bring with them a strong sense of self. Thai culture is socially oriented; its identity is on a very wide spectrum, and social relationships and sensitivities are very strong. Most of us don't have that. Our culture is quite different. Americans, anyway, are very individualistic. We demand our rights, stand up for ourselves and assert ourselves, and on and on like that. You can see this on an international level as well. Now, I am not saying that this is wrong, I am merely pointing to how it affects conscious experience. Recognize also the strong sense of self-criticism and self-disparagement that is common in the Western world. We are very aware of what is wrong with us, of what is not right — the weaknesses, the faults and flaws. We often see ourselves through these perceptions of 'something wrong' and 'I'm not good enough the way I am'.

The Thai Forest tradition has a strong disciplinary aspect to it, so Westerners tend to go into strict Vinaya monasteries with this sense of 'I am a flawed and weak person and need to purify myself through keeping these rules'. This, of course, has a certain effect. For one thing, by holding to rules or precepts that are given to us, we can easily become insensitive, because the sense of our self-worth depends on keeping these rules. If we cannot keep them according to the standard we have, we tend to feel worse than we did before; we feel we are not good monks, not worthy of the robe. As alms mendicants, we are dependent on the goodness of others, so we might find ourselves thinking, 'I'm not worthy of these alms . . .' and get into states of self-loathing.

This is a logical process, isn't it? If I am identified with being this physical body and this personality, and if I am very aware of what is wrong with these things, I might try to make myself into a better person by endlessly meditating and keeping the moral precepts. But then if I find I can't live up to the standard I hold — an ideal standard of what I *should* be — I tend to have this sense of, 'See! I'm too weak; I'm not good enough.' Living the holy life, then, can lead to an even greater lack of self-worth; and it all comes from the basic delusion — putting it in Theravadan terms — that 'I am the Five Aggregates' *(khandha)*, identifying with the five aspects of form, feeling, perception, mental formations, and consciousness *(rūpa, vedanā, saññā, sankhāra, viññāna)*. The Buddha used this five-aggregates teaching as an expedient means, a convenient way of simplifying everything. If you begin to break yourself down into these five aspects or groups *(khandha)*, you start to question the assumption that 'I am this permanent personality' from which you see through very critical eyes.

So, how do we get behind this? What do we do? It is not a question of going into reverse and saying, 'I *am* good enough; I am the deathless; I am the Buddha; I am a wonderful guy . . !' One can go into a kind of positive thinking mode: 'I'm totally wonderful and beautiful and lovable!' That is better than doing the reverse, I think, because you might at least have a few happy moments out of that. But the problem is not with thoughts or perceptions as such; it is with the way we hold to thoughts and perceptions, the way we identify with them and cling to them. If I have the fixed perception that I am a flawed person and am not good enough the way I am — if that is the assumption I make about myself — it tends to influence how I relate to the world, to other people, to monasticism and everything.

At one time I developed a kind of skilful means and intentionally thought, 'I am not good enough the way I am.' But instead of analysing this statement, I just reflected on it, just became aware of it. If you learn how to listen to yourself, to listen to your thoughts when you think, 'I am not good enough the way I am,' for example, you will begin to realize that this is actually just something you are creating in your mind. There is that which is aware of thought and there is the perception that you create, and you begin to separate the two. So the awareness is the focus. And this is the emphasis the Buddha made. Our ability in this present moment is to be awake and fully with the way it is, to be awake to how things around us are affecting us through sight, sound, smell, taste and touch.

Explore this sense of 'I am' — 'I am this physical body; this is me.' If we begin to listen to this sense of 'my body', 'what I look like', and become aware of the way we see ourselves — attractive or unattractive, male or female and so on — we realize that these are perceptions we create. We identify strongly just on the level of gender, for example. The 'I'm a man and you're a woman' kind of thing seems obvious, just common sense. The body is either male or female; that is the nature of the body. But is this body what I really am? I encourage you to explore what this body is. It has a momentum all its own — it is born, grows up, gets old and dies. And no matter how hard we try to prevent it from getting ill and old, it still does it, doesn't it? And then there is the inevitable death of the body. I can say to myself, 'Don't get old Sumedho!' I can say that, but the body doesn't obey. It doesn't obey because it isn't me, so it is like telling a leaf not to wither and fall off a tree. I can't do that; it is beyond my ability.

So then I realize it is foolish to identify, to cling, to hold to the Five Aggregates[14] *(khandha)* as some kind of personal possession. And if I really explore them, I see that they are conditions in nature; they follow nature's laws; they are what they are. Sometimes they are very pleasant and sometimes they are horrible. That is the way nature is — good and bad, right and wrong.

---

14 Five Aggregates *(khandha): rūpa, vedanā, saññā, sankhāra, viññāṇa* (form, feeling, perception, mental formations, and consciousness.

The point to see is that this world, the conditioned realm that we are experiencing, is 'like this'.

As you observe, as you listen to this sense of 'I am' just on a very personal level — 'I am not good enough,' for example — you begin to notice the effect it has on your consciousness. When you hold to a view like that, you begin to notice a sense of depression, embarrassment, or timidity — because that is the result, that is the emotional result of holding to 'I'm not good enough the way I am'. Now, this is not an analytical process; this is awareness. As I said before, it is not a question of trying to change the attitude you have towards yourself, but of getting behind any attitude you have, seeing it as a viewpoint, seeing it as something you assume or believe. Pure awareness is not dependent on what you are thinking, your physical condition, your emotional state, or the conditioned realm, because it is what you can always refer to or be. You can *always* be the awareness, no matter what the conditions are, externally or internally.

We have to really apply ourselves, however, really be fearless in our investigations, because there are a lot of subtle assumptions and things we might be very attached to, things we might not yet be ready to let go of. So just trust yourself in letting go of the things you *can* let go of in the present. I am not saying you should let go of everything during this Summer School, and that by the time you leave here I want you to be completely free from all attachments. That would be asking the impossible. I am encouraging you rather to have more confidence in your recognition of attachment — not as a judgement against it — but in order to realize what it is like, to see that it is wanting things to be what they cannot be, or holding to views and having to defend your views, maybe feeling threatened when your views are challenged.

Now, just as an experiment, we can sit for a while and try to make whatever comes into the mind fully conscious — happiness, sadness, uncertainty, confusion, inspiration, depression . . . It doesn't matter what the condition is, just listen to it, just let it be what it is and recognize that your relationship to it now is 'listening' not 'judging'. You are not trying to pass any kind of value judgement about anything, but just noticing, allowing even something unpleasant to be fully accepted in this conscious moment. Make a special note of the listening and the object you are listening to — listening inwardly to your thoughts, for example. Just notice the thoughts move and change. You cannot sustain a thought, can you? You cannot keep one thought, but you can be aware of its movement. This is separating the subject from the object by being the subject. Be the witness, the knower. And then the known is, say, thinking or feeling. Thinking is cultural conditioning ; we are conditioned to think about things. We are also sensitive and have feeling. We can feel lonely or sad or confused. And there is knowing these things, isn't there? You might think, 'I'm feeling sad today,' and there is an awareness of the feeling, what it is like, and also that it changes. So, there is that which is aware, and there is the object you are aware of. If you grasp the object, you become someone who is sad, say, and that is what we call 'becoming'. If somebody says something and makes you angry, angry feelings arise. Then if you grasp those feelings you become an angry person and might act on it. You could blow it, in other words, and start yelling, saying unkind things, and even getting physically violent — because of 'becoming'.

The point is to know the difference between the objects and the awareness of them (the Five Aggregates are objects). That is putting 'that which is aware' into the context of, say, *buddho* or the Buddha, the knowing, the awakened state. This sense of awakening is very significant. This is a 'wake up' teaching. We think we are awake because our eyes are open and we are not lying down sleeping, but we might still be completely lost in delusion and living in the realm of assumptions and habits. The Buddha, the Awakened One, woke up to this. It is not a question of saying, 'I shouldn't be like this; I shouldn't be ignorant and I shouldn't be angry.' That is making it into a personal judgement and getting stuck in the same realm again. We know we shouldn't be like that; our social values tell us we should conquer anger and lust, and comply with all the other 'shoulds'. We all know what we *should* do; that is not the point, is it? The point is to be aware of the way it actually is.

This is where I encourage you to trust yourself. And it is like an intuitive function. You can't get at it, you can't really say, 'Ah, this is it!' and hold it in your hand. It is something you have to trust within yourself; it is your awakenedness. What is it for you when you are awake? It's no good asking me what it is like for you, or asking me whether you are awake or not — 'Ajahn Sumedho, am I awake?' (It isn't for me to know that; it is for you to know it.) That is where the teacher-student thing can get in the way, because students empower the teacher: 'Ajahn Sumedho knows what's good for me. I'm so stupid and hopeless! I'm a clumsy person and I've done a lot of foolish things in my life, but Ajahn Sumedho knows what I need.' Then I say, 'Yeah, you've lived a pretty stupid life and you should never trust yourself. *I* know what's good for you!' That would be reinforcing the assumption that I am the expert and you are the student. It isn't a matter of assuming the opposite, either — 'I'm *just* as good as Ajahn Sumedho, you know.' With meditation, you are getting beyond that; you are learning to trust in your own intuitive sense, in the awakenedness of your own mind and really making that a fully conscious experience. (It is not just some idea in your brain, but something you really know, *really* know and trust.

At first, maybe your own intuitive sense doesn't seem all that trustworthy, because there is nothing you can get hold of in the way you want to. This is where I encourage you to trust more in your direct experience than in ideas you have from the tradition. No matter how good those ideas might be, as long as you grasp them, you are trying to interpret life from somebody else's point of view. We can easily get intimidated by what others think and say, or what we feel the world expects of us. We can become very frightened by that and mistrust ourselves.

And in our materialistic society, I have noticed, we can appear quite confident, but are not. We can give the impression of being an authority and an expert just by knowing a lot about things — 'I know all about Theravada Buddhism. I'm an expert!' And yet, if we never practise, the confidence fails when it gets to the realities of life, to the emotional stress, the loss of loved ones, the disappointments. All of these things are part of the human experience, and no matter how expert we are on the teachings of the Pali Canon, if we have not really applied those teachings in our lives and learned how to trust in our own intuitive sense, then they won't help very much when the going gets tough. And just to say to somebody that it is all impermanence, unsatisfactoriness and non-self somehow sounds like an empty statement when that person's life has got difficult, when he has lost his job, his wife has died, and his electricity has been cut off. Just to say, 'Well, you know, everything's impermanent . . .' sounds a bit hollow.

During this Summer School, then, I encourage you to really listen inwardly. If you are unhappy, full of doubts, low, bored, or maybe feeling elated, rather than trying to suppress it or just endlessly tell people about it, listen to it: 'I'm bored! I'm bored!' You can then begin to get in touch with boredom; you can accept it, in a way. It is not a matter of trying to figure out why you are bored or blaming it on somebody else — 'I am bored because of him; I'm bored because of the Summer School!' Just use the boredom to open to it, to understand boredom, to recognize it. And if somebody says something that offends or upsets you, use that to learn from.

When we start analysing, it gets back into the same problem of, 'Why do I get so upset when you do that?' We might think about it and try to figure it out — and it is interesting sometimes to do that — but it doesn't solve the problem, at least not until we learn how to recognize that being upset is 'like this', feeling lonely is 'like this'. But that which is aware — is that lonely? Is awareness lonely? Or is the object of awareness lonely? Investigate that relationship!

Fear is another important aspect of our lives to contemplate, isn't it? It is a basic human emotion. This realm that we live in is a realm of fear. We can create institutions to give us a sense of security, but the animal world is all about survival; it is the law of the jungle where we look after ourselves, where we learn the tricks of survival. It is a frightening realm to be born into, but that is just the way it is. We can think how it *should* be — the lion and the lamb should lie down together and love each other — but that is an ideal realm. We can create an image and an ideal, but this realm is not actually like that; lambs and lions don't do that. Nor are they supposed to, so it isn't their fault, either. We are recognizing the way it is on the level of just raw conditioning where we have to survive, have to give birth, procreate, raise families, eat, protect our things. All these are part of this human realm that we are experiencing, and there is a lot to fear in it in terms of pain and loss. But that is the way the realm of fear is.

Here in Britain, we have a sense of security. As much as people complain, this is a fairly well-run country. You can take a lot for granted living here that you can't in other countries. But then little things can jar. You want it to be perfect; you want it to be how it *should* be if it were a really well-run country and all the people were doing what they *should* do. You would like that, but that is not the way it is. And noticing the way it is, isn't excusing it or apologizing; it is just recognizing that this realm and this physical body are the way they are at this moment. Whether you feel healthy and strong, weak and sickly or whatever, is not the point, is it? The point is to willingly accept the way it is, to recognize it — even if it is not the way you want it to be — rather than being caught up in abusing society, or your body, or the world you are living in, because you feel threatened and persecuted by them.

Now, that which is awake and aware can be aware of your body, but your body cannot be aware of you. You can recognize — just by the body-sweeping practice, just by sweeping through

deathless

the sensations in the body — that you can be aware of the body as experience right now. As you sit here you can be aware of the posture of sitting, of the pressure of sitting, of the heat and cold and all sensations. 'That which is aware' can include the whole body in this moment. It isn't like thinking. When you think and analyse, you have one thought at a time. You have to think this one thought, then the next one, then the next one; and you can't think two thoughts at the same moment. Also, when you are attached to thinking you are caught in this time realm. Thinking is quite a gift, actually, but your thoughts can easily delude you because they are limited; they are linear and dualistic. Nevertheless, you can be aware of thinking, and you can deliberately think 'I am not good enough the way I am' or whatever. So what is it that is aware of thinking? Keep asking yourself: 'What is it that is aware of thinking? What is it that is aware of feeling? What is it that is aware of sadness, anger, lust, despair or anything? What is it that is aware?' It isn't a matter of coming up with some smart-alec answer, but of just trusting yourself to keep that kind of question floating in your consciousness so that you can begin to feel the connection, begin to get the sense of being this awareness, this pure subjectivity where the physical body is an object and no longer the subject, where you are no longer operating from the assumption that 'I am this physical body' or 'I am this personality', where you are actually in the space that contains all of this.

This is my own experience and interpretation of what I call 'the deathless'. I am aware of what changes, what is death-bound, such as thoughts. Thoughts are born and die incessantly. Thinking moves very quickly, as well as feeling, emotion, states of mind, physical sensations, pleasure, pain, aches, and so on. What is it, then, that is aware of them? What is it that is awake? Just by repeating that question, you are listening to the questioning as well as learning to trust in the simple act of paying attention. The question helps to encourage this attentiveness. It is not a matter of looking for an answer in the normal way; it is simply questioning in order to develop more confidence in your own receptivity, in your own awakenedness.

This awakenedness is natural; it is not a condition you create through meditation practice. It is a natural state of *being* and sustains itself as you begin to trust in it. That is why I keep reiterating this word 'trust'. Your thinking mind endlessly creates doubts about it. At least mine used to. I would think, 'It couldn't be this simple! It takes years for even meditation masters to get enlightened, and is said to be rare for anyone.' You read the scriptural accounts and dhamma books and think, 'I don't imagine anyone like *me* could ever do that.' You hear about the miraculous side of it, the great teachers that read minds and levitate. I know I will *never* be able to do that — would like to, though!

Recognize the limitation even of the convention we are using — the scriptures and commentaries, and the words of the great teachers. These are often taken out of context, anyway. Ajahn Maha Boowa wrote a biography about Ajahn Mun that makes him sound like superman. It is a very entertaining book and you cannot help but be impressed, but when you talk to disciples of Ajahn Mun, they say, 'Oh, that stuff doesn't matter. Just forget it! Ajahn Mun taught about waking up, being aware.' The other stuff is impressive and entertaining, and may inspire you, but recognize its limitation and trust in your intuitive sense. What is important? For you to communicate with all the realms in the universe and talk to the *devas* in the heavenly realms, be connected psychically to the arahants in the Himalayas, or be awake and aware in this moment, in this mundane, sitting, standing, walking, lying down, moment where you are washing the dishes or vacuuming the carpet? When I reflect in this way, I recognize that awareness is more important than trying to make myself into an extraordinary super-magician. I realize that that is not worth trying for; it is not what I want.

Test it out! See for yourself through your own intuitive intelligence. There is suffering *(dukkha)* and there is non-suffering. By just taking those two, by just exploring the unsatisfactoriness, you can make a point of becoming aware of, say, waking up in the morning and feeling a sense of dreariness or even a dread. Maybe there is something in the day you don't particularly want to face. Maybe there is a feeling of restlessness, of wanting something to do, of loneliness, of wanting somebody to talk to, of wanting some distraction. Things like this are just ordinary in anybody's life, and the awareness allows us to observe this, to know it is 'like this'.

The more I trust in awareness, the more my relationship to the conditions that arise in my mind change. Instead of being pulled into conditions or trying to suppress them or get rid of them, I acknowledge them, recognize them, and don't make a problem about them. That leads much more to a sense of being content and peaceful with life. I don't feel, 'Oh, there's so much I have to do!' We create problems for ourselves when we say, 'I've got an anger problem; I suffer from jealousy; I have a lot of fear; I carry resentments.' We assume from these identities that we shouldn't have the feelings. We think, 'I shouldn't be an angry person; I've got to do something about it. But if we listen to it, rather than just believe it, do we find that 'that which is aware of anger' is angry? Assuming you are really angry right now, *really* angry, and you are aware that there is anger, is the awareness angry? The anger is what you are feeling — it's 'like this' — but your awareness, is that angry?

That is the way I investigate that particular experience. And the more I investigate it, the more I see that awareness is not angry. Awareness is aware of anger but is not itself anger. I trust in the awareness more and more; I rest in it rather than make a problem about feeling angry. If I take it personally, then I start thinking, 'A good monk shouldn't be like this. I should have loving-kindness *(mettā)* for people.' And then somebody does something that makes me really angry and I try to have *mettā* for him. 'That's what I should do,' I tell myself, 'I should forgive him.' The point is, I know what I *should* do, but really I am very angry and I have absolutely no *mettā* for that person. I would actually like to punch that person on the nose! But that which is aware of the anger, is that anger? is that greed? is that frightened or confused?

As you question, just trust more and more in the awareness. This is an intuitive practice. This is where you have to trust yourself. You are the one that has to do this; nobody can do it for you. Don't be frightened of trusting yourself. Don't trust your opinions and views. Don't trust your views about Buddhism or Christianity or anything. I don't trust any of those things. I can still have viewpoints and opinions, but I don't trust them. That is not where my refuge is. I do, however, trust this awareness.

As you keep developing this, it gets stronger through your life experiences. This is not just an airy-fairy kind of idealism; it is something that, as you grow older, gives you increasingly more strength in dealing with the problems of this realm, in living in a human body in society. 'This' is the way it is. It isn't 'what it should be', but it is just the way it is. Notice that! At various fleeting moments, you might have the sense that life is just as it *should* be, but you can't sustain that.

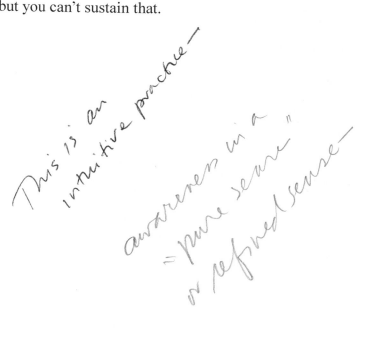

Dhamma is not an Ideal

I use this word 'reflection' a lot to imply the ability to observe and witness the way it is. It is not intended to mean analysing or wondering whether the way it is, is the way it *should* be, or whether one can make it better, or should keep it the same; it is rather a receptivity of the present as experience — simply because that is all there ever is! Experience is now.

You can imagine the experiences you may have when you go on holiday to Ibiza or somewhere. You can fantasize about future experience. But actual experience is always *now*, so you can reflect on now. Most people, however, don't do that; most people operate by either planning or doing something to attain a hoped-for result in the future. Society tends to perpetuate the idea that you work hard while you are young, save your money and then retire to enjoy yourself when you are old. The sense of 'now' in that case can be completely dismissed as unimportant, because the future — especially when you are young — holds the promise of success, wealth, fame, comfort, ease, and all the rest. The future has infinite possibilities and potential, but 'now' can only be the way it is. 'This' is the way it is right now. The same with the past. Past experience is a memory in the present, but you can kind of live in the past — in 'the golden age' or 'the good old days' — or carry resentments from being abused or misunderstood in the past. And if you have had a lot of negative experience in your life, you might see the future as the potential for more pain, more misery and more humiliation. Actually, though, all of it is always in the present. Whether you are remembering the past, hoping for success in the future or dreading the future, it is all happening right now. So, this is a reflection on how we perceive time as reality.

In Buddhism, there is this emphasis on mindfulness *(sati)*. And the thing that is very obvious in the present is this physical body. Wherever I am, this body goes with me, so it is always here and now. The physical body is an object I can actually refer to. It grounds me, in a way, because it is a heavy condition. It has more solidity to it than emotion, thought or feeling, so it seems much more like 'me', like 'mine'. But we might not like our bodies very much because they are coarse. Civilization — especially European civilization — has made a desperate attempt to ignore the body and live in an ethereal world of ideals. And when the body behaves itself, we can spend time in refined mental states. But when the needs of the body predominate, we have to deal with them. These things are natural, of course, and we are used to them, but still, the ego doesn't want to be identified with the coarser aspects of the physical body, especially in old age, sickness and death. Sickness is a humiliation, isn't it? When we lose control of our bodily functions, it can be humiliating — particularly if we think of ourselves as being finer than the coarse aspects of the body. Notice how much emphasis modern society places on glamour, fitness and fashion. We would like to be identified with beauty and youth, and wearing fashionable clothes. Covering up the body with beautiful textiles can give us this sense of being attractive and desirable.

In the present moment, however, the body is the way it is; we might be sick or in perfect health, young or old, or whatever. It isn't that there is any way the body *should* be. The point is to see that it is 'like this'. The body then is a kind of grounding mechanism for paying attention — not through vanity, not through comparing oneself with ideal, beautiful examples of men and women — but just through experiencing it in the present. In Buddhist meditation therefore we use the four postures (sitting, standing, walking, and lying down) as a way of grounding ourselves in the here and now. At this moment the sitting posture is 'like this'.

Now, we might idealize sitting perfectly; we might see pictures of yogis in the full lotus posture or impressive meditators sitting in zendos, and then try to emulate not only a way of sitting but also a particular way of standing, walking and lying down. This is one of the problems in monasteries — monks trying to act like yogis and forcing their bodies into what they think are perfect postures. Sometimes they ruin their backs and knees as a result. And sitting meditation has become an obsession with Buddhists in the West. We talk about 'sitting', and everybody knows 'we've sat!' 'How many hours have you sat? I have sat for three hours today.' Anyone who didn't know would regard that as a very strange thing to be talking about.

Reflecting on this, one recognizes that there *is* an ideal posture and it is to be accepted and appreciated. The way it is, however, is 'like this'. If you are causing stress to the body by trying to achieve some ideal, then reflect on what is actually happening — that trying to make your body live up to an ideal is also 'like this'. This is not a criticism, but a recognition. You begin to recognize what is happening rather than just operating from ideas acquired from teachers or books or whatever; you begin to develop an inner sense of trusting in your own intuitive awareness, realizing that what you are actually doing is adopting some ideal and trying to make yourself fit into it. This is why I emphasize learning to trust intuitive awareness. If we try to force the body into a kind of rigidity, we can see that maybe this is not what is meant. So we begin to recognize what is happening and to see that we are coming from a very wilful place; we are thinking of meditation as something we always have to do and gain from, and make ourselves, and force the body, and force the mind. So we recognize the suffering in that. Even though it is very good to meditate and be mindful and to practise the various meditation techniques — nothing against any of that — but it is worth asking ourselves whether we are relating to meditation through awareness (*satipañña*) or through clinging to views and opinions about it.

We might give a lot of importance to scriptural teachings and to what teachers say. If someone has a big title like 'meditation master', 'roshi', or 'guru', it can increase the sense of 'that person knows and I don't'. The point for us, however, is to be aware of that sense, to be aware of how we relate to the teachers that we incline towards. The emphasis then is on trusting intuitive awareness. When I look at the reality of this moment — just here and now in this room — the body is sitting here at this point, and I can be aware of what is going on in this formation; I can be aware of my feelings and physical sensations. But what is going on in *your* mind? I don't know, really. I can guess, maybe, through body language or facial expression. If somebody is looking really desperate I can kind of wonder . . ! But what you are actually feeling, what you are actually experiencing, I cannot be aware of; I cannot be aware of what you are experiencing as the reality of this moment, as direct experience. I can, however, be aware of this fact and recognize the limitation I am under.

I learn from this point here — this point of consciousness — rather than from external sources, rather than from thinking somebody else knows me better than I know myself or that what is written in the scriptures is infallible, that there can never be any mistakes or anything wrong with the scriptural teachings. I learn from this point of consciousness rather than from giving power to teachers and gurus 'who are enlightened and so must know everything and can never make any mistakes and can never be wrong'. Most of us have seen this happen and have ourselves, maybe, projected our hopes onto books or traditions or teachers — because we don't trust ourselves. We come from this position of 'I am a confused, screwed up character and really need to get my act together. I need to meditate more. Maybe I need to become a monk or nun and work on myself so that I become enlightened in the future,' and we go on and on like this.

Getting behind that basic assumption is what I am encouraging now. I have seen for many years how Westerners meditate, how many of them never get behind the basic delusion, the premise

'I am screwed up and need to practise meditation in order to become enlightened'. Sometimes that can lead to, 'I'm *not* screwed up any more. I'm enlightened now! I'm perfect the way I am.' But that is equally ridiculous, isn't it? It isn't a matter of trying to define ourselves through either negative or positive adjectives, but of recognizing, reflecting, on what is *actually* happening. The 'I am screwed up' is something created in the present; it is an assumption we take for granted and never question. We might actually *seem* screwed up. Maybe we have crazy thoughts or are over-emotional and feel insecure. Maybe we have neurotic fears, fantasies and desires, and then judge ourselves accordingly: 'I shouldn't feel like this! I shouldn't think like this! I shouldn't be this kind of person!'

When you reflect on that kind of thing, the conundrum (or *koan*) would be: 'That which is aware of "I am screwed up"— is that screwed up?' This is where you have to stop thinking about it and trust in the intuitive sense, because now you are learning to take refuge in intuitive wisdom or awareness rather than in ideas about yourself, about Buddhism, about what you should or shouldn't be, or should or shouldn't do.

So lack of self-worth, it seems, is a cultural problem for Westerners. I used to think it was a personal one, but after all these years I see that many people have the problem in one degree or another. So now I think that maybe it is cultural; maybe we are brought up in a culture that basically gives that sense of not being good enough the way we are and need to do better. What we want to blame it on, though, doesn't make much difference. The point is to recognize that which is *aware* of the lack of self-worth. If we reflect on this, we might begin to notice the sense that we are not very good — 'worthless in fact and all screwed up' — but then allow that feeling to become more consciously accepted. Or we might just operate from, 'Well, get on with life! Stiff upper lip! Make the best of a bad deal!' and have all kinds of ways of never really recognizing it as delusion. So we can meditate for years with these delusions; and then through willpower and discipline and so forth get the illusion that we are getting better —'I'm much better than I used to be! And that is through hard work, discipline, sitting for three hours at a time, going on retreats, giving up sensual pleasures, controlling my speech,' and on and on like this. But that is all still delusion.

I encourage you therefore to trust in the awareness of the present and to carry it through by working at it, by really questioning. When you start thinking about yourself, feeling you are worthless, not good enough, unlovable, stupid, silly or foolish, notice that that is a mental state you are creating and then notice simply that it is 'like this'. But then question: 'That which is aware — is that foolish, screwed up and neurotic? Or is the feeling "I'm neurotic" just a feeling I have in the present?'

This is inevitably frustrating because we would like to have an identity. One reason we give our authority to others is because we feel that they are qualified. Psychiatrists, doctors, teachers and so forth are trained and have experience — 'They know, and I'm just somebody who doesn't know. I don't know myself. I feel confused, anguished, depressed, and therefore somebody else knows what I should do.' It is not even that that is wrong. Sometimes psychiatrists, doctors, gurus and people like that really can help us. But if we think it is through somebody else's endeavours that we become enlightened, then of course we are going to end up very disappointed — because that is an impossibility.

Notice that the Buddha's teaching is always about the here and now. Mindfulness is now, enlightenment is now, awakenedness is now, the deathless is now. If, on the other hand, you create yourself into the now all the time as a person with qualities and characteristics and never question that, then of course you are deluded and endlessly fumbling around with the delusions you create. If you begin to trust in your awareness, however, you will see emotional confusion, feelings of inadequacy and worthlessness — it isn't a question of denying those things — but you will no longer identify or attach to them; you will rather recognize that it is 'like this'. As you allow things into your consciousness without comment, without making any problem about them, then you realize 'it is the way it is'. Then see what happens. In the awareness of inadequacy, for example, you are actually letting it go, you are allowing something that arises to cease, you are practising according to the law of dhamma — 'what arises ceases'. Confusion, feelings of inadequacy, the sense of 'me as a personality' — they are not self.

What are you really, then? What is your personality? I might assume I have the same personality all the time. When I am asleep I am Ajahn Sumedho, when I am with the monks I am Ajahn Sumedho, when I am with relatives, friends, enemies or whoever, I am the same person experiencing it. If you notice, however, the personality adapts to conditions and habit-tendencies. It is therefore conditioned and dependent on many factors; it is dependent on whether you are happy, sad, elated, depressed, bored, feeling good about yourself, feeling horrible about yourself, or whatever. In awakening to the present, you recognize that the conditions are 'like this'. If you have to attend a committee meeting in which you know there is going to be a lot of acrimony, in which you know difficult issues are going to be discussed and you are one of them, you notice that your personality changes. You would not be the same person under those circumstances as you would be if you were being presented, say, with the Nobel Peace prize. And when you go home to see your parents, that too is different.

My parents died many years ago, but I remember going to see them in America when I was fifty-five years old. To them of course I wasn't Ajahn Sumedho or anything like that, but just their little boy. Pretty soon the old ways of relating to each other started up again, and I found it really strange; it really affected me. Try to notice those kinds of relationships, the assumptions that go with father-son, mother-son, mother-daughter and so forth, just the assumptions and habit-tendencies that we have personally and emotionally. You could say that your parents shouldn't treat you the way they do, that they should accept you as an equal adult. But that would be a *should* of life; it would be an ideal. The way it actually is, is 'like this'. By allowing experiences to be consciously accepted, you realize that even if your parents can't change, at least you can; you can change your attitude and not get caught up in adolescent resentments that arise — when you are fifty-five years old!

To think 'I am screwed up', is a value judgement, isn't it? 'Screwed up' makes the 'I am'. It is identifying with a certain kind of condition, a feeling about oneself personally. If we leave off the 'screwed up' bit, we get more to the reality of the moment — 'Right now I am' — and there is this sense of being here and now. This is a recognition of conscious experience as an entity. There is an entity but it is not personal any more; it is not 'I am Ajahn Sumedho' or 'I am' anything at all; it is just this sense of 'I am', of presence. Being a conscious entity is — 'like this'. Reflect on that and sustain it for a while, that sense of 'I am', without adding any personal conditions to it.

In this sense of 'I am', the body is 'like this'. There is consciousness, there is the breath (one can be aware of just the breathing of the body, *ānāpānasati*[15]), there is the 'sound of silence', the ostinato, the background. And in this intuitive moment, one observes without adding any kind of personal quality. The breathing does not convey a high sense of personal attainment, achievement or identity. When you reflect on the body as experience right now, it is not like looking into a mirror and deciding whether there are a few more lines on your face or whether your nose is too big; the appearance isn't important. You are aware of just the experience of a physical body that is a conscious being, and holding that; you are able to reflect on the reality of it. And as you do so, you may become more aware of tensions in the body — the way your shoulders are or your spine, the pressure of the body sitting on a mat, or sensations of itching that come along — and you realize they are 'like this'. In terms of basic meditation, the awareness of your posture and breath, and maybe the 'sound of

15 *Ānāpānasati:* mindfulness on in-breathing and out-breathing.

silence', are ways of bringing you into the present moment where you are not trying to get anything, not trying to achieve or attain anything, not operating from some idea of 'if I do this practice, I will get enlightened in the future'; you are rather learning to centre yourself, to open to the present through these very grounding experiences, before they get into highly personal conditions like emotions. If you ground yourself in this way, then emotional states will come up — lack of self-worth, doubt, despair, anger, greed, and all the rest — but you will recognize that body, feelings, mind, and mind-objects (in terms of the Four Foundations of Mindfulness, *satipaṭṭhāna*[16]) simply arise and cease.

Try to have a permanent emotion. Depression seems permanent while you are in it, and the biggest fear is that you will never get out of it again — 'I'm in hell forever, an eternal hell!' That is the way it seems. But as you relate to feelings of depression or worthlessness, despair or negative states of mind in this other way, you will recognize that they are the way they are. And you will allow them to become conscious by no longer resisting these things, by no longer trying to analyse them, criticize them or distract yourself from them. You begin to recognize impermanence and to allow any condition to be what it is.

Now, you cannot do that if you are taking it personally. Just speaking for myself, my personality is based on the idea that I shouldn't be depressed — 'A healthy man is not depressed. I should be a good monk. I should be the ideal. I should be full of compassion and loving-kindness. I shouldn't feel mean or resentful.' The personality is always coming out with that kind of thing. The superego loves to tell you what you *should* or *shouldn't* be. We have these monastic reflections about loving all sentient beings and being totally selfless, and about respecting the offerings given by others (because we are alms mendicants and reflect from the position of the ideal monk). But Western monks and nuns, I have noticed, get into feeling guilty from these monastic

16 *Satipaṭṭhāna:* the four foundations of mindfulness: contemplation of body, feeling, mind, and mind-objects.

reflections. One reflection is: 'I am dependent on the gifts of others. Am I worthy of these offerings?' The Western personality will say, 'I don't think I am worthy.' The truth is, they might not really like what somebody is offering them and then feel guilty about it — 'I should be grateful for these generous offerings!' But actually they don't like them at all and then feel unworthy. That is the personality, isn't it?

Monastic or religious conventions often come from the ideal position, which is fair enough — not to say there is anything wrong with that — but how do we relate to this idealism? On a personal level we can feel intimidated by it, and that can make us feel even more worthless than we did before, because we *should* be compassionate and yet right now we are not feeling anything near that. But reflection is non-judgemental, so if I am feeling petty and mean, and relate to that through awareness, then it is seen to be 'like this'. Feeling ungrateful, resentful, mean and nasty, is 'like this'. It is a question of just allowing it to be the way it is without taking it personally any more. This is putting it into the context of 'the way it is' rather than seeing it as some personal flaw, some personal defect.

This is not playing games with the mind; it isn't trying to say it is something that it isn't, but is directly looking at the way it is in an uncritical way. Awareness is not a critical function; it doesn't tell you how it *should* be; it just allows you to see that it is 'like this'. Dhamma reflections on impermanence, unsatisfactoriness, and non-self are ways of helping you look at things in an objective way. If feeling mean and nasty is the way it is right now, then it is 'like this'. When you accept something, you can observe it and allow it to be, so that you can see its changingness; its impermanence becomes obvious. If, on other hand, you just try to get rid of what you are experiencing, you can't see its impermanence; there is instead a resistance to it which makes it seem as though it is a permanent problem and really is yours. Then you don't accept it; you fight against it and make it into even more of a problem.

This is where trust comes in. It takes a high degree of trust and faith to allow something that you are frightened of or don't like to become fully conscious. The tendency is to react to things like that, push them away, deny them, distract yourself from them, or get stuck in despair. I encourage you to really investigate this. In the Buddhist teachings terms like 'investigate' are used or 'look into the heart of the matter' or 'get to the source'. So I encourage you to get behind the condition that exists in the present. Right now our bodies exist in the present; they are 'like this'.

Reflecting on the experience of the physical body, changes our relationship to it, doesn't it? We usually think the mind is inside the brain — the mind is in the brain and the brain is in the head — so we assume the mind is up here. And we make the further assumption that consciousness is also in the brain. Yet we can be aware of the body as experience without assuming that the brain is aware of the body as experience. We can merely be aware of the body as experience. We then see that the body is contained in consciousness rather than consciousness being something that comes out of the brain. It is as though we are beginning to change from identifying with a little bit of physical anatomy to a more expansive perspective of seeing that the body is in consciousness.

Because I am aware of my body as experience, I cannot see my face. Douglas Harding[17] some of you will remember used to talk about having no head. I cannot see my own eyes. You can see my face and eyes, but I can't. That is the way it is. I can look at a photograph of myself or look into the mirror and get a sense of what I look like. But at this moment I cannot actually see my own face. And yet it is right here. I can see *your* faces. Now, these are just simple ways of examining experience, and they can help us break down a lot of the assumptions we make. 'I am my face' is a very strong assumption, a very strong identity, but just notice that consciousness is 'like this'. Consciousness is

---

17 *On Having No Head: Zen and the Rediscovery of the Obvious*, Douglas E. Harding, Inner Directions Foundation (2002).

not a personal thing; it is universal. We create personality into consciousness. When we are aware, however, we are not creating anything. When we are really conscious and aware, there is no personality. There is no personal thing involved unless I start identifying with it — 'I am conscious and aware. I'm a mindful monk.' Then I am creating some kind of identity into consciousness. As experience right now in the present, conscious awareness is 'like this'. Really notice this. It is alert, intelligent, here and now. But then I can create myself into 'I'm Ajahn Sumedho. I'm screwed up,' and on and on like that. I can create the whole world into consciousness.

As you investigate and explore consciousness, you begin to realize how it actually is. This helps in solving all kinds of problems — personal, societal, communal, family. So many problems arise around views and opinions, identities, the ideals we have of how things *should* be, or how things should *not* be, and so on. I think idealistic people have a terrible time living with each other, actually, because they are always coming from the top. I remember falling down as a child and skinning my knee, and then wondering why God created pain. I thought, 'If I were God, I would never create pain.' And I imagined what *should* be according to the ideal of being happy, of being without any unhappiness, of having the best without having to deal with anything less — idealism carried to absurdity. But dhamma is not an ideal, is it? It is the way it is.

There is a relentless, inexorable change going on, and there is nothing that can save you on a conditioned level. There is always this *dukkha*, this sense of unsatisfactoriness. Money, worldly achievements, prestige, whatever, are all going to fail you as refuges. There is nothing you can hold onto in this realm of conditionality that is satisfying. It may be temporarily gratifying, but that is the best you can say about it. This is not a teaching — I am not saying you should grasp this as a teaching — it is a reflection. Can you find permanent satisfaction through grasping the conditioned realm? This is something to investigate. Is it possible to find permanent satisfaction through grasping at an identity with your body, with your emotions, with your ideals? Can you find a place in the world where you are permanently happy, where there is no suffering? This is self-inquiry. You are looking into whether these things are possible.

Sometimes people say, 'Buddhists teach that everything is suffering and everything is impermanent. And they believe in *nibbāna* which is extinction. And it all sounds nihilistic.' Well, some Buddhists might actually believe in that kind of thing, but that is not the point of the teaching. This teaching is not for grasping; it is for exploring. And this exploration is up to each of us; it is something we can do and no one else can make us do. Whether we do it or not, of course, is up to us.

My experience is that as one becomes more confident in this practice, the subtleties start to come up. One becomes kind of world-weary. You go through a stage where you just look at this world and think it's crazy! 'I'm living in a madhouse! Society is nuts!' And it is, actually. But if you attach to this view, you get a feeling of weariness and a kind of longing to die, 'Oh, I've had enough!' And then something happens — another issue, another rotten meeting in the monastery — and you think, 'No! Not this again! Don't they ever learn? Do we have to go through this again?' And the mind starts complaining. This is where you have to keep with the present moment. If you attach to world-weariness, you attach to just another thing. It is quite a challenge to keep with the present moment; it isn't easy.

Many of us want to get enlightened and live happily ever after. We want to have the big moment so that everything will be plain sailing after that and we will perpetually live in this blissful state of moronic happiness. This is a kind of ideal. According to the Pali scriptures, however, this didn't even happen to the Buddha. Apparently all sorts of things happened to the Buddha after his enlightenment. People tried to murder him, scandalize him, abuse him. There is a story, in fact, about some monks being so difficult and such a problem to him that one day he told

them he'd had enough, and then went off to spend the rainy season with an elephant and a monkey. Elephants and monkeys are
probably easier to live with, actually! So, according to the scriptures, even the Buddha got pretty fed up with the world he lived
in. The point is not to attach to things. As much as we get weary
and fed up, the challenge always is not to attach to feelings. Recognize and accept that it is 'like this', but do that without holding
or grasping anything. Actually, there is something in me that
in a perverse sort of way likes to hold onto world-weariness. I
quite enjoy it, you know, thinking I've had enough, or that it is
another one of those meetings where issues are brought up, and
the grumbling mind takes over. I quite enjoy that, actually. The
point is to see through the grasping of it.

But sometimes it seems as though I am becoming incredibly
simple-minded rather than any kind of wise sage!

Disruption Belongs

I try to encourage this sense of trusting in the ability to reflect, the ability to bring into consciousness the way it is. This is not taking a position on any issue or any particular Buddhist doctrinal teaching, because that would be starting from something acquired. We read Buddhist literature, Buddhist scriptures, and tend to grasp ideas without knowing what we are doing; we tend to believe in doctrines and have faith or trust in them. But teachings, teachers and traditions at this moment are just objects to us. We are not born as Theravadan Buddhists with Buddhist ideas, principles or views. These are all acquired later. And most of us here have moved towards Buddhism out of choice. Something in us was attracted to the teachings of the Buddha which somehow resonated with us. The point, then, is to take the Buddha's teachings and use them to reflect on in terms of our own experience.

The first Noble Truth — 'there is suffering *(dukkha)*' — is not a doctrine that we are expected to believe in; it is simply pointing to a reality that we all experience. So it is a matter of noticing suffering, dissatisfaction, discontent, and relatively innocuous forms of suffering that we experience all the time. I find, for example, that self-consciousness is *dukkha*. The point, then, is to notice that. Much of the emphasis in my monastic life has been on formal meditation, and there was a lot of suffering at first for me when I tried to practise. It wasn't that there was any social pressure, and the conditions were tranquil enough, but there was pain in my knees from sitting cross-legged, frustrations of the mind, and obsessive thoughts and emotions. So even though I was in a serene and tranquil situation, when I reflected on these things, I saw the suffering *(dukkha)*. It wasn't a question of trying to convince myself of anything, but of just reflecting that *dukkha* is 'like this'.

This word *'dukkha'* — as John Peacock was saying yesterday — is not adequately translated as 'suffering', but I think it is good enough, actually. It gets the idea across. You don't have to be all that precise with terminology when you are looking at the reality. You might not have experienced any great crisis, tragedy or terrible thing that has shattered your life, but still there might be a general feeling of unease. Being critical of yourself is *dukkha*, isn't it? When you really look at self-disparagement and the feeling 'I'm not good enough the way I am', you can see that even that is *dukkha*. Maybe you are not aware of doing it, maybe it is just a kind of habit in the background that influences you unintentionally, unconsciously, but what is this sense of not being good enough or not being as good as somebody else? By reflecting on these things, you begin to notice feelings of inadequacy — not as something that you should not be feeling or as some kind of personal fault (another fault you need to get rid of!) — but that they are 'like this'. You might also notice subtle emotional habits — dread or a sense of loneliness, or feeling ill at ease — and that they are felt in the body, maybe in the abdomen or heart.

When we first start learning how to meditate, we are usually encouraged to practise some kind of tranquillity meditation — a practice to calm the mind, to tranquillize, to bring peaceful mental states — such as mindfulness of the breath. If we concentrate on the movement of breathing and learn to sustain our attention on it over a period of time, we feel a sense of calm, because there is nothing in the breath to stir up emotion. And the more concentrated we become, the finer the breath becomes, until it almost seems to disappear. It can become so calm, in fact, that we might think we have stopped breathing.

I have been through various techniques (there are all kinds) — mantra, mindfulness of breathing, tranquillity *(samatha)* practices, and so on — and I think now that what people generally regard as meditation is simply being successful at calming themselves down and going into a state of tranquil concentration. Now, if you have been meditating for as long as I have, you find that it is quite easy to do this. It wasn't easy in the beginning, but I gradually acquired a kind of skill at it. If I turn round now and look at the shrine, at this Buddha-image, and if there are no loud noises or irritating things impinging on me, I can become very tranquil. Then I turn round again, and there you are — and now the conditions are different, aren't they? Looking at you is different from looking at the Buddha-*rūpa*. The point to notice is the difference. Buddha-*rūpas*, to me (I have been looking at them for many years) are usually calming images; they are icons that convey this message of tranquillity and peace.

It is very pleasant, actually, living in a monastery where there are lots of Buddha-images. These are not passionate figures reminding one of greed, hatred and delusion; there is usually a sense of poised calm and awakened serenity about them — something we all long for. If we get into the aesthetics of Buddha-*rūpas*, of course, we might find we don't particularly like some of them and sit looking at them critically. And then we don't achieve tranquillity! If we are too concerned about the aesthetics of Buddha-*rūpas*, we simply miss the point. Some are obviously more beautiful than others, of course. The ones found recently in China, for instance, are all very lovely figures that please the eye[18]. And it does help to have something aesthetically pleasing to look at that doesn't bring up negative or critical mental states. So it is a question of just noticing the way it is and how we relate to things and people.

When we eat our meal at Amaravati two rows of monks sit facing each other and I sit at one end facing down the middle of them. A few years ago, the monk sitting on one side of me was always fidgeting and was basically a nervous wreck, and

18 Discovered in 1996 and exhibited at the Royal Academy of Arts in London in 2002 (Return of the Buddha: The Qingzhou Discoveries).

the one on the other side was depressed. And the messages they were giving off, I noticed, did affect me. It isn't that things like that have no effect on one's consciousness. Incidentally, the two monks that occupy those positions now are very serene, so it is quite enjoyable looking at them. Aesthetically it is pleasing to see happy faces and serene expressions. This is just the way it is. I don't consider this to be a personal flaw in my character in finding that. It is just obvious that the things around us affect us.

This morning after the meditation I walked into the lounge and saw Maxine reading a newspaper. She said she didn't usually read newspapers because of how they made her feel. And I agree. When you read newspapers you are generally absorbing dismal information, and it does affect your consciousness. If all the horrors, scandals and corruptions of the world are put into your mind, it does have an effect in the moment. That is just an observation, a reflection. So, if you read gossip and bad news, you get a kind of negative feeling — just by thinking about the horrible things that are happening in the world. Nevertheless, you can still reflect on the fact that it is 'like this'. By being aware of it in this way, you then cease to resent the world for not always looking like a Buddha-*rūpa* or being a serene paradise where everything is pleasing — because that is *not* the way it is. Much of the world is unpleasing; many things we experience are upsetting or depressing or unpleasant.

Now, it is possible to become a retreat junkie, an obsessed meditator with a 'leave me alone' kind of attitude. 'I don't want to know. I don't want to participate in the world because it just upsets me too much!' If you are too attached to tranquillity, you become a control freak; you have to control everything around you. The ability to reflect, of course, brings you into the present. Through trusting in awareness, then, you begin to recognize a state of peace that is with you all the time, that is not dependent on lack of impingement or sensory deprivation. You then see the dhamma; you get in touch with what you might call your 'true nature' or the 'Buddha-nature' — that which most people are not really aware of. You might also experience moments like this through sensory deprivation, of course. And it is possible to experience a sense of oneness, peace and calm, and identify it with a meditation technique you are practising, or a particular environment, or with lack of coarse impingement. If you think you can only have a sense of oneness through depriving your senses of harsh impingement, however, you will grasp the desire to control things; you will try to avoid anything harsh or unpleasant. That is the logic of it.

As you develop more insight and wisdom, however, you begin to recognize that whether you turn to face the shrine or remain facing the people, it doesn't really matter, because the dhamma — that sense of peace and calm — is something that is always here — once you begin to recognize it! And nothing — no matter how harsh or horrible — can destroy that; it is always here. This is not something you create through tranquillizing your mind or through any technique, but is a reality you tend to overlook when you are caught up in reacting too strongly to sensory impingement, or liking or not liking the things that you are experiencing.

There are different ways of talking about this, of course, different terms that people use. Some like to refer to 'the Buddha-mind' or 'Buddha-nature'. In the Theravada they don't use words like that. So being a Theravadan Buddhist, if I use such language, I get this feeling . . ! But, you know, it's good enough, actually — even though I *am* programmed by the Theravada school. Last night somebody asked, 'Can you see the mind? Can you see the Buddha-nature? What is the Buddha-nature? Where is the Buddha-nature mentioned in the Pali Canon?' Well, there is no such thing as 'Buddha-nature' in the Pali Canon, but to think we can't possibly allow that kind of terminology is like doctrinal dictatorship. The point is to realize or recognize the reality rather than to hold to 'if there is Buddha-nature, where is it?' Then someone might say, 'Well, you know, it's — in your heart!' And then you think, 'In my heart?' But irrespective of whether this is orthodox or not, you might still find it a useful term for directing your attention towards recognizing inner peace, non-attachment, cessation, *nibbāna*. That is the point. You have to trust in your own recognition of it. This is not something you create; it isn't as if you are trying to create the Buddha-nature or peacefulness and get *samādhi*, and get this, get that, and get rid of your defilements. That would be to miss the point and be caught up in trying to achieve, attain, become, or get rid of.

It is very clearly stated in the teaching of the Four Noble Truths that the cause of suffering *(dukkha)* is attachment to desire. Even the desire to become tranquil is a cause of suffering. If you desire tranquillity and get it, it might last for a while, but then it goes again. And if you are attached to that tranquillity, you feel the sense of loss. You might think you have acquired something through a controlled situation, but then you go back into London, back to the office and '. . can't meditate here! Too much stress. Too many difficult people. Too much noise.' You then decide that the marketplace is not where you can find peace, because that is the way it seems — 'No Buddha-nature in the middle of London. Amaravati is where it's at. There's plenty of it there.'

We tend to empower words, but the more we are aware, the more we realize that words are things to be used rather to be grasped as though they are somehow the most important thing — like the term 'Buddha-nature' for example. Is that important or not? It is two words — 'Buddha' and 'nature'. Is that orthodox Theravada? We can get into this question of whether it is orthodox Theravada or not. Or maybe it is kind of inclining towards Mahayana? We empower words like 'Mahayana' and 'Theravada'; but these too are just words, just concepts. 'Buddhism', 'Buddha' — these are things we create in the mind and then interpret them. If we are biased, we could think that all forms of Buddhism except orthodox Theravada is somehow not quite right, not the real teaching, heretical. We could put it in terms of 'heretical' and completely dismiss it. I have known Buddhist monks totally dismiss Mahayana — even though they don't know anything about it! — because they heard it wasn't ortho-dox, it wasn't the real teaching. But that is adopting the biases and prejudices that go with any convention. Whatever we incline towards, we tend to grasp. And then those things that don't align well within that structure, we dismiss. If we are orthodox Thera-vadans, we can be aware of how threatened we feel by Mahaya-na terminologies.

A few years ago there was a controversy going on amongst the Western monks here in Europe and in Australia and Thailand on whether Dependent Origination *(paṭiccasamuppāda)* was about one moment or three lifetimes. Some monks get pretty heated on this issue. If you are a person who sees things intellectually, the 'three lifetimes' interpretation seems safer than the 'one mo-ment' interpretation. Now, my inclination is more towards the intuitive so 'the moment' is what I incline towards, because the 'three lifetimes' thing seems rather pointless in terms of practi-cal use. It is too fatalistic and logical as far as I am concerned and doesn't seem to have any great importance at this moment in my life.

The formula of Dependent Origination begins 'ignorance conditions the *kamma*-formations'. Now, what is that? Professor Gombrich[19] in his talk was questioning why that sequence of 'through ignorance are conditioned the *kamma*-formations and through the *kamma*-formations is conditioned consciousness' *(avijjā-paccayā saṅkhārā, saṅkhāra-paccayā viññāṇaṁ)*, and whether it is a purely Buddhist thing, or stolen from the Hindus or Brahmins, or what? That can of course be historically inter-esting, but how do you use a teaching like Dependent Origina-tion in terms of reflective awareness? I find it more helpful to have a teaching that you can use in the moment rather than just as something you try to figure out intellectually.

At first probably most of us don't connect very well with the teaching of Dependent Origination. When I first came across it

---

19 Boden Professor of Sanskrit at the University of Oxford (1976-2004), Founder-President of the Oxford Centre for Buddhist Studies.

I wondered why there was that particular sequence of first ignorance, then the kamma-formations, then consciousness, then
mind and body, then the six bases, then feeling, and on and on.
How do they connect with each other? The point is, the intellect
is linear so you have to have one at a time — ignorance, kamma-
formations, consciousness — because that is the limitation of the
intellect. You cannot think 'ignorance' and 'kamma-formations'
at the same moment.

Recognize, then, that thinking is a limited function; it is linear
and dualistic. And as long as we hold onto thinking about and
analysing the Buddha's teachings, we will always be caught in
the assumptions we make from logic, reason and all the dualistic functions of the mind. In terms of ignorance or not knowing
the dhamma, you might think, 'Well, I know the Four Noble
Truths: *dukkha, samudaya, nirodha, magga* (suffering, the origin, the cessation, the path). But that is not knowing all about the
Buddhist teachings, is it? Knowing the dhamma is what? What
is that right now? If the dhamma is not a thought, some kind of
thing you can grasp, what is it? Show it to me. 'Dhamma' is just
a word, actually, but it is a word that includes the conditioned
and the unconditioned — everything. In that sense, then, it is
a matter of *knowing* the dhamma. If I don't know the dhamma,
then there is ignorance. Ignorance, to me, is being caught up
in my own views, opinions, identities, the sense of myself as a
permanent personality, thinking the material world is ultimate
reality, making assumptions, having prejudices and biases, and
emotional habits. If I am caught up in all that, then that is ignorance. And if I attach to ignorance, it affects everything else.

'*Sankhāra*' (kamma-formations) is another interesting word.
It is a term which includes all conditions. If I start with ignorance, I come from 'I'm a screwed up person', and the things
that come from that assumption will affect my consciousness.
So then I just automatically assume that I'm a screwed up person
and shouldn't be, that I've got to work on myself, meditate for
many hours, sit on a zafu and in some way or other unscrew the

screwed-up-ness. That gives me something to do as a person.

It is quite interesting to work on yourself, to come to terms with your own problems, to rectify your own faults, to get really interested in your own history or why you feel threatened by this or that, or why you feel insecure in particular social situations, and so on. One can get fascinated with oneself because the kamma-formations *are* interesting — actually. Well, some are and some aren't! So, inclining towards interesting kamma-formations, trying to live an interesting life — a life full of meaning and purpose, an exciting and fascinating life — is one way of doing it. When I was young this was what I wanted to do. I didn't want a boring old life like my mother and father. The last thing I wanted was to be a businessman and get married and buy a house and pay the mortgage. I wanted an *interesting* life. This was my goal when I was very young. No matter how interesting your life can get, however, you cannot sustain the interest. Interesting things are unsustainable, which is why you lose interest in them! So you have to keep looking for something else. But you cannot in a permanent way find anything that will keep your interest, so then there is restlessness and constant seeking.

Meditation is not interesting, is it? We might take an interest in it to begin with, but the direction of meditation is generally towards what we are not really interested in, like the breath or the experience of the body. I found that sort of thing really boring — 'Notice the sensation on the top of your head, and then notice the sensation . . .' so what! I was hoping to experience really interesting sensations in the body. But most of them were just irritating, like some itch or pain. The point is, you are directing your attention towards that which *is*; it is what it is, rather than it is interesting. So you are learning to pay attention, to focus, to sustain, to hold to something — not because it is interesting and holds your attention — but because you are willing to hold your attention to something uninteresting; you are beginning to develop a kind of inner strength, a sense of being able to concentrate on something you would not ordinarily bother to notice

— like the breath, the sensations of the body, the experience of sitting, standing, walking or lying down.

When it gets to the 'sound of silence', that is subtle, isn't it? Most people don't know what that is, or don't notice it. It is something that has a continuity to it which you could describe as a buzz, even an irritating buzz, in the ear. In some religious traditions, they make it into a kind of cosmic or primal sound, or Krishna's flute, or the Angelic Chorus. It becomes more interesting if you hype it up a bit, doesn't it? And that is fair enough if it helps you take an interest in it. The point is to learn to trust in awareness, to relax into life, in other words. And in order to do that we need to be relaxed and at ease with ourselves. If we try too hard to hear the 'sound of silence', for example, we are trying to find something we conceive, and that means we are not relaxing and not noticing it. What I am talking about is more a sense of relaxing into the present, a sense of relaxing the body, letting go of things, just letting go of all one's problems and personal difficulties, of not holding onto them or trying to fight against them but just relaxing with them, allowing this moment to be as it is. This way of awareness is a way of allowing life to flow through you rather than going into control mode and trying to get tranquillity through suppressing unpleasant, disruptive thoughts.

Meditation, then, is not paying attention in the sense of 'AT-TENTION!' like a military command; it is more like learning to be fully with the present. You don't have to pay attention to anything except this present moment, so there is this general sense of openness and receptivity rather than of striving to get things and controlling the mind. With mindfulness of breathing, for example, the point is to relax into the breath rather than 'PAY AT-TENTION TO YOUR BREATH! INHALATION! EXHALA-TION!' That is how I used to do it. I used to sit and just force my attention onto the inhalation and exhalation. That can be hard work and you always fail in the end because there is no sustaining anything very long with that kind of attitude. The attitude I am now encouraging is one of faith or trust, of being at ease and feeling safe.

In this position of being 'the meditation teacher', people sometimes project onto me this idea that I am judging them, and they don't feel safe around me. They think, 'Ajahn Sumedho's looking at me . . !' The situation brings up a kind of fear of being judged in some way. But recognize that meditation is not about making yourself live up to a high standard of physical conduct and practice in order to be a good meditator and please the master. If you see me as 'the meditation teacher', you can be aware of that, but then let go of the assumption that I am here to set you straight, to chastise you, to punish you when you are not doing it right or reward you when you are. Reward and punishment are part of our culture, aren't they? We are brought up on it; we are used to being rewarded for being good and punished for being bad; we are used to being rejected and looked down on if we are stupid and being raised up and praised if we are intelligent. This is a cultural acquisition, and we have to deal with it in our lives, so we also bring that into our meditation.

Relaxing, trusting and being open, is a way of moving away from ignorance. I am not asking you to believe this, but simply suggesting that 'right understanding' *(vijjā)* is not far away from you; it is not something that can only be achieved after many years of 'real meditation practice'. If you hold to the idea that really practising hard will bring you to right understanding and away from ignorance — 'I'll be wise rather than ignorant!' — then that is how you are going to interpret your experience. What I am encouraging you to do, however, is to recognize the attitudes that affect this present moment, the assumptions you make maybe about being an ignorant, unenlightened person who has to become an enlightened one. Not to say that you shouldn't think like that — there is no judgement in this — but I am suggesting you just notice the underlying attitude and assumption. So I am encouraging you to trust in that which is aware, the awareness — not what you are aware of, but the awareness itself — and be that awareness.

When people attend meditation retreats at Amaravati they take the Eight Precepts. Now, this in some ways establishes a zone of safety, a sense of how we are going to live together as a group during a ten-day retreat. People don't usually want to go on a meditation retreat in order to talk and socialize, to chit-chat and entertain each other. They are seeking encouragement to look inwards. So we keep the noble silence. This gives us a sense of not having to be at our best. In a social atmosphere you want to present a good face to the public and enjoy the social scene, but on a meditation retreat that is not expected. So, in a way that is a relief, isn't it? I find it quite nice to be in a group of people that you can just sit with and who in many ways support you without making any social demands. There is a sense of safety in that, a sense of being able to trust, and so one learns how to relax, to open, to receive, to be here and now — at least this is the constant kind of advice and instruction that is given.

How do you deal with the physical pain or emotional stress that comes during that time? It is not a question of fighting or killing the satanic forces, is it? It is more about learning to trust in your awareness and being able to let go of conditions. You are changing from that worldly attitude of wanting to control — wanting to get rid of the bad, wanting to kill off the pests, wanting to hold onto the good and to protect yourself from all the unsafe possibilities around you — to trusting in awareness.

I sometimes teach in Thailand, and it is interesting to see the difference between teaching there and in Britain. In a Buddhist country people already have a tremendous faith in Buddha-Dhamma-Sangha. They might not know anything about Buddhism *per se*. Their ideas might simply be about how their grandmothers take food to the monks on the full moon days and so on. But because Buddhism is part of Thai culture, they seem to have an intuitive sense of Buddha-Dhamma-Sangha and the moral precepts, and they have a lot of faith in the ajahns, the teachers. So when you talk to them about Buddha-Dhamma-Sangha, you don't have to define it very much; there is already a basic level of acceptance, receptivity, and trust.

In the West, on the other hand, where Buddhism is fairly new, that faith is not present. Here the cultural conditioning is more towards reward and punishment. So you all look at me and you don't know what I'm about. Maybe you have heard terrible stories about gurus that take advantage of their students. There is a lot of good gossip in the Buddhist world. The scandals can be big news, spicy, interesting and horrible. So, can you really trust me? Are you going to put yourself in my hands for ten days? If there is a level of suspicion and insecurity present, I encourage you to relax and simply pay attention to this sense of mistrust or suspicion. I don't ask you to have faith in me as your teacher, nor do I suggest that I am an impeccable monk who will never let you down, or that you shouldn't be suspicious of me because I have all the right credentials. That is not the point, is it? It is not a question of proving that I am trustworthy. And even if I am not, that wouldn't really be an obstruction to your meditation as long as you begin to trust yourself more. The point is not to ask me to be somebody who is never going to let you down or never going to make a mistake or misunderstand you; the point is to find a strength within yourself. This is not a matter of depending on a strong teacher or somebody outside to be impeccable and an example of a Buddhist success story. Being aware of your own fears, suspicions or aversions, is being aware. This is moving into understanding — it is 'like this'.

Ignorance affects the present moment. If I start with ignorance, if I am caught in feeling self-conscious and suspicious or frightened and try to suppress that, then ignorance affects my thoughts, emotions, physical body, the conditioned realm around me, and of course consciousness. So I encourage you to trust yourself to move more towards understanding, this sense of the dhamma, this taking refuge in the Buddha-Dhamma-Sangha. Experiment with it. Learn to relax. It is not a question of *trying* to relax. The idea of making yourself relax is ridiculous, isn't it? If you say to yourself 'RELAX!' you immediately stiffen up. So it is more of an awareness of tension. If you accept the fact that you are tense and not relaxed, you will find yourself relaxing. But if you have an idea that you *should* be relaxed and should *not* be tense, then you create more tension. By fighting tension you create more tension. You can drive yourself up the wall and be an absolute wreck after half an hour of trying to relax!

Now, the encouragement to be at ease, to relax, and to trust, is not an order from above. It is a suggestion which might help you move away from ignorance, from just adding ignorance to ignorance. You don't even have to know what understanding is. You don't have to think, 'Have I got it?' If you think about it, you will probably think you haven't. It is a matter of recognizing that even if you relax only a little bit, at least you are learning something; there is a kind of knowledge taking place, a kind of insight-knowledge arising for you. This is not any kind of knowledge you acquire through memorizing texts. It comes through reflection, through noticing the way it is. And noticing, as I said before, is not criticizing; it is not taking a stand for or against anything; it is not that there is anything you *should* be thinking, feeling or doing. It is a matter of being aware of the *feeling* 'that you should be more relaxed than you are', say. And of course only you know when you are tense and uptight. Relax with that. Allow tension to *be*, and see what happens. We are so critical that when we see we are tense, we just want to get rid of it. There is therefore always the feeling that we *should not* be tense and *should* be relaxed.

The point is, we have to learn from the way we are, from the kind of character we have. There is no perfect prototype human being that we should make ourselves into before we can really practise. It is a matter of learning to accept the way we are non-critically — the tensions in the body, the physical condition, the mental habits — whatever they might be. This attitude will incline towards knowledge, insight. And as you trust in this knowledge, you begin to realize that you are not creating ignorance — that ignorance which affects your life all the time — you are not operating from a bias, from an ignorant assumption, but rather from an attitude of learning what you really are. Buddha-nature is 'like this'.

The formula in the Dependent Origination is: Ignorance conditions the kamma-formations *(avijjā-paccayā sankhārā)*, and that affects consciousness, and then we react emotionally and interpret experience through biases, and then it always ends up as sorrow, lamentation, pain, grief, and despair *(soka-parideva-dukkha-domanassa-upāyāsa)*. When there is ignorance of reality, the result is always going to be some form of suffering. That is just the way it is. The point is to awaken from this ignorance. And again I emphasize that learning to trust in awareness is the way to do it. That is where you are awake. It is not a matter of becoming 'somebody who is awake'; it is learning to trust in the awakenedness that is natural to you. You don't have to train yourself to do this; it isn't something that you cannot do right now. You might think you can't do it, but that is another thought you create out of ignorance. So it is always a question of learning to recognize what is present.

For most of us this might be a bit frightening because we are trusting something we can't really get hold of. 'What is this Buddha-nature, this understanding and all that? How do I know it is there? Prove it to me!' That is the cry of the sceptic, isn't it? 'How can you possibly trust in something when you don't even know what it is?' But it isn't about defining it; it is just the simple act of trusting, relaxing, opening, receiving and being aware. As you begin to recognize that, it gives you an increasing amount of confidence and faith. So you develop faith *(saddhā)* and wisdom *(paññā)* together. They kind of cooperate with each other; they enhance each other. And that is because you are learning through experience.

Some of the foreign monks at Wat Pah Nanachat in Thailand are very much into tranquillity. They have this strong idea about attaining *samādhi*. One of them even wants to build an underground, soundproofed *kuṭī*[20] to shut everything out. It was

---

20 A kind of hut in which a monk meditates and sleeps.

twenty-six years ago when I first established that monastery, and at that time it was a fairly quiet place. There was a minor road about half a mile away, and that was it. But now that minor road is a major road, and there are motorcycles and lorries going along it making all kinds of noise. So some of the monks are saying they have to leave Wat Pah Nanachat because it is no longer a peaceful place and they can't practise there. I have, of course, been through that same strong desire to attain *samādhi* (concentration) myself, so I do know this attitude of trying to control the environment, trying to find the perfect place away from barking dogs, aeroplanes and traffic sounds. But the world is not going to allow that. Even the Thai jungle is noisy with its insect life and so forth. There is noise everywhere.

The point is, these monks are operating from a desire to attain. This is craving for existence — and is one of the three desires — which is not being observed. So this is 'ignorance conditioning the kamma-formations'. They are not getting behind the desire. They are not aware of what they are actually doing and have an idea of what *should* be — 'In a good monastery there should be no disruption, confusion or noise!' Years ago people used to say you could never meditate in Bangkok because it's too noisy! There is too much distraction! And I would think, 'That doesn't sound right to me. You're a Forest monk, you identify as a Forest monk, and you are saying that Bangkok is a place you can't practise in! That doesn't sound right.' If *nibbāna* depends on conditions supporting it, then it is just another condition, isn't it? If you have to depend on controlling the environment and everything around you in order to attain *nibbāna*, then *nibbāna* is a very unstable state, because the world is 'like this'. This is not a tranquil, peaceful place where everything is supporting 'my tranquillity practice' and 'my desire for *nibbāna*'. That word '*nibbāna*', after all, implies that which is not dependent on conditions.

Noise is a part of life. The howling of a dog or any other kind of so-called disruption, belongs. Whatever is happening right now is the way it is, it belongs. It is not that it shouldn't be like this. With this understanding, then, we realize that all things enhance mindfulness rather than thinking that anything can destroy it.

Being Human

What do we mean by this word 'self'? In English we say 'myself', 'self', 'selfishness', and 'self-centredness'. And then there is the Pali word *'anattā'* which means 'no-self', 'non-self'.

In this culture we have the ideal of not being selfish. So when you don't want someone to do what they are doing, you say, 'You're being selfish!' which is a way of getting at them, isn't it? It makes them feel ashamed; it makes them feel terrible to be seen as selfish. 'Self-sacrifice', on the other hand, is inspiring. To me, at least, the idea of sacrificing oneself for the welfare of others is an inspiring concept.

Now, what do they mean in the Pali Canon by the word *'attā'*? We interpret that word to mean 'self'. But do the translations of words like that from the religious texts, from Pali or Sanskrit, mean exactly the same as we do when we use such words? It isn't always possible to have exact equivalents in two languages; you can't necessarily have absolutely literal translations. If you translate Thai literally, for example, it doesn't make any sense at all in English. Buddhadasa (the old Thai scholar-monk who died some years ago) told me he helped some Christian missionaries to translate the Bible. They had tried to translate it from English to Thai but it had sounded like nonsense to the Thais. 'In the beginning was the word' translated literally just didn't make sense. Even in English, of course, that is a difficult one, isn't it? Buddhadasa, however, translated it as 'In the beginning was the dhamma.'

When we reflect on 'self', then, what is it, really? It isn't a matter of getting definitions from other people or trying to align ourselves with some Pali text definition of 'self', but of contemplating the moments when we actually become a person, a self, somebody, and also those moments when we don't, those moments when there is no self. This is a reflective practice; it is intuitive and not logical. Most of us assume we are a kind of permanent person, a permanent self, and we give a lot of importance to our past, to our attainments, achievements, failures and mistakes. So, 'self' is conditioned.

When I use the word 'self', I am talking about my thoughts and memories, and how I align myself with them. Our personality obviously changes according to the situation we are in; it adapts to whatever conditions are in the present. We don't really notice that, though, and assume there is a permanent self, a permanent personality. When we do not reflect and observe the way it is, we just operate from this assumption. That is why, on a personal level, I am vulnerable. When I abide in my personality — in the sense of myself as a person — people can hurt my feelings, abuse me, make me feel suicidal, make me very happy, make me jump for joy, or bore me — as a person.

Knowing this, then, we can begin to examine the personality. What is it? In the Ten Fetters[21] — the fetters that need to be relinquished for arahantship — the first three are personality belief, attachment to conventions, and sceptical doubt. The point is to really know your personality. So I encourage this inner listening, just allowing your personality to manifest in consciousness without reacting or attaching to it, simply accepting it. Whatever conditions arise — pleasant, unpleasant or whatever — just listen to yourself, to the way you grumble and complain, to your discontentments, inspirations, depressions, doubts and attachments.

The Western world is idealistic. So we have these standards

---

21 Ten Fetters *(saṁyojana):* personality belief, sceptical doubt, clinging to mere rules and ritual or conventions, craving, ill will, craving for fine-material existence, craving for immaterial existence, conceit, restlessness, ignorance.

about how things should be and then compare ourselves personally with the ideals of what a perfect Buddhist monk should be, for example. We let our personalities work with these things and can inspire ourselves. We want to be the best. We really want to be like the Buddha. We want to be calm and serene, wise, compassionate and unselfish, and even 'sacrifice *nibbāna* for the welfare of all sentient beings'. These are ideals that might inspire our minds on a personal level. But we can't sustain it because when we act in a lesser way — when we can't live up to the ideals — what happens? We become self-critical — 'I'm not good enough! I'm not a very good monk. And I'm letting people down. I'm weak and unworthy of the robe.' The gap between our human personalities and our ideals is vast and they can never meet. Can I make my personality into a *bodhisattva* or a Buddha? I think, 'Buddha's personality . . ? But I've got to let go of personality so that I have no personality. And then I am just . . ! But how am I supposed to relate to anybody in that state? I come to the Leicester Summer School and just sit here . . !

I have noticed, after teaching in the West for so long, that there is this common pattern of self-disparagement here. We generally have low self-esteem and see ourselves in negative terms. Even though we might be very good people in every way, our tendency is to make a big deal out of the things that are not so good. I am quite capable of doing this myself. I can take the flaw and make it an obsession of my mind. In monastic communities it is easy to put up a good front. You just put on the robe, sit like a Buddha-*rūpa* and give the appearance of this ideal that we all long for. Well, some can put on a good show anyway. Others can't even do that! The Zen tradition, I think, can do it better!

I was an eight-*vassa*[22] monk when I was made abbot of Wat Pah Nanachat in Thailand; only eight years as a monk and suddenly I found myself as the head monk and teacher. I immediately tried to withdraw into this role of my ideal of what a good

---

22 *Vassa:* rainy season; the way of measuring the number of years spent as a monk or nun.

abbot should be. So I suppressed everything and more or less hid behind the role I had been given. And that, of course, led to a sense of frustration and loneliness, because the role is appropriate to time and place, isn't it? Being a teacher is fair enough; it is appropriate for situations like this relationship here right now, for example. The problem arises when you try to hold to a particular role with close friends, say, or even when you are alone. If there is a tendency to perform like that, the sense of loneliness and isolation on a personal level increases. You can be in the midst of a large community and still feel totally alone, totally isolated.

I have noticed that the King's daughter, Princess Sirintorn, in Thailand is always being put on a pedestal — sometimes literally up on a platform sitting separately — with everybody around her. But I feel that to live a life where you are always put in that position must be very unpleasant. The human side needs to be respected also, the human being that is not just an image, a role model, or an archetype.

In formal meditation we often go into another kind of role — the sitting posture, being the meditator, being in silence and allowing a lot of emotion to surface into consciousness — and it is appropriate in that situation. But what happens in daily life where there are relationships and interchanges? Some people, you find, are very good as teachers; they can give very good retreats. Yet on a personal level they can't really cope. So it is a question of recognizing that this is how things work. I mean, if we are coming from awareness (the transcendent) to the archetype of the monk, or the archetype of the meditator, or the archetype of the *bodhisattva*, or whatever, it is a question of trying to align the awareness with the archetype, so that there isn't a gap between the personality, the human needs, and the rest — so that they are working together, supporting each other — rather than identifying with one or seeking the highest and ignoring the lower aspects, the seemingly less interesting or more embarrassing conditions of being human. This happens a lot, I think, especially with Westerners. But in Thailand you find teachers that are very human. They are an earthy kind of people like Ajahn Chah. He was not at all idealistic. Yet when you read books about him, he sounds like superman, like a kind of perfect Buddhist monk.

In Theravada Buddhism the tendency is to see the 'self' as something we have to get rid of. We talk about the defilements *(kilesas)* and the fetters *(samyojana)*. And there are all these lists of taints *(āsava)* and ways of talking about greed, hatred and delusion. All these things are interpreted in terms of what we have to get rid of. We have to conquer desire, ignorance, greed, hatred and delusion. We have to get rid of the things that are involved with personality, with being human. This humanity thing is embarrassing. If you are idealistic you want to be this wonderful monk — and then you have to go to the toilet! It's embarrassing, isn't it? One suddenly has to get up and leave the room. Going to the toilet is not a perception that we generate from the role model, from the archetype.

Ajahn Chah was very ill during the latter part of his life and it was interesting to see people's reactions to that. The frailty of his body, his humanity, was very obvious, and since he couldn't take care of his own needs, we all had to do it for him. Most monks and laypeople adapted to that, but some just couldn't bear it. They wanted the model Ajahn Chah, not the reality, not the human one. In Thailand they love to make these kind of Madame Tussaud models of monks. They have a museum in the west of Bangkok where there are all the great teachers in fibreglass. You can see Ajahn Mun sitting here and Luang Por Chah over there. Luang Por Chah looks really good in the museum. They gave one of these fibreglass models to Wat Pah Pong, Luang Por Chah's monastery. And this model of Luang Por Chah was put underneath his *kuṭī* where he used to sit in a bamboo chair and receive people (the *kuṭīs* are on pillars). So they put the model in this chair, and it looked quite realistic; it looked in fact just like Luang Por Chah. I remember on one occasion when I was helping to nurse him and dealing with the facts of life, the human needs, I was getting a bit weary and went over to sit by this model, and then — just for a moment — I thought, 'I wish Luang Por Chah were like this model all the time!'

Recognize, that as soon as you are born into the world, you are conditioned by the things that happen to you, so you develop a sense of yourself, the sense of 'I am a boy' or 'I am a girl', 'I am American', 'I am a good boy', 'I am not such a good a boy'. You get the messages from your parents, peers, society and the ethnic group you are brought up in. So you acquire a sense of yourself as a separate person. Remember, this comes after you are born; you are not born as a personality; you don't see yourself as a boy or girl when you are born, or as anything at all. You are a baby, but you don't see yourself as a baby — as I remember. I can't remember thinking, 'I'm a baby.' The sense of your self-worth, then, develops in childhood, and often gets fixed in adolescence.

Much to my, sometimes, disgust and shock I can see that my personality and some of the emotional habits that arise into my consciousness are quite immature. Some in fact are adolescent and even childish. The point is, the conditioning process often doesn't get resolved in any skilful way while we are growing up, and therefore tends to perpetuate itself through a lifetime. When my father was ninety-one, he sometimes acted like a little child. He had been a man of great authority and presence, a man who had the world under control. Then suddenly, as he lost his ability to control things, as he let go of the illusion of 'I'm an adult man in control of the world', those unresolved conditions of his life-time started coming into consciousness. And he had tantrums and sulked like a little child! I have seen these tendencies also in myself. As one listens inwardly, one might become aware of quite childish emotional reactions to situations.

The challenge, then, is not to wait until you are ninety before understanding such things, but to realize now that meditation includes all the conditions we are experiencing — whatever they might be. It is not a matter of trying to calm down the emotions and dismiss the defilements in order to get some tranquil state out of meditation. For men, I think, emotions are very frightening. Most monks feel ill at ease around emotions, so when anyone talks about them, it makes them uncomfortable. They would sooner brush them aside — 'Don't attach to emotions!' — but that quite often means 'suppress them'. If you just push away emotional feeling as soon as it comes up, however, that leads to a rather sterile result in monastic life. You become kind of dried up. If you can't be at ease with emotions — your own and other people's — you tend to petrify yourself. You become fixed and often very opinionated about things. Women are more aware of their emotions. They are not so frightened of them and seem quite willing to be emotional. But that can be distressing if you don't like it; it can be a threat.

I have dealt with this by listening inwardly to the resistance, to the fear I have around the emotional world and my own emotional habits. It is like inviting them in, welcoming even a situation where I am put under emotional stress and be willing to experience anger, say, or fear, jealousy and resentment — just listen to those things without judgement. Now, it is very difficult for me to listen to my emotional world, because a lot of it I would judge as immature. But that is a put down, isn't it? If I say, 'Oh, immature emotions!' that is a way of saying that as a mature man I shouldn't have them. So this is another judgement I am putting onto the situation rather than listening to it, feeling it, and allowing it to be fully accepted into consciousness. The acceptance of emotion is actually the letting go of it. And that letting go isn't pushing it away. I found this works well for me. It allows the sense of humanity to be appreciated and respected. It is a way of recognizing that this human realm is not to be despised, not to be put down as a lesser experience that needs to be got rid of.

So, what does it mean to be human? We can regard it as a way of justifying our weaknesses — 'Well, I'm only human!' — or we can think of it in terms of caring about humanity. Obviously, being human has something about it that we respect because we are often drawn to the idea that someone is fully human. We like to be around people like that. If people are too stiff archetypically, you can worship them, but you don't want to hang around them too much. They just make you feel terrible because you feel you are not that good. You can adore the guru that proclaims his divinity — and some people love to adore the guru — but Theravadan Buddhists generally are not that type; they don't adore gurus very much.

When you really contemplate the Theravada teachings, you realize that your humanity is to be recognized, to be respected. So there is no question of harming your body, of taking up ascetic practices and doing terrible things to it, with the idea that the body is an obstruction to enlightenment. The thought that you have to control the physical body and all its desires, that you have to make yourself completely desireless, would be another ego trip, wouldn't it? 'I'm totally rid of all my desires now!' — that would be just another ego prop.

In contemplating the way things are, you are looking at the world — the world that you live in — this realm with its four elements (earth, fire, water and air) and your own humanity and the limitations you are under as one individual human being, as this entity here, this single entity that seems to be a person. And as you develop this trust in awareness, you see more and more that the subject is not the person. Personality is something that comes and goes and changes; you become a personality according to conditions. But the absolute subjectivity of this moment is not personal; I cannot claim it as 'Ajahn Sumedho' in any way; it is pure awareness — not male or female, not even Buddhist — but 'like this'. The absolute subject of this moment recognizes the experience of being an entity in the universe incarcerated in this human form with the conditioned realm that we are living in, with the earth, fire, water and air realm, and the conditioned emotions and perceptions that we acquire after we are born. The absolute subject of this moment is consciousness and awareness that is always here to abide in once we begin to appreciate and trust it. This awareness is non-personal. And it is the same for all of us. We are actually one in that. Even though it seems as though the subject is 'here', when we abide in pure awareness, we are actually one — not lost in the realm of identifying with the body or the perceptions that we experience. This is what I call real refuge in the Buddha, or *buddho*.

I encourage you to listen to your personality non-judgementally, and if immature, emotional reactions come up — if anger and resentment or negative states come up or you get carried away with inspiration and all the good stuff of life — just say, 'Fine, welcome!' The point is not to judge any of it, not to cling to it, or prefer it, but to merely trust yourself to be the witness. Things arise and cease; they are what they are. And in this attitude of it-is-what-it-is, I find a way of accepting experience without judging it. As soon as I say 'immature emotion', I am making a value judgement about what I am experiencing. And the logic that comes from that is that I am an emotionally immature man. There is such a strong resistance to some mental states that it takes real determination in awareness to accept them. But, if you can, trust yourself to accept the things you don't like.

For me, it took real patience to do this. 'Patience' means, of course, allowing something to be what it is, something that you don't like or don't want. If you are impatient, you say, 'Oh, I can't be bothered. Get rid of it.' But patience allows you to bear with conditions that you don't want, don't like, and can't stand. The more you are willing to accept things, the more you can actually observe them, and then you find that they are nothing, really, just kind of changing energies that have arisen with nothing permanent in them.

The point is not to try to claim that which is aware. As soon as you say, 'I am somebody who is very aware,' you are back into the realm of identifying with awareness — and that is not to be encouraged. It is a question of *being* the awareness. And *being* the awareness is an act of faith because you can't find awareness as an object; you simply can't get hold of it. So you have to *be* it. That is where this attitude of relaxation and opening comes in. And if you can do that only for a moment, be grateful for it! If you are constantly losing it, don't be critical of yourself, just be more accepting of the fact that this is the way it is — but still with a kind of determination — and after a while you will find that you are learning to be with this natural state of being. This is not a creation of your mind; it is not a state that you attain merely from ideal situations or very refined conditions. Whatever you are doing — even if you are knitting on the Silk Road as Fiona did — does not preclude mindfulness.

I tried to go to Mount Kailash in 1998 but got turned back because the Chinese didn't want monks entering Tibet in those days. I did get to the northwestern part of Nepal, the Humla area, and then up through these very narrow, high mountain passes. There were no roads and, like Fiona, I became very frightened — agoraphobic, in fact. I looked down into this seemingly bottomless pit, and Kamali river was way down there at the bottom, and I was way up here. I realized then that if I took one false step I would fall down the cliff! By using this awareness, however, by paying attention to the 'sound of silence', this 'cosmic vibration', the fear went away. Fear is a conditioned reaction, so just by trusting this 'silence' I stopped creating the conditions for fear to arise. Then I was able to look down the cliff without creating the conditions for fear in my mind.

I finally succeeded in actually getting to Mount Kailash last May during Visakha Puja (the full moon day of May). Thousands of Tibetans arrived in trucks from all over, and we circumambulated the mountain — fifty-three kilometres, it was. It was hard going, I can tell you, but very inspiring, and so high up that you could only take a few steps before having to stop. I became really tired going up one particular pass, and two young men came up to me — one took my arm, the other took my daypack — and they helped me up. Now, they were wearing lay clothes, but they told me they were Tibetan monks.

Physical discomfort in general is bearable, I find, if I don't get lost in aversion, if I don't start grumbling or being negative about fatigue or difficulties. If I don't do any of those things, the awareness allows me to join in inspiring pilgrimages like going around Mount Kailash. And it was very inspiring to be with thousands of Tibetans who had total faith in what they were doing. Some of them were performing these full prostrations at the same time, which was an amazing thing!

In preparing for these trips to Mount Kailash, I went to Switzerland several times, and also, on one occasion, a *tudong* walk with Ajahn Anando and Nick Scott. We started at Harnham and made our way through the Pennines and the Yorkshire Dales. I wasn't very fit in those days and we had to carry backpacks, a tent and everything. Also I had borrowed these boots which were terrible. You may have noticed my big feet! One of them is quite swollen and I had to squeeze my feet into these boots which were much too small for me. That brought up all kinds of childish emotions — 'Oh, why do I do things like this? I want to go home!' These were the emotions that came up at the time. But when I look back I wouldn't have missed it for anything. I would go to Kailash again, even though when I was there I found it exhausting. The food, I remember, was also terrible. I lose my appetite anyway in high altitudes, but because I could not eat in the evenings, they gave me and another monk who was on the trip, a kind of packed lunch before noon (usually dry bread and a boiled egg), and after a while I got this aversion to eggs and bread. Even the word 'food' brought up a feeling of nausea.

Going to foreign countries, into unknown situations and exotic scenes, will bring up fears, anxieties, discomforts and culture-shocks — because you don't have the security of the known around you. As you trust in your meditation more, however, you begin to use this fear, anxiety, feelings of bewilderment and insecurity, for practising, for recognizing and accepting. Then the anxiety falls away. It isn't a question of suppressing anything and trying to be a 'good guy on the trip', but of actually learning from what you are doing.

So, consider this pure subjectivity of awareness, the absolute subjectivity. These are just terms, but this is what I call the natural state of awareness here and now. 'You' arise into that. When I become a person, I say, 'Ajahn Sumedho'. Then I can operate in the conventional world. I neither try to avoid the conventional realm, nor am I endlessly blinded and deluded by conventions. I just put it into the context of what it really is.

Sense the Sacred

I went to India this year for six months. And as soon as I arrived in Bombay I felt this sense of being at home. Monks, *sādhus*, holy men and so on are so much part of the culture in countries like India and Thailand that you feel unquestionably accepted there. Even though most people in India don't know much about Buddhism, they know you are some kind of *sādhu*, somebody who tries to live the holy life.

India, in any case, is a country that is very accepting of life. You fit in there no matter how weird, diseased, strange or eccentric you are. The mere fact that you are there means you belong. I find it a very pleasant country to be in because of that. And Benares, which is a holy city for the Hindus, is for me one of the most interesting places in the world. I spent two months there this year right on the *ghāṭs*, right near the main *ghāṭ* in fact, just watching life going on. You see marriages, corpses burning, devotional observances *(pūjās)* by the river, and people bathing. The Hindus love to bathe in the river Ganges, so they go there in their thousands. The cows and water buffaloes also bathe in the Ganges, and the sewage goes in, human and animal corpses are thrown into it, and people wash their clothes in it. It just takes everything. For me the idea of bathing in the Ganges was not particularly attractive, so I waited until I got to the northern part of India before I did that. But Benares is a city in which everything is sacred, *everything*, no matter how good or bad, clean or dirty, right or wrong. The sense of the sacred is palpable in that place. The whole city is just like a *pūjā* to the great river, the river Ganges.

Many of our common values in the West are based on very self-centred goals and materialistic values. But in a place like Benares you feel this devotion towards deities like Shiva, Kali and Ganesha. Whatever the deity, you feel the power of devotion, the sense of recognizing something beyond the material world and individual needs. In the American system, on the other hand, individuality is the priority. We are brought up to proclaim ourselves as individuals in such an extreme way that often we don't feel any connection to anything at all, not even to our own parents or families. For myself, I don't have any strong identity with race, ancestry or anything like that. And my family didn't have a close relationship. The sense of myself as an individual was very strong — 'my rights', 'what I think'. Because of that I was able to leave it all behind and didn't go back for thirteen years — nor did I really want to. So individualism does have its advantages. It gives you the freedom to do what you want.

But just endlessly trying to satisfy your own needs and thinking only of yourself can also lead to extreme loneliness. When you are young it can be rather exciting doing what you want, but as you get older it creates a sense of disconnection with the world, and depression and loneliness. Self-aversion and self-criticism can then take the mind over because the sense of yourself, your self-worth, depends on things that you cannot sustain or maintain. You might achieve them sometimes, but you can't keep them. In India, then, the sense of the sacred is stronger than the individual. And yet the individual — the leper, the eccentric, the low caste, high caste, king, the military, the communist, whatever, whoever — is also accepted. There is this sense that it all belongs. And this is a reference point I find very helpful.

The discriminative mind always tries to control things. You see this in the political scenes where the Americans are determined to wipe out 'the axis of evil' — 'It doesn't belong! We've got to destroy it. Get rid of it!' Of course, the 'axis of evil' is not in America or in any President; it is somewhere out there in some general direction — though it is very vague! But, anyway, it definitely points outside itself. In that logical sense, if good is right and bad is wrong, we must get rid of the bad and hold onto the good. That makes sense, doesn't it?

The Buddha, of course, very clearly pointed to the way it is, the dhamma, rather than to ideals of how things *should* be. Even though one felt that 'this is the way it is' in Benares, however, there were many things one thought needed to be done, many things one thought needed cleaning up or making more efficient. The American mind can rattle on like that. And yet in the end there was a sense of 'this is the way it is'. In its own way things do get done in India. Somehow the trains and buses and every-thing do function. And for a country with a billion people where everything seems so completely chaotic and erratic, it does work, actually. Maybe it is us, then, that have to look at things in a different way!

Comparing that to my own experiences in meditation, much of my early years were spent in trying to control the mind, trying to get rid of the bad thoughts, trying to hold onto the good ones, trying to retain the more refined states of consciousness, get the high levels of concentration, control the environment, keep out the noise and generally limit everything so that irritating, sen-sory impressions did not disturb me. It was a matter of trying to develop this ideal of *samādhi* and always feeling frustrated by the fact that even if I managed to get concentrated, it was unsus-tainable because the effort was on controlling, ignoring or deny-ing the conditions that destroy peaceful states of mind. People can get obsessed in some of these groups — 'shush! don't talk!' — wanting to control everything, not wanting any disruption so that they can gain tranquillity. Of course, you need the right environment for that because if you have distractions, noise, harsh impingements, physical pain or irritating things going on around you, you can't get it. It isn't possible if the conditions are not there. Sensory deprivation is ideal for this — one of these sensory deprivation tanks, maybe, where you float in a pool of body-temperature water with your eyes closed and everything shut off so that you can't feel a thing. When nothing is attacking or irritating the body or senses, the mind will go into a tranquil state — simply because it isn't being irritated. The human mind likes that and wants it. And once you have such an experience, you want more of it. You create a desire for it even while you are having tranquil or mystical experiences, even while you are experiencing a sense of oneness, or loss of self-consciousness, or whatever. We have the experience, then we remember it, then we grasp that memory and try to recreate it from what we remember. But it doesn't work.

If you are always trying to achieve some mental state — maybe something remembered in a previous meditation retreat — you will be endlessly frustrated. The first time these things happen, you don't know what is going on. Suddenly your mind drops but you have no inkling of what you have done. Maybe you have some vague idea, but you have never actually experienced it before, so you don't know. Once you do experience it, however, the danger is to desire it again. Whatever is pleasant, we want more of. If something is unpleasant, then what? People that only have pain and miserable states in meditation don't usually continue after a while because the memories are too painful. As soon as they think of meditation, they think, 'Pain! Misery!' and they are not going to do it unless they are masochists.

The Buddha, in pointing to the way it is, wasn't pointing to an ideal of the way it *should* be, but to the ability to open to the way it actually is right now — whether it is peace and tranquillity or noise and confusion. He was pointing to the ability to open to that which includes everything in the moment. When we don't use this ability, we are always trying to exclude things. All our efforts in meditation go towards controlling, trying to get rid of this or that, trying to get tranquillity, trying to get *samādhi*. So we are busy with the ideas, habits and techniques we have acquired. But the Buddha was pointing to the power of recognition, this awareness *(satisampajañña)*. I call it 'intuitive awareness'. It is an intuitive ability.

Now, the intuitive sense is natural to us; the ability to allow consciousness to manifest the things that are happening — seen or unseen — in the present moment is natural. But this is not a function that has been highly praised or respected in the Western world. We like the dualistic functions of reason and logic, right and wrong. We love that kind of mental exercise. So, even though we all have intuition and use it, we often don't know anything about it! We mistrust the idea of it, actually, because it is not a rational thing. Intuition isn't something that we can explain. We don't have any really good words or symbols to make it very clear to anybody. The best we can say is 'I have a feeling, a sense, maybe a sense of uneasiness'. But intuition includes everything. It is not discriminative. It is not us making moral judgements or value judgements about anything, comparing one thing with another, saying what should or shouldn't be, or what is right or wrong. It is the ability we have to open to life as we experience it, even if what we are experiencing is painful or unpleasant. Nowadays in the West our efforts are generally aimed at trying to control life, trying to make things perfect, and exploring the realms of science *ad infinitum*. No matter how far we go or how successful we are, however, we somehow never feel content with what we have. It is never quite satisfying in itself. There is always the desire for something more — one thing goes to another thing.

The Buddha, however, referred to awakenedness, to being awake and aware. When we trust in that — when we begin to trust our intuitive awareness — we get behind our conditioning , so to speak. I become aware of self-consciousness, cultural conditioning and the emotional habits I have. I am open even to the fact that I want to get something, maybe. The awareness gets behind any desire to attain or achieve, any disliking, criticizing or anything I might be feeling in the present, and therefore goes beyond cultural conditioning .

At a Buddhist monastery like Amaravati, many nationalities are represented, and in consequence many different ways of thinking. We have people from Eastern Europe and Russia now who have been brought up under the communist system. Because they look like Western Europeans, we tend to judge them according to our own experiences, but actually their way of looking at things can be quite different to those of us who grew up in the capitalist democratic systems of the West with its affluence, materialism and emphasis on individual rights. We also have Thai and Sri Lankan monks living at Amaravati now, and they have another way of looking at things. But Buddha's emphasis was on emptiness, which appeals to me very much, because the realization of emptiness, the reality of emptiness, starts with zero — no thing at all — rather than from some 'thing'. When you start from a metaphysical doctrine, you usually have something very inspiring — an ideal, an abstraction — something quite high. Then you look towards that ideal for inspiration. The emphasis the Buddha made, however, was on realizing cessation (as in the third Noble Truth where everything drops away). When you try to *think* about cessation, you go back to the dualistic structure of mind and think it means you drop dead and everything just vanishes into a void! That is the way logical conclusions work.

I was brought up to think and reason. So there was a great desire in me to know everything about Buddhism and figure it all out. But then I learnt to trust intuition. If your security lies in figuring everything out — in getting answers to every question and solutions to every problem — and you stop doing that, you could feel rather frightened. It might seem as though there is nothing to hold onto any more, as though you are vulnerable and raw in a rather frightening universe and you don't know where to turn. Instead of holding onto that state, however, just be patient and allow it to be what it is until you learn to relax into it, into this natural state of being, this emptiness where you can really be yourself for once. People say, 'I just want to be myself.' To me that is not trying to become something I think I would like to be, but rather being fully at ease in this present moment as it is, even if the conditions are threatening or complicated. From here, I begin to see through the idealism that is part of my cultural conditioning and the sense of individuality — 'my rights, my self, my judgements'. I am actually very critical of myself. And this is a constant source of suffering for me, because the critical mind is never content. It is always saying, 'No matter how good you are, you are not good enough!' You can either persecute yourself with this, or you can go into the empty place, go into it and learn to sustain it as you trust and recognize it. The third Noble Truth is just that recognition — the reality of no-self, of nothingness, of cessation. Instead of, on the logical level, that being a totally unconscious void, it is like a plenum — full, rich. Fullness and emptiness mean the same thing, really, because words are very limited.

Remember the great limitation of words and why you need paradoxes. On the level of real experience, nothing is just like *this* and not like *that*. Fullness and emptiness are at the same time empty and full. We hold to a view like no-self and then criticize our egos. If we have selfish thoughts or emotions, we tend to make value judgements about ourselves as personalities. But if we are aware of this tendency to make judgements, we get behind these habits. It is like being the background to the things that come and go, arise and cease in consciousness. We look at it in this way rather than getting carried away by the good and wanting to hold onto it, or the bad and wanting to get rid of it.

Learning to trust this, I think, is the big challenge for Westerners. From what I have seen there is a tremendous lack of confidence in people's own direct experience. There are so many in the meditation world — in this country and in the States — who trust external authority more than their own direct experience. They mistrust themselves so much, in fact, that they believe whatever the gurus say, or whatever is in the scriptures. They empower external beings and conventions, and are always looking to them for some kind of affirmation or verification of their own experiences. They do this rather than trusting not in their own views and opinions but in that intuitive wisdom which is natural to them. And this intuitive wisdom is not something that they don't already have; it is just that they don't trust it. Their personalities are conditioned in a way that makes them afraid of being enlightened or even of being right, and instead makes them look for confirmation from somebody else, wanting the teacher, the *guru*, the *swami*, the authority to say, 'Yes, you are now a stream-enterer!'

What is it that you can really trust within yourself at this moment? Don't try to find anything, but just see what that very question arouses. Thoughts come up, of course, and then feelings and reactions to them. But you can't trust those things. What about the awareness, this ongoing awareness? You can be aware that you are thinking; you can be aware that you are feeling; you can be aware of emotion; you can be aware of your body, of how it is; you can be aware through the senses of the things that are in this moment. Learning to trust that awareness, learning to put your faith in that awareness, I call 'taking the refuges'. The refuges, then, are here rather than in some kind of abstract Buddha-Dhamma-Sangha, or in some external thing. When you take the refuges, I encourage you to really see them. It need not be just some little ceremony, just a sentimental thing we do at the Summer School; it could actually have great value. It could be a reminder that your refuge is here in this awakenedness, in yourself, and to trust that, because the conditioning of the mind will tend to mistrust it.

I think some people are just afraid of being enlightened in case they have to change their lifestyles or something. But it isn't a question of becoming 'somebody who is enlightened', is it? It doesn't make sense on that level. The point is to learn to trust in the awareness, the enlightened awareness. This awareness *is* light, actually, and it is here and now. It is not created; it is not a mental image *(nimitta)*, a sign that you create out of imagination; it is real, something you have with you wherever you go and whatever state of mind you are in. This, then, is the refuge. The safest place to be, actually, is in this refuge.

From here you can get behind *kammic* conditions rather than just being totally lost or overwhelmed by what you experience in life. You can actually learn from tribulation and enjoy life without trying to squeeze every drop of happiness out of it. When you don't try to hold onto the joy of life, you don't create suffering about its fleeting and changing qualities. Always looking for happiness means you are never content. And even when you get it, you know you can't keep it, so there is a constant search for more. You become so obsessed with looking for happiness, in fact, that you simply can't enjoy it when it comes. Life in this realm is like this. Put it into perspective. It is beautiful, ugly, right and wrong, good and bad. And even the axes of evil belong.

In Benares every day we used to pass a Kali shrine. And Kali is one of the more interesting ones because she looks like a demon; at least that is how she is usually represented. She has a red tongue which hangs out of her mouth and she wears a necklace of skulls, and people put garlands of flowers round her. When the Christian missionaries first went to India, they were appalled by sights like this. They thought everyone worshipped demons and felt that they had to convert the people to God and Jesus Christ — somebody beautiful and loving. This is how the mind works when you are caught on that level of thinking Jesus is beautiful and good, compassionate, full of love and everything else. So when you put Mother Kali next to Jesus, what have you got? This hideous female eating her own children! But actually it is not about mothers eating their children; it is about time as experience. In the Hindu iconography, Mother Kali gives birth and then in time consumes what she gave birth to. So this is a metaphorical way of recognizing that reality. We are born, grow up, are nurtured through Kali, through this life, and then at the end she consumes us.

Another way of looking at it is to think that we should be full of love and light and happiness, and must destroy the evil forces. That is the thinking process again. We like the good and don't like the bad — 'Jesus is good! Kali is bad! I want Jesus! I don't want Kali!' And then the logic comes from that. Intuitively, though, when we stop trying to logically deduce what life is, we open to the reality of it. We have been coming to these Summer Schools in Leicester for fifteen years now, and we can see what is happening to us all! Time is like that, isn't it? We could say, 'Well, it shouldn't be like this.' But it is the natural experience of human beings on this planet. It is not ideal, it is not the way it should be according to what we might want, but it *is* the way it is. We are only discontented because the way it is isn't good enough for us. As we trust in the way more, however, we begin to feel this sense of contentment with ourselves and life. And feelings of somehow being cheated or being a victim falls away.

What I think surprises many people when they first go to India is that even though there is so much poverty there, somehow the average Indian looks happier than we do. Many of them don't expect very much — just to feed themselves and their families is enough — and in a place like Benares this sense of the sacred seems to bring a lot of joy into their lives. There is this sense that life isn't just concerned with oneself but is an expression. One belongs to the sacred and is sacred oneself rather than just some miserable, poverty-stricken beggar that should somehow feel ashamed for being in such a lowly state. It isn't like that there. The beggars in London seem to hate themselves. Maybe that is because being a beggar here is the pits according to our way of looking at things; it is the worst thing you can be. If you have to resort to begging, you are just a total failure; you are absolutely no good. It is all taken on an individual level here, which means you are somehow a worthless being. That is what individualism does to the mind, doesn't it? You have no connection to anything, and you justify yourself by being in line with the values of society; that is your worth. Whereas in Asia there is more of a resignation to the way it is. And this we can also criticize. But it has its good side. It allows people to accept things that we could not accept, and yet have to in the long run. Sickness, old age,

death and loss are inevitable for all of us no matter where we live
or how fortunate we are in the material world.

So the sacredness of life brings a sense of joy — if we know
how to tune into it. We can get outside of ourselves and our particular problems if we know how to tune into the sacredness
around us. 'The way it is' is not based on an ideal, but on a sense
of trusting and resting. It is based on having a sense of belonging
to this realm because we are what we are rather than because we
have achieved anything within it. It is not a question of being the
way we are 'whether you like it or not!' — that is not the point.
The way we are is the way we are, and that is the way it is, and
there is room for it all — everything belongs.

So from zero things manifest. In experience we are conscious
beings. We don't create consciousness. When we are born, the
experience of consciousness is natural to the state of birth, to
having a body. We do, however, create many of the things *in*
consciousness. Memories, passions, emotions and thoughts are
acquired after birth; they are the habits and ways of thinking that
we develop. But in emptiness you actually go back to pure consciousness before you create yourself as anything. There is this
pure presence of knowing and consciousness. Try to recognize
that. You can't find it in a form to grasp, but you can trust it; you
can trust *being* the awareness. When you see yourself as 'somebody trying to become aware', you are creating yourself again.
What I am talking about is more a sense of relaxing, opening,
receiving, than trying to attain. Pure consciousness is not an attainment; you can't get it; you can only *be* it. Recognize 'it is like
this'. It is natural and being at ease. You feel relaxed and at home
here. All the problems of being a separate person, a personality,
drop away here. So, as you begin to explore and investigate this,
you will find the way out of suffering.

This Pure Subject
Has No Name

We are now, it seems, in the information age. There is an overwhelming amount of information available now, all that anyone could possibly want to know about the world, science, art and everything. It is all praised, encouraged, and readily accessible. To me, however, the essence of education lies not in the acquisition of knowledge, but in understanding, 'right understanding' in other words, for which you don't need much information. The whole Buddhist attitude is one of awareness, of using awareness as a basis for understanding, and understanding your own mind which you can observe directly. I can acquire all kinds of ideas and theories, read case histories of people who have been through therapies or had religious experiences, but no matter how good or true any of it might be, it is still just acquired knowledge. It is not understanding.

The Four Noble Truths give the paradigm for that understanding, which doesn't mean you limit your knowledge to the Four Noble Truths; it is just that those truths give you the perspective in which to see and contain other information, in which to have the wisdom to be able to see what is worth studying, what is worth retaining, and what is just worthless. There is something we know, something we feel within ourselves that we need to understand but cannot if we are always going into something else.

I found my first experience of looking inwards terrifying, actually. My life had been all about acquiring things from outside, but a friend on a ship I was serving on started trying to get me to look inwards — and I freaked out! It scared the hell out of me. But it was also a kind of awakening moment. After that I became interested in psychology, meditation, and anything that moved towards introspection.

I think many people, actually, are frightened of anything which focuses on themselves. You can talk about the noble truth of suffering *(dukkha)*, for example, and people will just dismiss it — 'Well, of course, everybody suffers!' That is a way of brushing it aside, isn't it? It will of course touch some people because some are 'ripe and ready', you could say, whilst others just don't seem to be.

The terrifying part in meditation is when the ego is being threatened. At first there might be a lot of interest in 'solving my problems so that I can attain *nibbāna*, be free from suffering and be free from all the problems of my life', but I found that as all that began to resolve itself, there was quite a lot of myself, my ego, that I really liked. And the thought of not being anything, of extinction, of cessation of the ego — the ego that is based on becoming something, on reinforcing itself — was very threatening. People can have strong emotional reactions when their meditation gets towards the cessation of the ego. Panic and terror often become quite strong at those times. One can feel as though one is dying — that is the message you can get from the conditioning of the mind. Emotionally it seems like 'I'm dying! You're killing me!' In about the third year of my life as a monk in Thailand, I began to have this inner voice which kept repeating: 'I want to live! I want to live! I don't want to die!' It was like an obsession of the mind: 'This monastic life is killing me! I'm dying!' It was a very urgent and powerful voice, and a very convincing one. After the exoticness and newness of life in a Forest monastery in northeast Thailand began to wear off, it became pretty dreary, really. There you are living in this very simple environment and doing the same things every day, and your friends write and tell you about all the exciting things happening back home — and it stirs up this doubt.

Here in England I have tried to figure out what works and what doesn't work for those making a strong commitment to the monastic life. To take those vows is a pretty strong commitment, and yet for some it doesn't work at all. Now I have developed a kind of cavalier approach to the comings and goings of the Sangha — this one wants to ordain, this one wants to disrobe, and so on. When I first came to England I had profound faith in the practice of meditation and the monastic life. I thought that that was all anybody needed — just to get into the robe, live by the Vinaya discipline and practise meditation. That is why, in the beginning, I ordained almost anyone. But that turned out to be a rather naïve expectation. It didn't really work and brought doubts into the mind — 'Why isn't it working? Maybe it's because some are suited and some aren't. And, well, "there are only a few with little dust in their eyes".'

The point is, most of us in the West come to Buddhism as adults, so we have already been socially and culturally conditioned. At first we might just have an intellectual interest in Buddhism, or we might be fascinated by it. We might even have enough faith to come to a Leicester Summer School or go on a retreat. My basic cultural conditioning , being of a Judeo-Christian background and being brought up in a white middle class American Christian family, meant it was easy for me to interpret Buddhism with a Christian mind-set. That is all I had in terms of ideas. So without intentionally doing so, I interpreted experience through that way of thinking. I didn't consider myself a Christian at that point, but the patterns of thought, the assumptions I made were not all that conscious and therefore influenced how I interpreted or related to Buddhism. Training in a country like Thailand, which is very Buddhist, was a good mirror for that.

It was also easy for people like me to misunderstand the Thais. Westerners have a kind of cultural arrogance that can look at them and say, 'Well, they believe in all these things, and they're kind of faith types,' whereas we would consider ourselves to be more discriminative — the wisdom types rather than the faith types — and easily misunderstand the people we were living with in a Thai monastery. That is when I began to see that my thought-patterns were not really trustworthy, and that my emotional habits were based on those thought-patterns, based on the sense of a self, an ego. So I could easily be emotionally upset when someone said something that offended my ego. I could also feel threatened by other approaches and ideas, and become outraged when people criticized Luang Por Chah. And the way I had of dealing with the Vinaya discipline made me feel incredibly guilty all the time. I tried hard to live up to the highest standards, but couldn't sustain it, so I would be taken over by a sense of guilt and anxiety about myself. You see this all the time amongst Western monks and nuns — this terrible guilt problem. With the Thai monks, and I think with the Tibetans, this is not a particular problem. They have a sense of shame, but their cultural basis is in alignment with their practise of meditation. Thai people generally like themselves; they don't dwell on their short-comings. They accept their limitations as human beings with good humour and can laugh at themselves and their humanness with all that that implies — both its good side and its weak side. So there is a kind of earthy acceptance of life in Thailand.

Now, when Ajahn Chah taught, it was from a place of under-standing and a lot of faith, whereas most Westerners would be thrown into doubt because we were coming from ideas and in-terpreting Buddhism idealistically. So there we would be in a Thai monastery full of idealism about how the monks should be. Then you would see them and they didn't fit into the ideal forms that you had in your head, so you would be very critical of them. I would go into periods of criticizing Ajahn Chah after seeing things which made me think, 'If he is really an arahant, he wouldn't be doing that!' The point is, an ideal arahant is one thing, but the reality of an awakened being is based on the way things really are and not on ideas of how they should be. So I was being challenged by the realities of existence. Because we often

adopt Buddhism on the ideal level in the West, we become altruistic and see ourselves in comparison to the ideals we have of
what a Buddhist should be. Then what do we do? We feel guilt,
maybe, or despair because we are obviously not good enough.
We can't live up to our ideals. And those people who do try to
live up to their high ideals can be unbearable. You get some
monks who try to act like Buddhas all the time, and they're very
difficult to live with!

When the Buddha taught, he was reflecting on the way it is. It
was a question of looking at humanity. And in the Buddhist texts
there are lists of qualities that we all share as human entities —
as in the twenty-two faculties *(indriya)* in the Abhidhamma, for
example. But these aren't just abstract ideas; they point to the
reality of our emotions, physical bodies and sensory experiences. Yet these kinds of things are often ignored by us in favour
of concentration — the eye of concentration, meditative absorptions *(jhānas)*, the higher states, *nibbāna* — and all the rest is
suppressed, ignored, or just not noticed. Now, because Westerners are usually well educated, they often understand the theory
quite easily — this is just how I see it, anyway; this is what I am
reflecting on these days — but they don't have any confidence
in direct insight. They might have direct insight, but still their
ego-structure is based on doubting themselves. So they either
exaggerate direct insight by saying, 'I'm enlightened!' and think
that that is a kind of permanent state of the ego, an enlightened
ego, or they think, 'Oh, it was just one of those strange things
that happened.' Or, if the ego suddenly drops away because they
are in a very peaceful situation and they experience emptiness,
they think it is the result of those conditions, those circumstances. It is the way the ego-structure works.

My ego always makes me doubt. I have a sceptical kind of inner voice that is very critical. There came a time, however, when
I began to see that I needed to get some perspective on it, because
just developing an anti-ego attitude — trying to suppress the ego
— wasn't helping. I eventually realized that that was just the

ego again, that I was just developing a new ego-perception and trying to impose that onto experience. But structures like the Ten Fetters *(saṁyojanas)* can be very useful in one's reflections. The first three are: thinking which creates doubt, the personality belief, and the conventional structures we attach to. Once we see through these three fetters, that is stream-entry *(sotāpanna)*, which means we see the path clearly; we see the way to practise. So, what blinds us to the path, are these three fetters — the thinking process, the ego, and attachment to conventions or identification with conventional form.

Now, in insight meditation, we use impermanence, unsatisfactoriness and non-self as a way of not giving importance to the quality of experience. A lot of people who practise it, however, just seem to take the words and project them onto experience. They take the words 'everything is impermanent' and then bind themselves to the idea of that rather than trusting themselves to be fully aware of impermanence as it happens. 'Non-self' ends up with them feeling guilty about any kind of need or desire they experience, because for most people everything is highly connected with that sense of self. The hunger of the body can be thought of as some kind of personal greed, and the sexual energies can also be taken very personally, as with fear and all these kinds of primal, instinctual emotions. In modern life these things are generally interpreted in a highly personal way.

Yesterday I was talking about the sense of being identified as an individual, of everything being uniquely 'mine' as a personality and an individual creature. In Thailand the culture is not so individualistic; it has more of a social cohesion to it. Identities in Thailand are on a wider range, so their common humanity is accepted more. They don't seem to feel guilty about being hungry or having sexual desires and so on. For them it is just part of being human — 'Everybody's like that!' On the other hand, when one has developed a high sense of individuality, I have noticed, it all becomes very personal. One feels, 'I'm the only one that suffers from all this. It's just my problem. There's something wrong with me. Everybody else seems okay; I'm the odd man out; I'm the freak. There's something in me that's wrong.' I don't think that that would be the case so much with Thai people. Luang Por Chah was very good at laughing at human frailty — not in a derogatory way, not in a snobbish patronizing way of 'we monks are above that' — but in a kind of empathetic way of saying, 'We humans are like this. We all have these energies and emotions and instincts. Being human is like this.' He pointed at these very obvious things that we all experience.

I began to see that the important thing, actually, was to stop thinking. But that, I found, was a real challenge for me. My whole world was created through thinking. I thought all the time. It seemed as though I couldn't stop thinking, in fact. I wanted to figure everything out, know about everything, have it all nicely analysed — all the questions answered and all the problems solved — and I felt very ill at ease with vagueness or any sense of uncertainty or doubt. The scriptures refer to the greed type, the hatred type, the doubting type, and the ignorant type. I could see that, 'Well, I'm certainly greedy enough, and I certainly have enough hatred and anger, but doubt is an obsession of my mind.' I am a sceptic and there is nothing I can do about it. I tried to believe in Christianity by willing myself to do it, but couldn't.

In Zen they use the *koan* method as a way of nonplussing the thinking mind so that it stops in mid-air, so to speak. I started reading books on developing doubt and began to have moments when I actually recognized non-thinking as a reality; they were like gaps between the thoughts. Now, the nature of thought is such that one thought always connects to another. Thinking about thinking means you are still thinking. And thinking about not thinking is still thinking; it's a catch-22 thing, so you can't win on that level. All the planning you do to stop thinking — and knowing that you should stop thinking — is still thinking! So it is a question of recognizing rather than thinking, of getting to the point where your mind goes towards stillness; and making that a really conscious moment so that it isn't just a flash that goes unnoticed. I had these Charles Luk books on the *hwa-tou* — on asking questions like 'Who am I?' — and I started developing that. I then began to recognize where the thinking mind stops. When you ask yourself a question, there is a gap before the mind starts trying to answer it. The point is to consciously notice those gaps between the thoughts — before they connect, before the thought process starts again.

I found that developing that was very helpful, and I had some success in recognizing how thinking arises and ceases *in* consciousness. Previously I had regarded consciousness and thinking as the same thing. It seemed that they were bound together so tightly that there was no differentiation. But in this recognition of the gaps between thoughts I realized I was conscious yet there was no thought. From here I began to notice the cosmic sound — the background sound — and to recognize more and more a very natural state of being. Then I had perspective on my ego and was able to see how I created myself with thoughts, how I identified the body and emotional habits as 'myself'.

Over the years I have been developing this way of just seeing what the ego is. When I become 'Ajahn Sumedho' and operate from the ego, I am empowering something which is really not alive; it is just perceptions and habits that I have acquired. That is why, I think, as you get older the ego becomes boring. You get fed up with yourself. You have lived with the ego for so long — and it just says the same things all the time. I see how easily I am upset on the ego level, how I can get really angry if somebody insults me, threatens me or criticizes something that is very sacred to me, something that I have invested a lot of interest in. I can feel outraged and upset by all kinds of things. People might say, 'You don't have to be a monk, you know. That's the old fashioned way,' and I could react to that. A combination of thinking and emotion can develop around the sense of oneself. And in monastic life where you are living with others all the time, you find very childish emotions coming up — even when you are head of a community!

There is, however, this perspective on emptiness which does not depend on closing your eyes and shutting out the world. It is a natural state that we all have right now but maybe haven't recognized and don't know. Once that recognition comes about, however, then that to me is the path. And the rest is like they say 'the kamma[23] ripening'.

You have experiences in your life that are sometimes surprising. After many years you suddenly get very angry about something you thought was no longer a problem to you. Rather than taking it personally, however, you now know better; you just recognize that the conditions for this particular emotion are 'like this'. That makes it conscious; you allow consciousness to mirror the *kammic* habits and conditions that you have during daily life. And once you allow something to be conscious, you can let it be what it is. There is no resisting, judging or criticizing in this. You do not make any value judgements about it but just recognize — it is 'like this'. So childish emotions might come up, feelings of hurt and wanting to sulk for a while — 'I'm not going to speak to him . . !' To me that is childish, yet I can sometimes feel like that. Instead of judging it even as childish, however, it is a matter of getting to know it as you feel it, so that you recognize it. As soon as you say 'it is childish' you make some kind of value judgement about it: 'That is childish and here you are a grown man!' There is something kind of embarrassing about that. But if you just recognize it as it is, then it is conscious and you will see it changing. You cannot sustain it, in fact. It won't hold for very long before it starts dropping away. That I see as the way of not creating kamma with the existing kamma that arises.

Then, as you begin to enjoy not being anybody, not having to be anything and just trusting in this state of awareness, no more does the ego have a great hold on your experience of life. The ego still operates but is seen for what it is, and it's okay. It isn't that one shouldn't have an ego, but the ego is known; it is recognized and understood. The reality from that awareness is

23 *Kamma* (Pali); *karma* (Skt.): action; in this case the ripening of actions.

not ego, not personality belief — one of the fetters — but pure subjectivity, pure conscious awareness.

Now, one of the last fetters is conceit *(māna)*. This is not personality belief *(sakkāyadiṭṭhi)*, but a subtle sense of 'I am' that sustains itself. Then after that there is the arahant[24] — the one liberated through wisdom — the freedom from the fetters, oneness, non-separation, non-duality. The first three fetters (self-view, sceptical doubt, and attachment to convention) are created out of ignorance, so they are like our cultural conditioning and attitudes. These are not natural energies, but are artifices that we acquire. So the thinking process, the conventional world that we make assumptions from, and the sense of a self that is identified with the Five Aggregates — these we create through belief and ignorance. We create ourselves with these three fetters, and bind ourselves in this way. Once these are seen through, what remains are the basic primal instincts — desire, greed, and anger — but they are no longer interpreted in terms of the personality belief with egoistical perceptions. This is the experience of the once-returner *(sakadāgāmin)* and is the recognition of the natural energies that we have as human beings, energies that operate through these forms as basic human emotions. Anger and greed, sexual desire and fear are basic to the mammalian world. To see these in terms of what they are rather than judging them from some kind of moral or egoistic position, is to begin to trust in awareness. You actually recognize sexual desire and anger and fear; you know them but do not judge them.

For a celibate monk, it is necessary to recognize sexual energy. The relationship to that energy, however, is not one of identity, but of recognition, understanding. Living within the convention of a Buddhist monk determines how one acts or does not act, so even though one might experience these natural energies, because of recognition and understanding, they simply arise and cease. I do not identify with them, but I know them. The fact

---

24 *Arahant:* one who is liberated through wisdom, free from the fetters, and has understood and realized.

that a once-returner *(sakadāgāmin)* can still experience anger
and lust and so on, often challenges people's ideals.

In Thailand they think that even becoming a stream-enterer
(sotāpanna) is rare, but an arahant is such a rarity and *nibbāna*
so high up in Theravada Buddhism — it is exalted to such a
high level — that really it is impossible for any of us. That is
the way thought is. Thought is linear and can only go from good
to better, best, bad, worse, worst. And *nibbāna* can only fit into
the best. Well, that means it is really high. When you contemplate the teachings of the Buddha, however, you realize that he
was not pointing to height or refinement, but to reality here and
now, which isn't high, which isn't an achievement that you come
to by refining everything, by controlling your environment. A
high conscious state might seem like *nibbāna*, but try to operate
from that when you go into London on the underground! You
just feel 'this world is too ugly and coarse for me; I can't bear it
any more!' and you become someone who has to control things;
you become a control freak, because in order to get to that high
level, you have to control your environment. But *nibbāna* is not
high. You could use the word 'transcendent' instead, but that
also sounds high, so the worldly life is then dismissed as irrelevant and lesser, and one gets into wanting just to live in a refined state of consciousness because the coarse is too much to
bear.

We can get attached to tranquillity, to high levels of conscious
experience, but if we reflect from the empty point — from this
pure subjectivity — we begin to see through that. We see the
attachment to refined states of consciousness and to any experience. After contemplating this pure subjectivity, I began to recognize that the existential reality of *being* is that I am in this
place, 'I am' before I become anything, before I become Ajahn
Sumedho, before I become a Buddhist monk or an American.
Before I become anything, there is the sense of 'this is the subject
here and you are objects to me in this reality of now'. So I can

create myself into 'Ajahn Sumedho' and become 'a teacher' and so forth.

Now, for a while I resented this, because when you become 'a teacher', you can't learn from anybody. You always have to be the teacher and all your relationships are around being that. In a monastery everybody looks to you as 'the teacher', so you end up feeling lonely because a part of you just wants to be an ordinary human being and not always put into a position where that kamma takes place. From the 'I am' (and whatever I add to that) I make myself into somebody: 'I am an American. I am a Theravadan Buddhist monk. I am a disciple of Luang Por Chah. I am a person with limited qualities.' I become the very things that I create. If I just operate from that, however, without questioning it, that is how I see life. I become self-conscious, shy, or whatever personality trait I happen to be holding to. If I trust in pure subjectivity, however, then the ego can still operate, but I am no longer attached to it so I can come across in a personable way rather than just sitting here unable to relate. The personality then is a tool to use, and I don't have this sense that there is a real self operating. This is where I find Buddhism excels in its teaching.

I was brought up as a High-Church Anglican in Seattle, Washington. Now, in my childhood we were rare creatures indeed in Seattle, Washington, and very elitist. We considered ourselves better than everybody else, especially better than the Low-Church Anglicans, not to mention the others. One can get into a kind of exclusiveness as a way of experiencing life — 'This one is better than that one, and what I have is somehow the best.' I suffered a lot as a teenager because basically I didn't like that kind of attitude; it wasn't very nice. Always feeling 'I am superior to the rest' didn't appeal to me as a position I really wanted to take in life.

When I went to Thailand, I was supposed to ordain in the Dhammayutti Nikaya, which is the King's sect. All the rich people and aristocrats belong to that one, so this appealed to my High-Church Anglican side. And I was supposed to go to this teacher, Ajahn Maha Boowa (this was 1966), who at that time was also the best — 'All the rest in Thailand you might as well ignore. This guy has it. There's no point in wasting your time with anyone else.' Anyway, the High Anglican side of me thought, 'I've got the best and this is the King's sect, and this is the best teacher, and all the posh people belong to it.' The other sect, the Maha Nikaya — which is a collection of everything else — was dismissed as hoi polloi and not worth bothering with. So I started to reflect on this, and something in me didn't want to get involved in that kind of situation again. It seemed as though history was repeating itself. So I ordained in the Maha Nikaya — and no way can you feel superior if you are Maha Nikaya!

Later I went to stay in Ajahn Chah's monastery, and a similar situation arose. This was also an elite group. In fact Luang Por Chah was considered to be even better than the Dhammayut! And I could see the same thing happening yet again — 'We're very strict and very pure and our teacher is the best!' By this time I began to see just how easily I gravitated into that, and what a natural *kammic* inclination I had of moving into these elitist things. Because I am now aware of that inclination, I no longer have to follow it. But how does one use very good things? Luang Por Chah was a brilliant teacher and his monastic life was impeccable and good, but how do you use these things without identifying with them egotistically? Well, it comes with the pure subject. The ego will either say, 'I just want to be a common, ordinary monk and not be one of these hoity-toity types' — and I can get into a kind of righteous anarchism because I also have an anarchical streak — or I can get into a snooty position of thinking I must only stay with the very best and be an impeccable monk according to the purity of our tradition. But awareness includes both those extremes and you don't grasp either one.

When I talk about trusting in awareness, I don't mean trusting in your feelings or inclinations; I mean trusting in a simple awakened attention which has no quality to it that you can point to. You have to *be* it. It is something you recognize. And it isn't difficult. It isn't a question of getting some super type of concentration. It is so ordinary, in fact, that you don't notice it. One can easily get into trying to achieve a concentrated state, but that is not it. My main encouragement now is for people to trust themselves more, because one of the greatest problems I have had in the past — and I can see it in others around me — is the ability to trust in this awareness. The ego will always say, 'Maybe you're wrong! Maybe you're inflating yourself!' and desires affirmation from outside.

For years I wanted Luang Por Chah to tell me what I was because I was afraid of over-estimating myself. I trusted him more than I trusted myself. I wanted some great teacher to tell me who I was and where I was at. His way of dealing with this was by getting me to look at what I was doing, and this I found very helpful. Eventually, I began to see that he was getting me to trust in the awareness of the moment rather than being caught up in wanting answers from him, wanting affirmation, wanting verification, wanting proof, a certificate, a diploma with a red seal on it stating I was a certified stream-enterer!

This pure subject has no name; I cannot claim it as a personal achievement, and it doesn't make judgements or criticisms. And yet it is discerning. This is not like an unconsciousness blankness, but pure consciousness with awareness in which wisdom arises. So there is a discerning ability about it which at the same time is not a critical function. It knows the way things are and it knows the conditioned-unconditioned. They are together. One is not preferred over the other. In this way, the wholeness is reality — the changingness of the conditioned realm, the way things are — they all belong. They are not seen as obstructions or judged according to ideals, but are what they are. The *buddho* or 'the one who knows', the Buddha, is the ability we have to know the reality of this state in the present. As soon as you pass judgement, however, you are back into the ego again — 'I like *this* better than *that*.'

Trusting pure awareness is letting go of the world. At first that can be frightening because the world is what you are used to, even if it is imperfect. More and more, however, as you keep trusting in the awareness, it takes the stronger position, and then the force of your kamma is seen in terms of what it is. It will be recognized and understood without it being an obstruction.

How does that feel to you? Rather than teaching you, what I am doing is encouraging you; I can be a friend rather than a teacher. You don't have to always see me as your teacher and yourself as the student. In the reality of life, those conventions are appropriate at times — and I am quite willing to be 'Ajahn Sumedho' at the right time — but the ego-attachment to that perception is 'I'm a teacher' which is usually supposed to be a positive perception. The ego, however, might like that! Another aspect of being 'the teacher' is that you can feel lonely, or that you can't learn any more because you are always teaching. Yet the reality of life, like at Amaravati, is that you are learning from each other all the time. The nuns, monks and everybody are continually influencing and affecting each other. Only a junior person can teach me about my attachment to being senior, which is an important thing to know. When you are senior you can think, 'I teach you, but you don't teach me!' And that can become arrogant. Sometimes people can be permanently submissive; they can somehow only relate to you as a student. That can work in the beginning, maybe, when that kind of relationship is important, but if you hold them to it, they eventually resent it and leave; they won't stay. Nobody wants to be a permanent student. If we trust our intuition more, of course, our relationships — rather than being habitual — will be natural. We often feel obliged to play these roles with people, but as we trust in our awareness more, we don't have to play the game whether they do or not.

Knowing Not Knowing

Someone has just told me that their father-in-law died this morning. So this is an opportunity for us all to reflect on death — since this is what we are all going to experience sooner or later. As you get older you become more aware of death, of course, and I think Buddhism has a very practical and realistic approach to it. It is the end of one's life as a physical being. But at this moment now, as we are all sitting here in this room, we are all alive and conscious. So just reflect on the way it is. Consciousness *(viññāna)* and life is 'like this'. We are experiencing sensory impingement — what we see, hear, smell, taste and touch — and our thoughts and emotions come and go according to conditions. And this is the state we have been in since we were born. From birth — from when we separated from our mothers — to the death of the body, this is the period we all have of experiencing consciousness.

When there is a form like this, then there is form and consciousness together. Consciousness gives us this experience of subject-object. The sense of being incarnate in a form like a human body presents this experience — through sensing the objective world around us as well as the subject that is experiencing it. Our cultural conditioning takes place after we are born, so a newborn baby doesn't think of itself as English, Japanese or any nationality; it doesn't think of itself as male or female or have any views about politics, religion or anything else — yet it is fully conscious. There is simply form itself and consciousness. That is what we are born with. Then the conditioning process takes place through living with our mothers and fathers, brothers and sisters, the ethnic group, the social class, the country and so forth. All these are impressed upon us through the conditioning process which we identify with. They come to us in that package and it is from that that we form our class identity. Here in England there is a lot of class consciousness; it is more defined here than, say, in America. Here people talk about being working class, middle class, upper middle class or lower middle class. In the States it is easier; it is just middle class. It never occurred to me there was an upper or lower middle class. But this process affects how we experience life.

When we are young we are quite malleable. As we get older, however, we are not so flexible — unless we awaken during this lifetime. The ruts get deeper and we get more entrenched in our views, opinions, assumptions, fears and emotional habits. Emotions that haven't been resolved earlier in life, become problems when we reach old age. I saw my father at ninety throwing temper tantrums as though he were a four-year-old! When he didn't get his own way he would sulk like a young child. These emotional habits catch up with us if we have no way of resolving them with skilful means.

The perception of death — how that word 'death' affects us — is influenced by the cultural attitudes that we are conditioned by. There are various theories — 'If you're good you go to heaven when you die. But if you're bad you go to hell. And if you haven't been baptized you go into limbo.' That is what I was taught. Limbo seems to be the dreariest plane — neither heaven nor hell. And then non-Christians, they go to hell. And High Church Anglicans go to the highest heaven, front row centre; and the Baptists are up in the galleries. So when you are a small child, death is fascinating. I remember becoming interested in skeletons and things that society considered distasteful. Some people say, of course, that when you're dead you're dead! just annihilation, oblivion, nothing there! And others think we are reborn or reincarnated. But right now at this moment death is just a perception for us, isn't it? It is a word d-e-a-t-h. So recognize that.

When you say 'death', how does it affect you? In polite Western society, death is not a subject you are supposed to talk about. When somebody dies, you say, 'They've passed away,' which is a little easier to take because 'death' is too stark. If you say, 'He's dead!' it sounds a bit harsh; whereas saying someone has gone to another place or gone to live with God up in heaven, is a way of making it sound better — not so emotionally charged, not so scary — because death is the unknown to us. We are frightened of it and can imagine almost anything happening.

When I contemplate it, however, right now physical death for me is a perception. And that is a reality, a fact. I haven't physically died yet, so I don't know what it is. I haven't even had a near-death experience, so I can't speak of going through a tube into a bright light and meeting an angel. Physical death is totally unknown to me. Buddhists have various theories about it, and a lot of them are around reincarnation and kamma, so we speculate about what happens when we die. There is also a lot of mental proliferation around what might happen if you attain stream-entry, say, or become a once-returner. 'And maybe, if you haven't attained any of these but just made good kamma, you go to the heavenly realms; and if you've made bad kamma you go to the lower realms.' In terms of this present moment, however, these are just speculations. I might like one version better than the other — maybe I prefer oblivion to having to be reborn as a toad, or something like that — but the idea of having to live as this personality forever in heaven actually doesn't sound that attractive to me. I am not attached to my personality, so I don't see any reason why it should be immortal. I would just as soon let it go. The idea of being 'Ajahn Sumedho' for eternity is not an option I incline towards.

With awareness practice, however, one is not being asked to believe in anything or to operate from any theory — or even to regard one's own preferences for the afterlife — but to recognize the way it actually is at this moment. For me that is just recognizing that death is a perception. When I wonder what happens when I die, my thinking mind stops — ! I don't know what happens. This is developing awareness around language, terms, and the perceptions we have. 'Death' can be a loaded perception, because it is a mystery, it is — don't know! We tend to want to believe an authority and people ask me, 'What do Buddhists believe happens to them when they die?' They think, 'Oh, he's a Buddhist monk, he should know all about this.' Well, I can give the various theories that Buddhists have — and I don't deny them; I am not saying they are wrong — but at this moment, at this time, they are theories, just speculations, ideas. 'Death' right now is an idea, isn't it? It is a perception of the end when this body stops functioning, when it is no longer a conscious form. So this helps me to recognize that I don't have to know what happens after physical death, because I can't know, and it doesn't really matter. I am not asking for some kind of affirmation to make me feel better; I am just interested in opening to the present and seeing it in a direct way. I am even willing to look at the fear that might arise with this perception of death, though actually it doesn't frighten me.

My book, *Mindfulness: The Path to the Deathless*, was originally just called *The Path to the Deathless*, but the publisher said that 'death' is a dangerous word and people wouldn't buy a book with 'death' in the title. Yet the word was actually 'deathless'! Anyway, they insisted we put the word 'mindfulness' before it — I don't know if that helped. The strange thing is that the weekends held at Amaravati on death and dying have always been fully booked. I used to think that nobody would go to a death and dying weekend — 'Who wants to spend a weekend thinking about that?' but actually there is a lot of interest in it. And people want to know, 'What happens when I die? What is life about? What is the purpose of it? What am I here for? What am I doing, anyway? What's the meaning of it all?' If you just grow up, get married, have a family, get old and die — the end! — then none of this seems to matter. The Buddha, however, was pointing to the deathless reality.

For most of us this is another abstract theory. The deathless or *nibbāna* or the unconditioned — there are various ways of talking about it — sounds abstract. Yet, because we witness people dying — we have probably all experienced the loss of parents, relatives and friends — death is real for us. And it is something that we know is going to happen to us as well; we will eventually have to deal with it ourselves. Prior to that, however, we have to deal with the separation and loss of those we have known, loved, lived with and had a bond with. We might even feel a sense of loss when some famous person dies. I didn't know Princess Diana personally, but I had heard of her, and a death like that can have a strong effect. Awareness practice is noticing this, opening to feelings the way they are.

This experience of consciousness means we are in a very sensitive realm. This is a sense realm, which means it is continually changing and we have very little control over it. We have to experience life through the senses all the time as they impinge on consciousness, as sensations arise and cease in consciousness. So in one way or another we are in a state of continuous agitation. From the birth to the death of this body, there is always something affecting it. But this is the way it is. So I contemplate that my body is like this. There is always some feeling around it — pleasure, pain, heat, cold — and this is not a complaint; it is rather a recognition of being conscious and having a body. If you are unconscious, you don't notice. Whatever comes in front of you when you are unconscious, you are unaware of. Because of consciousness, however, whatever comes in front of your vision has an effect. If it is beautiful, you feel good; if it is ugly, it repels you, because the experience of impingement from sense objects is based on pleasure and pain, beauty and ugliness, like and dislike.

The conditioned identity we have with the physical body is what we mean by ignorance. 'You're this way, Sumedho, and you look like this!' You have a picture of your face on a photograph and 'you're a boy, and you are this way and that way, and your parents are like this, and your values are this way, and this is how you should be, and this is how you should not be'. The sense of yourself is conditioned by these things. Your personality develops around the perceptions you acquire. It all comes out of ignorance, out of not understanding the way it is, not understanding dhamma.

Now, in meditation we are exploring this; we are trying to get behind it. And if we were unable to do so, the Buddha would have been asking us to do something impossible. The whole point of the Buddha's teaching, is awakenedness; it is a 'wake up' kind of teaching. So, when you get down to it, all the Buddha was really saying was 'wake up!' — that is all. And that waking up is not affirming the conditioning we have around 'me being somebody who is awake or asleep', or of wondering who can wake up and who can't, or how deluded we are, in this endless way. My personality will create the self into someone who has many delusions 'because of my childhood and the things that happened to me and the mistreatment and abuse I've had in my life'. We can make a good case for being a victim. If we begin to recognize our true nature, however, we will have perspective on the conditioning that we tend to identify with. It is like awakening out of ignorance. And life is not always fair and just. You are not always going to get the best deal when you are born. You get what is around, which might not be very good at all in terms of quality. Awakenedness, however, is not dependent on any of that. This is why people who have had miserable upbringings or disabilities and problems, sometimes find it easier to wake up than somebody whose life is too easy, too pleasant, too perfect in the material realm. If you have had to go through a lot of suffering, you either get stuck in it or awaken. But pain can sometimes push you to awakening.

When we get into contemplating the unconditioned or the deathless *(amatadhamma)*, we might think, 'Well, those are just words, abstractions. Death is something I can relate to, but deathlessness — what in the heck is that?' Try to imagine deathlessness. No images arise in my mind — just a blank, maybe. And with the thought process, deathlessness goes towards annihilation. I can imagine heaven, at least. It is where I am happy all the time and have everything I want. It is a wonderful place where people are beautiful and everything is full of love and joy and as I would like it to be. Hell I can also imagine as endless torment and misery. In Thai temples they often have lurid pictures of what happens if you tell a lie or murder somebody — you go to these various hell realms where people are in anguish forever. But deathlessness, or *nibbāna* . . ! That is something else.

People who don't know anything about the dhamma do tend to create *nibbāna* into a kind of heavenly realm, and it remains very abstract. We can create abstractions with the mind; we can create ideas that have no form except for the words that we use to try to define them. But some people totally dismiss *nibbāna*. I have heard monks say, 'Don't worry about *nibbāna*, and don't worry about the deathless and all that.' One woman in Thailand said to me once, 'You talk about *nibbāna* too much! You shouldn't even mention it!' and she said it like that, too, with an angry voice.

What I am pointing to is that in awareness death for me right now is — don't know! I know I will experience death, so it is easy for me to contemplate it because I know I will definitely die, but deathlessness in terms of an object is something I don't know. I cannot define it or draw a picture of it. Often a circle or a blank, or a *tabula rasa* or something like that, is used to convey that sense of emptiness. What I can recognize right now, however, is that I don't know — and that is the *knowing* of not knowing. Now, that knowing of not knowing is not ego-building, is it? The ego wants to know, wants to have really good ideas and theories. People ask, 'What happens, Ajahn Sumedho, when you die?' And I say, 'Well, in the scriptures it says *this*, and Ajahn Chah said *that*, and *this* is the Buddhist perception, *this* is the Buddhist way to do it, and the Buddha said so, so it's true!'

And I say it with authority. Then they say, 'Thank you, Ajahn Sumedho,' because I know all about it; I am an authority. If I say, 'I don't know!' They would think, 'You don't know?' My ego is the kind that wants to know everything. But this 'knowing of not knowing' is not from the ego; it is from consciousness before the ego arises. So this is like pure subjectivity.

At this moment, right now, just trust in being aware and awake. It is not a question of trying to *become* someone who is aware and awake; it isn't a matter of thinking, 'Ajahn Sumedho says I should be aware and awake and I'm trying to do that.' In that case you would have missed it. That would be your ego grasping it and saying, 'I'm trying to become an awakened being.' And that kind of perception would be coming out of ignorance. Trusting in this awareness, however, is an immanent act of simple recognition, of attention in the present — it is 'like this' and it is like nothing. It doesn't have any quality to it. It isn't blue, green, red or any other colour; it isn't square, triangular or round. But it *is* real; it *is* reality. Then the conditions come from there. If you trust in this awareness, you can be aware of the ego arising — 'I think *this* and I don't like *that*, and I want *this*, and I don't want *that*.' The perception of death arises and you can see emotionally, maybe, that it is frightening — 'Oh, I don't want to think about it!' — or you wonder what it is, or somebody dies and you wonder what has happened to them. But if you trust in awareness, in the present, then you have perspective on the conditioning around perceptions and emotional habits that arise.

Now, is this the deathless? Is it as simple as that? My intellectual mind says, 'Well, the deathless is very abstract and very difficult to understand — and can you prove it? What do the scientists say? What does the Dalai Lama say? What do all the authorities say?' The point is, maybe we are afraid to trust the reality because the ego will come up and try to shake us. So this is where I keep reiterating and emphasizing this sense of trusting the awareness. Begin to recognize awareness as a natural state. It is very simple and uncomplicated. And it is sustainable because it isn't created, it doesn't depend on conditions to hold it together, which is why it is sustainable. If you create conditions that make you feel tranquil, when those conditions drop away you are confused again; you are agitated again. Refined states are dependent on controlling conditions. In recognizing the world the way it is, we can see that having a human body is not very helpful to tranquillity — if you've noticed! These are terribly restless and sensitive formations. So you realize what a job it is, what hard work it is, to be human, to be living in one of these forms for a lifetime. We struggle so much with it because we are in a constant state of sensitivity and never get out of it. And that sensitivity doesn't mean happy sensitivity; a lot of it is just very unpleasant. We try to control it by having beautiful things around us. But after living in this beautiful place for a week, you go back through some slummy part of London and can't bear to look! It hurts your eyes to see the ugly side of life.

This sense realm includes pain, disease, old age, sickness, loss, lamentation and grief. They are all part of the human experience. The Buddha was pointing to these as the very things we are always trying to control and get away from. We reason that if we could control everything, we would be in heaven, we would feel happy and safe; everything would be beautiful and we would never have to experience unpleasant, sensory impingements again. But that is impossible.

Knowing the world as the world means that you are fully aware of the existential reality of being a human being. A conscious human being is 'like this'. In this way we can bear it; it is endurable. Being in a human form — male or female — and having this sensitivity can be endured; it is bearable stuff. Even the pain and sickness, the old age and the loss of loved ones, are endurable conditions, because that is part of our human kamma; as human beings we share that.

What is unbearable is what we create. At least this is what I have found. What I can't stand, what I really hate, are the resentments and fears I myself create in life. As soon as something starts hurting I want to get rid of it, I want to get away from it. If I get sick, I want to be rid of the sickness immediately. If somebody upsets me, I want to get away from that person immediately. I don't want to be upset; I want to feel happy. If I am feeling threatened and insecure, I try to find a place where I feel secure and safe. I create this desire for sense pleasure, and because of that I fear and resent it when sense experience is ugly, unpleasant and painful. I desire to be happy and to live in a realm of love, safety and beauty. And I would like to go to heaven and be in a blissful state forever. But then I get caught up in things that prevent that — the irritations of life, the little problems that monks come up with, the petty little things that go on in monasteries, the endless committee meetings where you spend hours discussing trivialities. You think, 'I didn't ordain for this! I ordained for *nibbāna*. I want to get rid of all this silliness, all these ridiculous things, all this foolishness. JUST GET ME OUT OF HERE!' And I have this kind of thing going on — 'I want to go off and be a hermit in a cave. I'm going to leave Amaravati and go and live in the Himalayas, find a cave, leave all this behind. I don't want this any more. I want to get rid of it!' And emotionally I also want to get rid of my anger. I am ashamed of my anger and want to get rid of that too. I don't want to feel these foolish emotions — because I am idealistic — and I want to be a pure-hearted bhikkhu like the Buddha — 'and you've got these dirty thoughts!' You feel ashamed of yourself and there is the desire to get rid of it all.

But in reflecting on the way things are, you realize — as the Buddha pointed out — that it is identifying with desire that is the problem. So then your relationship to desire changes and you are willing to see the desire for sense pleasure, the desire to get rid of pain, the desire to become this beautiful, blissful saintly being, and it is 'like this'. Desire for achievement and attainment through meditation is one of the problems people have; one of the blocks is the desire for attaining states and achieving *nibbāna*, or getting away from negative mental states. Awareness, then, allows these things. If they arise, they belong. That is how I see it. If bad thoughts arise, they belong. My relationship to them is no longer one of 'I don't want you', but of realizing that if these are what are coming up now in my consciousness, then they belong. I might not like them, but they belong. So I don't add anything to them. And if I try to get rid of bad thoughts, I create aversion as well as the desire to get rid of them. If an angry impression arises in me and I start dwelling on it, I attach to that, get more and more angry, fall back into the habit of finding somebody to blame for the anger, and then start resenting them.

I used to go to India every six months. It is such an interesting country and has incredible beauty as well as incredible ugliness. It isn't a tidy country like this one. There is a lot to feel averse to and a lot you might be attracted by. So for a meditator it is a very interesting place to be, just for observing how the conditioned mind reacts to it. You go through these narrow lanes in Benares. It is cold and you have just arrived. Your personality says, 'They should keep these cows out of this lane. These lanes are too narrow. They shouldn't allow cows just to wander in these lanes.' Now, that seems just common sense. 'And they throw their rubbish out in the lanes. They should have rubbish bins set there (because I'm a very tidy person). And these motorcyclists come by — they're very aggressive! Get an Indian on a motorcycle and he thinks he's Lord Krishna riding his chariot. They shouldn't allow motorcycles in these narrow lanes!' and the voice goes on like that: 'I'm going to clean up Benares!' But after a couple of weeks you just let it all go; and after two months you don't mind any of it. You find yourself manoeuvring round the hind end of a cow in a narrow lane without finding it in the least bit onerous, because it is just part of daily life there. And it is endurable; it is bearable; it isn't something I can't bear. What I can't actually bear is that every time I see a cow in a narrow lane I go into, 'It shouldn't be like this!' That sense of 'I can't stand it! It shouldn't be like this!' is what I find unbearable. And I create that. I can't blame it on anybody else. I am the creator of that feeling.

The point is to get to know the way things are in their good, bad and neutral aspects, and to realize that what we *want* them to be is additional. Realize that we add the criticism and reactions to the world and environment around us. The realization comes from this point of awareness. Death, then, *is* the door to the deathless — this is a reflection not a doctrine — and whenever you really trust in awakenedness, a part of you, your ego, dies every time. That is one of the reasons there is a lot of resistance to being fully aware, because in a way you are dying, your ego is dying. Ego is conditioned through ignorance. It wants to live; it wants to perpetuate itself. That is how it is. It is a desire. So when your relationship to the ego comes from the deathless awareness, you begin to have perspective on what arises and ceases in consciousness every moment — on feelings, thoughts, memories, and the physical side. This awareness includes everything. It is not the same as thinking, which is linear and can only generate one thought at a time. Awareness is unitive; whereas thinking is divisive. By not attaching to thought, you recognize that your true nature is not something you can define. You cannot define yourself as anything; you cannot find yourself; you are no thing. At the same time, however, awareness is pure, intelligent and wise. So this is what I recommend you put your faith into. To me refuge in the Buddha-Dhamma-Sangha means this. What I am saying is, you are not really going to die.

Trusting yourself with just awareness is a natural state of bliss. But you have to give up trying to describe it or putting it into terms. When we talk about annihilation, that has a sense of dead emptiness about it, a kind of vacuous, sanitized nothingness, like an unconscious forgetting. But recognize that the Buddha was pointing to ultimate reality which has a fullness. That is about the best you can do with words. That ultimate reality is realizable for each one of us through awareness at this moment. In order to recognize it, however, you need to let go of everything. That is why, if you try to figure it out, you find you can't. You have to trust and be patient, and be able to endure the emotional reactions you have when you let go, because your ego starts resisting, it gets panicky.

I always find it helpful to think I can endure the physical side of life — the praise or blame, success or failure, good health and bad health. There are people who have chronic pain and horrible physical problems, and I am amazed at how they endure it. One woman I know always looks bright and radiant, yet she goes through terrible pain all the time, and this isn't something that lasts for a few moments. She doesn't want to take painkillers and spend her life doped up on morphine or whatever, because she knows she *can* endure it. She is tuned in to the present and does not create the aversion, fear and resentment around the physical pain she experiences. Loss of loved ones is also endurable. All these things are part of our human experience, and we *can* bear them. We can bear the loss of fortune, and we can endure humiliation and failure. These are all endurable experiences we might have. Enduring fame and wealth is also something many people cannot take; they get corrupted and lost in it.

Right now just ask yourself, 'The deathless is — what?' Just ask that question of yourself. It can't be merely an abstract idea. If we see the deathless as merely a Buddhist theory, then it is meaningless, really. But if it is more than that, then it is now; it isn't something lacking at this moment. What is it, then, right now? Trust your intuition rather than your thoughts and views about it. Be patient with the way you are thinking or feeling, but just ask that question. Then these things drop away and what remains is non-self, the selfless state of bliss, peacefulness. In Thailand they chant a reflection on impermanence when someone dies:

Aniccā vata sankhārā uppādavayadhammino;
Uppajjitvā nirujjhanti, tesam vupasamo sukho.

All conditions are impermanent, they arise and pass
away; and when they pass away, there is peace.

'Anicca' means 'impermanence'. All conditioned phenomena, all conditions, are impermanent. The body, the mental states and feelings, arise and pass away. That is the nature of the conditioned realm, the sense realm, the thinking realm, and the emotional realm. And when they pass away there is peace, ultimate happiness, bliss. In Buddhist terms, this is a beautiful reflection about death being nothing to be frightened of.

You can begin to recognize this as you experience death whilst still a conscious living entity. As you trust in your awareness, you will start dying. In this awareness, you will find that when you let go of your ego, it is like putting down a burden. Carrying the ego is like carrying the world on your back; it is heavy and burdensome. And when you let it go it is a relief, unless your sole identity is as this person here — and then it can be frightening. Who am I if I am not this person? Emotionally, I don't know who I am any more. But with this refuge in Buddha-Dhamma-Sangha, I don't need to know who I am any more. It isn't important who I am. Instead, there is a knowing, but not claiming the knowing in any kind of personal way.

Emotionally — this is how I experience it — I am personally conditioned for extremities. I like extreme things. My nature is always to go towards adventure, excitement, interesting relationships and interesting books. And I used to fast and put myself through a lot of extreme ascetic practices, because you can get some interesting mental states that way. But Ajahn Chah was always pointing to the ordinariness of life. Certainly the monastic life in a Forest monastery in Thailand was ordinary; it was so ordinary, I found, it was boring. That is why I had to go to the extremes of asceticism to get the highs I was emotionally conditioned for. But after a while I got tired of beating myself up and starving myself; it didn't work any more. And then I began to understand better. Because of my liking for extremity, there was the tendency to resist the boredom and restlessness — emotionally resist it — which was quite a powerful thing. So I really needed to trust in the awareness. I therefore kept affirming this refuge in awareness so that I could be more aware of the subtleties of habit.

If you want to experience death before you die, then this is the way to do it. The emotional side of life can be so alive, powerful and strong — and your sense of vitality and self so connected to it — that when that starts dying, there can be a real fear of loss and maybe a resistance to it. It is like dying. Notice that when some people get old and their faculties diminish — when the life force gets less and less — they struggle against it and maybe resent it. Other people just find it a relief — 'Oh, I don't have to be a scintillating personality any more. I can just be a boring old man!'

The point is, death is the end of something that began. It just means the end. The word 'death' conveys a sense of physical death, yet you are experiencing death all the time without recognizing it. There is always an ending to something; things are always changing. If you seek an interesting, exciting life and find things to be interested in, you will notice that sometimes you reach a high — it gets to the point where you can't go any higher, you reach a peak — and then it changes and starts getting boring, starts becoming uninteresting. Then you look for something else, but without noticing the cycle, without realizing that as soon as something reaches its peak, you start to lose interest in it and start looking for something else to inspire and uplift you. This running around, this *saṁsāra*, this constant search for the next interesting event or fascinating experience or meaningful relationship or whatever, is always related to the fact that the present experience no longer has that romantic, exciting quality to it. If you practise according to the dhamma, however, the downhill stage is seen to be the important part.

Seeing the Path

The Four Stages in Buddhism — stream-entry, once-return, non-return, and full liberation *(sotāpanna, sakadāgāmin, anāgāmin, arahant)* — are reference points. When people try to figure out whether they are stream-enterers or not, they miss the point, really. Of course the ego would like to be a stream-enterer. If you have been meditating for some time, you would like to get a title for it or a degree of some kind. It is the reflective quality that is necessary, however, and for that the Ten Fetters *(saṁyojanas)* are very helpful.

In the Abhidhamma Canon and so forth there are all these lists. They are like inventories of human experience. Sometimes such texts can be overlooked, and sometimes they can be given too much significance. We take the definition of a stream-enterer, say, and then we try to attain it. This is how we tend to misuse the conventions that we align ourselves with.

Because we are so developed in intellectual knowledge, we can figure things out quite easily. We can analyse, criticize, define, limit and compare. That is how we are educated; that is what our education amounts to. But I have noticed that people who spend too much time doing that, often end up in total despair; it all gets too complicated. The Abhidhamma can seem so mind-boggling — especially if you start with it — that it makes Buddhism look very complex and difficult. It gives the impression that to be able to differentiate the subtleties of mental states would take a very special kind of human being indeed. The intellectual approach, then, is one end of the spectrum. It is certainly interesting for people who have an affinity with that way of learning; they generally like the brilliance of that approach.

We can also make the practice of meditation sound complicated: 'First you do *samatha-vipassanā*, then you develop the *jhānas*, then you do the Four Foundations of Mindfulness,' and so on, and it is beautifully described. But it just makes it all sound so complicated; there seems so much to think about, so much to determine. And how do we pick up on the terminology, say, in Pali? Some of the old translations of Buddhist texts are not all that accurate. They were translated not by Buddhist practitioners but by academics, linguists and scholars. Maybe they were accurate as literal translations, but some of them just miss the point of what the words actually mean. Buddhism is a different world outlook, a different basis for experiencing phenomena, and this needs to be taken into account when translating.

The point is to let go of definitions and trying to attain states or hold to views about practice — trying to achieve according to the viewpoints we have — otherwise we shall never be very successful. It is much more a question of awakening the human heart to reality, a reality which has no name. It is not a matter of defining or naming, but of recognizing and realizing. And this is ultimate simplicity; it is not complex. The more we hold to complexity, the more we get caught in that realm of thought and ideas. They might be beautiful thoughts, beautiful ideas, but liberation from suffering cannot be achieved through clinging to those kinds of things.

It is very helpful, I think, to reflect on the Ten Fetters. The first three are personality belief, sceptical doubt, and attachment to rules and ritual. Now, personality belief is something I have talked a lot about; it is how we create this personality, how we identify with it and feel we *are* our personalities. This is rarely questioned or investigated by most people because the sense that 'I am this person' seems so real. But when you reflect on experience in the present, you find that the personality is something that is always changing. As someone was saying earlier, when she is with her mother she is like *this*, and when she is with her husband she is like *that*, and when she is with her pet cat she is another way, and it is not the same person.

When I was young I had the idea that I ought to be the same person under all circumstances, that when I was with my mother and father, I should feel exactly the same as when I was with my friends. This was an ideal of not cheating, of not adapting myself to other people, of being this same personality under all conditions without wavering. Well, that was an ideal! When I went home, I found myself very quickly submitting to the old ways with my parents. It was easier to go along with it, just kind of bear it rather than fight it. My parents wanted me to be their little boy again, and it would have taken too much to resist that, so I just kind of gave into it. Because of that, however, I seldom went home. And then I felt I was being dishonest and made all kinds of value judgements around that. But in Buddhism we have this term 'interdependency' *(idappaccayatā)* which means 'things arise when the conditions for them are present'. So, when your mother is present, the conditions are not the same as when your best friend is present; it is a different condition. You can reflect on this, just observe how you adapt to conditions and how much they change. So you cannot sustain a permanent personality through the changing conditions that you inevitably experience. The stability, then, lies not in the personality, but in the awareness.

The point, then, is to notice the personality belief *(sakkāya-diṭṭhi)* but without thinking there is anything wrong with it. When the conditions are good we have a positive, good-humoured personality. And when the conditions are not very good we become grumpy, angry or jealous. If there is no condition to make me jealous, of course, there is no jealousy, but as conditions change, jealousy might arise. Then the personality will lay claim to that, judge it and make some criticism about it: 'I shouldn't feel jealous! It's wrong and it's my fault,' and there is this self-disparagement that takes place. So looking at it through interdependency, I found, was a more useful way of investigating the experience of changing conditions. We can be aware of this changingness, and realize that the awareness is not a personality — yet it is discerning. There is intelligence, discernment and wisdom from that point of awareness. From awareness, then, we have the capability of either acting or not acting.

The other day somebody said they thought that if you were always mindful, you wouldn't really be able to do anything. So, you might see people starving on the streets and just say, 'Well, impermanence . . . watch the sadness in the heart and it will change . . .' It is possible to be like that, of course, but you might also actually do something. The action, however, would not be a reaction; it would be more spontaneous. Actions coming out of awareness have a spontaneity about them and are more appropriate to time and place rather than being reactive habits.

When we see poverty-stricken people on the streets we could develop a habit of, 'Oh, isn't it too bad for them . . .' and go into this kind of pity where we see life as unfair — but still without doing anything. Or we might feel compelled to act because if we don't we will feel guilty. Our actions then, even if they are good, often have some kind of delusion attached to them. It is of course better to do good through delusion than not to do anything, but it isn't necessarily going to be liberating for you, and you are then inclined to think, 'Maybe I should have done more? Maybe I should have done *this* or *that* . . .' I remember a sort of conundrum which went round some years ago: 'Should you give money to a tramp who is obviously an alcoholic? Because if you do, he'll just go and buy more booze with it, so maybe you should take him for a meal instead!' That, of course, puts you in a moral dilemma, 'Am I really perpetuating his horrible habit by giving him money, because I don't have time to take him to McDonald's?' Then you say to the tramp, 'I'm going to take you to McDonald's!' — and he doesn't want to go! He says, 'McDonald's hamburgers are carcinogenic, alcohol is better.' And you think, 'Maybe that's right!'

Another of the first three fetters is *sīlabbata-parāmāsa*, which is generally translated as 'attachment to rites and rituals'. Now, this has never been a great problem for most Western monks, because Westerners in general tend to look down on the rites and rituals that take place in Buddhist temples rather than get attached to them. We are, however, attached to views, opinions, ideals, and conventions. We get very attached to 'our form of Buddhism' or 'our way of keeping the Vinaya' or 'our teacher', 'our group', or 'our monastery'. If you invest a lot of your life in these institutions, you do get very attached to them, and to Buddhism itself.

Attachment to rites and rituals, therefore, isn't just a matter of believing that if you light candles and incense and offer flowers, you are purifying your mind in some way. That has never been one of my attachments, anyway. My attachments have been more around the Thai Forest tradition and Ajahn Chah, or 'our way of doing things'. I feel this incredible loyalty to Ajahn Chah and also to the Thai Sangha which has put such a lot of trust in me. I don't want to disappoint them; I don't want to let them down. Attachments, then, can often be quite noble-hearted and high-minded. But when you really look at even these, you realize that attachment itself creates suffering; it blinds you, and you can get stuck somehow through this blindness. Burdened by being dutiful, by trying to uphold and defend, by doing the right thing and saving the world, is a way of thinking and experiencing life that tends to be rather onerous. At first it can be quite inspiring to think like that, but after a while you just feel burdened, weighed down by some heavy thing that you have created.

People sometimes say to me, 'Well, why don't you just disrobe and leave it all behind?' But that is another kind of attachment, isn't it? The conundrum for me is how to let go of the conventions that I am representing. How do I stop holding on and carrying them around with me? I have found that reflectiveness and awareness is the answer, because it is not a matter of *doing* anything other than letting them go in my mind. It is a question of seeing through the illusions I have about myself and my tradition, of seeing the fear around betraying or letting down my group and disappointing people. The fear of failure goes with the sense of success, duty, and living up to things. You can't have one without the other.

The challenge, then, is to recognize letting go by becoming conscious of what attachment or clinging is. Reflectiveness and mindfulness allow me to witness in my mind the sense of myself being of the Thai Forest tradition, say, and how that perception affects my consciousness. What comes from thinking the thought that I am the representative of the Thai Forest tradition here in Europe, and that Ajahn Chah trusted me to come here, and that I am responsible? I can stop thinking about it and just feel this sense of 'I'm responsible for all this'. And if I stay with that feeling without justifying, denying or doing anything about it, I notice the energy changing. The tension I create about being responsible, drops away — just by noticing that attachment is the way we don't let go. We feel these burdens; we feel we are doing the right thing, that we are good and trying our best. We analyse and justify everything. But it isn't a matter of figuring it out; it is more about noticing how perceptions affect consciousness in the present. By making a perception fully conscious, by allowing it to be, by noticing the way we feel physically (maybe in the heart or abdomen), and by noticing the mood that generates from that perception — not critical of it, not analysing or judging it, but just noticing it — then it changes; we can't sustain it. We have to keep thinking something over and over again in order to get some kind of sustainable sense of it. If we just let it be, that tension of grasping is recognized and naturally drops away, because we are not doing anything to create more of it. I found this a skilful way of freeing myself from the kind of altruistic nature and attachment I have around the monastic life and Buddhism.

What is the monastic life really for? Is it to make me into an arahant? — 'I want to become an arahant so I'll join the monastery.' That would be using a conventional form to *become* something. 'I'm not an arahant now, but if I practise diligently for years in the monastic form, I might become one.' That would be personality belief and attachment to conventions both together; it would be using the conventional form out of ignorance and attachment on a personal level. You meet people who give up the monastic life after a while because it doesn't work for them. One can be inspired to begin with and really try one's hardest, but that kind of energy can't be sustained — not with the monastic life, or with marriage, or with a career, or with anything — it isn't possible. It is rather a question of noticing that the monastic conventions are there for awareness.

The point is to use this awareness in order to put into perspective the conventions that you adhere to — the way you hold yourself as a person, the attachments you have to the institution of family or to being English, Scottish, Welsh, Tibetan or American, the idea of being a man or woman, of being gay or lesbian, or anything. When you bring conditions into awareness, what are they? If you make them fully conscious but don't create anything out of them, they drop away. The need to define yourself falls away and what is left is liberation — the sense of being unlimited, not being bound by the limitations of identifying with the physical body, its gender, behaviour, ideas, conventions or personality habits. You somehow see beyond the delusions you create. However you define yourself is always going to create suffering. If I try to define myself as 'a good Buddhist monk', if that is my ideal, I can never be good enough. Actually, I've given up on that one because the critical mind will say, 'You dropped marmalade on your robe this morning — not very mindful!'

Now, the third fetter, *vicikicchā*, is defined as 'sceptical doubt', and doubt is created by attachment to thought. People have told me how they try to solve dilemmas in their lives — 'Should I do this or should I do that?' — and how they just get caught in doubt. They ask me, 'What do you think, Ajahn Sumedho, should I do A or should I do B?' Then we try to analyse it. 'Well, if you do A you will get *these* advantages, and if you do B you will get *those* advantages. Which do you really want?' 'Well, I'm not sure. Some days I want to do A and some days I want to do B.' So then I say, 'Well, just stop worrying about it. Let it go. Forget it for a while.' The point is, if you let go of trying to figure things out, the answer usually comes, and it is usually the right one. I have made many mistakes because of not liking that feeling of doubt, though. I have chosen arbitrarily — A! Then regretted it when it turned out to be the wrong choice.

We think and have retentive memories, and those things are not to be despised. Thought is a tool; it is one of our gifts as human beings. But it can also be a source of great suffering because a lot of our memories are very unpleasant. Somebody reminds us of something, an unpleasant memory arises, and then we feel depressed, saddened or angry — because of something that happened twenty years ago! Just notice how memory works. We don't usually remember ordinary things; we remember the extremities — the great times and the horrible, the successes and failures. When I look back on my life, I find it easy to remember the unpleasant things that have happened to me, those things I resent or feel angry about, or regret or feel guilty about. Sometimes I can cheer myself up by thinking of the good things in my life, but for some reason my nature tends towards the negative; it doesn't easily incline towards the positive. But recognize that memory arouses emotion. That is why we can remember something that happened twenty years ago and still feel angry about it now. The rational mind says 'Don't be so silly; that's over and done with; it was a long time ago — forget and forgive! — just let it go.' You can say all the wise things, give yourself very good advice and feel that you should definitely do that, but you still feel like *this*. So notice, awareness includes the rational as well as the emotional; and the rational is often very critical of the emotional because rational thought doesn't like emotion.

Men in particular, I think, prefer rationality. For many men it is embarrassing to be lost in emotion. Rational thought is very nice; it is rapid and intelligent and clear, and is a whole world that is quite enjoyable. And then emotion comes in and you find yourself resisting it. You don't like emotions because they aren't rational. So all you can do is rationalize and say, 'Oh, this is just a bunch of rubbish — forget it! — "Much ado about nothing!" — it doesn't really matter.' That is a way of dismissing things. But as you trust more in awareness, you begin to recognize your emotional life. If you just ignore and deny it all the time, it is always going to come at you in some way; it will pursue you and haunt you, which is why I think men get so depressed in middle age or later life. There is so much effort needed to hold down the emotional world that if it becomes too strong — if it becomes overwhelming — it just ends in depression. You cannot experience any joy if you are not free emotionally. Also, after a while the entertainment of thinking falls away. You get tired of just think-think-think all the time, of clever ways of thinking about life. It seems so superficial and meaningless.

Now, I have made many mistakes in the past by assuming that my memory of someone *is* the person. But if I remember someone who is not here, that is just a memory, isn't it? It is *not* the person. And memories are very selective. If the last time I met that person we had a terrible fight and parted saying terrible things to each other, that is the memory I am left with. Twenty years pass and then somebody mentions his name and I say, 'He's a — ! I'm having *nothing* to do with him!' He might have become an arahant in the meantime, I don't know, but I am stuck with the memory and the powerful belief in that memory. If the last memory I have of him is a strong one — positive or negative — that is what I am left with.

After somebody has died, we do of course have the memory of that person, but the memory now is connected to the word 'death'. If you notice, when people are alive — even though they might be in pain and very sick in hospital — somehow we can relate to them; the person is still alive. Of course we have sympathy for those who are sick and in pain, but pain is something we can understand. Disease and all these things are understandable in our own experience. Death, on the other hand — don't know!

Ajahn Chah was ill for about ten years before he died, and Ajahn Passano phoned me many times from Thailand to say he thought Ajahn Chah was dying. So I would get the first plane out — and then he would pull through. Pretty soon you get used to that. The idea of Ajahn Chah being sick and of Ajahn Chah dying — these I adjusted to. I knew he was going to die at some time — I wasn't expecting immortality — but when he did actually die and I knew he was dead, it was a different feeling; it was a feeling of real grief. For a long time there had been a feeling of 'he's dying but he's still alive'; there was hope there and I could relate to that. But 'Ajahn Chah is dead' — that was finality.

Just note how words affect us, how the power of perception affects our feelings. Some words are just neutral and don't arouse much feeling, whereas others have a very powerful effect. The tone of voice even or how people say things can also affect us. We are so sensitive that if somebody says beautiful words in an angry tone of voice — 'I LOVE YOU!' — we feel the anger, even though the words may be very nice. In the navy we used to call each other terrible names — 'You old son of a bitch!' — but it was mostly just expressions of affection.

It is a question of recognizing what sensitivity is and how memories can affect us. I found it helpful to notice consciously that memory is memory — whether it is a strong memory, a beautiful memory, or an ugly memory. Whatever it is, it is *not* a person; it is merely a memory. In that way I can actually recognize what is happening. I am here with you right now and this is not a memory. When I go back to Amaravati, of course, you will be a memory to me. Then the conditions will have changed because memory is different from direct experience. Remembering somebody, however, might bring up feelings of unease and resentment and endless fears might be created about meeting that person again. 'What will I do? He just upsets me so much and I don't think I can take any more! BUT WE'VE GOT TO RESOLVE OUR DIFFERENCES! I'VE GOT TO CONFRONT

HIM! I MUST SAY EXACTLY HOW I FEEL!' And I plan it all out ahead of time. If I let go, on the other hand, if I don't come from 'I'M GOING TO TELL YOU THE TRUTH!' or from a feeling of fear — if I trust in the awareness — then the conditions will be present for a genuine meeting when it takes place. If I go to meet him with a bias and I don't see what I am doing, then I don't see him, do I? I see my bias, project that onto him, and then act accordingly, maybe saying terrible things which are totally unrelated to him as he is in the present.

You can see this worldwide in terms of terrorists. We talk about 'the axes of evil', 'the war on terror', 'the evil forces'. We hear these kinds of phrases all the time now, and they are perceptions that bring up emotional reactions. So notice that. It isn't a matter of condemning it, but of recognizing how easily we are affected by what we hear, see, and experience through the senses and through the mind. Awareness, however, is the background of that and is our refuge. That is the stability. It doesn't change. It allows change and knows change, but it sustains itself. That is what we mean by refuge in Buddha-Dhamma-Sangha: *Buddhaṁ saraṇaṁ gacchāmi; Dhammaṁ saraṇaṁ gacchāmi; Sanghaṁ saraṇaṁ gacchāmi* (I take refuge in the Buddha, the Dhamma, and the Sangha).

When you take these refuges, try not to say the words just because you think you are supposed to, but *really* contemplate what they mean. I found it helpful to try to figure out those words intellectually and then to see the reality of them in the present moment. Buddha-Dhamma-Sangha is in here; it isn't some abstract thing. Through our own ability to recognize and investigate thinking, memory, personality and attachment to conventions, we actually remove the obstructions to the path. The stream-enterer is one who sees the path. We create delusions. We are not born with the delusions of being attached to rules and rituals, personality belief, and sceptical doubt. These are created after we are born. They are not natural in the same way that consciousness is natural.

When we are born we are conscious — consciousness and the physical body are natural conditions. What we acquire afterwards are greed, anger, hatred, resentment and delusion. These come mostly out of ignorance through reactiveness. And we create our personalities and attachments to conventions, views and opinions. By taking refuge in the Buddha as the awakened state of being, however, we begin to have perspective on both the conditioning process and the awareness that transcends conditions. So the conditions can be seen. What you *think* you are — you suddenly realize — is *not* what you are. This is not a matter of trying to dismiss or judge anything, but of recognizing that everything is what it is — it is dhamma; it is the way it is. All conditions arise and cease; so it isn't a question of denying, judging or criticizing, but of just discerning. The wisdom faculty develops out of that. And don't think that the recognition of stream-entry is such a difficult thing. In the Theravada it tends to be elevated to this level of being a high attainment, but I have found that to be very unhelpful. The ego would *like* to attain and become; my personality wants to *become* an arahant. But my personality will *never* become an arahant, so I can't trust that. We get attached to the conventions we use — to meditation techniques, ideas of Buddhism, schools of Buddhism, views about Buddhism — and we don't recognize the attachments we have. We align ourselves with a conventional form of Buddhism and then wonder why we are never liberated through it. That is not because of the school of Buddhism but because of the attachment to it.

I encourage you therefore to trust in your ability to be aware. Really explore that, really notice that. Then you will begin to recognize your own doubt, worry or whatever, but as the witness rather than the judge. And then you will not be so willing to buy into these states, or to follow them or be intimidated by any thoughts and memories. Just notice your emotional reactions. Rather than trying to figure out *why* you are angry, notice what it is *like* to feel angry. Notice that the anger is 'like this', and really take the opportunity to recognize and accept it. The same with greed, doubt, fear, or jealousy. To simply recognize these things is all that is necessary. You don't need to know why; it isn't necessary to know why. Just know — it is 'this'. And recognize non-thought as well; just recognize that. So be very patient with yourself and with the conditions you are experiencing. Eventually, if you are patient enough, they will drop away of their own accord. Then notice the feeling — it is like a state of bliss. It isn't high; it isn't like being over the moon, but it is a sense of being really present, really full and complete — no-self. So notice that. When you let go and allow things to be what they are in yourself, your practice develops this way. Then more and more you gain confidence in the practice. The practice becomes clearer, easier. It is not an artificial state that you are recognizing, but a natural one. Anything artificial, created, depends on other things to support it. But being present doesn't depend on other things to support it. The important thing is to recognize this.

In the Four Noble Truths, the third truth is about realizing and recognizing, and the fourth is about cultivating and developing. Just from one little insight — if you really appreciate it — more and more you begin to see the path. You might still get carried away with other things, of course, but don't trust that. And don't regret it, either. Don't make problems about your inability to really meditate. We can persecute ourselves about not meditating as much as we think we should, but just notice that; just notice the way you hold meditation. Notice the perception you have about how many hours you do and about the need to become more patient and so on. You might have very good ideas about meditation, but when you are attached to ideas from the personality belief, you are always going to feel guilty and doubt yourself. But as soon as you do that, just begin to look at it; look at whatever your feelings are, whether good or bad, high or low — 'I'm fed up with meditation; I don't want to do it any more but I should, I should practise!' Look at that. Your awareness of these things is the opportunity you have of developing the path in this present moment.

After you see through the first three fetters, the primal energies are still there, as with a once-returner. And as a non-returner you are still attached to refinement and tranquillity. Then finally the arahant is one who is completely himself or herself, at ease in being truly aware, just being *with* life as it happens, all delusions resolved. This is someone who doesn't make a problem about anything. So an arahant — in the Theravadan school — is not cut off, but is no longer deluded by the conditions that he or she has to experience in life.

I don't know what I will have to experience before I die — good health or bad, success or failure, whatever — but that doesn't bother me any more; it doesn't concern me. When one is willing to just live one's life, whether it is happy, successful and healthy or not, isn't a problem, because one sees that the kamma is 'like this'. The conditions for sickness and bad health are here, but one doesn't create a problem around whatever life presents.

Intuitive Awareness

I realize that the way I use words like 'intuition', 'thinking' and 'feeling' can be quite confusing so I will try to clarify what I mean.

Now, thinking is *not* intuitive. You can analyse with thought, but thinking is not a sensitive function. People that think too much are often quite insensitive. Cold-hearted scientists and intellectuals who have great thoughts about loving all sentient beings, can be as cold as ice — because thought itself has no feeling in it whatsoever. Acts such as genocide are quite possible from the ideal world of logic and reason. Apartheid and the Jewish holocaust were based on a degree of reason and logic, and not on feeling. If you have any feeling, you can't do those kinds of things. When we start from an idea, when we have a premise, then we can lock into that — and the logic comes from that. Some of these crazy fundamentalist groups are often made up of very reasonable people. They start out with a basic premise and the logic follows from that. So, if you follow their way of reasoning, if you are converted by their way of thinking, you could end up joining them.

But we are also sensitive creatures, so we feel things. We are sensitive to atmosphere, the tone of a person's voice, the power of words, language, spin — all of these things. A good orator can convince crowds of people to do very stupid things. It is said that Hitler was only brilliant in that he was a brilliant orator. Even before he had any kind of mission in life, he realized that once he started talking, people would gather round and listen to him. This is how demagogues can manipulate crowds — just by tuning into some kind of common fear or ideal that everyone shares. Someone like Hitler could catch the minds of masses of people to follow along and do atrocious acts in the name of some kind of ideal. There are many stories about charismatic people that can convince, convert, compel and hypnotize us. But how we feel about things might also come from our parents' prejudices and things that we have picked up as children. So when a particular perception is triggered off, we get caught in the feeling that is aroused from that. We can, of course, reason our way out of prejudices and irrational feelings. But when groups get together, the rational side can easily get lost and an incredible mass power can develop — as in the case of football hooliganism, for example. I am sure that this kind of thing happened in Rwanda where some kind of tribal common ground was reached and an emotion aroused that infected everybody beyond reason. It wasn't reasonable, and yet many people participated in mass slaughter. So 'feeling' can't be trusted, either.

Finally, there is this word 'intuition' by which I mean 'intelligence'. What I am talking about here is an intelligence that is not gained through learning but is natural, so it includes instinctual intelligence as well as the ability to be aware. Wisdom comes from that intuitive sense. There are many books on wisdom and wisdom teachings — and they are certainly wise teachings — but just memorizing them and repeating them doesn't mean we are wise. We can memorize all the words of Confucius and still be utter fools. Wisdom, then, is the spontaneous ability we have of dealing with time and place, the appropriate response to conditions of the here and now.

When you are meditating and letting go of everything, your thoughts cease, your feelings calm down, and what is left when there are no thoughts and feelings dominating consciousness is intuition, an intuitive intelligence. As soon as you try to think about that, however, you are lost again. Intuition is an act of surrender, a relaxation into awareness, which actually doesn't seem like anything at all. You have to give up the idea of trying to define it. Just trust the ability to recognize — this is it! This is mindfulness! This is intuitive awareness *(sati-sampajañña)*! It is an inclusiveness rather than a divisive function of mind.

Now, concentration practices tend to be centred on focusing on one object and excluding everything else. So when people take up tranquillity *(samatha)* practices, they usually have to find a place where there are no harsh impingements. That is because they have to concentrate all their attention on the one point by *excluding* everything else. What I am saying is that intuitive awareness is inclusive; it is the point that includes everything. Everything that happens — even the sound of an aeroplane or a lawnmower or whatever — belongs in this moment. And from here there is no attempt to control the mind, but rather to open; there is a sense of opening and relaxing with the present moment. Because this is not divisive, wisdom then starts operating, and we begin to observe how things really are. We notice the body, the breath, the mental state, the door slamming or whatever. All is included. If we concentrate on the point that excludes, on the other hand, when somebody slams a door, we just feel annoyed by 'the clumsy person who has disrupted my tranquillity!' because we think a slamming door doesn't belong. In the point that includes, everything belongs. It isn't a matter of how pleasant or unpleasant the conditions might be. The fact is they are here, and in this intuitive awareness, they belong. However we are feeling — physically, mentally, emotionally or psychically — whether we are in a crazy state of mind, calm and cool, or communicating with *devas* in the heavenly realms, demons in the lower realms or whatever — it all belongs. The quality of the experience is not the issue.

The wisdom faculty develops out of our reflection on impermanence — 'all conditions are impermanent' — and you actually witness impermanence. You do not just project the idea of impermanence onto experience, the wisdom is ripening and you are seeing the nature of all conditions by witnessing it; it isn't a question of holding the view that everything is impermanent or believing in it, but of seeing it for yourself. You see it! It's obvious! And that includes everything whether it is a beautiful *deva* or an horrific demon. As you trust in this intuitive position, you are interested only in changingness and will therefore not be overwhelmed by beauty or hideousness.

Emotional reactions are also included in this intuitive awareness, because everything belongs. So happiness and misery and all external and internal experiences in this moment are received. It might sound as though we ought to focus on one thing — because if we receive everything, we are just going to be overwhelmed! — but that is not the case. In fact, if we trust in the intuitive point that includes, our relationship even to chaos and confusion is one of wisdom rather than of being lost in the chaos. I find this a skilful way of going about things when life gets confusing — which it does sometimes — when things happen and nothing is very clear, when I am emotionally confused and everything seems to be in a state of amorphous obscurity. This can be rather frightening. Yet when I trust in awareness, I can totally accept that feeling. If I don't trust in it, on the other hand, I get carried away with resentments towards people whom I think are the cause of it. I might try to get at somebody: 'DO YOU MEAN *YES* OR DO YOU MEAN *NO?*' — I want clarity and definition; I don't want indecisiveness; I want clarity. My personality is such that I feel much more secure when everything is clear and defined — personally, as a person. When things are not clear, my personality gets wobbly. So I can't trust my personality because it is like that; it is just the way the personality operates. But awareness is beyond the personality. It isn't a thought, it isn't perception, and yet it includes feeling. So it isn't just a cold, icy kind of sterile witnessing of life like a cold-hearted scientist dissecting frogs or something; it allows for feeling. Feeling then comes out more through the *brahmavihāras*[25] — loving-kindness, compassion, sympathetic joy, and

---

25 *Brahmavihāras* (the four sublime or divine abodes): loving-kindness *(mettā)*, compassion *(karuṇā)*, sympathetic joy *(muditā)*, equanimity *(upekkhā)*.

equanimity — rather than through emotional habits of liking and wanting this, or disliking and trying to get rid of that.

Last night's talk about compassion for Hitler was very interesting because most of us would like to feel compassion — and maybe even compassion for Hitler — as an ideal. On an emotional level, however, I feel, 'Well, Hitler really deserves to be tormented in hell for an eternity.' I can be quite judgemental — 'He was so bad, how could anyone have compassion for such a demon!' But compassion is not, as John Peacock was saying, a sentimental feel-good emotion; it is understanding. When you really tune into yourself, how much suffering do you think you have created in your life — just from little things? I haven't killed anyone or done anything all that bad, but I have suffered enough even from being basically good. Imagine what it would be like to be really bad. I remember the mean or selfish things I have done more clearly than the good ones. You never forget those; they are always ready to come into consciousness. So there is a sense of 'I'm going to be careful just for my own good, just so as not to create too much misery in my own mind.' Somebody like Hitler, having done what he did, must have suffered enormously. You read stories about his fear and anger, about how he didn't have a sense of humour and took himself too seriously. And people were trying to kill him! His life was constantly under threat. At the same time he must also have had a sense of great power. Men can love that feeling of total power, to feel 'I'm King of the world!' But you can't sustain it. You might have moments where you feel really great, but you can't keep that feeling; it isn't something that sustains itself for very long. So most tyrants, it seems, live paranoid lives. They experience endless fear and anxiety, which is why they have to kill so many people. Saddam Hussein was obviously trying to kill off anybody that threatened him because he was so frightened; and he had every reason to be. You can control people with fear, but there is always going to be somebody who isn't frightened of you, and you have to find out who that is — and then get them! Just think what it would be like to have a mind like that. You wouldn't have many pleasant moments.

People sometimes say, 'The law of kamma isn't always true, is it? There are people who live very bad lives — they kill, are corrupt and dishonest — and yet have beautiful homes, big cars, swimming pools, go to Monaco every year . . . They've got everything!' But if we had to live within their minds, I don't think we would want it. All the stuff they get doesn't solve the problem; it is meaningless, really. I think all of us have experienced materialism to the point where we have simply got tired of it. Just having more and better makes you more bored with it all — because you spend your life just trying to improve everything.

The answer then is in the mind itself, in here. I am referring to this intuitive awareness. Mindfulness, awakenedness, is the kingpin, the axis, the real essence of the Buddha's teaching. And that is a very simple, immanent act, which is why I am encouraging you to recognize it rather than trying to become 'someone who is mindful'. As soon as you conceive yourself as 'somebody who is not mindful and has to become so', then you are holding to a *view* of mindfulness, which means you are not mindful — unless you are mindful that you are attached to a view of mindfulness. So this is something you have to find out for yourself, something you have to recognize. I can encourage and point, but that is about the best anybody can do.

Now, the teaching to do good and refrain from doing evil is so basic in Buddhism, it is kind of hackneyed. In Thailand everybody says it, every little kid recites: 'Do good receive good. Do bad receive bad.' You hear it over and over again. And after a while you don't want to hear it any more. But it is pointing to a reality. Doing good, thinking good thoughts, taking up tranquillity practices and developing positive qualities — if you really appreciate that way, have the right attitude towards it — then you feel happy. You develop bliss and beautiful mental experiences if you think good thoughts filled with loving-kindness and compassion. Just thinking good creates happiness. Thinking bad thoughts, on the other hand, creates unhappiness. So it is very immediate. When I start worrying, immediately it is like being in hell. But if I look at the sun coming up or the beautiful gardens here, it is different. Geshe Gedun[26] and I were walking through the botanical gardens this morning and they looked incredibly beautiful. We were both awestruck by their beauty, and it was a heavenly feeling. The Geshe said, 'This is the Tushita Heaven,' so we are already in Tushita here. But just notice that this is the way it is. We can conceive of the Tushita Heaven as being some kind of ethereal state, as some abstraction out there, but we experience these kinds of things here like in these gardens, when we open to the beauty. We can walk through the gardens worrying about what we are going to do when we get home and not get any joy or pleasure out of them whatsoever — maybe not even notice them — or we can open to them.

One reason we like nature is because we *can* open to it, and trust it. Nature is what it is, a tree is what it is and nobody has made it, a human being has not created it. So things are just what they are in nature and that gives us a sense of relaxation and trust. An artificial world that comes from the workings of the human brain is often produced for the purpose of making money and is for dazzling, exciting and stimulating, and that produces a different feeling, doesn't it? That is different from being in a place where nature is allowed to be dominant, where there are just trees, flowers, mountains and waterfalls. So Disneyland — not that I have ever been there — is different from the Leicester botanical gardens. This is just a reflection; you don't have to agree with me; it is a question of noticing how things work with you; you might be different, I don't know. What I am saying is find out for yourself; see how things are for you.

When you get caught up in worry, anxiety, mistrust, self-aversion and so on, just step back and ask yourself, 'What am I doing?' Intuition will then begin to take hold and you will no-

---

26 Geshe Gedun Tharchin, Lam Rim Institute, Rome.

tice that you are creating negative thoughts that arouse negative emotions. If you then say, 'I shouldn't do that!' you are creating more negative feeling. No matter how much you punish yourself for being foolish, you will just add to it; the very desire to punish and judge yourself will pile more negative feeling on top of that which already exists. Intuition, on the other hand, is non-judgemental; it just says, 'It is like this. Self-aversion, anxiety, worry, depression is like this.' Then you stop analysing states of mind and making them into something. You just recognize them. You just *feel* the kind of mood that hangs around you, the kind of greyness and dreariness. If you don't recognize the mood in its energetic form, everything you say will come out of that mood. You will see the world and talk to everybody through that cloud, and come across as bitter or anxious. By trusting in awareness, however, you will see that the anxiety or self-aversion is what it is, and you will also see that you are allowing it to do what it is meant to do, which is to change — it arises, it ceases. As you gain more in confidence, you will see states of mind drop away. If you are patient and willing to receive them, they will do that, they will drop away, and you will feel peace of a kind you perhaps didn't know was possible, a peacefulness that is not a tranquillity that comes from shutting out irritating conditions, but is from non-attachment and letting things be what they are. Then any powerful emotion that dominates your consciousness and which you accept, just drops away. What is left, to me, is like bliss. It is a real sense of being at ease like letting go of a heavy burden that has been weighing you down; you just let it go and there is that sense of relief and bliss. This is the way it is when you are not lost in blind grasping.

In the Pali we chant *paccattaṃ veditabbo viññūhi* (to be experienced individually). In other words, you can only know for yourself, and it is very simple. We tend to project dhamma onto ideals, and it gets beyond us. We cannot all come here and live permanently in this Tushita Heaven of Leicester. We are lucky to get six days out of the year here, and we appreciate it — it is certainly something I appreciate — but if I go away thinking, 'I can only be happy in the Leicester botanical gardens,' I am a fool, aren't I?

I have been in India this past year, which is the most interesting country in the world as far as I am concerned. I really love that place because it is such a challenge. Everything is out in the open. The people live more or less on the streets and are very friendly, so it is a country in which you feel an aliveness — at least I found it so. If you make the effort to smile at people, they generally smile back and seem delighted that you are interested in them. They have a lot of poor people there, of course, but even the beggars — even those that tend to be irritating — have a good sense of humour, and you can joke with them. You do see quite shocking things also in India in contrast to our part of the world which we have tidied up so nicely. Britain is actually a very nice country to live in, though I don't think everybody realizes it. It isn't perfect, of course, but it is better than most places, and I appreciate living here. When I go to India, I don't expect it to be like this. Yet India offers another way of looking at life. There I appreciate the sense of the sacred and the quality of the people. In England there is very little eye contact; people generally look away. But in India they just stare at you, and you can just stare at them — nobody minds. There isn't the fear in India of looking and receiving each other, so it feels much more open there, which I quite like. When receiving India from that intuitive position, everything belongs. Any feeling of foreignness or fear becomes more conscious, but it doesn't motivate or drive you any more, and you can let it go. Then you find a sense of ease, of openness and receptivity, and an interest in the people and the things you experience.

The Sense of Timelessness

I find that time goes by very quickly. I have been in the UK now for twenty-eight years and I look around and think, 'Why is everybody so much older?' Then I look in the mirror and . . !

This investigation of time, I think, is a very important reflection because we are a time-bound society; we really believe in the reality of it. We believe our age, the sense of history and the continuity of time. And we believe we have been born; we have this sense of going through the years and yet in some way remaining the same. We just assume that we are the same person throughout this span which we call 'our lifetime'. In awareness, however, we realize there is no such thing as time, and that all we do is project onto the experience of now. That is what we call 'time'. In reality there is only right now, only the here and now. This is where consciousness operates. Breathing is happening right now; feeling through the body and the senses is now; the thinking process is now. We can remember what we were thinking yesterday, but even that is a thought, a memory in the present.

Breaking down the assumptions about oneself and the cultural habits one has in regard to time I found very helpful in learning to trust in awareness and recognizing that liberation is now, freedom is now, *nibbāna* is now — rather than having this perception of practising now in order to attain liberation in the future. The point is, we create the perception of past, present and future, birth and death, beginning and ending. First we create the words to describe experience, and then we become attached to those words, often not noticing the reality behind them. So we create ourselves as personalities, and we create England, and we create our positions in society. When Christians ask whether we have a Creator-God in Buddhism, we say, 'Well, not exactly, because "I" am the creator of the world,' which can sound like a kind of megalomania. If one is claiming to be the ultimate creator, that is a sign of madness, isn't it? But in terms of the reality of this moment, we are the ones who are creating; we are projecting our habits and feelings onto this moment. So, in terms of reflection in awareness, we call this 'the creator of the world'.

I found also that just through the exploration of my own memories, just through remembering things of the past, I could arouse emotion in myself. When I started developing insight meditation years ago in Thailand, I noticed how angry and indignant I could become over past events in my life, events that had nothing to do with the conditions I was experiencing at the time. I could wind myself up simply by obsessing my mind with memories of unfair treatment that might have happened twenty or thirty years before. There I was in a Buddhist monastery in Thailand still angry! And I could maintain that anger by continuously remembering and dwelling on the memory. In terms of dhamma — in terms of 'all conditions are impermanent' — I realized that memories simply arise and cease, and that if I keep holding onto them I can feel the anger and resentment again and again. By feeding memories I can get just as angry as I did when those events originally took place.

Revenge, also, is based on remembering wrongs done to you in the past and holding onto them. There is a desire to get even. And vengeance has a kind of attractiveness to it — 'They should be punished! They shouldn't get away with it! They should be made to suffer! They should pay the price!' I began to watch this in myself — this desire to get even, this desire to make them pay — and realized that it too is based on memory. By putting memory into context through awareness, however, one can see what it really is — that it arises and ceases according to conditions. If you don't cling to memory, it is very brief. It flashes through consciousness and does not sustain itself. Nevertheless, a good memory makes you feel good, and a bad memory makes you feel bad. That is very clear and obvious.

Since there is only the here and now in terms of experience, of course, the past at this moment is just a memory. So try to put that into the perspective of perception. There is nothing wrong with memory — it is actually a great gift — so it isn't a matter of trying to wipe it out or destroy it, but rather of investigating its nature and not being enslaved and tortured by it. The point to realize is that the past *is* a memory. By reflecting in this way I was able to put the perception of time into context and began to see it quite differently.

Awareness is this sense of 'awakened here and now', this intuitive sense of embracing the moment. It is not a divisive function of the mind; it is not a judging faculty; it isn't something that decides which is the best and which is the worst or takes an interest in quality or quantity, but it is discerning, so it knows things as they are. And the wisdom comes from that discernment. The critical mind is cultivated through thinking and dwelling on the quality of things — 'This is more beautiful than that; this is a man and that is a woman; this is a Buddhist and that is a Christian.' Everything is divided up and compared, and there are preferences. You like some things better than others, and some conditions you detest. This kind of emotional range arises from dwelling on the quality of conditioned experience. The reality of conditioned experience, however, is seen when there is awareness. We have the ability to discern, to know that it is 'like this'.

Now, this Pali word *'tathatā'* that we use is sometimes translated as 'as-is-ness' or 'suchness'. It is a word that points to the present reality without having to define, name or qualify the present reality. So it can help you to see that 'it is like this' rather than 'I don't like the way it is' with the reactive mind when something unpleasant happens We think, 'I don't like this; it shouldn't be like this!' — that is the reactive pattern. With awareness, however, the reality of that same experience — the conditions you

are experiencing and the emotional reactions you are having —
are all included. And the only thing you can say about them is
that 'it is the way it is'. That is not a description or a definition;
it is just a pointer, a way of using thought to recognize that right
now being frightened, upset or confused is 'like this'. And this
is not some final judgement in a fatalistic way; it is the reality of
this moment; it can only be like this — the way it is.

For most of us there is a great deal of concern for the future.
We have this idea that the future holds all possibilities and all po-
tentialities for happiness, success, wealth, fame and all the best.
But with each potentiality goes its opposite — success with failure, praise with blame, and so on (in terms of the Eight Worldly Dhammas[27]). The future, therefore, is the unknown, isn't it?
There is possibility, potentiality, probability, all the could-be's
and might-be's, the hopes, dreads and anticipations. These are
the mental states we create around the future. However, the way
I see it — especially as a Buddhist monk — I don't need to plan
or anticipate the future because it is the unknown. The life of the
Buddhist monk is not about creating certainty and making great
plans; it is meant to be a flowing lifestyle rather than a controlled
one.

We can make a problem out of anything, actually. People generally want security, safety, certainty, things to go well, harmony
and peace. And yet to the worldly mind peace and harmony are
quite boring, actually. Conflict is exciting! To have a quarrel in
your group, a real problem to solve or a great issue to face, somehow gives a sense of 'this is important and this is real'. But as we
develop the way of awareness, there is no seeking things and no
functioning from desire. We see the difference between awareness and desire, even the desire to be enlightened, to get rid of
faults and defilements, to have perfect harmony and peace, to
have the ideal monastic community, or the ideal society. Our idealism tends to make us unhappy with the way things are, doesn't

---

27 Eight Worldly Dhammas *(lokadhamma)*: gain and loss, honour and
dishonour, happiness and misery, praise and blame.

it? We always think there is something wrong when we have the attitude that things should be like the ideal. Awareness, then, allows us to see what we are doing; it allows us to recognize that we are creating desire even for peace and harmony. If I am not aware and do not discern the way things are, I get caught in preferences. I don't want conflict and confusion, so when conflict and confusion arise I think, 'I don't want this! I don't like this! Monks and nuns shouldn't be like this! They should be peaceful, saintly and perfect.' Then I can only be critical of them because none of them is saintly, none of them is the ideal monk or nun, and nor am I, but that is the way it is, isn't it? This movement, this flux, this energy that we experience through consciousness and through the senses, is 'like this'.

So, as I was saying earlier, through the power of meditation I found this sense of timelessness. Time seems to have passed so quickly since I first became a monk and came to live in England. When I think in terms of the worldly mind, it doesn't seem I have been here that long, actually, and yet it has been twenty-eight years. Now, twenty-eight years sounds like a long time; I have never before lived anywhere for twenty-eight years. Then last week I turned seventy and people kept asking me about that. I said, 'I don't feel old yet.' The perception to my mind is that seventy *is* old, and yet the reality of a seventy-year-old body is that I can't say I feel old; I can't relate to myself as feeling like the perception of seventy suggests. And, actually, it is just the way it is.

We can see how conditioned ways of thinking influence how we experience life, and if we don't liberate ourselves from that — if we just continue to operate from the conditioning of the mind — we only experience life through the limitation of some perception we have, some conditioned reaction, some habit. Liberation, then, is through awareness, and that is not a created state. Awareness does not have form which is why trying to *become* aware, is not awareness. Most of us have probably been through some kind of struggle with the word 'awareness' or 'mindfulness' and then — thinking we have understood it — tried to become it. I remember trying to make myself do things mindfully. This inner voice would say, 'Be mindful NOW! Do it mindfully . . . mindfulness . . . mindfulness . . . mindfulness.' You get tired of hearing the word in fact. It is terribly good advice, right on the mark, but what does it really mean? What is mindfulness? In trying to find the proper definition of a word like that, we might find ourselves going to the texts and dictionaries to look it up. What did Ajahn Chah say? What did Ajahn Mun say? We want to know how the authorities define it. The reality is, of course, that it cannot be defined.

Mindfulness or awareness is knowing, isn't it? It is a direct knowing, immanent here and now. It is being fully present, attentive, to this present moment as is. But defining mindfulness tends to make it into something — and then it is no longer mindfulness, is it? Mindfulness is not a thing; it is a recognition, an intuitive awareness. It is awareness without grasping. With this recognition, we have perspective on the conditions that we experience in the present — our thoughts, identities, and the conditioning we have. Concentration, on the other hand, is usually on a form. We choose an object and then put our full attention onto it, in contrast to mindfulness which is formless and immeasurable, and does not seek a form. That is why describing mindfulness or awareness leads to the wrong attitude. Terms like 'wake up', 'awakening' or 'pay attention' are not definitions; they are suggestions to trust in this moment, to be present, to be here and now.

The way the scriptures read in the Theravadan schools tends to create an incredible ambition to attain particular states. I get quite despairing sometimes within my own tradition. The Western mind in particular can be very ambitious, and the sense of one's self-importance seems to emphasize that by wanting to attain the *jhānas* (absorptions) — this is the big thing! — and wanting to attain stream-entry and arahantship. I can understand this to a certain extent, of course, because I am also conditioned to wanting to attain things. I was brought up in the States where your whole life was about attaining something. So, for me, that was the most obvious way of dealing with it — you get the *jhānas*, you do *vipassanā*, you go through the four stages, and on and on like that. I can understand it and I have no problem with the concept. I have noticed, however, that operating from this sense of wanting to achieve and attain just reinforces cultural conditioning ; it does not reflect it but tends to reinforce it instead. The point is to recognize with awareness how one actually holds such concepts.

It is very common in Thailand and Sri Lanka (I don't know about Burma) to have strong views about practice. In Thailand, which I am more familiar with, there are many different techniques and ways of teaching *vipassanā* and *samatha-vipassanā*. So you get different cults and groups forming which tend to criticize each other. And this can be confusing. Naturally, I prefer my style because that is what I have learned from, that is what I have done, and when I teach, I teach from what I know; I can share that. If I put it in a context of my way being better than somebody else's, however, then that will be misleading. Somebody might actually believe me! It isn't a matter of one technique being better than another; it is how you use a technique or tradition that is important. For me, it is a matter of using the monastic discipline, or the tranquillity and insight *(samatha-vipassanā)* teachings, or the Four Noble Truths, for awareness and not for holding to opinions and preferences. I see this as the way of breaking out of the limitation of 'self' and realizing that the self-view, the sense of 'myself', is always formed through identifying with some kind of limitation.

When we really look at personality, when we examine and investigate it, we can see that it is totally based on the limitation of memory, views, opinions, preferences, fears, desires and habits. So the personality is not a living thing; it comes through conditions arising. In awareness we no longer trust it, no longer believe in it or identify with it. Awareness transcends the personality, and through that we see what the personality is in terms of experience. If we try to claim awareness, it is lost again; we have deluded ourselves. It is not a matter of it being some kind of personal ability or achievement that we have attained 'after all these years'; rather is it a natural state, our very nature, uncreated, independent of conditions. Wherever we are, whatever the conditions, no condition precludes awareness. It is therefore our refuge; it is where we find our liberation.

In the Theravada, words like *'arahant'*, *'nibbāna'*, or even *'sotāpanna'* (stream-entry) are defined as extreme positions. They are held to be great attainments. When you try to contemplate them with your thinking mind, when you are attached to thinking as your way of experiencing life, you are forced into some kind of limitation, because your thinking mind is dualistic. *'Nibbāna'*, from the position of the conditioned mind, can only be something very high, something which seems almost unobtainable. Reading about such things too much without ever practising them, will therefore make you think they are impossibilities. Even stream-entry will seem unattainable because it just sounds too complicated and too difficult. This is why it is important to reflect on your thought process. What is the function of thinking? How should you use it? How should you use it for awareness so that it is a tool rather than something that limits you, something that blocks you and binds you to these dualistic, divisive creations?

The Buddha made very clear statements about *nibbāna* being reality, about it not being an attainment. To put it simply we can say it means 'the reality of non-grasping'. Grasping is what we are involved with. The unaware, unenlightened individual is conditioned to grasp things, then be born into them, and then be limited by those grasping habits. In that case, one blindly grasps just out of habit, not knowing any other way of dealing with life. As we awaken, however, we see the suffering of that grasping. We have to know what it is first, though, we have to really experience what suffering is as a result of grasping. It isn't a matter of experiencing suffering through some ascetic obsession, but just recognizing what it is in very simple ways; just recognizing it in feelings of loneliness, sadness, anxiety or worry about even relatively minor experiences that make our lives quite unpleasant. We create these conditions through not understanding grasping. So when we realize the suffering of grasping, we can let it go. Then the reality of non-grasping is known. That is what we call 'nibbāna'. Does that sound like a very high state? It isn't refined. It isn't like going into the heavenly realms of bliss. It isn't dependent on conditions being very refined or very special.

Every day in the monastery we chant *sandiṭṭhiko, akāliko, ehipassiko . . .* (apparent here and now, timeless, encouraging investigation). *'Akāliko-dhamma'* means 'timeless'. What, in terms of right now, is timeless? It isn't a matter of thinking about timelessness or trying to decide whether there is such a thing or not; it is a question of learning to trust yourself to recognize, to value your own ability to be aware right now. That might not seem very much in terms of how you think, maybe, or your conditioned habits. The worldly mind thinks in terms of attaining something — stream-entry or arahantship — some qualification like a PhD. In terms of awareness, however, 'attaining' doesn't make sense. You don't attain awareness; you recognize it. It is a natural state of being that is recognized through receiving this moment without trying to control or limit it, irrespective of whether this moment is pleasant or unpleasant, wanted or unwanted.

Our culture believes in definitions, words, identities and time as reality. That is why this investigation is encouraged. What is time in terms of right now? It seems so obvious that there is only here and now. Tomorrow, yesterday — where are they right now? I can remember coming here yesterday, but that is a memory now. And tomorrow? Who knows! I just don't know! But there is a 'knowing of not knowing', there is an unwillingness to project some definite thing onto the potential. I am willing to 'not know', however, because that is the way it is. It isn't a question of trying to fool myself into having some kind of false guarantee about the future. Liberation comes through the realization that knowing not knowing is 'like this'. The future is the unknown.

I think that Buddhists, like anyone else, are quite good at grasping conventions, even though the teaching is about non-grasping. Non-grasping is built into Buddhism. Grasping things in order to investigate them and to see the result of attachment is one thing, but the reality — the deathless reality and timelessness — is recognized through awareness. And in terms of language, the deathless is a negation, isn't it? Is it a double negative? — 'death' is kind of a negative, and 'less' is a negative. Then we have the 'unconditioned', 'unborn', 'uncreated'. Notice that rather than trying to create an image of deathlessness or trying to create an immortal god or anything like that, the Buddha used the negation of language — 'unborn', 'uncreated' — to express the reality of his experience. Psychologically you can't imagine the unborn, because it isn't a thing, is it? Try to imagine the unborn. My mind goes blank! — no image comes — unborn, uncreated — it's just a blank nothingness. It can actually sound like annihilation or nihilism, but that is only because of the limitation of language.

The reality of non-attachment is recognized by exploring attachment, by becoming aware of the unsatisfactoriness and unhappiness we create through grasping. It is then that we let go. Non-attachment, *nibbāna*, the path, the way of non-suffering, the way of awareness, mindfulness, is then known; it is direct knowing, and letting go is realized. This is a knowledge which is no longer based on concepts or ideas, and it is very simple. It is also very subtle, because this is taking everything to cessation. There is, however, a strong resistance to that. The closer we get to that point of cessation, it seems, the more rampant our desires become. There is a sense of fear and terror that 'I'm going to

die! I don't want to die! I want to live! I want to experience life!
I want to enjoy . . . rejoice . . !' And then we get back into thinking we have to seek happiness in the world because we want the
things we don't have, and we are afraid of losing everything.

So there might be a sense of sadness and even grief in meditation because a lot of things that we let go of are very nice; we
are fond of them. But if we trust our awareness, the sadness also
ceases, and what is left is — what? What do you call it? Is there
a name for it? — it is to be realized each one for ourselves. We
call it 'the deathless' or 'the unconditioned', and that is simply
because we have to call it something.

Years ago when I was in Berkeley, California, I went to see
the Christian monk, Father Bede Griffiths, who was staying in
the Korean Zen Center at the time. He had had a stroke and was
lying in bed looking very joyful, actually, with these rosy cheeks
and white beard. He smiled when I entered his room and said,
'I had a stroke and I lost my memory — *thank goodness!*' He
looked overjoyed. His intellect was brilliant and he obviously
understood what had happened to him, but he wasn't frightened.
Other people are often terrified when that happens to them, but
he wasn't.

I was invited to a conference in Gloucestershire not so long
ago which was all about dealing with spiritual crises. There
were therapists, psychiatrists and counsellors there talking about
mindfulness, because this word 'mindfulness' seemed to be the
main topic of interest, which I thought was very good. The way
to liberate the mind is through mindfulness or awareness, and
this is the essence of the Buddha's teaching; this is the important
one. It isn't that people in general are never mindful or always
heedless and ignorant, but speaking for myself, it never meant
anything to me in the past; it wasn't raised up as anything significant. I would be mindful under certain circumstances, but
I didn't know what mindfulness was; I was just that way because the conditions were there for it. And in life-endangering
situations, I would be particularly mindful. People would ask

me afterwards, 'Were you frightened?' And I would say, 'No, I was very mindful.' It wasn't that I had trained myself to be that way; it was just that I was naturally alert on those occasions; it just happened as part of the life-preservation instinct. We didn't call it 'mindfulness', of course, and it wasn't appreciated even though it had happened. After developing meditation over the years, however, I began to recognize and understand the power of it rather than just seeing it as a technique or a way to gain some limited state.

Psychotherapy gives a forum for talking about things that you would not perhaps talk about in other circumstances. It can be quite useful for allowing fears to become conscious, especially the darker aspects of the psyche. You can't talk to just anybody about these things because you need someone who will listen to you without making judgements or giving advice, so having that facility can initially be quite useful as a skilful means. But if that process becomes addictive, you can get too interested in yourself as a person. In meditation, on the other hand, you don't find your personality that interesting after a while.

I can see as a result of teaching here all these years that Western Buddhists don't have a lot of confidence or faith in Buddhism, or in themselves. Some problems people face — and I can relate to this myself — are the results of having developed a critical mind. My tendency is to criticize myself, and that destroys any sense of real respect for my own ability to be aware and use wisdom. The critical faculty takes over and sends out messages like: 'You don't know what you're talking about! Who do you think you are? How dare you assume this or that?' Even after years of meditation and commitment, people might feel they just can't do it; and this seems to be a common problem. My conditioning was a combination of Christianity, modern science, and rational thinking. Reason and logic in my culture had been raised to such a level that it was the ultimate human attainment. So I gave a lot of importance to doubt and criticism, dwelling on what was wrong, on the faults and flaws within myself, the people around me, and the world.

Asian monks — because there is such a strong cultural base to their experience of Buddhism — seem to have a stability that we don't have. The *saddhā* or faith aspect is part of their cultural conditioning , whereas it wasn't part of mine. Their culture isn't based on making you feel guilty, whilst we can't even seem to accept our basic human drives without feeling guilty about them. This is where we are dealing with cultural conditioning that is quite complicated. In Thailand they are just as likely to say, 'Well, of course, greed, hatred and delusion are part of everyone's life. These things are natural.' They have a kind of cultural acceptance which is not approving, but recognizes that 'this is the way we are'. Because of our conditioning , however, we might say, 'I shouldn't feel hatred. I feel angry but I shouldn't.' This is what I call neuroses. Our tendency is to complicate the issue, because not only do we have the anger, but we also have the fear, resentment and guilt around it.

Unshakeable Stillness

Meditation is the beginning of breaking down the condition-ing process, but it is not getting rid of it; it isn't a rejection of conditionality. Until you can separate yourself from the con-ditions of body and mind, however, you will be caught in chang-ing conditions and have no perspective on them. That is what is generally referred to as 'saṁsāra', the endless cycle of birth and death where we are helplessly caught in the movement of thoughts, emotions and change, and which for many people, I think, leads to despair.

Cultural conditioning is very strong, and the ego — as far as most Westerners are concerned — is stronger than identity with family, country or clan. The identity of the Asians, on the other hand, is not so fixed on just 'me' or 'what I think and feel'; it is more on the family or clan. And being identified with oth-ers on a wider scale can be helpful in dealing with loneliness, because you always have this sense of belonging to a group. In my own cultural conditioning , however, the emphasis was on individuality, on 'my rights', 'my self' and 'my independence'; the ideal was to be completely yourself, to be nonconformist. But it was ideals like that that finally led me to an increasing sense of isolation and loneliness. Even though one's family is there, this sense of individuality is asserted as the important issue, and the family or society comes after that — or maybe dismissed altogether. 'My rights', 'my thoughts', 'my views' usually take precedence, and when that attitude becomes obsessive, one ex-periences what I eventually felt to be loneliness and isolation. There are good aspects to this, of course, because one is able to do what one wants without feeling bound by the demands of one's parents. I noticed this was not usually the case in Thailand and Sri Lanka where the influence of the family and group was so strong, an individual could not assert himself or herself against the group without creating a reaction.

By the time I was thirty my cultural conditioning in many ways brought me into a state of despair. I had taken the sense of individuality and personal freedom to its extreme and what resulted was a feeling of wanting to end it all. In fact, I couldn't imagine just continuing in that way for the rest of my life, just feeling this sense of 'me against the world', and nor could I imagine finding any happiness in it. Then I became a Buddhist monk and in the process committed myself to the group by taking refuge in the Sangha, by agreeing to live by the Vinaya (discipline) which made me a member of a group of monks. For the first few years of this, as it happened, I was the only Westerner in a Thai community, and that put me in the position of being the foreigner, the tallest, the whitest, and the American. People who came to the monastery would pay their respects first to Ajahn Chah — because he was the big boss — then pass all the monks and bow to me at the end of the line, even though I was just a junior monk! At first I took this personally and was concerned about it because I didn't feel worthy of that distinction. When I mentioned it to Ajahn Chah, however, he said, 'Well, they're just respecting what you are doing.' In other words, they were not just looking at me as someone worthy of respect as a person, because I certainly didn't feel as though I was; I was going through all kinds of angry and greedy states at the time.

The monastic discipline can bring up all kinds of things as a result of the restrictions of one meal a day, taking only what is given, celibacy and so forth. I quite liked the ideal of the monastic discipline, actually; I was attuned to it. But emotionally it brought out feelings of anger as, for example, when I watched the food being distributed once and there is something there I particularly wanted — and they don't give it to me! I don't ever remember as a layperson feeling such petty reactions, having always been able to choose what I wanted and arrange everything on my own terms. But here in this monastic setting I was being subjected to the whims and fancies of the group.

Luang Por Chah constantly pointed to the here and now. And it was through that continuous emphasis — in spite of a certain resistance to it and being caught up in my own views — that I began to get the point; I began to see what I was doing. I was creating suffering from just little things, from not getting my own way or not particularly liking the way other people did things. I could just sit and fume for days on end and create utter misery over something relatively minor, something that really didn't matter at all. But eventually I began to notice that I was creating this suffering *(dukkha)* by my own obsessions, opinions, pride and conceit or by feeling threatened and victimized by the system. It had been so easy to blame others, to say it was their fault, that they were doing it wrong, that they didn't respect me, or to blame the mosquitoes, the climate, the food, or anything. Yet Ajahn Chah never let me get away with any of it, and I experienced quite a transformation when I realized what I was doing. I realized it was me that was creating these perceptions, and began to reflect 'I am the creator of my own suffering', and to notice that even if somebody was treating me badly or unfairly and I had a justified case for blaming them, it was really *my* anger and resentment that was the suffering; it was my wanting to get even with them that was the problem, my wanting to tell them off, my feeling misunderstood, unloved or unappreciated; it was actually me who was creating these thoughts and emotions.

Much of the Vinaya is about morality, but there is also a social agreement in it about behaviour and restraint. When you take the ordination, you have to ask three times before they give it to you. Nobody is holding a gun to your head and forcing you into it. And, in fact, you have to kind of plead with them: 'Please accept me venerable sir!' And one can leave at any time. The Thai system is quite liberal about disrobing, and sometimes people will ordain for just one day and disrobe. Then they say, 'Well, I've been a monk! I've done that!'

At a monastery like Amaravati the problems are not really around Buddhism or monastic discipline, because when people enter the community they agree to live according to the rules and are genuinely interested in the dhamma. The problems are more about personal issues; and community life gives a very good perspective on that kind of thing. I often reflect on the fact that it is a good community at Amaravati, and it is in quite a beautiful place, and the people are committed and sincere in what they are doing, and yet one can feel such a lot of anger and aversion! It isn't that people break the rules or challenge the dhamma teachings or anything like that, it isn't around anything on that level, it is more to do with personality conflicts. Using my own personality as a reflection, I can see how the community affects me and how I affect them. This isn't a matter of just sitting there having ideas about how people *should* be or how they should change their personalities — I've given up trying to do that; it doesn't work! — it is rather about observing what irritates or frustrates me, what it is that I like or that appeals to me, and what it is that angers me. Learning from this kind of reflection over the years has given me a level of calm, centredness and inner stillness.

I have also noticed that when people direct certain kinds of mental states towards me, the stillness can be instantly forgotten and replaced by rage. I know what the conditions are that arouse feelings of anger, but this kind of fiery rage I find distressing; it surprises me. But by reflecting on this rapid anger — I call it rage! — I recognize that the people that trigger if off in me usually come from a position of righteousness; they are always 'right'; they always want to say, 'This is the *right* way!' and they have a judgemental kind of self-righteousness about them. And I also realize that I am quite prone to being like that myself. So somebody else's self-righteousness can trigger off this rage which is a kind of righteous indignation within me. I have learned a lot from people who provoke these kinds of feelings; I have learned by receiving them in a way that is not just reacting. I listen and notice the feelings that result from contact with them, and then I find a way of using those situations. One can see therefore that situations like that are opportunities for learning.

Now, the first Noble Truth is the recognition of suffering *(dukkha)*, and the second is the recognition of the cause of suffering (which is attachment to desire). When this or that monk comes at me in a very righteous way, I observe any feelings of being threatened, or that he has no right to do this, and I also recognize my own blindness — 'HE'S WRONG AND HE SHOULDN'T BE LIKE THIS! HE SHOULDN'T ACT LIKE THIS! HE SHOULD BE AWARE OF HOW HE UPSETS ME!' I begin to notice the attachment I have to my own views about him and about what should or should not be. I can see a strong desire to ask him to leave because I find his presence difficult. That is the desire for something *not* to be *(vibhavataṇhā)*. By just observing the desire to get rid of him or for him not to be the way he is, I can let it go — just by reflecting on the feeling of not wanting him to be this way, or not wanting this experience. So I observe the feeling of 'not wanting' within myself, and I allow it to become conscious. Then it loses its potency naturally; it resolves itself in the reality of cessation — 'What has arisen has ceased.' With awareness, then, you recognize when something that is present, ceases — its presence and its absence. And the second and third Noble Truths are in connection with this reflection on the presence of a condition and then the absence of a condition.

Thought moves, but the quality of emotion can linger; it is an energetic feeling in the body — a mood or some kind of distress — and then one has the tendency, maybe, to resist it or try to get away from it. But now I have this welcoming practice — 'Misery, welcome!' This is a skilful means *(upāya)* for reversing the strong resistance to the feeling of distress. When you think about somebody who has caused you some kind of sadness or suffering in the past — even if they are on the other side of the planet —

attachment to that memory brings up the same feeling. I could go to Thailand and think of this or that monk, and, 'Ohhhh! — there's that feeling again!' But we have the opportunity to open to that, to receive it, and this is where words like *'satisampajañña'* (mindfulness and clarity of consciousness) come in; this is where they become very meaningful.

In our modern Western world we seem to idolize intellectual ability — the ability to discriminate, analyse and rationalize. Yet our discerning faculties are not that highly developed, so we hold strong views and opinions on practically every issue — about ourselves, politics, religion and everything that we think or feel. The discerning ability that comes through intuitive awareness, on the other hand, is not a cultivated state; it is what I might call 'natural intelligence'. This is not something we learn from studying texts or that comes from any conditioned perspective; it is an understanding or wisdom that operates when there is openness, non-attachment and seeing things as they are — 'discernment' in the Buddhist context, that is.

So, instead of seeing the feeling that I tend to put into that category of 'rage' in terms of being a personal flaw or being caused by the fault of another monk, I see it simply as 'this way', and note that it has a certain vibrating, resonating effect, a certain kind of energy. Using terms like 'the way it is' or 'this way' helps me to recognize and discern it without making any judgements about it, without evaluating it. It is just the discerning of that which is present in consciousness in this moment; and in that discerning there is the receiving of it. If there is no mindfulness *(sati)*, then I tend to react to the rage — I try to get rid of it or resist it — whereas mindfulness or awareness allows for even misery, for even the sense of rage or guilt to be what it is in the present. Then I find — much to my pleasure — that in that receptivity there is no suffering. The suffering has gone. It is only when I lose the mindfulness and get thrown back into the momentum of habit, that I feel suffering.

Experiment in life. Learn to apply this paradigm of the Four

Noble Truths to the flow of your life. I have found it to be such a brilliant teaching; it is useful, practical, and something that one can learn from throughout one's entire lifespan. The point is, we don't reach a state at any stage of our lives in which we just float in bliss. This is a realm of suffering where there is continuous impingement on the senses. The human body itself, the sensitivity we experience, this sense-realm that we are conscious of — none of it is meant to be paradise or a place of eternal bliss; its very nature is change — arising, ceasing, birth and death. The sensitivity that we experience means that we are constantly irritated by the impingements we receive from the things around us; and that is just the way it is. There is nothing wrong with that. It is pointless just complaining or putting it down in any way; it is simply a matter of recognizing that this realm that one is experiencing as a human individual with a human body, brain, nervous system and all the different organs and conditions is 'like this' — and to accept it the way it is.

Now, when you put it into that context, it would be foolish to say, 'I don't want it to be like this.' That is a desire that can never be satisfied. The way it is can only be 'like this'. And by receiving the way it is, we do not create suffering even from physical pain or humiliation, not even from the worst possible things that can happen to us. The suffering that the Buddha pointed to in the first Noble Truth was from not being aware, from wanting something one doesn't have and not wanting something one does have.

When I first started meditating, the conditioned realm seemed incredibly powerful to me. I reflected on this body, and it seemed overpowering in every way — just the needs of this physical form and the emotional world that I live in; it seemed to be like a series of tidal waves, tsunamis, that completely engulfed me. And when I heard about 'the unshakeable deliverance of the heart', from the perspective of those early years it seemed a totally impossible goal to me. I couldn't find *anything* unshakeable. In spite of feeling overwhelmed by the sense world, however, there was something that kept me going; I just didn't want to resign or give up. Even though I wasn't all that conscious of it at that time, there was some force that kept me at it. One can have a love-hate relationship with any conventional form, and sometimes I just hated monastic life; I could get very critical of it and see all kinds of things wrong or silly about it. And yet in spite of that, there was something in me that didn't really believe any of the criticism. Once I began to tune into the simple immediacy of attention, once I became more confident with awareness, I found that I really respected the monastic life, even worshipped it in a way. It was like being devoted to awareness — 'refuge in Buddha' I call it — by putting it into the terms of *Buddhaṁ saraṇaṁ gacchāmi* (I take refuge in the Buddha); I began to have this sense of really treasuring and respecting this moment of awareness.

At first it was just like having momentary flashes, and then I would fall back into the old patterns. But as the awareness began to connect, it also began to sustain itself. Awareness is not a created state so it doesn't depend on conditions to support it. The tranquillity practices, on the other hand, I found frustrating because special conditions are needed for them. One would get a sense of peace and tranquillity from concentrating on refined objects, but when those conditions had fallen away, one would feel angry or upset because the conditions had been disrupted — maybe somebody had slammed a door, or a plane had flown over. I remember one monk would get angry with the birds for singing!

Gradually, I began to realize that I didn't really want to live in a sort of sensory deprivation tank for my whole life, just shutting everything out and being the ultimate control freak. This realm is not like that; this is not a tranquil realm, but a sense realm. And sensory activity is always moving and changing from happy to miserable, from beautiful to ugly, from day to night, from hot to cold, and from beautiful sounds to cacophonous noises; it is just the way it is. To expect to live in a kind of *deva*-realm of refinement and bliss is foolish. I *could* arrange it sometimes; it is a conscious experience within this realm, though an extreme one. But it cannot sustain itself; you can't depend on it.

The Buddha emphasized this awareness which *is* sustainable. Awareness is natural and not simply an attainment. So it is ordinary — so ordinary, in fact, that we don't really notice it. Our cultural conditioning moves towards extremities. We are always trying to *get* something or get *rid* of something. On a cultural level I am conditioned to seeking extremes, to finding interesting things, to getting rid of the cacophonous noises and the ugliness of life, and trying to hold onto the good. There came a point, however, when I began to recognize that awareness is quite empty, and that even though it allows everything in, it doesn't have any boundaries and doesn't control anything. So, rather than trying to control forms in order to make myself feel good, I began to accept both external impingements and internal reactions. And as I reflected on that, I noticed that by resting in awareness, I didn't suffer even if the impingements were miserable. I could feel pain or any kind of irritation to my senses and mind, and yet not suffer in the way that I would if I tried to get rid of those things or tried to change or control them. The way of non-suffering, then, became clear to me in terms of experience — it is 'this way' and isn't a matter of getting rid of anything or attaching to anything.

There are, I think, always things we would dearly like to get rid of like rage, jealousy or fear. So we might have subtle attachments that seem perfectly all right. As someone who was trying to establish a monastery, I would feel intimidated when anybody accused me of not being responsible. I am from a cultural background where the ideal is responsibility and accountability, of getting the accolades, of 'being somebody' and having a special ability. And over the years I have been given honours and honourable titles in Thailand which then gave me a feeling of having to live up to a standard and be an example to others. Some of these things are quite good in themselves — they are what *should* be, how you *should* be — and yet by attaching to the ideal of, say, being a teacher, or the head of a monastery, or a preceptor, or whatever, it can become an onerous task. One can feel burdened by always having to be 'the example' for every-body, by feeling obliged always to perform in the right way and be the 'good monk' that everybody wants. It wasn't that I was unwilling to do it, but there was an attachment there which I had not quite seen. And the unsatisfactoriness *(dukkha)* arose when I felt a sense of resentment at being burdened, by always having to be the example, by seeing more monks and more nuns as more burdens, more problems. The whole thing just seemed to increase and multiply.

When somebody ordains, they have to say, 'I am your burden and you are mine.' I am not sure the translation is all that good, but this is how it generally comes out. The point is, even with the best conditions and the most high-minded intentions that one can have in the conditioned realm, any attachment to them will be the cause of suffering. Even if you create a paradise, a heav-enly realm, attachment to it will mean suffering — even from living in paradise!

This reflection, then, points to letting go — not in the sense of getting rid of or destroying anything — but in seeing the way one holds and grasps even very good things, even good people or ideals. We begin to see that attachment of any kind is the cause of suffering. We might then of course go to the opposite extreme and wonder whether we should just not bother about being re-sponsible any more — 'to hell with it!' I realized, however, that I wasn't going to attach to that either, because that is still coming from the same position — first the sense 'I have to be responsi-ble,' and then the reaction 'I'm *not* going to be responsible.'

It is awareness, then, that is liberation. In that natural resting in awareness, problems disappear; they are just gone. The sense of myself and the resentment about having responsibilities ceas-es if I trust in the awareness. And it affirms the refuges because that is what is left. Putting it in an agreed vocabulary I call it

'Buddha-Dhamma-Sangha'. But it is what it is. You don't have to agree to the terminology. Since I am a Buddhist this is the language I use, but one simply recognizes the stillness, the unshakeable deliverance of the heart *(akuppa-cetovimutti)*, the still point. One recognizes it through awareness not through seeking it or trying to get it, but just through relaxing, opening, trusting and receiving both pleasant and unpleasant experience.

I encourage you to trust in your own awareness. Don't believe the perceptions you have about yourself, about whether you have attained or not attained, or whether you can do it or not. Your mind will always create problems about yourself, about Buddhism, about meditation, and about life in general — but don't believe it! Life is what it is. My personality is conditioned to be critical and suspicious. And the personality still tends towards that. I don't believe it any more, however, but trust rather in the awareness of it. Sometimes I have lovely moments where I find my personality ranting on and on, and then suddenly realizing that I am not that; that that is just that 'thing'. I don't make a problem about it but just realize that there is no self — and yet there is awareness; and awareness is oneness not two, so there is that sense of oneness. But what is the reality of oneness? Well, you can't think about it, can you? Thinking will divide everything in consciousness. It seems as though there are two — 'me and you'. The appearance is of division. When people talk about 'oneness', or 'mystical union', or use any of these terms that one uses to describe it, however, simply recognize that the words themselves are inadequate. The reality of 'oneness' is recognized through awareness rather than through thought or definition; so consciousness now seems to have no boundary.

This form here can be compared to a radio, in a way; it picks up things. How I interpret them, though, is according to my kamma, according to the way I have been conditioned to think, to see and to react to sensory experience. It is these things that determine how I interpret experience. The unshakeable stillness which is before birth — before the conditioning , before anything starts happening — is, however, the stronger. It might seem that the senses are the stronger, it might seem that the influence of the body and emotions are so powerful and so overwhelming that getting beyond them would be impossible, and yet through the power of meditation comes the recognition of the strength of awareness. Awareness holds everything. It is unshakeable. It allows and is not a controlling, judging or manipulating function. It allows even the worst things to be what they are. All conditions are allowed to have their span in consciousness and then their cessation. When conditions cease, however, the awareness does not cease with them but rather transcends all the conditions that we experience.

Sometimes I question how Westerners interpret meditation. I have noticed that most of us start out wanting to shut everything out — at least I did. I just wanted to get out of my misery and thought that by becoming a monk, by going off into the forest and getting away from it all, I would be able to get that *samādhi*, that concentration. And I did! I lived alone for a year and got into this very fine state. But there wasn't any wisdom in it. And as soon as I left that controlled environment, I just fell apart. It seemed I had become too sensitive, and all the defences and protective mechanisms had gone. On the one hand I experienced a kind of bliss, but on the other when unpleasant things happened, I fell to pieces, became overwhelmed — even by relatively innocuous things that wouldn't have bothered me in the least before that time.

We have this desire for peace, tranquillity, bliss. Using drugs is one way people sometimes have of trying to get it. Maybe cocaine and heroin can take you to a kind of beautiful state of emptiness, but when you start taking drugs, you have to take more and more and become addicted. Trying to control the environment can also become a form of addiction; we can become obsessed with trying to keep things the way we prefer, and resenting any disruption. I was fortunate to have a teacher who didn't allow any of that. His emphasis was always on ordinariness, and he would use this word 'dhammada'. The word 'dhamma' is day-to-day vocabulary in Thailand and means 'ordinary', 'the way it is'. So, if you ask a Thai what the weather is like, the answer might be 'dhammada', just ordinary. Anyway, Ajahn Chah never encouraged me to practise heavy concentration even though I wanted to. I kept trying to move into that, but he would pull me back. Although I didn't actually want to do what he wanted me to, however, something in me knew to trust him.

His emphasis was on learning to be with the breath and the body without trying to get anything out of it, without trying to get the *jhānas* (meditative absorptions) or trying to heal the body through being aware of it. It was more to do with just being with the posture and the breath the way it is. Later I became conscious of the 'sound of silence', this background sound — or is it a sound? — is it rather a vibration? Whatever it is I started meditating on it and found that it is where I am quite empty. It pervades everything, and if I stay with it, rest with it, the sense of self is gone; the suffering is also gone, and the emotional state I am in is gone — not through suppressing any of those things — but just in this natural sound of silence, this natural movement. So I began to cultivate this by recognizing and using it.

Since living in England, I have not had much silent retreat time. I used to go off and spend months in retreat, but now it doesn't really seem necessary; it doesn't seem to matter where I am or who I am with. I find it just helpful to work with my life as it happens rather than thinking I have to go off and do something special in order to get something out of it. And in terms of teaching, I used to have more confidence in technique and in the word 'practice'. Now I trust awareness more — though it is difficult to teach that.

I don't want to experience anger and hatred, pettiness and jealousy; I loath those states in myself. My personality is such that I want to be good, wise, compassionate, forgiving, fair and all that is best. And I am very inspiring when coming from that kind of place. Speaking in a positive way from ideals inspires people when you are teaching on a meditation retreat. You have a certain position and can sell these wonderful things. Of course, everybody is quiet for maybe ten days and then they leave. When you live in a community, however, it is quite different. You can't hide the blemishes in a community, so in a way I consider community life to be the real practice. The people I inspire the most, I discovered, are the most critical when I don't live up to expectations. And that can be very painful. I feel I have failed — 'I'm just a hypocrite!' — and the self-criticism would come up.

With awareness, there came a time when I began to see the importance of making my negative side more conscious. But there was a resistance in me. There was so much resistance in me, in fact, that under certain circumstances I couldn't hold it; I would just blow it and say something terrible! Then I felt that if I kept resisting this negative side and not allow it to become conscious, I would die inside; I would become completely petrified with a kind of botox smile on my face! So I decided to make these negative states conscious, and to do it without directing them towards anybody, without being confrontational. So sometimes I would write out all my angry thoughts — unedited, unexpurgated — in all their meanness and nastiness. I would write and keep writing until I reached a point where nothing more would come, and I realized that that was the end. Then I would read the whole thing through and somehow — just by making that resistance more conscious — it would fall away. Rather than just suppressing those negative feelings therefore I had actually resolved them, and I was left with a sense of having released something.

Awareness doesn't have preferences, so the nasty stuff belongs as much as the saintly. When it gets into picking and choosing, I don't want the nasty stuff, I want the good stuff, but I can't trust that any more because I know the result is not liberating. Even calling something 'nasty', even labelling it or saying anything about it, makes it more than it is. The fact is, it is what it is. So, feeling really grumpy and resentful is — ! You don't even go that far any more; it just is what it is. This feeling is 'like this', and if there is no movement towards adding anything to it, if you have patience with it, it naturally ceases.

I use this word 'patience' a lot because resistance — that wanting to get rid of something because 'I don't like it', wanting to get rid of it *right now* — is very impatient. I have learned to accept and receive uncomfortable, unwanted feelings; I have learned to let them be what they are. If I think about them, they become complicated. Just being aware of this present mood or this energy, is enough. By resting here and allowing negative states a right to *be*, by seeing them for what they are, one realizes they don't have any solidity to them, they don't have any core or essence even. Then one sees them to be just like mist, just empty.

Seeing the Nature of Form

This morning I would like to reflect on space and form. Oscar and Alicia have donated a modern sculpture to Amaravati which is of the Buddha represented by space, and space represented by solid form. It is interesting to see people's reactions to it. They look at the form first and try to make sense of that; and they generally interpret it as two people making *añjali* (putting their palms together in greeting). That is because the mind is conditioned to grasping form and trying to perceive it as something. Forms, concepts, thoughts, emotions, creations of the mind and the sense world are what we regard as reality. Yet space and consciousness — that which does not have any form — is with us all the time. The reality of space and consciousness is why we are here; the experience we are having right now is a conscious experience. And space is the most important thing in this room, isn't it? — but we don't always notice the most obvious. We usually only look at the people, the walls and the things in the room.

Thought is form, isn't it? When we try to think about emptiness we go round and round and end up with some logical deduction that it is a kind of void, a nothingness, a kind of vacuum of nothingness. But thought is limited. We create it and then have attachments to it. We have attachments to memories, attitudes, opinions and views; and what is absolutely essential goes unnoticed. We are conscious but usually interpret consciousness with some kind of definition, so we think *about* consciousness, speculate on it, have views around the word, but cannot grasp it as a thing. We can grasp the things that arise *in* consciousness — thoughts and sensory impingement. But consciousness itself — can we grasp that?

The tendency in modern life is to invest one's interest in forms — the body, the sense realm and conditioned world. Reflectiveness or awareness is what the Buddha emphasized as the way of liberation, however, and this is formless. And because it has no form, it has no limit — and yet it includes all forms. Awareness does not destroy or annihilate anything. It doesn't have preferences. It is the ability we all have of being present without attachment and without connecting to any condition that appears. But developing or cultivating awareness isn't an easy thing to do because we don't recognize the importance of it and what it really is. We therefore develop methods or attach to views and techniques, and these inevitably blind us to the reality.

In the Theravada teachings meditation — that English word 'meditation' — is divided into 'tranquillity' and 'insight' *(samatha* and *vipassanā)*. Now, in Thailand there are all kinds of views about *samatha* and *vipassanā*. And within the *vipassanā* world there are all kinds of views about how to practise it. Some people think that *samatha* isn't necessary, whilst others think it is *absolutely* essential. Some say you have to get the *jhānas* before you can do *vipassanā* (there are certain elements that think like this) and others say, 'Well no, don't do *samatha* — just straight *vipassanā*; that's all that's necessary,' and there are arguments about it. Now, teachers speak from their own experience and this has to be taken into account. It isn't that all these opinions are wrong or that one is absolutely right or absolutely wrong. As Ajahn Chah used to say, 'True but not right, right but not true.' Looking at the opinion-making process in one's own mind, one's own preferences, the way 'I' do it, the way 'I' practise, 'my' experience, tends to present this sense of 'this is the way to do it because I know this and everybody should do it like I do.' This is the logic that results. But if you really recognize awareness as the central issue and appreciate it, you will notice attachments to your own style, your own group, your own way, or your own opinion.

Westerners tend to pick and choose from the traditional forms of Buddhism. Some would even take Zen out of Buddhism and say, 'We're not Buddhists; we're Zenists.' They take *that* much but don't want the rest. This also happens in the Theravada in terms of *vipassanā* — 'We're not Buddhists, but we practise *vipassanā*.' It's all right; I am not complaining or condemning it, but the arrogance in our cultural conditioning makes us want to take what we like and dismiss the rest. *Vipassanā* in the West, therefore, tends to be practised according to highly evolved techniques and strong views. But this limits you. If you cannot see what attachment is and the limitation it puts you under — as well as the suffering that results from that attachment — then your efforts at practising *vipassanā* might lead to more refinement but then you become addicted to *vipassanā* retreats and the special situations that help you practise that technique. In the Theravada scriptures you see statements like: 'Go into the forest and leave the world behind.' There is this encouragement to leave the busy world and seek solitude which is represented by the forest. But of course 'this is true but not right, right but not true', as Ajahn Chah would say.

Then you hear the other extreme: 'You don't need technique, you don't need religion of any sort or any convention, just be aware — that's it!' That is another 'true but not right, right but not true' opinion. Whatever position you take and grasp binds you to that particular view, and that binding — that attachment to a view — creates division. You then always feel this sense of having to *do* something or *get* something or develop or cultivate something; there is always a feeling that if you sit on a zafu long enough and attend meditation retreats or live in the forest, you might get something you haven't quite got yet — hopefully — if the world doesn't disrupt you too much!

But the whole Buddhist ethos is around this sense of awakening. The word 'Buddha' itself means 'awakened'; and that is significant because it is not that difficult; it is not like developing psychic powers or special abilities. That attitude of 'I am not awakened but will be if I practise' is often the *modus operandum* that we start with, but if we don't see beneath that — if we don't get behind that position — then we are stuck with it, and no matter what technique we experience or great teacher we come across in our lives, if that basic delusion is never challenged, we will always be under its limitation — even with the very best teacher or the best technique. So contemplate 'I am', just this sense of 'I am somebody', just the thought 'I am' before you apply any identity to it. We all have this sense of 'I am here and now', this presence. But then we add to that — 'I am Ajahn Sumedho' — and then the limitation is there. I am now a form, a person, a position. There is this sense of 'I am this body', and this is binding oneself into the identity and limitation of a particular body — 'I am a Buddhist monk', 'I am an American', 'I am . . .' whatever, good or bad, high or low. How do I put that way of thinking — that sense of 'I am' with the limitation of 'I am Ajahn Sumedho' — into the context of awareness? I have created a form, haven't I? 'I am Ajahn Sumedho' is a creation; it is a thought-formation. Everybody says, 'You are Ajahn Sumedho,' and I generally refer to myself as Ajahn Sumedho — so it is obviously right! And it works like that on a conventional level, in conventional society, in the formed world. But is it really true? Is that what I really am? To reflect in this way allows me to be aware of myself thinking this.

I have practised over many years just listening to myself saying 'I am Ajahn Sumedho' and seeing that this is a form I create, a habit-formation. So, on the intellectual level I can say it is all empty and I am not really Ajahn Sumedho; I can see that Ajahn Sumedho is a delusion and can go along with the theory of emptiness or non-self. But just going along with the theory is not liberating. The point of the teaching is to awaken to the reality of this moment. And the reality of thinking 'I am Ajahn Sumedho' is that it is a condition arising and ceasing in consciousness. Consciousness, then, is not something I can claim. It transcends the forms that arise within it. Our emotions, habits, thoughts, memories, and the body itself, is the sensory world that we experience. Our experience is conscious, so we can recognize, we can name, and we can attach to various forms through consciousness. Consciousness therefore has no boundary, no form, but is a fact here and now. Trying to pinpoint consciousness and say what it is exactly — trying to define it, describe it and show it to someone — is impossible. We can, however, be aware that consciousness is 'like this'. When I reflect in this way, my thinking is not defining consciousness or arguing about the nature of it in some abstract way; it is awakening me to the reality of consciousness and the form 'I am Ajahn Sumedho' that arises and ceases.

Visual space also I found a good reflection, just contemplating the space in this room. Can you say that the space in this room is somehow different from the space outside the room? The room itself is in space, isn't it? The building is in space; the planet is in space; space includes everything and doesn't have any preferences. Whether things are good, bad, right, wrong, beautiful or ugly — whatever their quality — space has no preferences; it is where whatever is formed can appear. Our attention, though, is culturally attuned to judging the forms in space. We also have other uses for the term like 'I need space' or 'this is a good space' or 'that's a bad space'. But actually space doesn't have any quality to it except spaciousness; it is just that we project perceptions onto it. When we are not thinking but just present and aware, then space has no limit or boundary to it. We put up the boundaries with the walls in this room, don't we? I say, 'This space is just *this* big,' and that is because the walls are all I am willing to notice. But where does space really end? Where are its limits? The fact is, it just goes on and on, and I can't see its wholeness. I can recognize its infinity through this awareness, however. So this gives perspective on the forms.

Insight meditation, as it is often practised now, concentrates

on the nature of the forms too much — this is just my thinking on it — and a great deal of emphasis is placed on noting
that conditions are impermanent, not-self and unsatisfactory.
But that can lead to merely becoming obsessed with form. As
you develop increasing levels of concentration, you find yourself
dealing with the minutiae of form — the more subtle forms that
you might never have noticed before — and that can be in just
an ordinary moment. The tendency then is to become fascinated
by the groups of existence *(kalāpas)*, the different movements
and subtleties of form, and seeing their impermanence. But what
is the result of that? It doesn't liberate. It is interesting and is a
good practice, but in terms of liberation, you are still only concentrated on form; your attention is still limited to forms, coarse
and subtle. But the formless or the immeasurable is also here and
now, and that you cannot conceive. Even the words are negations
of form. This is where you need to trust your intuitive sense, your
awareness, your ability to receive the moment. At first I found
this rather distressing because my emotional habits were attuned
to trying to figure things out, trying to grasp things, trying to
have them in the palm of my hand in order to say, 'This is reality and I can show it to you,' like an empirical scientist who has
got hold of God and shows him to us as some kind of scientific
fact. Since you can't do that, however, the mind thinks, 'Well,
there isn't one!' Or you just live in a kind of projection of hope.
Or maybe you create a form of God. I am using the word 'God'
right now not as a theological expression but more of a pointer
to the unlimited, the uncreated and the immeasurable. I am not
referring to a Father, a Trinity, a person, or a deity — whether
there is one or many, or a right one or a wrong one — but taking
the English word 'God' and applying it to the present moment in
terms of experience. Awakening to the present, then, leaves you
with nothing, because there is nothing to grasp. We chant the
words *'paccattaṃ veditabbo viññūhi'* (to be experienced individually), meaning you have to see for yourself, because even the
Buddha was unable to enlighten his disciples. He could point out

the way to them, but he couldn't zap them so that they became Buddhas.

The point is, the Buddha didn't create a metaphysical teaching. His teaching is a pointing, an awakening, rather than a definition. And because there is no statement, it looks like a denial of God or atheism, and is therefore greatly misunderstood. In a theistic approach, the metaphysical position is stated in the beginning: 'I believe in God!' That is where you start from. But the Buddha's teaching is the encouragement to awaken. And meditation is looking into the way things really are. So that is looking into the nature of form, isn't it?

The discriminative mind picks and chooses. I like some forms better than others; I think some are beautiful and some are ugly. And I can create strong views about right and wrong, good and evil. Whether good or evil, however, forms are still forms; they are still impermanent and not-self. So it isn't a matter of preferring one over the other. Everything arises and ceases in conscious awareness, but I can't claim that on a personal level. As soon as I say, 'I am a very mindful monk,' it becomes part of 'my form'. Letting go of form is trusting in the immediacy of awareness. And awareness is real. It isn't abstract; it isn't just some kind of concept I have that I don't recognize immediately; it is more like the space in this room and the forms in space. They are what they are. And I no longer go from one thing to the other saying, 'I like this; I don't like that,' but recognize that whatever is in this space belongs here at this moment. It doesn't matter whether I approve or disapprove of it, or whether it is good or bad. If it is here, this is the way it is; and this is learning to trust in awareness which doesn't pick or choose. It is choiceless awareness.

From awareness, we have the ability to see the nature of form, and to discern it through wisdom rather than through habit and conditioning which are based on liking, disliking, approving and disapproving. This doesn't mean we are completely neutral about everything, but our passions and preferences are in context. They are no longer the dominant conscious experience, and they no longer blind us to the reality of this moment. We still like this and don't like that; we are still aware of the different qualities of things. But it is all in perspective, and we recognize that the real refuge is in this awareness which is not conditioned, which is not dependent on any particular technique or religious convention, and which is the natural state. No religion can claim it. To say that this is Buddhist and isn't Christian is getting into religious arrogance again. Awareness is a natural state and we can't say the Buddha discovered it. He pointed to it, though.

So, in the Theravada they emphasize the four elements — earth, fire, water and air — but space and consciousness often get left out. Within the Tibetan Dzogchen and other forms of Mahamudra I think these things are fully recognized and encouraged, but it has baffled me how very few people within my own tradition seem to recognize the fact that if we start from awareness, then the Five Aggregates and all the different teachings are in a perspective that we can relate to with wisdom, and that there is no need to take a position for or against any technique or view.

In the paradigm of the Four Noble Truths, the third truth is the realization of cessation. And the truth of cessation is what we would call 'stream-entry', which is the recognition of emptiness. The problem with using the word 'cessation' is that it sounds like the ending of everything. And sometimes people have this idea that they have to get rid of everything. We don't all agree on how to interpret the word 'cessation', of course, even in English. You might think it means Armageddon, that everything ceases, that it is annihilation. In terms of awareness, however, in the context of informing consciousness through wisdom, through discerning, there is the arising and ceasing of thoughts or emotions that you experience as part of your *kammic* lesson. So when you trust this awareness, you actually accept whatever comes to you.

When I first started training as a monk in Thailand, I would sometimes think, 'I can't stand this any more! This is too much! I can't stand another minute!' The voice would be very forceful

and I started believing it, 'I can't do it!' Then I realized that I
could, actually. While that voice was saying 'I can't stand it another minute', I was actually standing it. Then I began to recognize that that voice couldn't be believed, that that voice was limiting me; it was placing too many restrictions on me. My personality says that I can't do all kinds of things, 'You'll never be able
to do that; it's too much!' It always has this tendency to make me
feel I don't want to even try 'because it is just *too* difficult, *too*
much for somebody like me'. Coming from the spaciousness of
awareness, however, made me realize that this is just a habit pattern; it isn't really true. It sounds true if you grasp it, but then you
are binding yourself to limitation and also to the fear of going
beyond it because you might fail, you might make a mess, you
might make a mistake and do something wrong and be humiliated, so it is better to stay in a safe position where you know your
limits. You therefore stay within those limits and never expand.
But then you are dead! You are a kind of walking corpse. And if
things change in a way that you can't control, you lose it; you are
shattered by the challenges that life sends your way.

In this refuge, then, of Buddha-Dhamma-Sangha — in this
awareness of the Buddha (awakened consciousness) and the
dhamma (the way it is) — the Buddha knows the way it is. The
Buddha is the wisdom, is discerning. Now, that is not a kind of
cold attitude towards conditioned phenomena. It isn't that conditioned phenomena are in some way a pejorative — 'Oh, that
is just conditioned phenomenon; get rid of it!' — which is how
we often interpret it. One can become a cold observer of life and
think that all conditioned phenomena are impermanent and not-
self. But that is not the way it is. The unconditioned, awareness,
includes all conditions. It doesn't say anything about whether
they should or should not be — it doesn't care! Whatever conditions are present belong because that is the way it is. So when
it is raining it is 'like this', and when it is sunny it is 'like this'. I
might think, 'Oh, I don't like the rain; I want the sun.' But then I
am creating another condition; I am reacting on a personal level

to rain; I am reacting without awareness. If I trust in the awareness, however, then rain is 'this way', and there is an awareness of how it affects me. The feeling of the wetness or coldness is still the same — it is still wet and cold — and even the emotional reaction of not wanting rain might arise. But resting in awareness is where the strength lies in contrast to the reactiveness of my habit patterns. So, even on a cold, rainy, damp February afternoon at Amaravati I can create suffering or not, because it is all bearable. I can bear the cold, the wet and the damp. And it isn't a state of suffering unless I think, 'I wish I were somewhere else!'

This, you can prove for yourself. It is 'to be experienced individually', to be known not through believing me but through trusting in your own awareness. I hope that what I am saying is an encouragement to you. That is all that I really want to offer. I am not trying to convince you that the way I think is the right way, but rather encouraging you in your own recognition, in your own sense of what is taking place. The most valuable gift we have is 'the jewel in the lotus' — this very precious reality. It is a jewel, a great blessing, and it is here and now. We all have it. Never is it gone, never absent, and we can never get rid of it no matter how bad we are. But we forget and create suffering; we become suffering creatures.

Now, in all of this we have to face the kamma of our lives. This can be seen in very personal ways — 'my kamma' — and we can theorize about it: 'Oh, in the past I did so and so, and I will have to pay the price for that in the future.' But this is speculation again, isn't it? It can be interesting, of course. People are always talking to me about past lives and I am quite curious about that myself, but I know that it is just curiosity. I also know it isn't important. Past life is just another memory in the present. If you remember being a caveman it might be fascinating, but the discerning faculty knows that 'it is what it is' — arising, ceasing, not-self. The sense of 'I am' then no longer connects to memories or the specifics of the conditioned world. But this 'I am' is still not liberation yet. It is worthy of reflection, though, because one is acknowledging the pure presence of being. And this English term 'I am' is a powerful thought in itself. Just notice that it isn't suffering until you add something to it. It still isn't liberation, however, because it binds you to thought. In the end even the 'I am' drops away and there is just pure awareness where there is no longer a need for supports or skilful means.

Personality belief is one of the fetters that one needs to recognize in order to see and know the path. There is awareness and there is personality, and I see that my personality is conditioned; I create myself; I am my identities — who I think I am, my abilities or lack of them, my self-criticism, my preferences. These are all conditioned in the sense of 'me and mine' and depend very much on attaching to thought and emotion. I feel anger or greed or whatever, and then I think 'I am greedy' or 'I am angry'. That further proliferates into, 'I shouldn't be angry; I should love everybody.' But this is all my creation; it is part of my kamma; it is the way I am conditioned and the assumptions I make about myself from identifying with the body — 'This is my body. This is my space.' People nowadays say, 'This is my space; don't come into my space! The space belongs to me! This belongs to me and that belongs to me. And this is my view; this is what I think and what I feel.' All this has a lot of emotional power. The point is, when anger arises, I can say, 'Yes, it feels like this!' and realize that the awareness is not angry. If I grasp the emotion of anger, then of course I *become* angry.

Thoughts like 'I can't stand this! It's just too much! I've had enough! I'm fed up!' is personality belief talking. By trusting in the awareness of that, however, the 'self' becomes an object. And when you see it as a mental object, what do you see as the pure subject? The subject is not a self, is it? It is not identified with anything. This is an act of surrender to awareness, but your personality can be frightened of that. In order to be a person, you have to have conditions to support the sense of yourself as a person — 'Am I a likeable person? Am I acceptable? Am I presentable? Is it all right for me to be here?' The 'self' is like that; it is very shaky. And it also changes, so you find yourself acting differently under different circumstances. You might go home to see your parents, spend time with your best friend or go to a football game, and in each case your personality adapts to the conditions you are experiencing.

While I was at university I took on this idea that everyone should just be themselves. People would say, 'Don't be a phony! Get real and be yourself!' I liked that idea, but I didn't quite know what it meant. So I formed some notion of it and tried to be like that with everybody — and it didn't work! I simply couldn't sustain it. The point is, conditions with one's parents are different from conditions with one's colleagues, or conditions in India. The conditions in India are not the same as those at home in England. When people love and respect you it is like *this*, and when they hate you it is like *that*. How do I maintain a constant personality that never changes? It is impossible because the personality is a conditioned thing based on changing conditions. When you are attached to 'this personality', therefore, you can be easily hurt or offended. As a personality I am very delicate and people have to be careful around me because they might offend my personality. With some people you feel you are constantly walking on eggshells, they are so easily upset. But I have found that there is a fearlessness coming out of awareness because it is non-personal. As a person I can be easily hurt and have to protect myself. From the awareness, however, I still get hurt, but I know what is happening. My refuge is not in the hurt or the sense of myself as a person, but in the awareness. As you trust that awareness and recognize it more, it will support everything so that there is nothing to fear. You realize that whatever the forces might be, whatever the kamma or the conditions that you might experience from now until you die, the awareness will be your refuge and will give you the right perspective on whatever happens.

'Self' is a word which gives the impression of something limited, but you could also refer to 'the pure self'. In Hinduism they use the word '*ātman*' and refer to the big self and the little self, and that is fair enough. However, you don't really need any term at all because it is not a thing, it isn't a matter of identifying or defining anything; it is rather about recognizing. So it is immanent; it is here and now; it is reality, like space. Space is here. Space is through us and everywhere, so it is just a matter of recognizing it. You might think, 'Well, in order to get a proper view of space, I should ask everyone to leave so that the building can be destroyed. Then everything in sight should be destroyed so that the space becomes vast and has nothing in it.' But we don't need to do that in order to recognize space. Space is a reality and without it forms would not be possible. Consciousness also has no boundary; the present moment is 'like this' and includes all forms. We can be totally deluded, insane or whatever but still conscious. It isn't that I am more conscious than you are, or that my consciousness is purer than yours; it is the amount of attachment we have to what we create within consciousness that is the point.

Contemplate birth itself, birth into a form. A human baby is conscious and sensitive, but it does not have personality belief yet. The self-view is inculcated after birth through cultural conditioning . As I get acculturated, it takes me over and my experience of life is interpreted from the position of personality belief. My personality is then the centre of the universe and everything affects 'me', 'me' as a person. And that is rather frightening because 'me as a person' is just something conditioned; there is no way I can make myself perfect; there is no such thing as a perfect person, a perfect personality. I become like the people that affect me on a personal level, as in the case of being a monk. I became a monk by living with monks all these years. As an identity, however, being a monk is not very satisfying. If my monastic conditioning is coming from the personality belief, it is wretched. My personality can be endlessly critical about monasticism, because the monastic life does in many ways seem limiting and binding — particularly for someone like myself who came from the American scene where one wanted to experience everything and 'be oneself!' You can feel suffocated by monastic conventions if you operate from some ideal, if you imagine yourself being spontaneous, being totally 'yourself'. That would be an ideal, and a very attractive one. But in terms of awareness I find that spontaneity comes out of emptiness rather than out of some kind of cold, clinical personality which says, 'All that arises ceases, and is not self,' and 'Everything is suffering!' like an old grump. The spontaneity, the joy and love, come from emptiness. So emptiness doesn't stop these things; it isn't a kind of suicide.

The American system is a competitive prove-yourself kind of society. And failure is terrible; it is terrible to be a nobody. So this sense of being somebody — being a self-made man or woman, proving yourself, getting somewhere, being a personality-plus, being a charmer — is an ideal that is held from the very beginning, especially when you start going to university. Trying to make yourself fit into these moulds, however, is self-defeating, because you never succeed. In your heart you know you are a phony, you know it is just an act or a put-on and that you are just trying to be something you are not. You might think, 'Well, be yourself!' But your mind goes blank — ! You don't know what that is. Which one of those things is me?

Much of your personality is based on fear, and so in awareness where there is no personality belief or self-view, fear ceases. As a personality your happiness depends on whether you are liked or disliked and on conditions being a certain way. Awareness, on the other hand, is not dependent on conditions being any way. Whatever the conditions are, awareness has the strength to carry them, to support them, and to allow them to be. And as the nature of conditions is to change and cease, there is no permanent condition.

Don't Make a Problem About Yourself

This word *'satisampajañña'* (mindfulness and wisdom) has an embracing quality about it. It doesn't refer to discrimination like picking and choosing; it rather means 'apperception' or 'apprehension' and is what we call 'intuition'. So an intuitive moment is not a rational moment; it isn't a moment based on common sense and habitual ways of looking at things; it is rather based on an openness through being conscious, receptive and aware. Intuition, then, receives the reality of this moment, the here and now; it includes what is happening emotionally and physically, and it also includes those conditions which are impinging on one's senses through the eyes, ears, nose, tongue and body. The value of this is that it *is* inclusive; it is not divisive. Words fail at this moment because intuitive awareness is to be recognized — it is reality. And words themselves, even the most embracing concepts, can get in the way. That is why it isn't a matter of defining or analysing, but of recognizing.

Now, the Four Stages (stream-entry, once-return, non-return and arahant) as described in the Pali Canon are reflective teachings aimed at getting perspective on our own experience. They are not positions. It isn't a question of thinking in terms of *becoming* a stream-enterer or *becoming* an arahant, or wondering, 'Have I attained stream-entry yet? Am I a non-returner? Will I ever become an arahant?' This is the worldly mind grasping the concepts. Sometimes you hear people say, 'This monk — he's a stream-enterer!' and everyone goes 'Ohhh! a stream-enterer!'

'And that one's an arahant.' 'Wow, an arahant!' (that's like super-man). But the Pali Canon refers to these Four Stages in connection with the Ten Fetters, these Ten Fetters which I have found to be a very valuable reference point in relation to the Four Stages. The point is, it is easy to conceptualize stream-entry as some kind of attainment. The ego grasps the concept and the Western ego in particular tends to want to *become* what it grasps, looking upon such things as kind of achievements or goals. If you have invested many years as a monk practising meditation, you want something to prove it has been worth it, you know. 'Give me a title! After all these years I don't know whether I'm a stream-enterer, or not.' It is by investigating and recognizing the first three of the Ten Fetters, however, that you come to recognize stream-entry, and stream-entry is the path.

So, what are the first three fetters? These are artificial conditions that we create. The first is personality belief, and this is not a natural phenomenon. We are not born with a personality. And the second fetter is attachment to conventions *(sīlabba-ta-parāmāsa)* which is from our cultural conditioning ; we are born into a particular family and acquire the values, conventions, views and opinions of that family. And then the third fetter is *vicikicchā* which is translated as 'doubt'. *Vicikicchā,* of course, is the result of thinking. If you think, then you doubt. People that think too much are too critical, too analytical, and that is their attachment, their identity. They are always in a state of being unsure. Thinking is like that. It is a function of the mind and has its purpose, but as an end in itself it does not lead to stream-entry. We can't think ourselves into stream-entry. So doubt is the result of being attached to thought, ideas, views and opinions.

Notice that these first three fetters are not natural conditions; they are not part of nature. Greed, hatred and delusion, on the other hand, are part of natural conditioning . This realm that we live in is one of anger, greed and delusion; these are part of the package of this realm. It is the basic energies of this realm that bring the primal emotions into play. The procreative energies, the self-protective energies, survival, and so forth are just natural to this realm. When we are born into a body like this, there will be fear as well as all the primal emotions that we share with the other species. But these primal emotions are not a self; they are not attachment to conventions; and they are not caused through thought, through thinking about things. The first three fetters, on the other hand, are the artifices of society, culture and the sense of self.

When we get a perspective on these three fetters, we begin to realize that awareness is not a culturally conditioned ability — it is not Asian or European, male or female — but is actually a natural state of being, something that is part of being in this form. And the essential point about this awareness is that it is also a way of freeing ourselves from the energies of greed, hatred and delusion. So, the sense of a self is a created thing; we create our egos. We also create the conventions — the artifices that we put onto this moment — the identities we have with our group, family, culture, ethics, religion, whatever. And if we never get beyond doubt, then even if we have insight into the path, the doubt seems to be our obsession — 'Maybe it isn't the path!' When we think about it from the position of the ego we are never quite sure — !

Now, investigation into these three fetters is not for the purpose of getting rid of them; it is not an attack on the intellect, or the conventional world, or the sense of a self; it is not a question of trying to destroy these as if they were enemies, but of recognizing them so that the awareness allows us to get a perspective on them in this moment. The sense of myself, my personality is 'like this'. Conventional conditioning , cultural conditioning , religious conditioning — the whole range of conventions that are created by human beings — are recognized. It is not a matter of determining whether they are good or bad. They are just what they are. So we recognize our attachment to conventions, not from an anarchist view — 'down with all conventions!' — but as something we create and can be bound to. We might find we are always coming from a conventional position like being nationalistic, or being a Theravadan Buddhist, or a Mahayana Buddhist, or a Roman Catholic, or a Protestant. There is nothing wrong with any of these as conventions, but the attachment to them separates, doesn't it? To think, 'You are Theravada and he is Mahayana,' makes a division in the mind. And then we have a preference for one or the other.

Now, the ability of awareness is to actually see this sense of committing myself, say, to Theravada monasticism or to the Thai Forest tradition. This is a lifetime commitment and is an investment on the ego level. How does it affect me and create the sense of myself in this society? I have followed this particular convention and given myself to it, and I can see that when somebody starts criticizing it I begin to feel threatened or defensive. Maybe I feel I have to prove that this is the best and that someone else's convention isn't quite as good as mine. But this is just the operation of personality belief, sceptical doubt, and attachment to conventions.

The point is, it can be witnessed; if we trust ourselves with awareness it can actually be observed. Awareness is not discrimination; it isn't deciding which is the best; which is the best is not important. 'The best' is merely a condition we create with thought. When we think about which the best is, we are going into opinions, preferences, conditioning and attachment. It is not important to figure out which the best is, but to recognize that convention is 'like this'. Attachment to convention, identity with it, is all very good — it might be a very noble, inspiring thing to do — but it will limit us if we cannot recognize the sense of the convention limiting us, the sense of being bound to the convention and not seeing attachment. That very attachment will always separate. We will always be put in a defensive position when our convention is under attack or being criticized.

These days here in England the Sangha is continually being bombarded with new ideas, challenges and criticisms. And these things can be quite intimidating on a personal level. I noticed that when somebody criticized Ajahn Chah, or the Thai Forest tradition, or Theravada in general, I would feel threatened or defensive, or even get caught in doubt — 'Maybe I've chosen the wrong one! Maybe there's a better one and I've missed out! Maybe I should have joined the Hare Krishna lot?' So I trained myself to observe that sense of threat and defensiveness when somebody challenged me. I would go to that feeling, that emotion, and begin to see the attachment and clinging to conventions, ideas, methods of practice, Ajahn Chah, the Thai Forest tradition, the Ajahn Mun tradition — all good stuff (still just as good as ever) — but I began to see the attachment to these things and also that attachment limits. Whatever we are attached to we become, and that binds us to the world. In consequence we cannot see the path; we cannot transcend. If we only go that far, we get stuck there.

So explore this sense of 'me and mine', the personality *(sakkāyadiṭṭhi)*, the views you have about yourself, the habit tendencies, the character tendencies and so forth. Awareness receives all that — the good and bad, the skilful and unskilful — and never selects. If some kind of unskilful emotion and characteristic arises in consciousness and you think, 'That's unskilful,' then you make more of it than it is. You don't have to regard anything as unskilful — it is what it is. If you trust your intuitive wisdom, you will know how to respond to a situation rather than just reacting to it and creating some kind of 'bad trait' that you have to get rid of, and feel that 'there is something wrong with me because I have this characteristic'. That just leads to complications. It becomes conceptual proliferation. It becomes more than it is, and you create a mountain out of a molehill. I am sure you all recognize that as one of our human problems.

Attachment to conventions I found to be more subtle, actually, than personality belief, even though they are intertwined. Our conventions are often very sacred, very good, and we might have a very strong sense of loyalty to them. Thinking of the Thai Forest tradition and Ajahn Chah and so on can bring up this sense of loyalty and gratitude within me, this feeling that I have to protect it. After Ajahn Chah died in 1992 some monks became interested in preserving the purity of his teaching. They wanted to make sure it didn't get distorted, which all sounded very good and right — it was coming from a righteous position, from good intentions — but is that what Ajahn Chah was teaching? Was he teaching us to grasp the idea of him as the latest infallible sage and that we must give ourselves totally to his memory? After living in his monastery for ten years, I never once got that impression. And yet it is an easy thing to do — not want the Thai Forest tradition to degenerate and feel we have to protect it. It is the awareness of that, however, that is the refuge.

Occasionally I talk about purity, and people feel exasperated because it sounds like such a high-minded thing, being pure; it sounds so impossible. What is purity, anyway? You might think of some ideal form of purity. A perfectly pure monk *(bhikkhu)*, for example, would be like a Buddha-*rūpa*, an idealization of goodness and all that is best. All the best things you can think of and create would be put into that form of the perfectly pure monk. And yet, in terms of each one of us, we are not ideals. We are not made of white marble. We can't make ourselves into the very best conditions. So recognize that the basic nature of the conditioned realm is impure, unstable, and always changing. In dualism, in the conditioned realm, if there is good, there is going to be bad. Everything has its opposite. So, trying to divide everything — which is what dualism tends to do — trying to get rid of all the bad stuff and hold onto the good, creates division, which means war, doesn't it? It means violence. Even holding onto the purity of the tradition can lead to violent action. You can be very insensitive and cruel to those you feel are unworthy or degenerate, or threaten the purity of 'my' group. You can get into this very self-righteous attitude — 'Burn the witches! Kill the heretics!' — and it is all based on righteousness and the preservation of purity.

So I contemplated: 'Well, what is pure in terms of this moment?' because if purity is just an impossible ideal then I give up on it; it's a hopeless concept if it is applied merely to ideas and the conditioned realm. When we explore conditionality we know that its very nature is change, that it is unsatisfactory *(duk-kha)*; that it is impermanent, unsatisfactory and non-self. That isn't a criticism of it; it is just pointing to the way it is. Purity, then, is awareness. Purity is our true nature, in other words, and can never be tarnished or soiled no matter what we think or do. The problem is we don't recognize this and attach to impurity. Personality belief, sceptical doubt, and attachment to conventions are impurities that we are bound to. Even attachment to the best convention or the highest thought or intention is attachment to something that is unstable and changing. And that can only disappoint us. So when we seek purity and security from the impure and insecure, that is blindness; that is not seeing things as they are. Beauty is beauty, goodness is goodness. They are the way they are. The conditions for goodness and beauty arise, and we can appreciate and enjoy them without holding onto them, without asking them to be fixed or 'mine'. Then we can rejoice in the beauty and goodness of the world we live in, and in the goodness and beauty of ourselves. Once we grasp them, however, they are no longer there. They are lost. They are no longer joy, but just doubt and worry and fear.

Grasping the concept of 'the purity of our tradition' immediately creates the potential for it to be tainted by 'monks who are not very good', or by changing conditions, or by monasteries that don't live up to 'my standards.' One can also feel threatened by other groups, by New Age Messiahs, new religions, psychologists and all the rest. Some of the Sangha are very intent on maintaining that purity — 'There's just the Theravada tradition, and that's it! We can't allow anything else in. It's all there. We don't need anything else!' They can be quite pleasant guys, normally, but when they get into that mode there is something not so pleasant about them.

This is why I say 'trust this awareness'. Recognize it. Don't look for anything. Give up trying to find anything. Just trust yourself to be in the present, relax into it instead of thinking, 'I've got to trust mindfulness!' With that attitude you won't recognize it. I find the most conducive attitude is to trust myself. That isn't trusting what my personality says — I know that one! The personality can say, 'How do you know you're really mindful? Do you think you can trust yourself? You should sit more. You should practise more. You should . . .' and it goes on like that with a whole scenario about 'what I *should* do'. I've listened to it for years and recognize it now.

Relaxed attention sounds like an oxymoron, doesn't it? We think of attention as 'ATTENTION!' and you suddenly go rigid. But 'attention' doesn't mean 'stress'; it isn't an imperative: 'Pay attention!' It is trusting, relaxing and letting things be what they are, whatever way they are in the present. Even if you have confused emotions, attention allows them to be what they are. There is no question of trying to get to purity by ridding yourself of conditions; it is more learning to recognize the state of being which is natural to you. You can't create it; you can't make yourself pure. It is merely a matter of recognizing it. And you do that through attention and awareness, through listening in a relaxed and open way. There is nothing to protect or defend, to get or get rid of. I found that kind of suggestion very helpful to me in the past because my tendency was on the 'ATTENTION!' level — 'Got to practise! Got to get rid of these bad thoughts and purify the mind!' — these imperatives which came from the inner tyrant.

The Bodhisattva Avalokiteśvara listens to the sounds of the universe. This is an image I find quite meaningful. It is like a suggestion of being this in the present and letting whatever is going on be what it is. I now no longer fight the pain in the body or the imperatives from my ego, but recognize them. This awareness is what I regard as pure. It has no flaws, no blemishes. The warts and diseases as well as the good stuff come and go, but what remains is always this awareness, this natural conscious awareness of non-grasping and non-identification. In this way I have affirmed it: This is it! This is the way it is! The high-minded ideals, the altruism, the fears, the desires and the dark side have an inner perspective of dhamma. They are seen for what they are and are no longer threatening. I am threatened as a person. My personality gets threatened; I still feel this sense of being threatened. But the awareness of it is what I rest in. I am no longer trying to figure out what I am afraid of, how to get rid of it, or who to blame.

I would like to emphasize that we acquire cultural conditioning from the time we are born, from our families and social backgrounds. We acquire this sense of ourselves, this sense of what we should and should not be, of what a good boy is, of how we should relate to our parents, to authority, and so on. And these things are not always inculcated in us in any direct way. They are often assumed from those around us. So a lot of cultural conditioning is not all that conscious; it is just part of how we see and interpret life. The only way to get perspective on this, therefore, is through awareness.

Many of us, as we grew up, became very critical of our cultural conditioning , of our parents and our society. We could see that 'they shouldn't have been like that; they shouldn't have said that; they shouldn't have done that; they should have been this other way'. We were probably very good at criticizing and knowing how it *should* have been if we could have had the best of everything, if everything had been fair. We complained because we didn't get the best. But that is like getting angry with God, isn't it? 'Why didn't you give me the best?' — that is the ego again. The way it is, is not always the best in terms of quality, but it is in terms of the opportunity for understanding, for knowing things as they are. And this is what is important, what is liberating.

When you begin to trust in the awareness, you see personality belief, doubt, and attachment to conventions in terms of dhamma. You also see that *you* create them. They are not natural energies; they are artifices that you add to the present moment, that you put onto your experience. Once the illusion is broken and seen through, you see the path; you see the way. So that is stream-entry. Now, when people think about stream-entry egotistically, from the personality belief, they think they can actually train to *become* stream-enterers. You hear people say things like, 'Well, you know, I went on a retreat in Sri Lanka and attained stream-entry! I went through all these stages and finally reached the sixteenth stage and now I'm a certified *sotāpanna!*' And that always rings false to me, because it just sounds like another artifice; it sounds like a Pali convention that has been adopted and clung to so that if a recognized meditation master says, 'You've now attained stream-entry,' you think, 'Well, it must be true; he's a wise master.' The ego loves that. I could see that in myself — that wanting confirmation from outside — and went through a period of desperately wanting Ajahn Chah to tell me what stage I was at. On a personal level I didn't trust myself at all and put all my trust in him: 'He's the wise man. I'm the stupid one. He knows and I don't.' But whenever I mentioned it to him, he always threw me back on myself: 'Well, are you or not? How do you expect *me* to know?' He had ways of not reaffirming that basic delusion I had that 'he's the wise man and I'm the stupid one; he's the enlightened master and I'm the ignorant disciple'. I never heard him once affirm that delusion. And now I really appreciate it. When I was a child and made a mess of things — when everything was a wreck and I didn't know what to do — I always wanted my mother to come and straighten it out for me, or the Messiah, or some authority that would straighten everything out and make me feel secure. I could see the same thing in monastic life, that wanting the master to approve of me and tell me I am a good practitioner and doing it in the right way.

Every day we chant in Pali: *sandiṭṭhiko, akāliko, ehipassiko, opanayiko, paccattaṃ veditabbo viññūhi* (the dhamma is apparent here and now, timeless, encouraging investigation, leading onwards, to be experienced individually). Ajahn Chah constantly used the Pali word *'paccattaṃ'* in the Thai context. He would say, 'This is *paccattaṃ*,' meaning it was to be experienced individually. He would say that insight is *paccattaṃ*, which is the Thai way of saying you have to know it for yourself. It was one of the things I picked up very quickly in the beginning of my time there — because of the chanting and because it was a Pali word used in a Thai sentence structure.

So reflect on your own life with this kind of questioning, with this kind of self-inquiry: 'If purity is real, then what is it for me at this moment?' By challenging the moment with questions like this, I began to realize that purity isn't my thoughts, or my emotions, or my body — it is awareness. Awareness is reality. Awareness is a fact and not an abstract idea. So this awareness is the refuge *(saraṇa)*. And a refuge is a safe place. One goes to a refuge because one is frightened and wants to feel secure. Well, I can't find security in personality belief, doubt, and attachment to conventions. Those things just make it worse; they just increase my sense of anxiety and fear so that I have these fears following me around all the time.

By learning to recognize and trust awareness, you realize that it is this that is purity, and you affirm it: 'Purity is this!' It isn't the personality belief saying 'I am pure!' but 'Purity is this! Then you are awakened to it; you recognize it. And through that recognition the impurities are seen in terms of what they are. You can still use conventions and language, and you can still analyse, but the conventional world becomes more functional. You do not identify with it or become limited by it. So, rather than being taken over by the conventions you create, you use them; you use the conventions skilfully.

After stream-entry, comes once-return. When the artificial conditions have been seen through, one is still left with the basic human conditions of anger and lust. These are primal energies that we have through having a human body and living in a sense realm. But they are no longer interpreted on a personal level. In the West we tend to take things too personally. Sexual desire becomes one's personal problem, and people make endless problems around anger, jealousy and fear. These things are taken to be 'my fault', 'my problem', 'my obsession', and all the shoulds and should nots arise in the mind. The ideal of purity is that we would not have any sexual energy. Purity would mean being celibate, being a *brahmacariya*, and being an arahant. We wouldn't have any of these things going on if we were pure; we would be beyond it all! In terms of the reality of this realm, however, we are here because of the procreative energies. And sexual desires are pretty much part of being human. Anger and hatred are also part of it. We usually take them personally, but are they? Or are they just the natural processes of self-protection and survival? When something attacks us, we have to protect ourselves; we have to resist, fight. That is the law of the jungle. Jealousy is also a basic emotion; animals feel jealous. Probably your dog gets jealous if you pay attention to another dog. And fear too is a natural emotional experience.

These energies are what I call 'primal', and they continue to operate with stream-entry. But now you have broken your identity with them. You have broken the artificial attachment, the judgement about yourself in regards to greed, hatred and delusion. You no longer claim them or create problems around them — once you have seen the path. The agreement of a celibate monk, of course, is not to act on these kind of energies — but you still have them. Your relationship to them then is with recognition. But whatever, your refuge is in the awareness, not in the energy itself. The energy arises and ceases; it is what it is. Anger, lust, and fear still arise in consciousness when the conditions for them are present, but you don't identify with them. And as you develop that, the resistance or attachment to them is no longer reinforced, and you begin to have more confidence in the awareness, in the refuge of awareness.

Following on from this there is what is called 'non-return', and this is where you get into the blissful states, the states of tranquillity and refined conscious experiences that one really likes to be in. Then, finally, the last fetters before arahantship, are conceit *(māna)* and ignorance *(avijjā)*. *Māna* is an interesting one because you might not immediately see the difference between *sakkāyadiṭṭhi* (ego) and *māna* which is translated as 'conceit'. Reflecting on this, you will see that *sakkāyadiṭṭhi* is personality, it is culturally conditioned, and it becomes very obvious what that is. But this sense of 'I am' is still the vehicle. Now, this subtle sense is what I call *'māna'* (conceit). As your trust in awareness increases and expands it becomes very strong. Then even the sense 'I am' drops away. The subtle sense of 'I am' just doesn't make sense any more in the context of awareness. To think, 'I am Ajahn Sumedho' is *sakkāyadiṭṭhi*, isn't it? 'I am a Buddhist monk' is both *sīlabbata-parāmāsa* and *sakkāyadiṭṭhi* (attachment to conventions and personality belief) — because I have a quality, a position, and I am good, bad, wise or stupid. But in terms of *māna* (conceit), I have seen through the 'I am Ajahn Sumedho'; there is no 'Ajahn Sumedho'; I realize that that is merely a condition arising. So when the conditions for 'Ajahn Sumedho' are present, then I say, 'I'm Ajahn Sumedho', but it isn't something that has any continuity to it. The sense of 'I am', however, *does* have a sense of continuity to it, even though it isn't identified or qualified. This then is translated as 'conceit' (I don't know whether this is the best translation or not). Anyway, this is not the same as the *sakkāyadiṭṭhi* conceit where one thinks, 'I'm the greatest,' or 'I'm better than you are,' it is just the conceit of 'I am'.

Now, the word 'ignorance' as used in Pali means 'not knowing the Four Noble Truths with their three aspects and twelve insights' (that is the formula of the Four Noble Truths). And the path is in terms of being eightfold (the Eightfold Path). But the Eightfold Path is really just awareness. Awareness is the path, and the eight parts are more or less positions for reflection rather than actual steps on an actual path. It is not a matter of taking this whole conception of a path too literally, thinking that one step leads to the next — first you do this and then you do that.

Taken in personal terms, you might start wondering, 'Do I have right view? Is my speech really right speech all the time?' And then maybe thinking, 'Oh, I'm not on the path! I said something the other day I shouldn't have said.' If you start thinking about yourself in that way, you just get confused. My advice is not to make a problem of yourself. Give up making a problem about yourself, or how good or bad you are, or what you should or shouldn't be. Learn to trust in your awareness more, and affirm that; recognize it and consciously think, '*This* is the awareness — listening — relaxed attention.' Then you will feel the connection. It is a natural state that sustains itself. It isn't up to you to create it. It isn't dependent on conditions to support it. It is here and now whatever is happening.

This Endless Rebirth

A s this is the last day, I want to reflect on the perception of separating, of leaving, of the end of the Leicester Summer School 2004. On the first evening there was a sense of something about to happen; and that was a different feeling from the one now of being faced with the inevitable separation, of leaving. So this is an exercise in reflecting on just the simple experience of meeting and separating. It is not a matter of making value judgements or statements about it; it is merely recognizing the reality of this moment with this sense of the conditions having arisen for separating — it is 'like this'. The separation is still in the future, of course, at about twelve o'clock today or something like that, so we are not talking about a memory. We might remember previous Summer Schools, but this is recognizing the conditions that exist at this moment, this sense of the end of something that began on Monday and is ending today, Saturday — the actual physical separation being a couple of hours away.

One's life is a continuous experience of meeting and separating, isn't it? When you think of your life from birth to death, it is this process of coming together and separating, of starting and finishing. The realm that we live in, this sense realm, is impermanent, so every beginning has an ending. The beginning is the potential, the possibility, and the ending is remembering what *has* been experienced — the people we have met and the things we have done during these past five days, for example. Now the future is no longer connected to the Summer School; it is about going home, going back to the monastery. Tomorrow afternoon I have to give a talk! The tendency is to mix our awareness with wanting to define it, qualify it, or compare it with something else. Hardly ever are we fully appreciative or tuned in to the reality of life as we are experiencing it; and during the ending of something we usually start planning our next move so don't fully experience ending and separating.

This is the *saṁsāric* (round of rebirth) tendency of attachment. When you become bored — and you don't observe boredom unless you are practising mindfulness — you seek something interesting or exciting, or at least something to distract your attention from the boredom of the present moment. Life is a process of searching for rebirth in this way, a continuous sense of being reborn again into some new thing, something that interests you. But try to sustain an interest for a long period of time. What happens? Inevitably you become bored even with the most interesting conditions or experiences. Too much pleasure, actually, becomes boring. If you live an exciting life with lots of adventures, romance and pleasure, after a while you become bored with it all and think, 'I just want to go off to the mountain top and be alone.' So you go to the mountain top, you are there for a few minutes, and then start planning how to get back down to the next thing you think you want to do.

This is rebirth in terms of what we might actually contemplate within our lives. The word 'rebirth' doesn't necessarily mean physical rebirth — being born again in the next life — it can mean the mental rebirths that are so ordinary we don't even notice them. As soon as life becomes boring or unpleasant, we seek rebirth into something else. That means beginning again, choosing something that has the potentiality for fulfilment, for happiness, for entertainment, for being totally mesmerized and taken over — like those pop movies about sex and violence. Sexuality, physical violence, war and conflict excite the mind. You don't have to concentrate on them; they just hold your attention. Not that there is anything wrong with that — I am not complaining about it or condemning it — but just talking about taking notice of how the mind becomes excited. Much of life isn't exciting, is it? It is just this moment, just nothing much. If we are not aware, the tendency is to want to fill our lives with plans, possibilities, distractions, eating, drinking, television and many other things. Peacefulness, calm, emptiness and stillness, we can't stand, actually; they are just too hard to bear!

Because of the tendency of the mind to wander, to plan the future or remember the past, most meditation techniques are related to concentration exercises. This is a way of training the mind to stay with an object and absorb into it. When you absorb into something you actually become one with it, and the sense of separateness falls away. By doing a colour-*kasina*[28] meditation, for example, you become that colour through absorbing into it. Years ago I did one on the colour green and started to see green in everything, even when I wasn't concentrating on it. I absorbed into it and the result was a heightened sense of greenness. It was a beautiful colour, too. At least mine was! It wasn't one of those murky greens. And in the *jhāna* (absorption) practices, you take a subject and by concentrating on it, you experience rapture, a sense of physical oneness with the subject, a kind of physical pleasure, then mental happiness, and then one-pointedness. So these are like meditation exercises. It isn't right to refer to them as 'attainments', because they are actually relinquishments. So, in the *jhāna* practices you recognize how to let go of the coarser factors until there is nothing left but equanimity or one-pointedness, instead of trying to get rapture and happiness through conceiving them and aiming for them. You let go of the desire to achieve and go towards an increasing sense of surrender and relinquishment to the object of concentration. Like any form, however, this is limited; conditions that support tranquillity and refined levels of consciousness are limited. The world we live in is not a tranquil realm; it is a sense realm full of stimulation and irritation. The senses are constantly being impinged upon from birth to death. Even pleasurable impingement, when you look at

---

28 External device for developing concentration.

it, is a kind of irritation to the senses; even sensory experience at its best when seen from emptiness, is irritating; it is kind of inadequate.

This word 'meditation' can encompass almost anything, any kind of mental training you can think of, and the tranquillity practices are basically about concentration — one chooses an object and focuses on it. Very often a lot of the insight meditation techniques also end up as concentration practices, because the technique tends to dominate. One absorbs into the technique rather than using it for awareness. This is why during this week I am pointing to this sense of trusting yourself to intuitively recognize natural awareness. You can't see it, but you can know it. Awareness, then, is formless. And this I think is what we find difficult to accept. Our whole conditioning process is aimed at seeking rebirth in form, attaching to some form, becoming something. The ultimate freedom of formlessness can therefore seem quite frightening, especially at first, because all forms, boundaries and identities fall away, and our emotional habits cannot cope with that; our emotions don't know what is happening. It might seem that we are having a breakdown, losing our minds, and suddenly we don't know who we are. So this can be frightening.

I have met people who don't have a very good self-image, and yet they know who they are — 'I'm a Buddhist; I'm a Theravadan.' People take on identities and that gives them a sense of security. But when those identities fall away, then what are they? Their emotions are conditioned around becoming something, around happiness and suffering, so when they reach this point of emptiness — or even just get near it — emotionally it can be very frightening. They want to find a place where they can feel 'Well, I know what I am now! I know who I am now!' This sense of not knowing with awareness, however, is not a state of stupidity; it is centred on consciousness knowing the way it is. It isn't a judging, critical factor — it doesn't seek to evaluate, criticize or prefer — it is the direct knowing of the way it is.

Now, I find that the way insight meditation is often taught leads to people becoming obsessed with the idea that all conditions are impermanent. In some ways it can be like an intellectual projection. I have heard people say, 'Well, everything is impermanent,' as though it isn't worth grasping anything at all because 'it's all just going to disappoint me!' That is a kind of wet-blanket approach, isn't it? 'I'm going to fail and I'm going to die anyway, so what's the point?' This is not *vipassanā* (the word literally means 'insight into the nature of things') or *yoniso manasikāra* (getting to the very root, the very cause of the thing, direct knowing rather than knowing *about*). *Vipassanā* isn't a function of thinking, but rather of trusting intelligence — and that is a universal. Intelligence is not a personal thing; it isn't cultivated in the sense of having to increase anything; it is more a matter of learning to recognize and appreciate the natural ability we already have. We have the potential for enlightenment, for seeing in this clear way without attachment to anything whatsoever.

I found that reflecting on space gave me some insight into infinity. I thought I knew what infinity meant, but it was just an abstract idea; it was defined but not recognized. I am not making a statement about infinity in the way a scientist might; nor am I trying to philosophize about it. I am simply talking about recognizing the reality of space at this moment. Space has no boundaries, does it? It is infinite. So, as I open to just space — starting with the space in this room — I realize that although the walls look like boundaries, they too are in space. Infinite space is reality in this moment; and when I contemplate that, I don't dismiss the conditions that are here. I don't have to shut all of you out for that because infinite space can receive everything — all forms, all conditions — and forms do not hide the spaciousness of this moment. I also used to regard consciousness as being in my brain, in my head. But then, in reflective meditation, I realized I couldn't say that consciousness was in my brain, because it seemed to be everywhere. The fact that I can actually see you at this moment means you are in my mind, you are in my consciousness. Consciousness holds you at this moment because that is the way it is. But you are not in my brain. At least I don't think so!

These things are so obvious that we don't usually notice them. That which is most simple and most real can be overlooked because we always move towards extremity, towards certainty, towards wanting something that doesn't exist right now, towards getting something we imagine would be wonderful to have but don't have yet, or looking around and thinking we need to get rid of what is here in this moment — because it is all an obstruction to 'my peacefulness and enlightenment'. The realities of space and consciousness are here and now, however, they are a fact. So if we use that for reflection — if we notice it, pay attention to it — we will have perspective on the forms and conditions that arise and cease throughout our lives. We will have perspective on thoughts, emotions, the sense of oneself as a person, love and hate, greed, hatred, delusion, fear, pleasure and pain. And it is impossible to define infinity, because language itself is not infinite; it is form. This is why I emphasize trusting in awareness. Before we learn to speak and before thoughts arise, awareness is present; awareness and consciousness are always here and now.

Deathlessness is another term to contemplate. Death right now for all of us is what has not yet happened. We haven't died yet. It is therefore a concept, isn't it? We can think of Catherine Hewitt now. Last year she was alive and she was here; and she was sitting right there. The perception now is that Catherine Hewitt is dead. And that is different, isn't it? It has a different feel to it because death is what we don't know. We might like to know what happens when we die, and there are various scenarios about reincarnation, heaven, hell or oblivion. I might go along with what the Buddhists say, or the Hindus, or the Christians, or whoever, but the reality — at least from this position right here — is that I don't know. I am confident that my body *will* die, though; I am not trying to make my body immortal, a deathless form. That, I know, is not possible.

So, is deathlessness just a wish in the mind? Is immortality just a wish because we are afraid of death? Or is it reality? In Buddhism we have the words *'amatadhamma'* (the deathless reality) and *'amarāvatī'* (the deathless realm). And the Buddha pointed to deathlessness as liberation. He didn't point to some kind of perfect state or formed state as liberation. If we explore the beginning and ending of conditions as we experience them, we will have the insight prior to physical death that what arises, ceases. Conditions arise according to other conditions. So when the sun shines, it is like 'this', and when it is raining it is like 'that'. When the conditions for happiness are present, we feel happy, when the conditions for sadness are present, we feel sad, and when everything is going well and no threatening warning signs envelop us, we feel secure — as a person. As soon as threatening signs recur, however, we again feel insecure. So, the conditioned realm is all about beginning and ending, birth and death — that is its very nature. The sense of a self, the personality belief, is also a condition. It also arises and ceases and changes according to conditions. And insight meditation is a way of reflecting on conditionality, of getting to recognize that conditionality is 'like this'.

So what is the flavour of the world? What does the world taste like? My mind would try to make that into some kind of complicated, maybe even poetic, form. But the flavour of the world to me is always unstable; there is always this sense of something missing, of incompleteness, of unsatisfactoriness. Even at best — even when everything is just fine, even when I have good health and everything is just the way I want it to be — there is this kind of fluttery experience.

Some people I know have been very fortunate in their lives, but some of them also have a lot of fear because they know it will change. We can't sustain security and the best conditions, and we know that; we know that we can't hold on, no matter how hard we try. The more we try, in fact, the more miserable we become, because the very act of grasping is an unpleasant state of mind. This means we can't even enjoy beauty; we suffer even with beauty because we want to hold it and keep it. The point is to notice this without criticizing it, just as a way of awakening to the way it actually is, awakening to the dhamma.

Deathlessness, then, is our true nature. My personality gets born and dies all the time. I used to think, 'What part of my personality would I like to live with forever?' — and I couldn't find anything. The idea of being a unique soul that would last forever made me wonder, 'Well, what is it in my soul — the soul that is unique to me as a person — that I would want to be eternal and never die?' And I couldn't think of a thing! There was nothing in my personality that I wanted to have, first as a unique person, and then to go up a grade and become a unique soul so that when we are all dead you would say, 'Oh, that's Ajahn Sumedho!' And I would say, 'I'm a soul now; I'm glad you recognize me!'

What if we all had to live here in the grounds of this beautiful garden forever with no option of getting out — all good people, beautiful place? If we were permanently what we are on the conditioned plane, we would still have anxiety and insecurity, because the result of absorption into conditioned phenomena is our identification with it. The only way to resolve that problem is to understand it, to know it, and to awaken to it. And that awakening is Buddha. It isn't Buddhism in the sense of knowing all *about* Buddhism or knowing all about being a Buddhist; it is actually the reality of Buddha, of awakenedness. Try to imagine deathlessness and all you get is some kind of immortal fantasy where everything is beautiful, where you are young forever and there is no disease. This is a childlike fantasy of paradise. As you trust awareness more, however, the formless and unbounded is not seen as a kind of unconscious annihilation, but is where you are no longer obsessed with ignorant grasping. Right now we are all experiencing forms arising and ceasing from this emptiness. It is like a miracle. And that is just the way it is. We are not trying to seek annihilation so that all forms die and no form ever arises again. That is the desire for annihilation, for extinction.

Sometimes when we are fed up with ourselves and the world we would like to just become nothing, just disappear into the void; but that is a wish, another desire that we create. Suicide is not the answer; you simply get reborn, because that is the nature of desire.

Every moment we recognize awareness — and really trust and learn to appreciate it — joy comes, compassion comes, and love. But it isn't personal; it isn't based on liking, preferences, or *kammic* attachments. The dhamma is not the destruction of conditioned phenomena, but the container of it. All possibilities of conditioned phenomena arise and cease in the dhamma; and there is nothing that can bind us once we see that, because the reality of the dhamma is seen rather than the forms that arise and cease. Mindfulness reflections are skilful means the Buddha developed for investigating experience, for breaking down the illusions we hold, for breaking through the ignorance we grasp at, for freeing ourselves from form, the limited and the unsatisfactory. Rather than teaching too many techniques now, or giving too much structure, I prefer to encourage people just to trust themselves with mindfulness and awareness. Often meditation is taught with this sense that one has to get something or get rid of something. But that only increases the existing idea of 'I am somebody who has to become something that I am not, and has to get rid of my bad traits, my faults, my defilements.' If we never see through that, it will be a hopeless task. The best we will ever do under those circumstances is maybe modify our habit-tendencies, make ourselves nicer people and be happier in the world — and that isn't to be despised, either — but the point of the Buddha's teaching is liberation.

Generosity and morality will of course help us to create more happiness in the world; they will lead to self-respect and good relations with others. When you are positive and happy, people like you, and you tend to have more friends and more worldly happiness — just by being good and happy. Being miserable and bad, just creates the opposite. Nobody likes you if you are like that, and you live in a world of fear and resentment. The point is to notice how it is. Happy thoughts, good thoughts, make you feel happy; and when you are happy you are a lot easier to be with. When you think negatively, then you think of what is wrong with you, what is wrong with others, and what is wrong with the world. So when you meet people you start grumbling and complaining and making *them* unhappy as well. This is where kamma comes in. In the West the word 'kamma' is often taken to mean 'fate'. People talk about 'my kamma', meaning 'my fate, my destiny', but the word actually refers to cause and effect, action-reaction. And so we have the simple, 'Do good. Refrain from doing bad.' Good *kamma* is doing good and receiving a good result, and bad *kamma* is the reverse. If I harm, lie, steal and disrespect people, people will hate and resent me and I will live in a hell-realm of negativity.

You hear of these power-of-positive-thinking kind of cults where you are told to just think 'happy' and you will be happy. But there is something in us that sees the superficiality of that — of simply suppressing negativity by obsessing our minds with positive thoughts. If we know what we are doing, that is fine. Using mantras, *māla* beads, chants and these kinds of things, can be a skilful means; they can have a good and calming effect on the mind. But they won't if we are just using them to suppress fear and anger. In Buddhism they are used for reflecting on Buddha-Dhamma-Sangha, and can bring a sense of gratitude towards the Buddha, for example. I do in any case feel a lot of gratitude towards not only the Buddha but also towards Ajahn Chah — this sense of real gratitude for having been given so much in my life. And a sense of gratitude is also very positive; it gives one a reference point to something other than just resentments and criticisms. Monasticism itself, monastic training, is all about contentment, learning to be content with very little. Every day we reflect on what the Buddha allowed a bhikkhu: 'A bhikkhu is allowed a meal, a robe, shelter for the night and medicine for illness (the four requisites).' If you reflect on these over the years, you find this sense of contentment. You are not just trying to get the best robe, the best shelter, the best food; it isn't a matter of whether it is your preferred meal or whatever. This is very good for someone like myself who was brought up in a society where contentment was almost despised.

In America we think that anyone who is content is a bit stupid, like a cow chewing cud. To be discontented, on the other hand, is a sign we are trying to progress — 'Don't be content with anything except the best!' But even when we get the best, it doesn't stay that way, because we always see somebody with something better, and then the best changes. This kind of movement of the mind is the way we create endless discontentment with the material world, with our families, with the conditions we are living in and with society — because we can always imagine it being better. Contentment is not, however, a matter of just ignoring things or deluding ourselves; it is a reflection on the fact that we don't really need very much. My needs are minimal, actually. If I have high standards, high expectations, then I have to struggle to get them and keep them. That takes a lot of effort — and I wouldn't have any time for meditation! If I suddenly win the lottery and find myself a multimillionaire, I would still be programmed for 'now what do I do with a hundred million pounds?' — and maybe begin to wonder why people are being so nice to me! But notice that contentment comes through the recognition of what is important in your life, what is really worthy of your attention; you can't *make* yourself grateful. So, what are your needs, really? And what are you conditioned to feel you *must* have? This is a way of not being caught in the obsession of getting more and more, an obsession that really blinds you.

How, then, does one teach mindfulness and awareness? It can be pointed out, and situations can be presented for people to reflect on; but apart from that I think it is a question of confidence, which is why I keep saying, 'Don't trust what you think you are. Don't believe it!' What you think you are, is not what you are. Whatever you think or believe you are, you are not that; that is

just a perception you might be obsessed with or attached to —
but you are not that. Keep reminding yourself. It is so easy to
believe 'I am this person'. It seems real to me when I am attached
to such a perception; and it seems that to deny it would be wrong.
Of course, it isn't a matter of saying 'I am *not* anything', either,
or of adopting some kind of denial of the conditioned, but rather
of recognizing conditionality, receiving conditionality and letting it be. Let whatever you think you are, be what it is — but relate to that in terms of 'the knower'. Whatever you think you are
or believe yourself to be is your creation — but you can actually
be aware of that. And that isn't to criticize it, but to realize that it
is no more than a bubble, no more than foam on the sea without
essence or substance.

In a monastery there are opportunities for solitude as well as
community life; the lifestyle itself has those options to it. But
people can get very attached to solitude — 'I've got to be alone!
I can't live at Amaravati; there are too many people here!' That
is binding oneself to the idea that in order to really practise you
have to find a place where nothing is going to irritate or threaten
you. The truth, of course, is that it doesn't matter where you are,
or who you are with — if you trust your awareness. If the only
time you can ever really feel you are mindful is under ideal conditions — in some nice meditation hut *(kuṭī)* where everything is
properly arranged for you and you feel quite safe and secure, and
all your wishes are fulfilled — then something will come along
to ruin it!

I went to an ideal place once and thought, 'I'm really going to
get my *samādhi* (concentration) together here.' Then one morning I couldn't get up off the floor! I didn't know what had hit
me. Later I discovered I had malaria, and the recurring attacks
lasted a year. During that time I kept thinking it was ruining my
practice and that I couldn't practise with malaria. Then Ajahn
Chah came to see me and he said, 'That's your practice, now
— malaria!' I hadn't thought of it like that before and had just
kept thinking, 'I can't practise because I feel so terrible.' In the

end I learnt a lot from that episode. I learnt about the fear and suffering I was myself creating around having the disease, and eventually realized that when I opened to it, the symptoms *were* bearable. They were uncomfortable but nothing I couldn't bear. I was surprised about that. The personality is conditioned for 'I can't stand it! I can't practise! I don't know whether I'm going to die. It goes to your brain, doesn't it? You go crazy with this, don't you? I've heard of monks losing their minds. They get cerebral malaria and get taken off to the mental hospital — no possibility then of enlightenment!' The worst case scenarios came to my mind. Fortunately it didn't go to my brain; it was certainly an unpleasant physical experience, though. And yet it also had its quite nice moments. The fever would reach a peak and then suddenly break, and when it broke there would be this incredible sense of coolness — and that was very pleasant. So even within the experience of malaria, there were pleasant moments on the physical level.

The flavour of the world, then, is unsatisfactoriness *(dukkha)*. Now, this isn't meant to be a put-down of the world. I am just pointing to the nature of it. And its nature is change — birth and death, coming together and parting. The world is like this; it is an ongoing experience of coming together and separating, of meeting and parting. Notice that when we part we don't usually like to say 'Goodbye forever!' We say, 'See you next summer! See you again!' However we put it, it usually amounts to 'See you again! See you soon! Let's keep in touch,' with that sense of 'in the future we'll meet again'. Because the perception of never meeting again is too stark, too hard to bear. Emotionally, we *would* like to meet again; we don't want a total separation — unless it is from somebody we really can't stand!

During this next year, then, reflect on these things and try to trust yourself more in your practice. Don't criticize yourself; don't believe your critical mind evaluating your ability to practise, because *that* you can't trust. It will say anything, and will usually be in terms of not being good enough, or needing to practise more, or not really being a good Buddhist, and on and on like that. This is the conditioned mind. Most of us are very self-critical; most of us see ourselves through the flaw, hold to that, and then make it into an enormous problem. So I encourage you to let go of that habit. Recognize it for what it is, but then don't perpetuate it. Learn to trust in your own goodness and awakenedness — and see what happens! See what comes! Whatever state you experience doesn't really matter because your relationship to it is 'knowing' rather than identifying with it or judging it.

Sometimes in meditation, negative states come up that have previously been suppressed. Well, see that as a process of purification rather than as a sign that you are practising wrongly. There is a lot of commitment to suppressing negativity in our lives, of just denial, rejection and resistance. When you stop resisting in meditation, however, when that habitual rejection lessens, then the states that have previously been held back come into consciousness. But see that as a purification rather than as something wrong with you. What I am pointing to is a level of faith, of confidence in the human ability to be awake and aware. It is the same for everybody; there are no exceptions. It is a matter of recognizing your true nature and finding that you are not what you think you are. Every thought and every attachment gives a sense of limitation. The very fact that you can open to infinity, to space, to consciousness, however, gives you perspective on that; it frees you from just this endless rebirth, this habit of going from one thing to another.

Receiving Praise and Blame

Looking back on my life in Thailand and England, it all seems to have gone by so quickly. It doesn't seem that long ago that I came to live in the UK, but this is my twenty-ninth year here now. It sounds like a long time, but in hindsight it doesn't feel that long — I think that might just be part of ageing. We can probably all relate to that! Actually, I can't believe I'm so old. When I was nine I remember waiting for my tenth birthday — which seemed like a hundred years away — because I wanted a two-digit age; I wanted to be ten. And my last year in the navy (I was four years in the US Navy) was one of the longest I have ever spent. I had this calendar with a page for each day on which I marked the number of days I had to go: 365 days, 364 days . . . I was so eager to get out. And that year moved at a snail's pace. But looking back over my life as a monk — which is nearly forty years now — I find I quite like the result of that. It was a way of life I was attracted to and now feel very grateful for. In any situation, of course, human life is always the experience of what we call the 'Eight Worldly Dhammas' (good fortune, bad fortune, success, failure, happiness, suffering, praise and blame); they are the four positive and four negative aspects of life.

Ajahn Chah encouraged people to contemplate these Eight Worldly Dhammas because on the conventional plane we experience them continually. But his advice was always to see them as of equal value — praise and blame of equal value, success and failure of equal value, happiness and suffering of equal value, good fortune and bad fortune of equal value. This isn't just an intellectual exercise, but a way of developing awareness when these things arise. Our refuge is in our awareness rather than in our feelings of happiness at praise, resentment at blame and so forth. And this was emphasized over and over again during my monastic training in Thailand.

Ajahn Chah died about fifteen years ago, and when a good monk like that dies, they get placed among the stars; they get apotheosized. So Ajahn Chah is up among the stars now. You never hear any criticism of him now; all you hear is praise. This is what happens when you are dead. When you are alive, it isn't quite like that. Maybe, if I don't mess up my life too much before I die, I might get placed among the stars! At this point, however, I am not in that position. The realities of being human and having the *kamma* one has, means one can be praised or criticized, have good health or poor health, success or failure and various forms of happiness and suffering. These are all part of an individual's experience. The aim, however, is to use experience for reflection, to develop awareness, to recognize and learn to trust it. This isn't something precious, remote or refined; it doesn't depend on ideal conditions, success, praise, good health and all the best. It serves us no matter what is happening externally and internally. This is why the Buddha emphasized the value of mindfulness and awareness, of being present here and now, of being fully present to the way it is.

Life experience, as we know, changes according to conditions. And in my life here in England over the last twenty-nine years, the periods of success and failure have alternated. In the first ten years everything went kind of magically. I lived in Hampstead Vihara for two years and spent some time at the Oaken Holt Buddhist Centre. Then the English Sangha Trust acquired Chithurst and Amaravati. More and more monks and nuns came, the Sangha grew, and I was the one that everybody looked to to make decisions. One of my friends called me the 'supreme commander'. After ten years, however, this way didn't work any more; you can't keep people in that relationship of being subject to a 'supreme commander' forever. As monks and nuns became more confident, more capable in their own practice, they needed opportunities to teach, to take on responsibilities, and to question, so I had to learn to handle things differently. The following decade then became one of criticism — mainly of me for being domineering. So how does one deal with that? On a personal level, I like praise and I don't like to be criticized; I like success and I don't like failure; I like happiness and I don't like suffering. So, of course, when the successes were coming my way I felt a sense of happiness, buoyancy and purpose. And that wasn't just a sense of indulging in happiness; it was a pleasurable time during that first decade, even though it had its moments of difficulty like when we acquired Chithurst — this big derelict worm-ridden Victorian house — which was in a deplorable state. We spent the first five years renovating that place because much of it had to be gutted and rebuilt. So most of our time was taken up with tearing things down and repairing things. And we lived very frugally at that time. This kind of activity I found quite stimulating, actually, because there was a kind of group spirit about it. When a community is poor and you share things in common — difficulties and obstructions — it is easy to work together for the common good. After those early years of hardship and success, however, another wave came along of 'we don't like this and we don't agree with that'. The Thai Forest tradition was criticized, the Theravada Buddhist tradition was criticized, I was criticized, and on and on like that.

The point is to use the praise and blame that comes our way for developing awareness and insight. This was how I got to the root of the problem. I was unable to take criticism from others and began to realize that the Sangha I was leading was what you might call 'dysfunctional' — this is a word a came across when I visited California in the early eighties! I remember sitting in somebody's house in San Francisco and being shown a video of an American psychotherapist talking about 'dysfunctional American families'. It was quite interesting and I thought '. . sounds like Chithurst monastery to me.' So then I had a word for it.

When a Westerner goes to an Asian tradition, it is interesting to see what affects them in that tradition. Most of us were taken by the strictness of the Vinaya (the rules of the order), the way everything is laid down in the Thai Forest tradition. Right, wrong, good and bad are very clearly defined in terms of behaviour in the Vinaya; and this was something we all took up. The ideal of the bhikkhu was very attractive to us and we tried to become these perfect Buddhist monks, keeping the rules very strictly and trying to be the models of perfection — because we grasped the ideal of 'the bhikkhu' and the '*dhutanga* bhikkhu'. In Thailand there are different kinds of monks. Some are academic and others are more ceremonial. But the kind that attracted me was the alms mendicant tradition, the monks who live out in the forest and walk barefoot in the jungle. This appealed to my romantic image of how I wanted to develop.

Now, I am from a White Anglo-Saxon Protestant (WASP) family. And the white Anglo-Saxon Protestants from my generation were always the privileged ones. We were the founding fathers of American society, so I came from not a wealthy background but a racially and ethnically privileged one based on very strong ideals. American society is very idealistic anyway about how things should be. Then I went to Thailand and lived in a remote area of the Northeast which was at that time the very poorest. So this idealism of 'the Buddhist monk' became very strong in me, and I saw the Thai Forest tradition with Ajahn Chah in terms of the ideals I had chosen from that tradition, somehow either not noticing the other side of it, or looking down on it. The point is Thai society is not idealistic; it does not have the white Anglo-Saxon Protestant type of cultural conditioning . Thai society — especially in those days being an agrarian, rice growing society — was much more down to earth and far more easy-going than we were. You constantly heard them say, 'It doesn't matter! We forgot to do this or that, but never mind, it doesn't matter!' Everything was 'never mind, it doesn't matter!' — the mañana syndrome — 'Oh, we can do it tomorrow. If you put it off today you can always find time in the future.'

The conventional forms in Thai society, however, are very highly developed. They have a fine sense of etiquette and highly developed manners and ways of behaving in public. Yet behind the scenes they are these easy-going, laid-back people that are quite at ease within themselves. This was something many of us didn't quite pick up on. In fact, we kind of looked down on that kind of thing. I was practising meditation by driving myself on, and when I saw some of the Thai monks not seeming to do that, I dismissed them as unworthy, at the same time regarding myself as a really serious person, a really serious monk and practitioner. So that was a kind of cultural arrogance; I was grasping a lot of the ideals of Buddhist monasticism but without the cultural conditioning to balance it out. My conditioning tended to perpetuate a sense of being driven, of always feeling I should be doing things, trying to get, attain or achieve things. When you are young and inspired, these kinds of energies are quite exciting to follow, but after a few years it doesn't work any more; you can't do it any more and you tend to just criticize the system. Many monks leave at that time.

I actually liked the Thai culture, and the people and society, so I didn't have any resistance to adapting to it. But a lot of the subtler things — their easy-going ways, their earthiness, the balance points — I didn't notice; they didn't register with me. So it was much more the ideal form of Buddhist monasticism that I had picked up on by the time I came to England, without those balancing qualities that seemed to be part of the Thai cultural attitude. The point is Ajahn Chah was never rushed; his actions were never compulsive. In fact he just seemed to flow with life. He was an impeccable and quite impressive monk, and yet he never seemed self-conscious, intimidating or arrogant in any way; he was just completely at ease with himself in his own society. We were to come to England together in 1977, and I was curious to see how he would survive outside of Thailand where he was so highly regarded. Thailand is a homogeneous society (ninety-five percent Theravadan) so the Thais don't have a lot of experience dealing with ethnic minorities or other religions. When we arrived in London I noticed that Ajahn Chah simply watched how people moved and how things were done, and I was very impressed with the way he adapted himself so easily to situations; it quite surprised me, and pleased me.

Ajahn Chah's emphasis in life was always on knowing time and place and situation. He wasn't just concerned about keeping the rules in terms of things having to be done in the Thai way and 'you have to do it this way otherwise you're wrong!' That was the tendency I found in myself — holding to the ideal and feeling that any lessening of that was like betraying it — that was my cultural conditioning , and it was very dualistic. I was brought up to believe that right and wrong, good and bad, heaven and hell were opposed to each other and that you had to do what was right and get rid of what was wrong. So, the dualistic thinking process was very much part of my cultural, educational, and religious conditioning . But I noticed that Luang Por Chah didn't really have that way of looking at things; he was much more tuned into time and place and what was suitable and appropriate, rather than to what was 'right' and what was 'wrong'. His emphasis was on praise and blame, or any other opposite, being of equal value. It was quite pleasant, actually, travelling with Ajahn Chah in England, because he pointed out things that I would never have otherwise noticed, things that we just take for granted. He had never travelled abroad before, so this was his first experience of going to a foreign country, and coming from the Thai Forest tradition of northeast Thailand was quite a leap.

When in Thailand I noticed that Ajahn Chah was criticized and blamed for many things, but I rather idealized him. I thought, 'This is the greatest monk probably in the world. My teacher is the best!' Americans always want to put things in these superlative terms — the best, the biggest, the greatest! — so the tendency from my American conditioning was to put my teacher into this high position above everyone else. I couldn't understand how anybody could want to criticize him; and yet people did —

even some of his closest disciples. I watched him at those times, and it seemed to be all right with him; he didn't have this attitude of, 'How dare you!' or 'You can't do that!' None of it seemed distressing to him. On the other hand, criticism of me was something I always dreaded; it always made me feel as though I was being rejected. Maybe that was because my life had always been dedicated to succeeding and making myself likeable, acceptable and presentable, so that I would get the praise. If I didn't get that positive side, the criticism was unbearable. One word would throw me into a depressed state of mind; and I would feel hurt or wounded by negative feedback.

Now, when this is a great part of your character, you can give talks on praise and blame and say they are of equal value, yet when the reality of those things arises, what do you do? Praise was manageable, but blame — ! I realized how frightened I was of that and also that I presented myself in a way that created what might be called 'a dysfunctional situation'. In other words, because most of the monks and nuns at that time were quite sensitive and good people, they didn't want to hurt me, so they didn't say anything. They didn't give me any feedback because they were afraid I would become aggressive, blame them, or feel hurt; and they didn't want to do that. But I began to see the problem and asked myself how I might receive blame without simply reacting to it; how I might receive praise and blame equally? This was the conundrum I became conscious of whilst living here in England. I recognized that if I didn't know how to receive criticism, then my position as head of the community was useless; there was no way I could really fulfil that role if all I was going to do was create dysfunctional situations. And being the most senior monk in the group, I also couldn't expect anybody else to do it. So I knew I needed to work with this and get to the root of it.

I started by experimenting with just listening to myself, listening to the way I criticized myself, because part of the conditioning process in me had created an inner tyrant. I had this relentless inner critic, and I began to realize that, actually, this inner critic was worse than any other. Nobody ever criticized me as much or as relentlessly as I criticized myself. So I began to listen to this judging, righteous thing in me that said, 'You shouldn't have done that! You shouldn't have said that! You're not a good monk! You shouldn't feel jealous of anybody! You're a hypocrite and just a fake, a phoney.' I simply started listening to this inner voice — which, by the way, wasn't a symptom of schizophrenia — and I did this rather than getting caught up either in the power of that voice or in trying to suppress or reject it.

Now, in the past I had had an experience whilst walking down Haverstock Hill one afternoon in London (this busy street across from Hampstead Vihara). I had been going past the Haverstock Arms, in fact, when I had this sense of what I call 'the sound of silence'[29] and with it a sense of boundlessness and emptiness; it was a powerful experience. After that I began to recognize the 'sound of silence' with this emptiness more and more. I also began to recognize more the difference between pure awareness and the personality-view. It became clear to me that my conditioned personality was this frightened character who liked praise and couldn't stand criticism, and who was very judgemental and full of anxieties, worries and self-consciousness. As I aligned myself with the 'sound of silence', I recognized that which was aware of the personality, then the sense of myself as a person kind of faded so that there remained just this pure awareness — and in that the personality seemed to come and go.

When I began to fully appreciate this, I recognized it was a way to deal with blame. When I listened to someone blaming me and criticizing me, and was in that silence, I realized that I was aware of my own reactivity without acting on it; I realized that if I trusted this awareness, I could receive my own reactions

---

29 The sound of silence: A kind of cosmic background vibration; a sound unlike sound as we generally think of it (with a beginning and ending); a stream-like, ongoing, flowing sound. [Ajahn Sumedho]

to what others were saying. This gave me the spaciousness in consciousness for the world to come and go with all its pleasure, pain, praise and blame. And I put this to the test in the monastic community one winter. I was not on good terms with the nuns (*sīladharās*) at the time and asked them to give me some feedback. So we arranged some meetings. I told them there would be no forbidden subjects, and that they were free to say whatever they wanted — especially around their relationship with me. The meetings were open-ended so that they could start in the afternoon and go on until the evening or until it was obviously time to stop. I was determined not to defend myself, not to blame others, and not to follow any feelings of wanting to set them straight. I did, however, allow myself to apologize if I felt an apology was appropriate. I decided that, even if I didn't agree with them or saw things differently, I would not argue the point. Each one of us sees things the way we see them, and I knew that none of the nuns was going to tell me a lie, so it wasn't a question of trying to prove whose angle was the right one, but of just listening — which I did.

They told me things that were quite painful to hear, actually, about how I had disappointed them, failed them, lost their respect. Things like that can break your heart. To receive the criticism and your own reactions at the same moment, however, is possible. Awareness gives us that capability. It was hard going sometimes, of course, and I would occasionally go back to my room feeling as though I had been in the ring with a prizefighter. But I didn't chicken out and the following day went back again. At the end of a month there was nothing more to say and it seemed to have resolved itself; it seemed that an amazing kind of transformation had taken place. Everybody had had an opportunity to speak, and I had found my own strength to receive blame. The blame no longer frightened me, and that experience later helped me to receive praise as well. I get a lot of praise, but no longer depend on it in order to feel worthwhile.

If awareness is your refuge, the personality will be received and accepted; and you can learn from it. But you will no longer be limited and bound into those habit patterns or that cultural conditioning you acquired while growing up.

This is the Deathless

S it quietly, compose the mind, adopt an attitude of relaxed attention, mindfulness, an attitude of letting go, of being at ease, of letting the world disappear.

Now, to talk about 'relaxed attention' sounds like an oxymoron, doesn't it? You might think attention puts you into a state of not being relaxed; and relaxation often means *not* paying attention. But in this context these two words 'relaxed attention' are pointing to an attitude of being present without trying, without having some preconception of becoming attentive or making yourself meditate, or putting yourself into the usual striving attitude. For most of us, when we think of paying attention, it is usually with a sense of striving, of making ourselves do something as an act of will; whereas the kind of attention I am talking about has nothing to do with willing ourselves to pay attention; it is a natural state of ease, of being present, more like listening but not controlling.

'Letting go' is another concept that might help us understand this sense of relinquishing rather than holding onto anything. We are allowing ourselves to be present without getting caught up in ideas that we have to *get* something out of this, that we have to control everything or get rid of negative thoughts. All these attitudes are part of our cultural conditioning . We have these tendencies to want to control, to judge, to discriminate, to try to get something we don't have yet — some idealized state, something called 'enlightenment' that we imagine we don't have right now — or try to get rid of bad thoughts, greed, hatred and delusion in order to become this enlightened being in the future.

But with the attitude of relaxed attention, we let go of all that — all our concepts, ideas, views about ourselves, about Buddhism, about meditation, about enlightenment, about everything — and there is nothing we have to get or get rid of.

What I am pointing to is simply learning to trust, learning to recognize a very natural state of being rather than coming from some idea, some opinion, some view or assumption which is the result of a culturally conditioned mind. The thing to keep remembering is that mindfulness is always here and now; it isn't something we have to attain. When we try to conceive of awareness or mindfulness, we create an idea of it and then try to achieve it according to that idea. Maybe we have a definition of it from a Pali dictionary or from what some teacher has said — and we grasp that. We grasp the ideas of Buddhism very quickly because intellectually we are well developed, but this can get in the way of awareness which is beyond definition. Awareness is more of an attitude, a natural state of being, yet we can take the word and say, 'Oh, I'm not very mindful; I should be mindful,' and form views about it.

Rather than trying to define awareness or figure out what it is, therefore, I suggest you just become aware of the present moment and the way you are right now. What is happening? You are sitting! — it's as obvious as that — and the posture of sitting is 'like this'. Notice, just be aware of the experience of sitting, your own body sitting on a chair or cushion. Awareness isn't a critical function; you are not saying, 'I don't sit very well,' or 'I should sit better.' If you start thinking like that, well, forget it! Don't create a problem about sitting. Just be with the way it is right now, the experience of your body sitting in this posture. I am aware of the pressure of my body on the cushion, the sense of weight on this zafu, and now my hands have suddenly come into consciousness — the right hand touching the left. Maybe I become aware of my breathing — inhaling and exhaling at the nostrils — or the movements of the abdomen. I am not trying to be aware of anything in particular, but just allowing awareness to *be*. Then that which is present here and now, the way it is, is allowed into consciousness. The ordinary, everyday, experience of the body sitting, or the body breathing, or the sensation of feeling hot or cold right now is 'like this'. Simply notice rather than react to things. You might think, 'Oh, it's too hot,' and then react. Before you do that, however, use the opportunity to simply notice 'feeling hot is like this'. Also be aware of your mental state, your emotional state or your mood — not criticizing or trying to define it — but just noticing it. You don't even have to describe it; simply trust yourself to recognize that it is 'this way'. Awareness is an embracing ability we have. It isn't discriminatory or judgemental, but is discerning. It sees, knows and allows even pain or negative mind states to be the way they are.

The Buddha's teaching was directed towards recognizing what we have not created out of ignorance. We are conditioned to trying to get or get rid of things. Our ability to think and reason — the conditioning of the mind from birth — is dualistic; it functions on this dualistic spectrum of best to worst, good to bad and right to wrong. We have developed our critical faculties to a high level, so we know 'what is best' and 'how things should be', 'what is right and what is wrong'. We can create the highest ideals of conditioned phenomena at their very best; and because of that we fear their opposites. So we have the concept of heaven and hell. And we say that heaven is the best and hell is the worst. But thinking is a dualistic function of the mind. Just contemplate your own thinking. If you have 'good' then you have 'bad'. We would like everything to be good and be rid of all the bad, but this creates a great division in us because we are always trying to get rid of what we think is bad. This we can see even on the international level — 'Destroy the evil forces!' That is the dualistic way of operating; the thought process is like that. Emotionally, ideologically, politically and economically there is always some kind of struggle and resistance going on — trying to control, trying to get rid of the bad forces, the bad thoughts within us, the anger and greed, the fear and depression.

Recognizing awareness allows us to put this dualism into perspective. Because dualism is created through thinking, we can be aware of ourselves thinking. If we had no way of being aware of thinking, we would be stuck in our conditioning ; there would be no way out of it. If we are born into a good family with wise parents and enlightened teachers, we might get some very good conditioning , but I don't think many of us have had that good fortune. In any case, we learn from the parents we have, from the society we are born into, from the experiences we have, and from the teachers we have throughout our lives. Some of it has probably been good, and some not so good. There are people who are unwanted right from birth, who don't have loving parents, and live in a cruel and insensitive society; and because of that they often acquire very negative attitudes from their early lives. But the Buddha pointed to an awareness which transcends conditioning . So no one is just a helpless victim of fate. It might seem that our lives have been ruined through the tragedies, abuses and misfortunes we have experienced since childhood, it might seem like that on a personal level, but the Buddha pointed to ultimate reality in which the conditioning of our minds can be resolved. In other words, we have a way out of conditioning ; we are not just victims of misfortune.

Buddhism is about awakening, paying attention to life, being aware, being present here and now. Thinking, on the other hand, is about ideals. I am not trying to stop myself thinking, of course. This is not an attack on the intellect. I am not anti-intellectual. I am talking about learning to use the intellect in a way that it does not become the dominant delusion from which we operate — like good and bad, right and wrong, praise and blame, happiness and suffering. The personality is created out of praise and blame. The sense of who we are, our self-worth, is associated with the rewards and punishments we have received from our parents, from society, from our relationships with others after we were born; the society we live in is a reward-and-punishment society. I was rewarded for being a good boy and punished for being a bad one. In school I was rewarded for getting good marks and punished for not. In the military I was rewarded for being a good soldier and punished when I was not a good soldier, and on and on like this. I am just pointing to the dualistic structure of our society, and of the intellect, and of language itself.

What *is* natural is consciousness. That is something you don't create. You can create ideals, and you can create negative mental states out of all the terrible things that have happened or might happen to you. You can dwell on unfairness, mistreatment and abuse, as well as on all the wonderful things that have happened. But it all takes thought. We have to remember, and we have to believe in our assumptions and memories. The proliferating tendencies from these memories then create our sense of wellbeing or misery. Awareness or mindfulness (I use these terms interchangeably to mean being present here and now) allows us to be aware of whatever we have created — the mood we are in now, the physical realities of this moment, the sensitivity of the body at this present moment, the breathing (inhalation, exhalation) and so forth. With awareness we can embrace the whole of it — the good, the bad, the right, the wrong, pleasure and pain — they all belong. It isn't a matter of trying to control the mind; it is more like 'choiceless awareness' in Krishnamurti's words. There is awareness and we don't choose anything; we don't try to hold onto this or get rid of that.

During the Summer School here at Leicester, I encourage you to contemplate this. Just notice — it is 'like this'. This isn't difficult; it isn't terribly refined; it doesn't depend on absolute silence and control of the environment; it doesn't depend on absorbing into refined mental states; it isn't *jhāna* or high levels of concentration; it is just 'this' — this sense of relaxed attention. I experience it sometimes as listening, but it is a sense of openness, receptivity and wellbeing, and it is relaxed. I don't try to do it in terms of 'You've got to be more mindful, Sumedho!' If I start that, then what happens? When I say, 'YOU'VE GOT TO BE MORE MINDFUL, SUMEDHO!' I go into a state of tension.

That is the inner tyrant again. When that starts, I go tense.

Notice these things through awareness. The instructions on meditation that I have heard — or even that I have given — often came out as 'meditate! meditate! meditate!' When you first begin you hear these things — 'You've got to be mindful! You're not very mindful. Your mind wanders all over the place and it shouldn't, so practise — practise mindfulness!' And you can get into a very tense state of mind from that; the body can contract from that. That is why I am emphasizing this sense of relaxing, opening, expanding, letting go, listening. It isn't a question of *trying* to be mindful; let go of any ideas about whether you are mindful or not; don't make a problem about mindfulness. Trust yourself, just trust your ability to relax and open. You don't have to prove anything, get anything, control anything, or achieve anything. If those kinds of thoughts arise, be aware of them and let them go. If there is this sense of 'I've got to get my *samādhi* together', just let it go. Begin to recognize the natural state of consciousness. It is pure consciousness before you become anybody. There is no self in it. The Buddha called it 'the gate to the deathless'. Mindfulness is the path to the deathless. 'This' is the deathless. You are recognizing dhamma, in other words, *amata-dhamma* (deathlessness). Reality is 'this'. Affirm it to yourself. Inform consciousness at this moment in this way. If you start thinking 'I'm enlightened now', just let go of that. It isn't a matter of 'me' any more or of 'I am something' or 'I am not anything'; it is just 'like this'. Learn to affirm that this is the way, this is the path — this awareness — so that your conscious moments are informed with wisdom rather than with the perceptions of yourself, of how you see yourself, and your ability or inability to meditate.

This is pointing to what in the Pali teachings they call 'the first three fetters'. There are ten fetters or habits that tend to block us from our true nature, the deathless reality, liberation. The first of these is personality belief which is also referred to as the ego, and it is conditioned. You are not born with a personality belief.

A baby doesn't have a personality belief; it acquires one. This is what you get after you are born. When a baby is born it is conscious; that is natural, isn't it? But consciousness is not male or female, Asian or European, English, Swiss or Tibetan; it is just natural; it is just the way it is. This is a conscious realm; and the human body is a natural condition. When it is born it is like this, and then it goes through its ageing process; but it is a natural state. Nowadays people try to create their own bodies — probably without much success! They expend a great deal of energy on trying to sustain the illusion of a perfect physical body. However, the state one's body is in right now — whatever way that is — is just natural. And ageing is the natural process. So we notice the way it is rather than coming from an ideal. If I think, 'Well I want a youthful body my whole life; I want to be young, vigorous and good-looking, and die aged one hundred years in a state of perfect beauty and youth,' this, I am afraid, is not going to happen. But you can certainly create an ideal of how it *should* be. In fact, you can create an ideal from any fantasy and live by that, probably ending up quite embittered, because you have created something that cannot possibly manifest.

The Buddha pointed to the dhamma, or the way things are, the natural movement and changingness of the conditioned realm that we are experiencing. He wasn't saying it is good or bad, right or wrong. And we too — without making a judgement about being human as something wonderful or horrible, good or bad — can see that it is 'like this'. We can recognize in our humanity certain pleasurable experiences. We have memories of happiness, success and security. And we also have memories of failure, loss and misery. So, when we are reflecting on the way it is, it is good and bad, right and wrong, true and false, beautiful and ugly, wonderful and horrible, heaven and hell. They all belong! That is the way conditioned phenomena are. You don't get one side without the other. On an ideal level you can create a heaven — an eternal heavenly state where all the apples are perfect, where there is never a worm in an apple and nobody gets old, everyone remains young and beautiful, lions are the best friends of lambs which love each other and kiss each other — but this is like a child's vision, isn't it? It is pretty and pleasing, but it's a fantasy, a picture; it isn't the way it is.

When the Buddha pointed to the way of liberation, he was encouraging people to wake up and notice. He wasn't *telling* them how it is; it isn't a question of believing what the Buddha said according to the Pali Canon — 'These are the words of the Buddha!' Then somebody says, 'I don't know — maybe they're not?' And someone else says, 'Heretic! Get out! We don't want you here. If you're going to join our club you have to believe that these are the words of the Buddha! You're evil, you are. You're going to be banished to the fiery hell for questioning these things.' The Buddha instead encouraged investigation. But I have heard Buddhists say things like: 'You've got to believe this!' And the Pali Canon becomes a kind of reference point. 'These are the words of the Buddha so you can't question them; you've got to totally believe them!' What attracted me to Buddhism — and probably most of you here — was its encouragement to awaken and not to have to accept a set of beliefs.

So awakening is what? It isn't getting into high levels of concentration and performing psychic miracles or doing fantastic things. The Buddha didn't praise psychic phenomena such as walking on water or flying in the air, or any of these fantastic abilities that some people might have. He pointed to just ordinary awareness here and now, to awakened attentiveness to the body, to the mental states, to the emotional states, to the experiences we have through seeing, hearing, smelling, tasting, touching, and thinking. The only way things can be put into perspective is through awareness. If we are not aware, we just think about life and the mind goes round in circles. Trying to figure everything out intellectually has certain advantages, but it can't be liberating because we are caught in the conditioning of the mind.

What I am encouraging is recognizing and learning to value awakenedness in yourself instead of endlessly dwelling on your failures, weaknesses, and seeing yourself from a critical perspective. This is what we tend to do. The personality-view often has this very judgemental element to it. And there is no wisdom in the critical mind; the critical faculty doesn't allow wisdom to operate. You can see in our Western civilizations the emphasis on the intellect and modern science. We consider ourselves to be terribly clever the way we manipulate the conditioned realm. We can create atomic bombs! Sixty years ago we dropped bombs on Hiroshima and Nagasaki and destroyed thousands of people just like that! We vaporized them. And we are polluting the planet right now, aren't we? Look at just this society here in Britain. Everybody has a car now. Travelling up the other day with Rocana I noticed how affluent Britain looks now. It didn't look like this thirty years ago. This is a well run society and has many good things in it — things that are praiseworthy — but you can see it is still deluded. Even with all its affluence and security, we are still living in an age where a lot of fear is being generated everywhere. I was in the United States last month — the first time since 9/11 — and I noticed the fear level there. Nobody seemed to trust anybody any more. They have this 'homeland security', this agency, that spies on everybody. And you get this fear that maybe it's getting to be like the KGB was in the Soviet Union. Is this room bugged right now? 'Big Brother is watching you!' So, we are very clever at manipulating the conditioned world, but we are not very wise.

But the Buddha's teaching *is* a wisdom teaching. And wisdom is knowing things as they are; it is the discerning faculty; it is 'the Buddha knowing the dhamma'. The Buddha represents pure consciousness in a physical form; it is pure undeluded consciousness — but within a human form. So, the Buddha knows the dhamma, the truth of the way it is. When we took the refuges the other day it was in Buddha-Dhamma-Sangha. These are the symbols we use, but they are not to be grasped in themselves; that would be another intellectual activity. So, what is the Buddha now for yourself in terms of this moment? Do you believe in the

Buddha as some historical sage? Or do you believe Buddha is some kind of abstract force in the universe? Is there some kind of Buddha-energy operating in the universe out there that we have to contact? We can create all kinds of abstract ideas about Buddha-mind or Buddha-energy or Buddha-nature. What is it right now, though, in terms of this point here where I am, where you are? What is it right now in terms of the way your mental state is right now? It isn't a question of being a certain way, is it? It is just seeing the way you are experiencing this moment right now — the body is 'like this', the mood is 'like this'. You begin to recognize that Buddha is 'this'. And when we say *'Buddham saraṇaṁ gacchāmi'* (I go to Buddha for refuge), it is this awakened consciousness, knowing the way it is, the dhamma. The dhamma is then seen. Your body is dhamma. The nature of the body is to be born, to get old, and to die. That is dhamma rather than some personal problem. When it is personal, I say, 'I don't want to get old!' and create it into a problem. I want to stay young and good looking for a hundred years, and die with a very handsome, youthful looking corpse. Then everybody will say, 'Ajahn Sumedho aged very well.'

Notice, also, how mind states arise through conditions. In last night's talk we looked at the question of praise and blame. People say, 'You're wonderful!' and I feel like *this*. And then they say, 'You're horrible!' and I feel like *that*. The mind goes up and down, doesn't it? If the sun is out and it is a beautiful day, I feel like *this*. If it is cold, wet and rainy, I feel like *that*. That which is aware within yourself, however, is what I am pointing to. And being able to see this awareness is your refuge. We have very little control over conditions. We can't control the weather; we just have to accept it! Sunny, rainy, hot or cold, it is 'like this'. And the human body also is the way it is. Some people are born with good constitutions. They are strong, healthy, vigorous and never get sick. Whilst others have all kinds of physical problems from birth. On the ideal level, it isn't fair that some people are born with all the benefits and others with a bag full of disabilities. But in terms of dhamma, it isn't a problem. The point is to awaken from the way we are, from the way it is, from the way the body is now, the way the mind is right now.

This reflection on 'the Buddha knowing the dhamma', then, is internalizing it. Buddha is coming from the heart. In Thailand they use the term *'citta'* — this is a Pali word which also means 'consciousness' — but in Thailand they always talk about the *citta* as the heart and point to their own hearts. To use the English word 'mind' as a translation of this tends to be too cerebral, doesn't it? To say, 'He has a good mind,' means he is very good at thinking. To have a good heart, on the other hand, means much more than that even in English; it means generous, loving, benevolent, kind; it means relating to the world in an open, compassionate way. So the Pali word *'citta'* (as used in the Thai tradition, anyway) is one of the common statements that you hear in Thailand. The Forest monks will say, 'watch your *cit!'* meaning 'look at yourself!' — not in a critical way, it isn't used in terms of looking at yourself and saying, 'Oh, that's not good; that's terrible, you shouldn't think like that,' but in terms of recognizing that 'this' is the way it is right now. The feeling of happiness is 'like this'; the feeling of being blamed is 'like this'.

I have found that Westerners generally have a lack of trust in themselves. We are caught up in ideas about how things should be and are good at criticizing or dwelling on what is wrong with us and the world. As a society we are very much aligned to the intellect, but the intellect is untrustworthy. There is no point in just forming some nice idea about dhamma being our refuge. We have to actually recognize that 'this' is dhamma, 'this' is the way it is; we have to actually recognize that which is aware of anger or fear or whatever. Awareness is not fear; fear is an object. When we feel frightened or angry, we know that we feel angry and recognize that. The awareness of it is the path; the awareness is the refuge — not the anger. Anger is not a refuge. The more you investigate this point, the more confidence you will have in awareness. You will realize it is a natural state and isn't anything you can't do, which is why I am encouraging you to value it and trust it completely. Don't take my word for it. Just put it to the test in your own life experience. Find out.

Personally, I seem to gain the most insight when I am under the most pressure, when life is at its most unpleasant. There is something in me on those occasions which feels that there is nothing left but to be aware of 'this'. Sometimes that can be a blessing!

Before 'I Am' Arises

I want to begin by encouraging an attitude of relaxed attention, an open receptivity. Sometimes the word 'meditation' or the idea of it can put us into a contracted mode of 'I've got to meditate!' And then we try to concentrate the mind on something. We associate meditation with doing things like being mindful of the breath or a mantra, or getting involved in some kind of technique. It isn't that that is wrong, but the whole attitude of the Buddha's teaching is awakenedness, awareness here and now, being fully present, being fully with this moment as it is.

When you come into a room like this which this week has become associated with dhamma instruction or meditation of some sort, just be aware of how that affects you. There might be a kind of expectation around it, or an anticipation, a resistance, or even a feeling of faith. It isn't a question of trying to find anything wrong with your reactions to coming into this room, but of just recognizing that it is 'like this'. I am encouraging you to simply notice what you are feeling. Be aware that it is the way it is.

The English word 'meditation' is a generic term which includes almost anything you do with the mind. But what do *you* associate with that word? Ajahn Chah emphasized practice. In Thailand you would hear this word 'practice' all the time. They took the Pali word *'paṭipadā'* (which translates into the word 'practice') and say *'paṭipā, paṭipā*; you are *paṭipā* monks, and you should be mindful and practise.' These were the imperatives. At least that was how I interpreted them. And that was fine with me. I had no problem with the idea of practise, practise, practise. In the beginning it put me into this habitual compulsiveness which was already developed in my life. Everything I did tended to move towards compulsivity; I therefore became a compulsive meditator. Whenever I didn't feel like meditating, resisted it, wanted to put it off, I would feel guilty — 'I should be meditating now and I'm not! I'm just chatting about nothing with these monks. I'm not serious!'

Our monastic lifestyle in Isan, northeast Thailand, was very primitive. We made all our own robes and dyed them with natural dyes from the jackfruit tree[30]. This is a method recorded in the Pali Canon and goes back to the time of the Buddha. The jackfruit wood is made into chips and boiled until it becomes a yellowish colour. This robe is jackfruit colour. It takes days to do the job properly and I would think, 'I'm wasting my time doing this. It would be much easier if I got my mum to send me some cloth this colour,' (this is how the American mind works). Anyway, while doing this, the monks would talk, and when I got to understand the language better, I began to think, 'You're not supposed to talk about politics, or women, or anything frivolous; it's against the Vinaya!' It is listed in the Vinaya what good monks don't talk about, and you are not supposed to talk about kings or wars or any of this kind of stuff. So when I heard what they were talking about, I thought, 'This is not . . !' and my judgemental mind would get working. 'I'm not going to be like them! I'm going to practise, practise, practise!' And this probably made me unbearable to be with. When you are too serious you are not a very nice person any more and nobody can stand being with you.

One day I questioned the frivolity at the dyeing shed and a Thai monk told me, 'The dyeing shed is like a psychological release centre for the monks. It is where they can be silly and ridiculous and talk about things they shouldn't talk about, and smoke cigarettes.' I thought, 'Yeah, maybe I should relax a bit more!' One can grasp the ideal of 'practise, practise' — and practise is

---

30 The jackfruit tree is a common tree in India and South-East Asia. It has huge jackfruits growing out of its trunk.

good; I am not saying it is a bad thing — but *grasping* the idea of it can lead to obsessiveness and losing one's sense of humour, 'Because it isn't funny, you know! Practice is a serious business! Being a good monk is really serious!' So you lose your sense of humour and joy of being. Then pretty soon you become arrogant and feel superior to others; you just become critical and then guilt-ridden about deviations you yourself make from the very strict, obsessive ideas about practice. This isn't a very pleasant mind state, but I could see it was a tendency in my life. Whatever I did tended to move into that, so even very good things became sources of great suffering to me.

It was through Ajahn Chah's encouragement to be aware rather than just conforming to tradition and trying to make our-selves into ideal Buddhist monks that the dilemma came for me about idealism in monastic life. After each morning *pūjā* some-one would read from a book about what makes a good Buddhist monk (it was a series of stories about monks), and my mind would always grasp the ideals of what one should be, what was right and praiseworthy. Then I would feel guilty when I had im-pure thoughts or feel angry or jealous, stubborn, arrogant, proud or commit any other kind of human sin. Part of my cultural in-terpretation of experience — having been brought up as a Chris-tian — was as 'the sinner'. In the Thai Buddhist culture they don't have concepts like that. They admit to human weaknesses, but that isn't the same as seeing oneself as a sinner, which in my way of interpreting things meant you were in a rather hopeless state, as though you had been born with some incurable disease.

The emphasis the Buddha made was to use suffering *(dukkha)* as a noble truth. And Ajahn Chah's emphasis was always on in-vestigating the Four Noble Truths. So I would ask myself, 'What is suffering? And what is the cause of suffering?' and then reflect on that. 'Why, if I'm such a good monk, do I suffer so much? If I'm practising, keeping all the rules and doing all the right things, why am I so miserable?' There was a kind of logic there. 'Surely, if I am doing all the right things, I should get rewarded for being good, for being a good boy, for behaving properly.' But the way I was holding the monastic life made me feel more and more guilt-ridden and critical. It was not a joyful life. Monastic life can be quite joyful, actually, if you are not attached to it, if you are able to relax with it. Then it can be a very pleasant life-style. By reflecting on the suffering, however, I began to have insight into its cause and I realized that the cause was 'grasping the ideals of monasticism', grasping the Vinaya. Because I was grasping something good, it seemed like the right thing to do, but as the Four Noble Truths points out, grasping anything at all is the result of ignorance. So you can grasp ideals and the highest altruistic thoughts that human beings can have, and be utterly miserable. Why? Because it is from ignorance, ignorance of dhamma, ignorance of the way things are.

I lived with mostly Thai monks for three or four years, and during that time I noticed that they had a kind of acceptance of humanity. The Thai culture isn't an idealistic one, so they have a way of accepting the limitations of being human. This at first seemed irresponsible for a high-minded idealist like myself — you can become very righteous when you are holding onto the best — and someone like myself can feel rather superior. When you look at the grasping, however, and the sense of being superior, when you really recognize it as experience in the present, you see that that is not a peaceful mental state; it isn't peaceful to feel better than somebody else. What I was grasping was a sense of myself, which is an illusion, and an ideal so high that I couldn't possibly live up to it — because I am human not an ideal; I am a human being. Buddha-images are ideals. Anything could go on in this room and that Buddha-*rūpa* would just sit there serenely. Ideals are not living conscious forms; they are not sensitive forms; they might be beautiful forms, but they have no sensitivity. And people that are very idealistic are often not very sensitive. You lose that sensitivity when your investment is in an ideal so high that you are always comparing the reality of the here and now with how it should be, which of course it very seldom is. In peak moments things are what they 'should be', but try to sustain a peak moment — the peak moment of happiness, bliss or success, for example — and see how long you can hold it. Peak moments go up and then as soon as they reach their peak, they go down again — and that is the way it is.

In terms of dhamma, the Buddha was pointing out that this realm is 'like this'. Being human, having a human body and consciousness and sensitivity is 'like this'. Contemplate simply being the way you are right now. Have a sense of opening, of receiving, of just the reality of your own being at this moment the way it is without analysing, judging or comparing. Just trust yourself to be the way you are, the way the body is, the way the mental state is, the way the emotions are. Bring your attention to the breath or the mood you are in, just with this attitude of accepting and allowing, rather than feeling you have to *do* something or *change* something. Notice any reactions you have to what I am saying, any sense of doubt, frustration, resistance. This is a willingness to know what is happening without judging it in terms of what should or should not be, just with this attitude of 'the way it is'.

In Buddhism there is the teaching on the Ten Fetters as I have mentioned before. The first one is what they call *'sakkāyadiṭṭhi'* which is personality belief, or ego, a conditioned sense of yourself as the Five Aggregates, the identity you have with body, thoughts, memories and habits. Now, this self-view is a creation. You aren't born with a self-view. Babies don't have self-views; they don't think, 'I'm a baby.' We say, 'You're a baby,' and tell them what they are, so they get a self-view after that. But how do we get the self-view into perspective? When we are not being aware, we tend to operate from the self-view all the time — 'I'm permanently Ajahn Sumedho'. 'Ajahn', incidentally, means something like 'teacher'; it is a respectful title I am stuck with. And the name 'Sumedho' was given to me when I was ordained — I quite like that. Before I was 'Sumedho', I was 'Robert', and that was the Christian name given to me by my parents; I acquired that after birth. They didn't name me before I was born. What I am pointing to is that these are human creations. 'Ajahn', 'Robert' and 'Sumedho' are the creations of human beings. 'Robert' is a Christian name and 'Sumedho' is a Pali name, but whether Pali, Sanskrit, French, English or whatever, it is a created concept. The sense of 'me' or 'I am Ajahn Sumedho' or 'this is my clock, my robe, I am this way, I am that way' — I create these concepts in the present. The point is to see the difference between created concepts and pure subjective awareness.

Pure consciousness is uncreated; it isn't man-made; it isn't Asian or European or anything; it is a natural phenomenon which we are born with. We then put the created subject into consciousness. To say 'I am Ajahn Sumedho' is the conventional way of thinking and operating in society. But when we investigate it, there isn't an Ajahn Sumedho in any permanent way. Particular conditions arise and these words come up in the mind, but there is nothing permanent or ongoing about it. 'Ajahn Sumedho' simply depends on conditions for its manifestation. So, am I Ajahn Sumedho all the time? Actually, you get tired of being Ajahn Sumedho and being put on a pedestal. Sometimes you just want to be plain old Sumedho. Your ideals can change, of course, from wanting to be the best ajahn to wanting to fade into the crowd and be an ordinary bloke; and you create the sense of yourself accordingly. When you get tired of holding yourself up high, you just want to be an ordinary guy in a group. But these are all creations. We create that sense of identity with the body, with the personality, with cultural conditioning , or with a particular generation. I am one of the old generation living in the monastery now! Everybody else is considerably younger. When these young monks come I sometimes feel I can't figure them out. They have a way of thinking which I don't quite understand because my conditioning in my generation was very different. The delusions are the same, of course, the sense of yourself; and whether this is in terms of being a member of the old generation or the young, it is still a created concept.

What I am pointing to is that which is, before we start creating anything, before 'I am' arises in consciousness. This is an investigation, a self-inquiry. 'I am' is not very personal, is it? It is more a statement of being which has not been defined yet. 'I am Ajahn Sumedho' is getting into personality; it is becoming a separate personality. 'I am American-British' (none of you can say that) defines me as a separate personality, doesn't it? 'I am the abbot of a monastery, I'm a Theravadan, I am a monk of the Thai Forest tradition' — these are all adjectives which make me a separate person. But notice this sense of *being* before the pronoun 'I' is defined, before it becomes personal, before it becomes 'my body', 'my mood', 'my memories', 'my emotions'. When you are aware and trust in your awareness, you begin to see this sense of 'my emotions' or whatever as concepts which you are creating. It is a question of learning to recognize pure conscious subjectivity in which creations are seen as mental objects. This is in contrast to putting mental objects into the subjective position. *Sakkāya-ditthi* (personality belief) is putting a false creation into the subjective position. When I become 'Ajahn Sumedho', I interpret experience in a very personal way. Life is then seen through my personality, through my preferences, fears, desires and habits. On a personal level — getting back to praise and blame — I like praise and I don't like blame. When the personality becomes the subject, I am a victim of praise and blame; I have to constantly demand praise and run away from situations in which I might be criticized or blamed. One can see how easy it is to develop a way of life which concentrates on protecting oneself as a person, on just trying to be with people that give one the necessary you're-a-nice-guy-I-really-like-you kind of feeling, avoiding the critics and only doing those things that one knows will be successful.

As a student I learnt how to manipulate the university system. I figured out what I was good at and how I could get through. So I became manipulating and controlling. The point is, no matter how successful you are in getting what you want, it still leaves this sense of lack, of fear, of anxiety, in your consciousness. Even a peak moment, one realizes, cannot be sustained. A sense of despair arises after a peak experience because you have had it and it becomes a memory. Then the downhill slide can be quite depressing — when taken personally. But one can get outside the personal by putting the creations you have into an objective perspective; you see them as 'objects'. And you do this by means of awareness. That is the only way you can do it. Then you have consciousness and awareness together. The personality *(sakkāyadiṭṭhi)* then is not judged, because it isn't a question of trying to get rid of personality or determine whether you have a good one or not; it doesn't matter what the personality is like as long as you recognize that it is impermanent, unsatisfactory and not-self, as long as you recognize that the sense of 'me and mine' is created out of ignorance.

Ignorance of course in this context means not knowing the Four Noble Truths, not having any insight into the Four Noble Truths. Under those circumstances, no matter what our educational qualifications are or what position we hold in the world — beggar or king — we experience life out of ignorance, out of an identity with the conventions of personality *(sakkāyadiṭṭhi)*. Someone thinks, 'I'm only a beggar,' and someone else thinks, 'I'm a world Emperor.' But these are both creations, aren't they? I might think I'm no good or I'm the best. Whether it is arrogant self-congratulation or a sense of humility, whether we think in terms of being just an ordinary person — 'nobody special' — or the worst person in the world, we are still operating from ignorance. With awareness, on the other hand, we are informing conscious experience with wisdom. Wisdom then operates through awareness and consciousness. So the Buddha's teachings are conventions, but they are also skilful means for developing wisdom. The teaching of the Four Noble Truths is a skilful means the Buddha used. He created it. But it isn't meant to be grasped; it isn't some kind of doctrine that you operate from as a belief system. It is rather an expedient means for pointing to something *now*. Suffering *(dukkha)* is a noble truth. This is not a metaphysical truth; it is an existential truth. We have this experience in varying degrees of feeling incomplete, worried, despair, afraid, or whatever. It is the awareness of suffering *(dukkha)*, however, which is the point. Suffering is an object, isn't it? If you totally identify with it, with *dukkha*, you are not aware of it as such and become lost in it. You become caught in the suffering that you are creating — 'I'm this miserable creature. Life hasn't been fair to me. It's your fault! God should pay for this!' We can create endless dramatic scenes with our anger and resentment about the unfairness and injustice of life as we experience it. But in awareness, in this awakened state, suffering is 'like this'.

I find that any sense of feeling superior or better than others — 'I'm a better monk than that one!' — is not a peaceful state. When I really observe it I see that it is actually a form of suffering *(dukkha)*. It is not a question, either, of thinking the opposite — 'I am *not* as good as somebody else' — or of clinging to the desperate belief that 'we're all as good as each other', just trying to be totally fair. I am not asking you to believe any of this, but to trust yourself more in your ability to reflect. What is it that brings peace and a sense of ease with yourself, with the realities of having a human body the way it is, with your personality the way it is? It isn't a question of judging your personality or holding up some ideal personality that you would like to become, and then trying to get rid of the present one. Whatever way your personality manifests, awareness of it is what I am encouraging you to trust in. Then there will be what I call 'pure subjectivity' — and that is uncreated, that is reality.

The created subjectivity, the personality, is changing all the time and is not a reality. You can't always stay the same person. If I am caught in my personality and somebody says, 'Ajahn Sumedho, you're wonderful!' I feel happy. And then if somebody else says, 'Ajahn Sumedho, you're horrible!' I can't sustain that happy feeling. So my feelings change according to praise and blame. That is how the personality is. It is reactive and dependent on conditions (the Eight Worldly Dhammas). When you experience success, health, youth, you feel 'like this' — on top of the world! And then bad health, failure, old age come along, and they don't have that same vibrant, uplifting feeling — because conditions have changed.

It is very common now to regard ageing as a kind of dreaded experience, isn't it? 'What are they going to do with all the old people?' Maybe they should allow more immigrants in to take care of us all. The point is, one gets the sense that old age is another failure, in a way, something that shouldn't be. But awareness doesn't age! Awareness has nothing to do with how old the body is or how one is feeling personally; awareness transcends the conditioned. And meditation is the way of learning to recognize that. It isn't that under normal circumstances we are never aware, but we tend to give our allegiance to the personality and generally operate through that. So, what I see as real meditation is not a process of trying to get rid of personality, but of learning from it — personality *(sakkāyadiṭṭhi)* is 'like this'. Then I can listen to myself: 'I like this and I don't like that!'

This year I am at Chithurst. I haven't lived there for twenty years, and it is quite different from Amaravati. Some things annoy me at Chithurst and some things I like, personally. Now, am I going to get caught in the annoyance, or try to suppress it, or try to set everything right according to the way I want it? Should I just barge into Chithurst and say, 'I'm here now! I want it like *this,* and I want it like *that,* and I don't like the way Ajahn Sucitto did it; I want to do it *this* way, and you *should* do it this way.' I can't do that any more. I could once, but they told me to get lost! The refuge, then, is in the awareness of this. And that I trust. I totally trust that. I haven't always trusted it, but you find that the more you recognize awareness and operate from it, the more you realize what is meant by 'refuge', the *saraṇa* (refuge) of *'Buddh-aṁ saraṇaṁ gacchāmi'* (I go to Buddha for refuge). You realize that awareness is what that refuge is. It allows you to flow with experience, with the changing conditions that we experience until we die. Awareness is not dependent on being praised or blamed, on being in good health or bad, on being young or old; it transcends all those things. We can learn from even the pain, the failures, the lack of appreciation, the unfairnesses that we experience in the worldly conditioned life — because our refuge is in awareness and not in an idea of being successful or appreciated or anything else.

Things arise and pass away, but the awareness is constant. Even when we are not aware, there is pure consciousness. We create impurities out of ignorance, but consciousness itself is stainless; it cannot be contaminated. So we begin to recognize that our refuge is in this purity of consciousness which has never been stained no matter what we have done and no matter what we have thought in our lives. Wisdom, then, is the ability to discern the difference between consciousness *without* attachment, and conscious experience *with* attachment. It isn't a judgemental thing; it is a discerning ability. If I am attached and then I get lost in my attachment without awareness, I become what I am attached to. When I recognize pure consciousness with non-attachment, however, there is just this simple reality of attentiveness here and now. Then this is it! This is the path! This is the way of non-suffering! You actually recognize it, insightfully know it. It is no longer a matter of holding to an idea of 'enlightenment' or of 'the path' or of having attained anything. All of that drops away and there is just recognizing and operating from the natural, pure state of your very being here and now — a pure state that is always with you, that never lets you down, that is totally trustworthy. You can see why the Buddha emphasized awareness as the way.

The third Noble Truth, then, is the recognition of this pure consciousness which is empty of attachments. It isn't empty in the sense of being in an unconscious or trancelike state; it is just that consciousness is pure. And then things arise and cease within that. Rather than finding your refuge in the habits that come and go according to conditions, therefore, you find it in consciousness, in awareness. When there is praise — 'You're wonderful!' — you can still feel happy, but you are not lost in that happiness; you are not bound into that limitation. And when there is blame you can be aware of the unpleasant feeling of somebody criticizing you, but still your refuge is in the awareness.

By investigating this, you prove it to yourself. This is provable. It can be verified through your willingness to investigate dhamma. I am trying to encourage you to do this because I think we need a lot of encouragement. We tend to get caught in seeing ourselves through critical minds or idealizing Buddhism, teachers and methods, and then feeling intimidated by them. Teachers get a lot of questions: 'Should you get the *jhānas* before you practise insight *(vipassanā)* meditation?' I am so fed up with that question! Another one is: 'Does Dependent Origination *(paṭiccasamuppāda)* take place over three lives, or is it simultaneous arising?' These questions were being asked forty years ago when I first came into Buddhism, and they are still being asked now. They are, of course, related to how people interpret the Pali Canon or their views about Theravada Buddhism — not to mention their views about the Mahayana and other forms of Buddhism. But we can see the views and opinions in ourselves. I can be very opinionated as a person, because Americans are like that. We have opinions about all kinds of things we don't understand; that is our culture. I can find myself contending with those who don't agree with my opinions. It is a question of seeing, however, that the problem is in grasping any opinion. And once you see that as the cause of suffering, you have the insight into letting it go.

The Point Includes Everything

If we reflect on our experiences in life, we will see there is only 'now'. We might think of time as a reality and the past as somehow more real than just a memory; after all, we can remember the past and feel happy, sad, elated, depressed, outraged or indignant. But it is all happening *now*. That I was born seventy-one years ago is a perception that I have now, isn't it? That is a perception, and a memory. I can't even remember being born, actually. My sister can remember it; she remembers my mother bringing me home. But whether it is my sister or my mother telling me about it, or whether it is a memory I have — if I could remember my birth moment, which I can't — it is conditioning in the present. The future also is right now. We have the idea of 'tomorrow' or 'after the Summer School', but these are just perceptions we create in the present. So it is always here and now. By reflecting in this way, we can break down the delusions we have of time.

The English word 'meditation' *(bhāvanā)* is a term used for any kind of mental exercise, but *'bhāvanā'* in the Pali context means 'cultivating awareness'. And awareness is always here and now; we are aware now. But aware of what? In the practice of insight meditation we are usually taught to focus on the movements of the body — sitting, standing, walking, and lying down[31], and the inhalation/exhalation of the breath *(ānāpāna-sati)* — which is bringing attention to what is happening now and related to things we don't tend to create into an ego. Even if we have a terrible posture we can be aware of it just as it is; I

---

31 Known as the Four Postures.

am not even emphasizing good posture. But the sense of a self is dependent on identities of the past — where I was born, what I have done, the memories, the emotional habits I have acquired throughout my life, and the way I react to the Eight Worldly Dhammas (success and failure, praise and blame, happiness and suffering, gain and loss). The constant factor, though, is always the awareness. This we don't create. We don't create it and we can't find it; we can't objectify it; we can't see it as some kind of object. Nevertheless it *is* recognizable. And this is very important, because when we try to make ourselves aware, we cannot be aware. When we think, 'I've got to be aware! I've got to practise awareness and I've got to make myself more aware!' we are merely grasping the *idea* of awareness. Awareness is an act of trust. It is recognizable but not as an objective reality; it is recognizing 'this is it'.

So I am encouraging you to recognize this natural state of presence, this openness, this relaxed attention which includes everything in this moment — the body, the breath, the mental state you are in, pleasure, pain, the beautiful, the ugly, the memories, whatever you are experiencing in consciousness — see that it is the way it is. 'The way it is', then, is noticing but not defining. How am I feeling right now? My emotional state is — ! I can recognize it, but how can I describe and define it? I could say, 'Well, it's peaceful and calm' and find some suitable words for it, but that isn't it; it isn't the words. Reality doesn't need to be defined, only recognized.

Trying to know things through definitions, through the conditioning of the mind, through perceptions, perceiving them as this or that, is ignorance. Things that we have no perceptions for, we try to fit into recognizable ones, or we dismiss them. We want to say what is right or wrong, what should be done or shouldn't be done, what is good, bad, acceptable or unacceptable. We want to spell it all out and live according to that. This is what we call 'conditioning ' or 'institutionalizing'; it is like computer programming. We put in the programme and operate from that.

The Buddha, however, pointed to liberation, not to acquiring a Buddhist computer programme — well, some Buddhists do create a programme. They go along with the convention without using it for awakening and become the convention itself. That isn't liberation, is it? Even though it is a good convention, it is still a convention; it is still impermanent; it is still basically subject to change, to birth and death.

Before I ever meditated, I wanted to define everything; and this was mainly because of my sense of personal safety and my own intelligence. And anything I could not clearly define, I tended to ignore. Some people get very upset about modern art because it challenges their perception. You hear it all the time: 'What is it? What *exactly* is that? A child of five could do better.' We have a standard of what art is or what beauty is, or what is right or wrong. That is our world and we feel safe within those boundaries. So if the standard is challenged, we feel unsafe and want to dismiss it, reject it, kill it, destroy it — anything that doesn't fit is the enemy. But the conditioned realm is like this; it is constantly changing. Everything is in the process of movement, this flowing movement. And this we can see through intuitive awareness, this inner sense of awareness. We can't see it through defining and projecting Buddhist ideas onto experience but by taking Buddhist teachings and using them as guidelines and a way of bringing into focus another way of looking at things.

In the teaching on Dependent Origination, ignorance is given as the cause of all suffering. The sequence begins with 'ignorance': 'Ignorance conditions phenomena, and conditioned phenomena conditions consciousness . . .' and so on. When you start from ignorance, the result is always suffering or some kind of disappointment, some sense of lack, despair or anxiety. In this context 'ignorance' means ignorance of the Four Noble Truths; it doesn't mean ignorance of worldly conditions or being illiterate. It means that insight into the noble truths has not yet arisen so there is lack of understanding. The ego — the sense of yourself, the self-view and cultural conditioning — is the result of ignorance, and the thinking process is conditioned through learning words, definitions and the ability to analyse and reason. You create a world of feeling, perception and conditioned phenomena *(vedanā, saññā, sankhāra)*; you create it from memory, preferences, liking, disliking, and identifying with the body — 'This is my body; I am this physical body.' Everything is around 'me', things happening to 'me'.

In terms of this moment, that is true. The reality of this moment is that 'this' is the centre point; consciousness is operating from this body. And by recognizing this you are opening yourself to the way it is. For me right now, you are objects in consciousness. Some of you will remember Douglas Harding. He really explored this one. He would point out that you can't see your own face. I can see your face, but I can't see my own face. Now, something as obvious as that is a profound reflection because it is true. We operate as if we all have the same ideas about 'me being here' and 'you being there'. We operate on the conventional mode of 'being here at the Leicester Summer School' and identifying with our names and memories and so forth, as if we are actually these things. In meditation *(bhāvanā)*, however, we recognize this unique position of being in this centre point, yet not claiming it. If we claim it, if we think 'I am the centre of the world', we are mad; this is megalomania! In another way, it is true, of course. The reality of this experience is 'I *am* the centre of the universe' — but not as an ego, not as 'me as a person'— but rather as the reflection on this moment. This is the centre point; and this is the way it is. It isn't a matter of saying it is good, bad, right or wrong, but just of reflecting on it. At this moment it is 'like this'. This stops the tendency to project all kinds of habits and ideas onto the moment such as 'You are like *this* and you are like *that*; this place I like and that place I don't like; this is good and that is bad,' or whatever. Awareness is not a matter of liking, disliking or remembering, but of recognizing. Awareness, then, is this central point.

Now, we tend to think of a point as a little dot, but actually awareness is a point that includes everything. It has no boundary. When we practise tranquillity meditation, we usually focus on an object, and then we exclude everything else. I would have to exclude you in order to absorb into an object; that is one-pointedness. But why keep the point so small? Why not include everything? 'Oneness', 'unity', 'universality' — we have the words in English — and the point that includes the universe at this moment in terms of this limited body, from this position, is 'like this'. It gives me perspective on the cultural, personal conditioning that I have acquired these past seventy-one years. And consciousness to me now is something I experience as inclusive, unlimited, and not as a mental factor in terms of the Five Aggregates (form, feeling, perception, mental activity, and consciousness).

Much of *vipassanā* practice emphasizes the four elements in regard to the body (earth, fire, water, air). In Thailand, they practise a lot of meditation on both the physical body and the sensory world experienced through the eyes, ears, nose, tongue and body. But there are two more elements — space and consciousness — which not many teachers really emphasize, or at least not the ones I have known. So, *vipassanā* — this is just my view of it, anyway — is often limited to the four elements and the contemplation of impermanence, suffering, and non-self. The way many people practise it therefore tends to bind them to the concept of impermanence and does not bring these other two elements — space and consciousness — into the practice. But space is also here now, isn't it? Space is the most obvious reality that we experience — unless we absorb into it and just go from one thing to another without noticing it. When we do that it is still here, of course; it isn't that it isn't here, but we just don't notice it. We might think, 'Oh, this is a big room; this is a spacious place,' without really opening to space as a reality in this present moment. But when we do reflect on it, what happens? I have noticed that I withdraw my attention from the things *in* the space. I don't have to get rid of anything, I don't have to go where there are no buildings, no people, no trees, nothing in the space, I just withdraw my attention from things. A couple of years ago I went to Svalbard up in the North Pole. It was wonderful being up there in the silence, but I didn't really need to do that in order to find space, because it is here and now, isn't it? This room is not the problem, and you are not the problem. The problem is my going from one thing to the next.

I have actually done a lot of space-contemplation in my life. While I was living in Thailand, I would think, 'Now, this monk I like; he's a good monk. And that one I don't like very much; he's not a very good monk. This one is really troublesome, and that one really practises hard.' So I would go on like that in my own kind of judgemental way. It was easy to create personalities and believe that my perception of this or that monk was the person, which meant I lived in a world of delusion in a Buddhist monastery which is supposed to be a place for breaking through delusion! I then started noticing the space *between* the monks. I thought, 'Why do I always get stuck with a particular monk and then go to the next one? Why not just notice the space *between* them?' When I did that, it was different; suddenly I wasn't creating people in the space. The space is a reality; it isn't a fantasy. Space is spacious — that is a kind of truism, isn't it? But it doesn't have any quality to it; it isn't red or blue, pretty or ugly, right or wrong — and yet it includes all these things. Space can include the beautiful, the ugly, right, wrong, war, peace, everything. So this room is *in* the space, actually, because the space isn't bound by the room — unless I decide it is and say, 'This is a big room — or is it a small one? Is this a big space or a small space?' And then we can get into our views about what is big and what is small, which of course is relative. Space is space whether we are in a very confined space, or just the spaciousness of consciousness.

Consciousness, then, has no boundary until we put boundaries onto it. If I attach to the body itself, I experience consciousness with a sense of 'I am this body'. And this I never questioned before I started meditating. I used to think, 'This is my body. This is what I am.' But that is just cultural conditioning . My mother said, 'You're a boy and this is your body. And you've got to take care of your body. You've got to brush your teeth every morning, keep warm, and have three meals a day,' and on and on like that. So it was obviously my body; if anything was mine, this body must be! Then when I went to school there was competitiveness about who was bigger and who was better looking. So gradually we identified more with our appearances. Little boys can be really cruel and will happily yell out, 'Your ears are too big! Big ears! Fatso!' And we all developed neuroses about the size of our noses, ears, and so on. The sense of self can then become fixed in that reality unless we start meditating, unless we start waking up, unless we no longer just operate from the convention of 'my body' but question, 'Is this really my body?' It isn't a matter of just thinking the reverse, thinking that this is *not* my body and somehow rejecting it. As Professor Gombrich was saying the other evening, it isn't a denial in terms of we either believe in God or we believe there isn't a God. This way of going from believing something to not believing something is really a mental trick we play on ourselves. The Buddha wasn't taking sides on that level of proclaiming anything or disproving anything, but of awakening to the way things are. It is very subtle. Awareness, even though simple, is quite subtle. Conditioning , on the other hand, is not subtle. In conditioning we are bound into assumptions, viewpoints, opinions, positions, biases, prejudices and preferences which make us feel we *are* somebody. Our self-worth, our world, our universe, depends on supporting these illusions.

Awakening, then, is sometimes rather frightening because the world that we have created and which seems so stable and certain suddenly falls apart. Have you ever had that experience where you don't know who you are any more? That can be frightening. I could say, 'Well, I'm the tall one with the big feet.' That might not be a terribly glamorous view of myself, but I could depend on it for some kind of certainty — at least I'm that; I'm big and I have big feet, and that's it! We form these identities because not knowing who we are or not having any identity might seem unbearable, frightening. So we fix our place — 'I'm Jewish, I'm Protestant, I'm Catholic, I'm Theravada, I'm Mahayana, I'm a man, I'm a woman, I'm English, I'm American-British — I don't know what I am!' These are conventions; and I am not criticizing them. There is nothing wrong with them. But ignorance — not understanding dhamma or the truth of the way it is, and the attachment that comes from that — is the cause of suffering. In awareness we begin to recognize this; we begin to see how we create suffering, and that the cause is ignorance and attachment which binds us to the conditioning we have, to the identity of the body, to the pleasure-pain principle, to praise and blame, to memories, religion, class identity, racial identity, ethnic identity, and so on. These are all conventions, all basically unsatisfactory and ultimately untrue.

How can we ever feel complete, whole, or liberated, while attached to things that are delusions, that are not real? Human suffering is the way it is. This age that we are living in is a time of great confusion. The old cultural boundaries, the racial boundaries and identities, nationality and ethnicity, the sense of superior and inferior, the prejudices that have been instilled in us through our cultural conditioning — these are all being challenged. Everything is under investigation. Yet consciousness is here and now; and it is boundless. We don't create anything with awareness, so are not attached to anything. We just receive this moment as it is. At the beginning of this session I encouraged you to have a sense of relaxed attention. This is a suggestion which will, hopefully, have a good effect on you. But what I am really trying to do is encourage you to trust yourself more, to open to this moment and receive whatever you are personally experiencing from where you are, even if it is unpleasant.

The insight I had through reflecting on space and consciousness is that consciousness is universal; it has no boundary —

and space has no boundary. So, when you trust in awareness or mindfulness, when you don't get caught up in thinking and trying to figure things out, when you learn to recognize just this much — just this natural state of pure presence — and rest in it, then that is dhamma. It has no boundary unless you put boundaries into it. If I start thinking and attaching to my thinking, then I am caught into the thinking process again. If I am not thinking, however, there is still knowing. Thinking is limited to knowing *about* things but does not *really* know those things. You might think you know certain people because you remember them, but you don't actually know them through memory. To really know somebody, you have to be open to that person the way they are in the moment rather than through some kind of memory you have of them from the past. Awareness, then, includes everything and is not divisive; it does not prefer one thing over the other, so everything belongs. But it is discerning. It is direct knowing *(ñāṇa)* rather than knowing *about* things through concepts. And *bhāvanā* or meditation is learning to trust this, to develop it.

Reverend Taira Sato[32] in his talk referred to the relationship of the *dharmakāya* (truth body) with Amida's Pure Land. These are terminologies, of course, but they point to this reality. They are not just philosophies, just ideas, just terms to get tangled up in and battle over with other people; they are pointers to this very simple natural state. The Theravadans like the term 'the unconditioned', and there are many references to this: 'There is an unborn, unconditioned, uncreated, unoriginated. If there were not the unborn, unconditioned, uncreated, unoriginated, there would be no escape from the born, the conditioned, the created, the originated. But because there is the unborn, unconditioned, uncreated, unoriginated, there is an escape from the born, the conditioned, the created, the originated.' This is, I think, one of the most profound statements ever made. It is so very simple and so very clear.

---

32 Reverend Professor Kemmyo Taira Sato, The Three Wheels, Shin Buddhist House, London.

Now, escape from the born, the conditioned, the created, the originated — what is that? Obviously, the body is the born, the conditioned; and thoughts and feelings, pleasure, pain and neutral sensations, are dependent on conditions. In order to feel pleasure we have to have pleasurable conditions supporting it; and in order to be miserable we have to have miserable conditions — neutral sensations we generally ignore; we just don't pay attention to them. So, most of our lives are spent seeking pleasure and running away from pain, looking for happiness and excitement, romance, adventure, interesting pastimes, fascinating friends, meaningful lifestyles, enjoying the senses and exploring sensuality as far as we can — the *gourmet*, the *connoisseur*, the best — always moving towards the extremity, because that is how we are conditioned. Our sense of self-importance depends on having the best, being the richest, being the most clever, having the finest taste, the best manners. It is from that that the sense of ourselves develops, but then we get into states of doubt because there is always somebody better, richer, more clever, somebody who can sit in meditation longer and never move! In the monastic world there are 'better monks than I am', so you can't win! Try as I might to be the good monk I think I should be, I have never succeeded in being the best. But that isn't the point, is it? That isn't what the convention is for. The convention is not for attachment but for reflection. So the way it is, is 'like this'. Looking, seeing, noticing this object here through eye-consciousness is the way it is. Now, there is something accepting in that, in not feeling that I have to judge or define what this is. It is peaceful just to be with whatever is and not say anything about it or think, 'I have a better bell than this at Amaravati.' — I do, actually; it's bigger!

So the unconditioned, to me, is consciousness. Consciousness is not conditioned. And this is not something I have made up; it is just to be recognized. The thinking process, memory, feeling, sensation, sight, sound, smell, taste and touch, arise and cease. My refuge now, however, is in the awareness. Professor

Gombrich used terms like *'cetovimutti'* (liberation through consciousness), and *'paññāvimutti'* (liberation through wisdom). The whole Buddhist convention comes together at this point. This emptiness, this pure state of awareness is not a void of annihilation; it is empty of attachment, of ignorance, but it is pure, uncreated reality — it is dhamma, in other words. There is room then for the created within that. But it is in perspective. The created arises and ceases according to conditions. Whether it is sunny or rainy, whether we are feeling healthy or sickly, whether our loved ones are with us or have all left us — there is room for it all, for all human experience in our lifetime until the death of the body. But our refuge is in the deathless reality not in clinging to things and then feeling frightened, worried or upset when they change or are lost to us. That is just the world of ignorance and fear that we see in ourselves and in the world around us, that is just the desperate grasping of illusions that are part of modern life, that is just ideas, opinions, democracy — 'We are going to force democracy down the throats of those Iraqis even if we have to kill every single one of them to do it!' Democracy is a great idea — I have nothing against it — but is that the way to do it? Is my view something I should force on others?

The Buddha did not force anything on anybody; he merely encouraged awakening, this sense of wake up! pay attention! notice! observe! The teachings of the Buddha are meant for that. They are for investigating reality in the present.

The End of Suffering

'All conditions are impermanent' — this is an important phrase, not as a doctrine to grasp, but merely as something to remind us to see the changingness of conditions. So what do we mean by it? What are conditioned phenomena in terms of now? The answer is 'everything'! Everything is included in the category of 'conditioned phenomena' whether subtle, coarse, physical, mental, emotional, psychic, good, bad or indifferent. When you look at the infinite variety of qualities and quantities of conditioned phenomena, it all just seems to go on and on into endless permutations, details and refinements. It is a question, then, of bringing this to the one point where everything ceases, where all conditions cease. Ajahn Chah used to call it 'the end of the world'. He would ask, 'Where does the world end?' — this would be like a *koan* or conundrum that he would challenge us with — and of course the answer was always 'it ends here, in this one here'. This is pointing to consciousness *(citta)*. In consciousness, or awareness, everything ceases. But that cessation is not annihilation; it is just that the grasping, the identity, the ignorance and illusion ceases here at this point. It isn't like the end of the world where everything collapses into a black hole, so don't worry about that! We are looking at cessation as a practical reality rather than as some inevitable Armageddon or total end to everything.

The point is, annihilation is a concept, isn't it? The subtlety the Buddha pointed to, however, was not concepts but awareness. So all concepts cease here; thinking ceases here; attachment, the sense of self, the ego, the conditioning of the mind, cultural conditioning , emotions, fears, desires and everything ceases here. This is where everything ends. And its ending, its cessation, is peace, *nibbāna*. Deathlessness *(amatadhamma)* is then recognized.

The third truth in the Four Noble Truths is that there is an end to suffering (this is a statement). And the recommendation is that it should be realized. The end of suffering, the end of the world, the cessation of conditions — in terms of direct experience here and now — is reality; it isn't a fantasy or an abstraction; it is reality so it should be realized. Each noble truth has these three aspects: the statement, the prescription (what to do about it), and the result. Notice that each of them is a paradigm of reflection. So, in the case of the third Noble Truth, first there is the statement that there is cessation, then cessation should be realized, and finally cessation has been realized. This is the essence of the Buddha's teaching, this whole reflective mode of witnessing, observing, noticing, being awake, and seeing how things really are. It isn't a matter of convincing yourself there is cessation, or believing in it as some kind of Buddhist metaphysical teaching; it is real; and the reality of cessation is insight.

Now, to have that insight — the reality of cessation — involves mindfulness and the acceptance of the present moment as it is, whatever it is, whether you are experiencing pleasure, pain, boredom, excitement, or anything. It is not a matter of controlling conditioned phenomena in order to realize cessation, but of trusting awareness to the point where it is the refuge. And it isn't just a fragmentary refuge, just a flash of insight that you forget; you recognize the continuity of it. Otherwise you have moments of insight — rather like flashes — but then you are right back into the old habit-tendencies again. This is where you might feel despair with your practice; you understand the idea, but the reality evades you.

The Buddha used words like 'emptiness', 'non-self', 'cessation' and *'nibbāna'* to point to this reality. You will notice that these are all negations, really. Non-grasping, non-self, non-identity, non-suffering, non-desire are reflections on the absence of desire, the absence of greed, the absence of hatred, the absence of delusion. We usually don't notice when there is an absence of anything; we are more interested in the presence of things. When there is greed, we are not generally aware of that greed, but just *become* greedy, or angry, or deluded. The unawakened human being who has never really stopped to observe or question or look into the way things are, will become whatever conditions come together in any moment. Then we are just conditioned beings, just victims of conditioning . You hear about the victim syndrome — 'My father used to beat me every day and because of that I have these neurotic fears.' This sense of being a victim can be justified by the fact that there was ill treatment. In terms of liberation, however, that justification doesn't help. A lot of our conditioning , of course, is the result of getting the parents we got. I don't know how I was born into my family or why I chose that particular couple; that was just the way it was. Anyway, the sense of questioning and this awakenedness have taken place in this lifetime; I didn't just think I was stuck with that *kamma* or that I was simply that way and there was nothing I could do about it. That is often how it seems on a personal level, that is often the way we look at ourselves and our predicament, but we have awakened moments even before we become aware that there is a reality beyond our habits and identities.

So, non-self is emphasized in the Theravada as well as *nibbāna*, cessation *(nirodha)* and desirelessness *(virāga)*. When we become bhikkhus and take the *upasampadā* ordination we say, 'We are doing this for the realization of *nibbāna, nirodha, and virāga.*' Now, is this just altruism, just hoping that the magic of the monastic life will transform us, that by living as Buddhist monks the convention of monasticism will take away all our faults and delusions, and at the end of our lives we will have realized *nibbāna, nirodha* and *virāga*? But that would be just superstition or attachment to conventions. Thinking that if one just changes from being a layperson to a monk, the power of the tradition will transform one, is a bit like thinking that taking a certain number of baths a day or eating a vegan diet will do the same thing. But that is not the case, that is not the way it is. The life of a Buddhist monk is a skilful means for awareness, for mindfulness; it is a convention to be used for helping and aiding mindfulness rather than as some kind of magical formula in its own right.

The second Noble Truth is that the cause of suffering is desire (the statement), the insight is to let go of desire (the prescription), and actually letting go of it is the result (you know what letting go is). And the third Noble Truth is that what has been let go (desire) ceases; its nature is to cease — 'All conditions that arise cease and are not self.' When we personify anything, it becomes more than it is. We like the sense of being a person; we want to have a direct, personal relationship with God or a deity or a force in the universe; we might even feel influenced by the devil or Māra or agents of evil. We can get into all kinds of personification, of anthropomorphism and ways of explaining what we are feeling and experiencing through consciousness, the tendency being to see things as external forces. God, Buddha, the personification of Avalokiteśvara, Chenrezig, and all these different *bodhisattvas* and deities can be externalized as forces 'out there'; they can be seen in terms of physical forms with personalities, because that is how it seems in terms of the conditioned world. The conditioned world has this sense of 'this is personal, this is feeling, this is good, bad, right, wrong, refined, coarse, heaven, hell'; the conditioned world has the whole gamut, the whole range of sensitivity. So sensitivity is the realm that we live in, and we are experiencing a relentless march of sensory impingement from the moment we are born — even before we are born when we are in the womb — until the body dies. This is the way it is. This realm of the senses, of consciousness, of eyes, ears, nose, tongue, body, memory, thinking, the intellect, all these things are the range of experiences and qualities we have of pleasure, pain and neutral feelings. But if we personify

God, we think he should be all-loving like a kind of ideal father, because God as generally perceived in the Western mind is patriarchal. Even though modern feminism has tried to counter this, the basic cultural pattern is the image of an old man with a white beard up in the sky, which is childish, isn't it? It might work when we are four or five years old, but later in life we tend to look down on that kind of thing, or joke about it. Even so, the assumption of a benevolent father is actually a great part of our cultural conditioning . It might be that as we grow up we wonder exactly how benevolent he is, of course. When that tsunami hit last year in Asia, people said, 'How could God allow that to happen?' A good father would have stopped it, wouldn't he? If we had the power to stop that tsunami — if there was this great threat to our children's lives and we could stop it — all of us would do so, wouldn't we? I would, at least.

The point is, when we talk about non-self, cessation or *nibbāna*, the thinking mind tends to conceive of a kind of blankness. Logically it sounds like annihilation, and the Theravadan formulations — if taken too logically on the level of pursuing the concepts — also make *nibbāna* sound like extinction, the end of everything. Thoughts are like that. When you depend on reason and thought for experiencing life, you get caught in dualism. I have heard people criticize Buddhism for being a negative philosophy, for being pessimistic and nihilistic. In the theistic approach, the logic goes towards a kind of eternal, personal relationship with this wonderful, benevolent father up in heaven — which doesn't sound very attractive to me, actually. So taking it just on the level of reason and logic, there is dualism, and that is the nature of thought; thought is a dualistic function. Obviously, then, by not attaching to that, thinking is put into perspective. Then you are not bound into the limitation of thoughts, but neither do you try to annihilate or deny them. Instead, you put thinking into context, into perspective, so that you are no longer deluded by your own concepts, views and opinions.

Now, how do you do that? How do you get beyond thinking?

One way is to ask a question. If I ask any of you how to get beyond thinking, what does your mind do right now? It stops thinking, doesn't it? At the end of a talk I say, 'Any questions?' and people stop thinking at that moment, even though they might have had a question before I asked. So notice the non-thinking; be aware of that. Thinking can either be a useful tool or just habitual proliferation, just endless thinking, thinking, thinking, and you don't notice when it stops because you are conscious through thinking; you become your thoughts. When there is non-thinking, then, it isn't noticed; it isn't recognized or appreciated. In Zen they have these who-am-I kind of approaches and ways of consciously stopping the thinking process. The aim is to recognize this sense of 'there is no thought but there is awareness'. You ask yourself, 'Who am I?' or 'Who is aware?' or just 'who?' or 'what?' and for a moment the form of the question stops the thinking mind. Some of you who are getting older probably have these 'senior moments', which is a euphemism for not being able to think of something. This happens to me sometimes. I might be standing next to a monk I have known for maybe thirty years and decide to introduce him to somebody passing, so I say, 'Oh, I'd like you to meet — er — er — a very good friend of mine.' I can't even remember my very good friend's name! Now, we can either see a situation like that as a sign of growing senility, of something terrible happening, or use it as a point of recognition, noticing that in this space there is non-thinking. Somebody at the end of a talk asks, 'Do you have any questions?' and I have personally experienced these incredible inner struggles — 'Do I have a question? — er — well er — shall I ask about — ?' I might feel I ought to ask a question, you know, because this is a social scene here at Leicester and somebody has given a good talk. The trouble is I either don't have a question, or the thinking process simply ceases! So, in the who-am-I type of questioning, one is not trying to define oneself, but simply noticing the cessation of thought at that moment, just that nonplussed moment, that gap where thinking does not operate. More and more then there is this sense of stillness and silence in awareness.

In a similar way I remember being in a room once where there was no light whatsoever; everything was completely black. I put my hand up in front of my eyes and just couldn't see it, not even a shadow, and I thought, 'I can't see!' Then suddenly I recognized that consciousness is light. I had never thought of that before. Even though my eyes were not operating they could see blackness. In terms of the objective world, my eyes couldn't see colour, shape or form without light, but as I pursued that inwardly, I realized that the light is consciousness; it is awareness; awareness is not dark. When you bring your attention back to this point here rather than creating a 'real' world for yourself out there, when you no longer seek absorption into the objects of the senses, there is consciousness and awareness with the ability to reflect. I found also that just by learning to listen — whether I am in the dark or in the light, by myself or in a crowded place, or whether sounds are melodious, beautiful and sublime or cacophonous and horrible — everything is embraced, everything is included in this poised attention. And this I find to be a valuable technique. It is not a matter of listening *for* anything; I am not trying to listen just to the sound of the traffic or just to one thing in particular; I simply have this attitude of poised, relaxed attention. Then I notice a background vibration or what I call 'the sound of silence'. This isn't a sound, really — though to me it seems like one — it is more like a vibration. I usually use the word 'sound' to try and describe it, but people then sometimes try to identify it with the ear. The reality, though, is that it is more like something in the background, something that includes and permeates everything like a flowing stream. It has a flowing quality to it that you can rest in. This is not something you create; it isn't a refined thing that depends on specially refined conditions for its support; nor is it exciting or sublime like the Hallelujah Chorus or a sound that dominates and stops other sounds. Once recognized, therefore, you can develop it wherever you are, and it integrates into the flow of life, into washing the dishes, going on the alms round, washing your robes, or whatever. Even now, while I am sitting here talking, I am aware of this 'sound of silence'; it is like a background that has no boundary, that has this sense of infinity, and that stops the thinking process. Having been addicted to thinking and desperately trying to stop it, I used to drive myself crazy with my own thoughts. They just seemed to wind me up and keep me going until I, hopefully, fell asleep and forgot about them. Then I got this great determination to go beyond obsessive thinking, and that led me to the 'sound of silence' where I noticed 'I'm not thinking!'

So, what is the reality of consciousness now — not in terms of concepts, ideas, or doctrines; it isn't a matter of looking for definitions — but what is it as a reality right now? When we make God into a patriarchal figure, we get a white-bearded old man up in the sky, but if we don't personify God or reality, if we don't create forms but just open ourselves to this present moment and rest in awareness, there is formlessness; and formlessness has no boundary because boundaries are what forms are all about. Personality, the self-view, always has a boundary, doesn't it? My personality is a boundary by which I describe myself. My abilities or lack of them, my emotional character, the judgements of how good or bad I am, my identity with a culture, with conditioning , with education, with the things that I have done or haven't done in my life, with the positions I am in, are all boundaries and forms that are part of my personality. But space and consciousness are not personal. You can't claim emptiness and say 'I am this!' or 'I am the sound of silence!' If you do, you have missed the point. Once you claim it, you lose it. The personality ceases in awareness; it no longer operates. But there is still consciousness and there is wisdom, so then I have perspective on the conditions. 'All conditions are impermanent' is true; and I am not just going along with the Theravadan party line on this; this is a true statement. Of course, it isn't up to me to convince myself or anybody else about it, but to question, 'Is this true or not?' Logically you can say that anything that begins must end — and we can go along with ideas of impermanence

— but actually witnessing cessation is . . !

In terms of emotional habits, when somebody insults me or does something I find offensive, I feel anger, and then maybe think, 'How could he do that? That's disgusting! He was supposed to be my friend but he's betrayed me, he's disappointed me, I'll never forgive him! No, I'm not even going to speak to him again — but I'm going to confront him! I'm going to seek revenge!' and I can go on and on like that. Then the rational mind says, 'Oh, just forget it! He's trying his best,' and there is a feeling of magnanimity, a grand gesture of understanding. But you can't sustain that for long before it goes back into, 'How could he? I'll never forgive him.' And there is a struggle between the magnanimous, generous 'Forgive! He's just doing the best he can. Don't make it personal. We all have our bad days . . .' and 'I'LL NEVER FORGIVE HIM!' At least this is how my mind works. I have heard all the good advice, but the hurt, the pain of disappointment, the sense of betrayal is still there. So I contemplate these things. And then in this emptiness or this 'sound of silence', the thinking process stops. Then I no longer create thoughts from anger or try to be magnanimous. There might still be some residual energy, I might still feel some tension within myself, within my body, but by staying with the 'sound of silence' and this energy of anger, I can actually witness its cessation. The energetic anger — what I call anger — ceases. So what is left when that has gone? Peacefulness! 'All conditions arise and cease; and their cessation is peace.' This is a reality to be realized; it isn't just some poetic view I have.

The point then is to sustain the awareness. And that isn't trying to keep it going like some wilful act. To me it is more a matter of learning to trust the sense of open, relaxed attention in which the 'sound of silence' becomes recognizable and I rest in the stillness. Then the acrimony and emotional conditions that are part of my *kamma*, that come in accord with other conditions, are in the context of cessation. This is non-suffering; and the Eightfold Path (the fourth Noble Truth) starts with this insight, with 'right understanding'.

When you live in a community you have plenty of challenges and opportunities for feeling betrayed, disappointed, let down, irritated, frustrated and all the rest — because monks and nuns are just like anyone else. Now, taking that personally would be an unbearable way to live; I wouldn't be able to find any joy in the life if I did that — not unless everybody behaved themselves and pleased me all the time! Rather than making that demand — which I know is an impossible one anyway so there is no point in making it! — it is better to simply trust in awareness. This is a natural stillness. And once you begin to trust it and cultivate it, it stays with you. When you forget it, however, you go back into those habits of liking, disliking, loving and hating.

In cultivating *(bhāvanā)* the fourth Noble Truth, then, there is the path (the Eightfold Path is the statement), it should be culti-vated or developed (and we have this word *'bhāvanā'* which is the prescription), and the last insight is that the path has been cultivated (the result). Notice that this reflective paradigm of the statement, the prescription, and the result are the three aspects of each noble truth. The first Noble Truth is 'understanding', the second is 'letting go of the causes', the third is 'realizing cessa-tion', and the fourth is 'cultivating awareness in the ordinariness of life'. No longer is it a question of depending on special situa-tions, meditation retreats, monastic conventions, mountain tops or caves. Those things are fine — there is nothing wrong with them — but you no longer depend on them.

Now that I am getting older I say to the monks, 'What are you going to do with me as I get more senile?' This is a problem, you know. We all used to be quite young; now I am the oldest. I say, 'Well, if I get too obnoxious just put me into a nursing home,' and I mean it! I know they won't do that, but I have this willingness to take whatever life sends me — because I know how to learn from situations and understand them. So, whether I die in the arms of the Sangha with all my wits at a hundred years old and get apotheosized up into the heavens as one of the great teachers, or get sent off to an old people's home — I don't care any more. I trust in this path, in this awareness, and feel confident in dealing with the things of the body and the emotional habits that can still manifest.

In Buddhism we talk of the four *brahmavihāras (mettā, karuṇā, muditā, upekkhā)* and this is sometimes translated as the 'divine abodes'. They are a Brahma-world *(brahmaloka)*, a kind of beauty and goodness that is natural to our experience, but they are not to be taken as forms of idealism or personal qualities that we identify with. You hear people sometimes say things like, 'I have a lot of *mettā*, but I don't have much *muditā*, and *upekkhā* is beyond me!' claiming these things as personal attainments. From this emptiness, however, this awareness, the *brahmavihāras* are more like natural responses to the conditions that we experience. They are not created by us and they are not forms of idealism or sentimentality; they are responses. You could get the idea that in cessation an arahant just sits there and doesn't care! — you know, people in war situations are being dragged from their homes screaming, yelling and crying, and an arahant is just indifferent — beyond it all — *upekkhā* — ! But compassion is empathetic, isn't it? It isn't sentimental, though. Holding to an idea of compassion *(karuṇā)* and going into, 'Oh, I feel *so* sorry for them,' doesn't go very deep; that is more of a pretty thought that one holds to. Real *karuṇā* operates from here, from the mind, from consciousness; it is an empathetic understanding of suffering, a suffering that you share with all creatures and in which you no longer see yourself as an isolated human individual. And empathetic joy *(muditā)* is our response to the beauty and goodness around us. We find the joy and beauty in others and the world without claiming it, identifying with it, or trying to hold onto it.

Just awareness allows loving-kindness because there is no judgement in it; it simply accepts everything as it is. This is what *mettā* is. But the formulas for *mettā* in the Pali Canon can sound terribly sentimental, and when I first came to London I remember starting the *mettā* meditation with the usual 'May I be well; may I abide in wellbeing', and people were quite cynical about it. It can sound rather sentimental, as though one is trying to be terribly nice about everything. But *mettā* goes much deeper than just nice ideas and thoughts; it is a way of allowing things to be what they are both internally and externally. It is not about approving or liking anything, but of allowing the world to be the way it is without resenting, hating or judging it. That applies also to having *mettā* for one's own cynicism, for example. On an ideal level cynicism is not a quality that is praiseworthy in Buddhism, but I can be quite cynical myself. I might think, 'I should have love for *all* creatures,' and then I would think, 'Rubbish!' If I trust my awareness, however, I receive those feelings for what they are without judging them. I have found that refraining from judging myself, to be one of the hardest things for me. I am a terrible self-critic. To me, it just seems so honest to *admit* and even emphasize the fact that I have faults and weaknesses. But the attitude of *mettā* is about receiving weaknesses, faults and negativities, and allowing them to be 'this way'. Then of course everything ceases, because if we receive life, its natural flow is towards cessation.

Luang Por Chah liked to say that the world ceases here in consciousness *(citta)*. And I encourage you to take this as a teaching. Realize, that this is a reality in *your* experience of life and that you can tune into it. The more you have confidence in awareness and in your own ability to pay attention, the more you let go of the need to control or be caught in helpless reactions to experiences. This is cultivating the way of non-suffering, which is the fourth Noble Truth. You will still experience age, sickness and loss, of course — the natural flow of *kamma* will still operate according to its nature — but you will no longer create suffering, the suffering which comes from ignorance and not understanding the Four Noble Truths with their three aspects and twelve insights. Because you don't want suffering, your world is centred around looking for happiness and security; and in a sense, this is the materialistic mind, isn't it? Looking for *nibbāna* or non-suffering is like thinking that having all the money in the world will do it, or that we can control things and avoid what we don't like. There is a longing there for happiness, peace, perfection and fulfilment. And in that attempt to find happiness, we struggle with the very conditions which create more unhappiness.

To take refuge in Buddha-Dhamma-Sangha is to internalize it. It is here; it isn't something we don't have, but maybe we don't recognize it. The way to do that, of course, is to wake up — and then we know what it is. Consciousness is an ongoing reality and operates whether we are attached and caught up in selfish desires or not. But attachment to conditions out of ignorance blinds us to that fact so that our conscious experience is always distorted. It always seems as though we are struggling with the world, with ourselves, with idealism, with immature emotions and on and on like that, in a kind of war that never seems to resolve itself — or at least not in the way we, personally, would like it to. So, instead of operating from the personal which tries to get more control, puts a greater demand on life, and leads to the inevitable disappointment that goes with not getting what we want, we can let go of everything. Then there is a sense of flowing with life, flowing with the *kamma*-result *(vipāka-kamma)* of our lives as it manifests in its good and bad forms. Our refuge then is in the deathless, in the dhamma, rather than in death-bound conditions.

No Person in the Present

As this is the last day of the Summer School the mind easily gets caught in thinking about going home or wherever, or about the future, or remembering the past. So when we talk about *bhāvanā*, or meditation, it is really in this sense of composing the mind, of bringing it to the here and now, to this one point. One-pointedness is always here and now; the world ceases here. This is pointing at yourself, at your own heart, at consciousness in the present. The world ceases in the present. Now, terms like 'the world', 'the present', 'the heart' or 'the *citta*' are just words, just symbols, and they can be helpful reminders, but that is all they can be. They are not in themselves anything to grasp, so it isn't a matter of clinging to ideas, but rather of trusting yourself to recognize reality.

I am at Chithurst this year because Ajahn Sucitto is on sabbatical leave. I haven't lived there for twenty years or more, so all the memories are coming up about it — Ajahn Anando, the early years, the refurbishing of the derelict house — all these memories from the past. Some people are wondering whether Ajahn Sucitto will return. Maybe he will like his freedom so much he won't want to! But that is in the future, isn't it? I think, 'What will I do if he doesn't come back?' Then I come to this point, the here and now, and trust in dhamma rather than getting caught up in the possibility of things not going the way I want them to. I trust that by being with the 'here and now' the future will take care of itself when the time comes.

In the monasteries we regularly chant in Pali: *sandiṭṭhiko, akāliko, ehipassiko opanayiko paccattaṃ veditabbo viññūhi.*

'*Sandiṭṭhiko*' means something like 'apparent here and now', and these are the words we use to describe dhamma. You might think, 'What is apparent here and now? Where is the dhamma now?' But that is like looking for something you are already familiar with — this is a clock, this is a glass, this is some new-fangled microphone Dick invented. 'Apparent here and now' is a phrase which reminds me to pay attention; it isn't pointing to something secretly hidden under the cushion, maybe, or under the carpet. 'Apparent here and now' means I don't have to go looking for it, but just need to awaken, to pay attention, to put myself into a state of openness and timelessness.

Will Ajahn Sucitto come back to Chithurst next year? Now, that is about time, isn't it? That is about next year. What will I do if he doesn't come back? Should I stay at Chithurst or go to Amaravati? Or should I just go on a sabbatical myself? But that is about the future, about 'what if?' The past is remembering Chithurst house when it was derelict and the shrine room fell into the cellar! Sister Candasiri invited her brother for tea, and when we were sitting there the windows fell in . . . nearly killed him! These are quite fond memories, actually. But 'apparent here and now' and 'timelessness' are not terms referring to the past, and they are not referring to Chithurst or Digby Hall or any place. This is awareness; and it is timeless. If you start remembering yesterday you are back in the time realm. This afternoon I am going back to Amaravati — that is about time, isn't it? 'This afternoon', 'yesterday', 'when we first moved to Chithurst' — all these thoughts are about time. Will Ajahn Sucitto return? That is about time. But timelessness is now, isn't it? If you decide to meditate for an hour, say, and you *are* aware for that hour, then that is timeless, actually, if you notice. But if you start wondering what time it is and sit there thinking, 'I've got to sit here for an hour; I don't know whether I can take an hour of sitting!' This is about 'me' and 'time', 'me as a person who has a past'. You have a past and a future as a person. In the present, however, there is no past, no future, and no person. By reflecting in this way, you begin to value and recognize just this very natural state of being — it is here and now, timeless.

And then we chant *'ehipassiko'*. This is translated as 'encouraging investigation'. I don't think that is a very good translation, actually; it doesn't have that quality of 'come and see!' about it which is what *'ehi'* means. *'Ehi'* is an invitation: 'Come and see right now! Wake up! It's here! See for yourself!' 'Encouraging investigation' doesn't have the same umph to it; it's kind of bland. The Buddha would say *'ehi bhikkhu!'* (come bhikkhu!) meaning you have been accepted into the order. That was it! They didn't have all these ceremonies. We have this incredible ceremony to perform now, and of course as Westerners we have to do it perfectly, so we have a kind of choreography as well; it is almost a formalized dance that we do. Originally it was just *'ehi bhikkhu!'* (come here bhikkhu!) and that was all.

Then we chant *'opanayiko'*, which at Amaravati is translated as 'leading onwards'. Ajahn Amaro and Ajahn Passano in California translate it as 'inwards', 'leading inwards'. But whether it is 'inwards' or 'onwards' I hope you get the idea. It isn't a matter of getting the translation exactly right. The point is to recognize the meaning. Once you recognize this 'come and see!' it will lead you, and you can trust that. This morning someone asked me, 'What do you do after you have realized *nibbāna*?' When there is a sense of dhamma, of course, there is no question of what you do next; that becomes irrelevant. Realizing *nibbāna* is recognizing the stream and trusting it. Then it leads you in your life. Your age, your *kamma*, your position — all these things are not really the issue. If I say, 'Well, when you realize *nibbāna*, you should ordain; in the scriptures it says that if you attain arahantship and you're not a bhikkhu, you should become one immediately!' that is all about what people say; that is just scriptural teachings and ideas. The point is, we don't need to wonder what will happen to us if we become enlightened, because it will resolve itself. Don't worry about it. Just trust the awareness — that's it! It's as simple as that.

The final phrase we chant is *'paccattaṃ veditabbo viññūhi'* which means 'to be experienced individually'. In other words, to realize the dhamma for ourselves. No one can do it for us; no one can wave a magic wand and enlighten us. Only we know what it is. It is no good asking someone else — 'Am I enlightened, Ajahn Sumedho?' The important thing is to trust your own awareness. And this is what I encourage more than anything else. I can see that Westerners fail, really, in developing practice. We believe the teacher or the scriptures or anything, but not ourselves 'because I could be wrong, couldn't I? I could be trusting my ego! Maybe I'm a megalomaniac! Maybe I'm just a deluded nobody — and how can you trust that?' Then sometimes people look at me and think, 'Ajahn Sumedho seems more trustworthy than I am . . .' But why do they think that? Maybe I'm deluded! Maybe this is all rubbish! If I start wondering whether I have attained stream-entry or realized *nibbāna*, I don't trust that. It isn't a question of attaining or realizing anything any more, because I see that that whole sense of 'me' is a delusion, a created convention. I made a determination once to trust this, to recognize that awareness is 'like this', because I began to realize that it is as simple as that; I began to realize that awareness is a pure, natural state of being. There is nothing complicated about it, nothing difficult. It is very simple, so simple in fact, that we overlook it all the time; we look for something complicated or terribly refined and special. This is the problem with the ego; the ego always seeks identity with extremity, with something esoteric, with something very special.

You sometimes hear people talking about lights they have seen in meditation, and heavenly beings *(devatās)* appearing, and special messages from the cosmos — and that's the first time they meditate! At the end of the sitting they say, 'Oh, that was fantastic! I saw this bright light. And this kind of radiant being came into consciousness and blessed me.' And you think, 'I just sat there in pain wondering when they were going to ring the bell!' Even if you do have moments when special things happen, they come and then they go again, they are just impermanent like everything else. And there is no point in expecting them. If you expect them, they won't come. It is more a question of learning to recognize just this moment as it is. When you look for special things happening and they don't, you feel bored with what you *are* experiencing — just breathing in and breathing out and sitting for an hour being still. That might seem terribly boring because you would like some marvellous experience, some great effulgent light and Lord Buddha to come and congratulate you. But if anything like that does happen, don't trust it. That is another delusion. You might know the saying, 'If you meet the Buddha, kill him!' The point is, a Buddha from outside is delusion. Buddha is not something that is going to come from out there.

So, become aware of any kind of expectation, any longing for special signs or beautiful experiences. Observe the desire *for* something or to get rid of something, and realize that that awareness of the desire is it; that is the dhamma. Be that awareness. Just notice your body — the way it is right now — and notice that which is aware of your body. You can be aware of your body because the body is not really you! You can't be aware of being aware, of course, because awareness is not an object; it is this centre point of awakened attention. You can experience your body as it is — the sitting, the sensations, the pressures, the pain, the posture at this very moment — but what is it that observes them? This observing is not judgemental; it isn't saying anything is bad or good. As soon as you say, 'Oh, my sitting posture isn't any good; there's this pain and so on,' you are identifying with whatever is being experienced. There is something you don't like about it and you become critical: 'It's bad! It's painful! I don't want it!' But before you put anything onto experience, just be aware that 'it is the way it is'. The posture, the breath, the mental states, the 'sound of silence', consciousness, space — these are all pointing to this pure presence of being. And when you recognize that, it is just 'this'. There is nothing fantastic about it. It isn't beautiful or ugly, marvellous, absolutely fantastic or anything. It doesn't have a quality that you can observe. But you can recognize it; there is a recognition. And by recognizing this natural state of being, you begin to trust it. So I say, 'Trust this! Don't trust anything you think *about* it, just recognize that this is the reality; this is it.

I encourage myself in the same way. Years ago, I had this insight about just trusting this, trusting it at all costs, because I realized this is the only thing you *can* trust. And I affirmed it. Then I knew I would be put to the test — and I was! Problems in the Sangha developed, and disrobings, and all kinds of things. But still I knew 'just trust this!' And I remember something happening which to me was quite wrong, quite disgusting, and yet I thought, 'Just trust the awareness of it.' After a while, though, I began to think, 'No! I've got to do something about it. I've got to act on this.' So I did. I told this person off — and I made a complete mess of the whole thing! It was a total disaster, and I realized I should have followed my original insight. When you don't trust awareness and act from righteous indignation or whatever, then even though you might have 'right' on your side — 'I'm right! He's wrong and I've got to tell him "You're wrong!" And I've got to make him admit that he's wrong and I'm right!' — it doesn't work very well. Anyway, I made a complete mess of this thing and had to bear the consequences of it. In the process, however, it confirmed my insight; having got caught up in my own sense of righteous indignation and following it, and seeing the result of that, made me more confident in trusting awareness.

Now, being aware doesn't mean that I don't do anything; it just means I don't act from a position of being 'right'. Righteous indignation is a very dualistic thing. There is 'right' and then there is 'wrong'; and the thing about that is that there is no mindfulness in it; you are unaware of the other person and simply caught up in your emotions: 'I'm right! I'm right and he's wrong! And I've got to let him know it. He's not going to get away with it!' And then he comes along. 'There he is, that wrong monk!' and

I say, 'You're wrong! You are wrong! And I want you to *admit* you are wrong!' And he gets this pounding from me. He may not even know what I'm talking about, except that I am projecting all this onto him, abusing him, insulting him and coming from a very heavy, righteous place. So who is right? Even though what I am saying might be right, if my tactics are aggressive and abusive, the other person will just feel the anger and aversion. What I am saying will have no meaning for him; he won't be able to hear it. That is why the world is so bad, isn't it? We are always trying to punish the bad ones, get rid of the terrorists — 'They should bring back capital punishment! Get rid of all the criminals. All the paedophiles should be castrated. We should completely cleanse ourselves of all the bad people — ethnic cleansing!' This is what it leads to, doesn't it? What is more evil than ethnic cleansing? And yet it is probably based on a sense of being right — 'We're right!' In awareness you might feel things but not necessarily act on them because your refuge is in the awareness; you become conscious of your emotions but see them in terms of what they are in the present. You recognize that grasping righteous anger and acting on it will lead to more confusion, more pain, more division and greater problems, and so your sense of trusting in awareness increases. Some of you have been practising for many years and probably know this anyway, but we all need reminding sometimes, we need encouraging, because we live in a society that tends to act from positions, from right and wrong, from reward and punishment. And we do it to ourselves; we are self-critical and judgemental towards ourselves.

Teachings like the Four Noble Truths and Dependent Origination are very skilful, but they are not for grasping; they are not for learning about in order to pass any kind of examination — 'What are the Four Noble Truths?' and you write them down: one, two, three, four. They are for what I call 'internalizing', for helping us to look at something in a way we would never have previously thought of. The same with the Four Stages. There are many opinions about becoming a stream-enterer, once-returner, non-returner, and arahant, and they often get elevated into these very high attainments — because that is the way the thinking mind works, isn't it? *Nibbāna* becomes so very refined and high when you think about it that it is beyond you. You hear these comments: 'Has anybody realized *nibbāna*? What about the Dalai Lama? Has he realized *nibbāna*? Is the Dalai Lama a *sotāpanna*? But he's Mahayana so he must be a *bodhisattva*,' and you get tangled up with all the terms. 'Are *bodhisattvas sotāpannas*? Maybe they're *anāgāmis*? Can an *arahant* be a *bodhisattva*?' — and on and on like this. People form views and opinions about these things without even knowing what they are talking about. The word *'nibbāna'* sounds like a superlative, like the best, the absolute highest attainment that any human being can arrive at, so it can easily be put into that category.

In Buddhist cosmology the highest is the Brahma-world *(brahmaloka)* with *avīci* hell at the bottom. There is this structure of the *devaloka* (realm of the gods), the *asuras* (jealous gods), the animal world, the *avīci* hell, the *petas* (hungry ghosts), and the human realm. These are categories that we can all relate to. We all have these six realms within ourselves, so it isn't a matter of trying to decide whether there is a Brahma-realm somewhere in the sky — 'Can you get to it by rocket ship or shuttle? Should the Americans spend a lot of money trying to discover where the Brahma-world is?' These are really about human conscious experience. If you look at these six realms of existence, I am sure each of you will be able to relate them to experiences you have already had. We generally assume that we are human beings all the time, don't we? We just take it for granted that because we have what we call 'human bodies', we are ongoing human beings no matter what. So when people torture or persecute other human beings or commit murders and do terrible things, we think, 'How can they act like that? They are inhuman!' And they are; they are inhuman. What they are doing is more like something you would expect to take place in a devil-realm or a demonic realm, isn't it? The word 'demon' usually refers to a being who loves to torture, persecute, harm, seek revenge and enjoy watching others suffer in pain and agony. But we are all capable of those things — all of us — because they are within the possibility of consciousness. This sense-realm includes the full range from the heavens to the hells and all the variations in between.

Whatever we align ourselves with or absorb into, we tend to become. So if we play around with evil or demonic forces, those energies will take us over. That is why the five moral precepts *(pañcasīla)[33]* are considered to be the greatest protections in the universe against the evil forces. Now, are the evil forces outside us or just part of the energetic realities of this realm? I have seen within myself that becoming fascinated, enthralled or frightened by something, gives it tremendous power in consciousness and I become like that. The five moral precepts are therefore guidelines for behaviour because sometimes we do find all of that fascinating; evil is fascinating, let's face it. Violence, sex — it is all exciting stuff, isn't it? That is what all those shockers and thrillers are about, the Dracula and Frankenstein films. Fortunes have been made from films like that because they evoke compelling, exciting energies which take us out of the boredom and dreariness of ordinary life. The same is true of refined tastes in art, music and high-minded thoughts. They can take us into the *deva* realms; we can become like *devatās*, these lovely, refined creatures. But the human body is not a *deva* body, is it? *Devas* are ethereal and our bodies are not. We can become ethereal mentally, but not physically; and being human is recognizing the humanness of having this body, this rather coarse condition that has to be fed and taken care of, that gets old and has diseases and various problems.

The Buddha, as we know, was aiming his teaching at awareness rather than the attainment of anything. Buddhism isn't about becoming terribly refined or being reborn as a *deva*, but about learning the truth of the way it is. So, all these realms are

33 *Pañcasīla:* abstaining from killing, stealing, sexual misconduct, false speech, intoxicants and recreational drugs.

dhamma; they are in terms of 'what arises ceases' and 'all mental formations are impermanent'. Whether the forces are coarse or refined, demonic or angelic, boring, dreary, depressing, ordinary, fantastic, true or false, whatever arises ceases. This is the liberating reflection on the conditioned realm. By being aware, we no longer identify with conditions; this is the freedom we get through awareness. If we are not aware, we tend to identify with what arises — 'This anger is mine; I would like to become a very refined *devatā* (heavenly being); I wish life were nothing but spring flowers and fairies dancing on the lawn!' You can either become very sweet and sentimental or frightened by the demonic forces that you sense around you. Awareness, then, opens you to this deathless reality where all conditions in their varying degrees are seen in perspective. That is why you can trust it. It isn't dangerous; and nor do you have to spend a lifetime cultivating some refined taste in order to recognize it. It is simply a matter of trusting yourself to recognize it.

For you right now, what is awakenedness? Ask yourself. It isn't a matter of answering the question in order to determine whether you are awake or not, or wondering whether you are just fooling yourself. That is all just thinking again, isn't it? Awakenedness is 'this!' And when I say 'this', I mean awakenedness is reality. This is not a matter of creating a false illusion that 'I am somebody who is awake', but simply of recognizing the presence of now, being now, which includes everything from the physical state you are in to the mental conditions you are experiencing. This is also what the Four Noble Truths are about. Suffering *(dukkha)* is a key to be used; it is the key to the door, actually. We take something quite ordinary like suffering and don't have to believe in it because we all have it. Then, by looking at it, by observing and receiving suffering, we let it go. If we don't let it go, we tend to get caught up in reacting to it — 'I don't want this; I want happiness!' — and we develop a life of running away. As soon as anything unpleasant happens, we try to find something pleasant; and if too much suffering overwhelms us, maybe we take to drink — 'I can't take any more of this!' — or we get terribly depressed because the suffering is too much. We feel overwhelmed by it and we can't get away from that.

Instead of trying to get away, however, the Buddha said 'understand!' And understanding suffering *(dukkha)* is receiving it — *dukkha* is 'like this'. I have found from observing my own experiences that there are mental states I simply don't like. But when one of these mental states arises, I now trust in the awareness of it and welcome it: 'Welcome!' And, actually, I don't suffer if I do that — if I really mean it, that is. Somehow it is all right. The fear and not wanting particular mental states is the real suffering, just being caught in the bad habits I have developed in my life and blindly reacting to them in very inadequate ways, ways which might have worked when I was a child, but don't work so well now. Yet I might still sometimes react like I did when I was five years old — even though I am seventy-one! It's just a habit. When you are a child you develop ways of dealing with problems that work at the time, that have a certain validity for the situation at the time, but you might get caught in those same habitual patterns later on in life.

In this awareness, however, we see the patterns. And if we don't judge them as personal flaws or failures — if we simply see them for what they are — they are bearable. We no longer empower them, and neither do we reject or follow them. That is the way to resolve them and let them go. Then they cease. Letting go is allowing things to go in a natural way. Everything ceases in the heart, whereas 'out there' it all seems too complicated. Trusting 'here' is ultimate simplicity; it is cessation, *nibbāna*, and it is now. You might think, 'Is this right according to scripture?' But trust yourself to know! The scriptures are meant to help, but they are not infallible. In fact they are quite limited because they too are conventions; they too are imperfect. They are good conventions for awareness, of course, and this awareness is what I encourage you to learn to trust. But it is possible to become attached to any conventional form, even to the monastic form. You can empower the form and identify with it so strongly, in fact, that it gets in the way. Then you merely become that form — you merely become a monk or a nun, or whatever — and that is not liberating. It is better than becoming a drug addict, of course, but the point of the monastic life is awakenedness. Recognize that! trust it! and then — *nibbāna*? 'What do you do after *nibbāna*?' You don't do anything, or you could say you do whatever has to be done.

The word 'Buddha' itself means 'awake'. And this is significant to me. Rather than making the word too sacred or thinking of Buddha as a kind of sage of the past or some mystical energy in the universe, recognize that it is awakenedness; it is the natural state. We might think of a Buddha as some special being and also create these illusory Buddhas that are beautiful and perfect in form and concept, but what are they right now in terms of our experience? What can the Buddha be as a refuge right now that isn't some abstract idea? We can't take refuge in an abstract idea. The point to recognize is that when we say *'Buddhaṁ saraṇaṁ gacchāmi'* (I go to the Buddha for refuge), what we are really doing is taking refuge in awakenedness.

Buddha knows dhamma — the way it is — and the way it is, is apparent here and now. This gives one the sense of being in this infinite awareness that embraces everything 'the way it is'. Whatever way you are — the body, the conditions around you, what you are seeing, hearing, tasting, smelling, touching — is the way it is. Your refuge is in dhamma and not in anything that is happening apart from the awareness of the way it is. This is one-pointedness. Everything ceases here. The world ceases in the 'unshakeable deliverance of the heart'. Now, all conditions are shakeable — body, emotions, ideas, everything — so what is unshakeable? Awareness is unshakeable. And as you recognize this, you cultivate it in terms of the flow and movement of your body in conscious experience. Awareness then is like the background to everything and includes everything. It isn't a judging or criticizing faculty, but it is discerning.

According to the scriptures even the Buddha after his enlightenment had to deal with the problems of living. He had backaches, headaches and stomach upsets just like everybody else — he didn't get out of any of that! And finally he got old and died. According to the scriptures, after his enlightenment he was blamed for things he didn't do — much worse than I ever have been! The difference between most people and the Buddha, however, is that the Buddha saw things in terms of dhamma. Most people take things personally — 'How can you treat me like this when I've tried to help you? All you do is criticize me. I wish I didn't have a body. I've got a backache and a headache, and I don't like it, and I don't want it!' That is personal, isn't it? But in terms of awareness, it is what it is; and within that there is no ignoring, pretending or dismissing, but rather an embracing, recognizing and knowing everything as it is.

I hope this encourages you. What I am saying is that you can do it. You might get the impression that it is too difficult. Often Buddhism is presented in such a way that it sounds terribly complicated and difficult, and you might think, 'Well, I'm just an ordinary person; I'm not a scholar and it's beyond me.' But it isn't. You might think that, but don't believe it. Awareness is quite ordinary. It doesn't make you high; you don't get spaced-out on it or blissed out; it isn't like ecstasy or anything like that, and in fact it usually isn't noticed. I have experienced pleasure, happiness, excitement, having lots of success, the best, and wanting more of it — and then being worried about losing it all. So when it all changed and suddenly collapsed, there was a feeling of despair and grief. But after that came a sense of relief, a kind of coolness, a feeling that I didn't have to hold on any more and it was finished! This, I find, often happens when things go wrong in life — when it all just seems to pile up and become hugely burdensome — suddenly it stops and there is a sense of relief. Now, in recognizing this relief, you see that it is nothing special. It isn't high or low; it is just quite ordinary. Awareness is like that sense of relief. And that is the most you get out of it. It isn't, 'Oh, this is fantastic!'

Begin to trust yourself to open to life as you experience it in its ordinariness, just in daily life, just living at home, going to the shops, whatever. Begin to feel this sense that all you have to do is *be*. Relax and be yourself without getting caught up in the compulsiveness of trying to *do* something, trying to *prove* something, trying to be approved of by others or feeling you are never good enough. Relax with the breathing and consciousness; just relax with that. Then you will start awakening to the way things are rather than always moving through time and not noticing, not paying attention but merely aiming for goals in the future or being caught up in compulsive, obsessive habits.

In my tradition there are categories of realization that are referred to like stream-entry which is considered to be a very high position. People are always wondering who is and who isn't a stream-enterer, or whether it is even possible to be one. Some believe that, actually, nobody can attain stream-entry at this time. Others feel that they are themselves stream-enterers and somehow superior to the rest of us. I know people who think like that — and they kind of feel sorry for me! And then there are those who would never dare believe they could possibly be a stream-enterer. But these are all just ways of thinking, aren't they? This is all 'me and mine'. And what is a stream-enterer really? Is it that difficult or remote? Whatever, it isn't something we can claim personally; it isn't an attainment. I can't say 'I have attained it!' as some kind of personal success story.

The more I trust awareness, the more I let go of the fetters that block reality. It is like a relinquishing, a letting go, rather than any kind of attainment through practising hard and getting a lot of concentration or being 'a better meditator than you'. That, I don't trust! The idea that I am better at meditation than you are or that I should get rewarded because I spend more hours sitting than you do, is the ego at work — 'I've spent so many hours a day sitting . . . got the *jhānas . . . samādhi . . . sotāpanna.* Now

I'm working on the *sakadāgāmi-phala*. So where are you?' I have heard monks talk like that. But just defining the words and descriptions and then trying to make yourself attain what you think those words mean, isn't how it works; you can't do that, really. The best you can do with that is just fool yourself. The words are actually pointing to the here and now, to awareness, to relaxing, opening, trusting; and that is a relinquishing, though not in terms of rejecting anything. I find this more helpful than just saying, 'I've got to attain this, get that, get rid of the defilements.' Though that is how my ego works. The sense of myself as a person is that I have these defilements and I have to get rid of them and develop these virtues. We Americans are like that; we are self-improvers. How many books do you see about self-improvement when you go into an American bookshop? We are never good enough the way we are. I can never see myself on a personal level as being good enough; I can always improve myself. But there is no end to that. How improved can I get personally? It just never ends! And I am getting old now; I don't want to keep trying to improve myself.

When one reflects on the Buddha's teaching it becomes clear that he didn't ask anyone to improve anything, but rather to let go of the conditions that one blindly attaches to through heedlessness. You can be blindly attached to the idea that you are not good enough and therefore have to spend your life trying to improve yourself. That is self-delusion. To think, 'I'm not good enough; I need to practise harder in order to become better,' is a creation; it is just you thinking those words, you creating that illusion. The other extreme is, 'Well, I *am* good enough the way I am. I'm perfect, actually, and I don't need to do *anything*; I'm against all self-improvement; just love me as I am!' But that isn't it either, is it? The point is to see through the illusion that 'I'm not good enough', as well as the illusion 'I *am* good enough'. This is all just language, just thought — 'I'm good, I'm bad, I'm not good enough, I'm all right, this is better than that!' — these are words that we create, and they are dualistic and always judgemental. But awareness is whole, complete. It isn't a matter of comparing, achieving or attaining, but of relinquishing blind attachment to concepts, ideals, views, opinions and all the things that we tend to bind ourselves to out of ignorance.

Buddha awakened from ignorance. So, when the ignorance drops away, there is awakenedness. My encouragement, then, is to keep pursuing this. Be awake! Trust yourself more and begin to appreciate it. This is something to really treasure, just 'this'. You might think, 'Well, it doesn't seem like very much, you know. I don't see *devatās* or angels coming to me, or bright lights.' But personally I don't want that. You can see that kind of thing in special effects movies, so if you want that just go to the movies now and then. What the Buddha was talking about was something ongoing. You don't have to be in a particularly good state for awareness. There is no state, in fact, that is an obstruction to awareness. Only ignorance is the obstruction.

Three Fetters

The Buddhist path is not towards some egotistical attainment or goal, but towards liberation. The intention is for liberation from all delusion, from suffering, from birth and death. These are just words, of course, but they convey the intention most of us have when practising.

The word 'Buddha' itself means 'awake', the 'awakened one'. And this is significant. The Buddha was a conscious individual human being not lost in delusion or the conditioning of his mind. Awakened consciousness knows the truth of the way it is, the dhamma. We have this word 'dhamma' which is unrelated to esoteric teachings or mysteries of any sort, but is something to be realized or recognized through awakened attention; it is getting down to the realities of our own minds — the way we think, the assumptions we make, the problems we have in our lives. We are, for example, caught in the assumption that we are actually 'this person here', 'this person' with these problems, with this body, with these habits, and we therefore think we should practise meditation in order to become an enlightened or liberated person. But this whole attitude of being a person, of taking for granted that we are what we think we are, is to be examined and questioned, and we do this by being attentive to the way it is, with this attitude of awakened attention.

Paying attention is not of course forming an opinion about anything; it is not coming from a position of 'I've got to prove something', but is the simple act of opening, listening, allowing yourself to be receptive instead of projecting, expecting or demanding anything. If you are trying to get something or trying to get rid of something, the point is to become aware of that. Many of us start meditating with the idea that there is something wrong with us and we have to make ourselves better or become somebody else, or become enlightened. When I first started I was convinced I was an unenlightened, ignorant person. That seemed to me to be an honest appraisal of myself; that was the way I seemed to be as a person — ignorant! — and I wasn't going to pretend I was anything special. But then, coming from that attitude of being an unhappy, ignorant, confused person, I hoped I would *become* happy and enlightened by meditating. So, notice, this is a way of thinking, an assumption that most of us make in our lives; it is an assumption based on language, memory, unquestioned identity with the physical body, social conditioning and everything. Now, paying attention is not criticizing or saying there is anything wrong with any of this, but is just noting it, just observing it here in the present, here and now, the way it is. Whatever you think or feel — intellectual, emotional, psychic, important, nonsense or whatever — will change. So what I am talking about is paying attention to those changing conditions that we experience in the here and now.

It seems so realistic to assume that I am a person, that I am a separate individual personality, soul or self, and also that I am this same person under all conditions. Right now I am sitting here and you are sitting there, and everything seems very separate. I am separate from you and each of you is separate from each other. Now, that is a conventional way of seeing; and if I operate from the assumption that you are 'this person', then I see you always from memory; and if I think of you when I am not at the Leicester Summer School, I assume you are always 'this person'. But that is just a memory of you; it is not a person; it has no substance and no essence; it is more like a soap bubble, in fact, floating in the mind. In terms of paying attention to the way it actually is, you are in my consciousness. So, this is the way of observing, of investigating reality in order to begin to break through the assumptions we make and the ignorance we tend to be attached to.

So I am encouraging people now — even those who are just starting to meditate — to ask themselves why they are doing it, why they want to practise meditation. Do you want to meditate because you are unhappy or feel some sense of danger? Do you want to become something else? This is just a way of making more conscious the sense of why you think you should meditate. Maybe you are here to become enlightened, or maybe you feel that enlightenment is beyond you. Maybe you see yourself as so screwed up that it will take at least 84,000 more lifetimes to get there — but at least you're starting! Whichever way you want to put it amounts to the same thing, to this sense of 'I am. . .' something, 'I am this person, this being; I am this way but I don't particularly like the way I am and have to become something better'. By intentionally thinking these things, you begin to notice the difference between the awareness and the thinking process. Your thinking might be, 'I am this unenlightened person who needs to practise hard in order to become enlightened.' But awareness isn't thinking, is it? It is intelligent and conscious, but it has no words. And as you trust yourself more in awareness, you begin to realize that it is nothing more than being alert, being attentive to the present, being aware of the changing conditions of your own thoughts and emotions whatever they might be. It isn't a matter of having right thoughts or right emotions, or intelligent ones or stupid ones, but simply of seeing that all conditions are changing; nor is it a matter of having certain conditions. The point is to investigate them all — from the refined, subtle movements of your mind to the coarseness of the body and material world.

I used to think I was an unenlightened person who had become a monk in order to dedicate my life to the dhamma so that I would become enlightened in the future. But this idea that 'I am this person' was holding to views from the past, to memories from my past history about where I was born, what I had done with my life, the way I had regarded myself, the sense of myself as good, bad, lovable, unlovable, or whatever. When we investigate this idea of doing something now in order to become something else in the future, we begin to realize that, out of ignorance, we are fully committed to time as our reality. The personality is always a time-bound condition. It was born and has a future — 'In the future I hope to become . . .' Or maybe I dread the future. Now that I am old, the future for me is increasing ankylosis, stiffness of the joints and death. So that is the future for an old man. Now, if I take this personally it could be quite depressing, but when I see it in terms of dhamma — in terms of the way it is — I simply see this sense of myself 'as a person' who was born years ago and who might now still be practising Buddhist meditation with the idea of attaining and achieving.

The Western mind is very much an 'attaining' mind; at least most people I know seem to see everything in terms of achievement — 'What have you achieved? After all these years of being a monk, what have you attained? Have you attained the stages? Are you a stream-enterer? You know, having spent forty years in the monastic order you should be at least a stream-enterer!' What a gyp if after forty years you are just as screwed up as you were when you started! But that is about attaining, isn't it? I know monks and lay people who regard these stages as attainments, and they ask, 'Do you know any stream-enterers, once-returners, non-returners or arahants[34]?' as though they are qualifications, university degrees. This is how the thinking mind is. Thinking, as a dualistic function of the mind, has 'good' and then it has 'bad'. If you have one, you have to have its opposite. That is the very nature of thinking, and that is also its limitation. Thinking is useful — and is certainly not to be despised — but trying to realize the truth through analysis or the thinking process will lead to terrible disappointment because it is merely a tool of the mind. It can take you so far, but then you need to let go of thinking and just trust in pure awareness, pure attention.

Now, most of us are so conditioned into thinking, our identities

---

34 The Four Stages: stream-enterer *(sotāpanna)*, once-returner *(sakadāgāmin)*, non-returner *(anāgāmin)*, noble one *(arahant)*.

are so strong as a result of holding to memories, views and opinions, that we have created 'this world' and are also firmly committed to it. In meditation, however, 'this world' starts falling apart. And I have seen people getting a bit panicky when it happens. If you are fully and unquestioningly committed to an ignorant view, you do at least have a kind of security. But you don't want it shaken! One of the most unpleasant mental states is to feel uncertain and insecure, and then there is this attitude of 'tell me everything is all right even if it isn't! Just tell me it is because that will make me feel secure. It doesn't have to be, you know, but I have to believe everything is going to be all right and everything will work out.' That kind of affirmation will make me feel good, but if I don't get that affirmation, then personally I can start worrying; if I hear there are unsolvable problems and dissentions in the Sangha and difficulties and scandals — ! 'Oh, I can't deal with it. Just say it's all right so that I can forget it!'

All conditions are impermanent, but who is it or what is it that knows this? Is that personal? Or is it pure conscious knowing? You begin to realize that in order to become a person you have to think and grasp ideas like 'I am Ajahn Sumedho, I am a Buddhist monk, I am a Theravadan Forest Sangha monk, I am a . . .' and on and on like that. On that level you define yourself, you create yourself as a separate person, an entity. But if you don't do that — if there is just pure awareness, pure consciousness — you don't create anything that causes separation; it is simply 'like this' — pure awareness. Now, that pure awareness isn't yours or mine. We can't claim it as some kind of attainment. If we do, we are deluded again; we are claiming something that is natural, that is dhamma, that is the way it is, and that has nothing to do with 'me' or 'you' as a person.

You find people deluding themselves sometimes. They think they have attained stream-entry or arahantship. But thoughts like that are to be mistrusted. So how do you use teachings like the Four Stages? The point is, the Four Stages are not for

ego-development or attainment; they are a skilful means for recognizing the way we cling to things. And they relate to the Ten
Fetters. So, if we see the first three fetters for what they are and
let go of them, we enter the stream; we see the path and know
it for ourselves; we know the way because these three fetters no
longer blind us to it. So, the first fetter is the personality belief.
You could also call it 'the ego' or 'the sense of me as a separate
person'. And this sense of 'me as a separate person', as I have
been saying, is to be investigated so that we begin to actually
observe how 'I' create 'my personality' through attachment to
memories and so forth.

People ask me, 'Where were you born? You're the one that
went to Thailand and became Ajahn Chah's disciple, aren't
you?' And then I create an entire history of my life as a person.
But that is only a convention. It isn't ultimately real. If I believe
that that convention is the reality, I am caught in ignorance and
bound by praise and blame and the success and failure of 'Ajahn
Sumedho'. When you take on responsibilities as head monk of a
Sangha and so forth, you inevitably put yourself into that position of being the receiver of praise and blame. On a personal level, praise makes me feel good and blame makes me feel terrible.
I like praise, and I don't like blame; I like success, and I dread
failure. But if I trust in the awareness of those feelings, I am no
longer bound by the limitation of the personality — the limitation of 'Ajahn Sumedho' — and am able to receive praise, blame,
success and failure, because the illusion of a separate person is
something I am no longer committed to.

During this Summer School, I encourage you to investigate
what this personality belief is. I am not saying there is anything
wrong with it — there is nothing wrong with having a personality or an ego; it isn't a matter of trying to get rid of it so you don't
have a personality or anything — it is rather a matter of recognizing personality belief and realizing that it is a creation that
comes and goes and changes according to conditions. You will
then no longer be enslaved by the personality, by conditioning

and memories, and begin to free yourself from those kinds of limitations. If you see yourself always in that personal way, you will be bound into limited states that will cause suffering for you in your life. So, once you see the suffering of grasping the idea of 'self', you can let it go. That doesn't mean the personality dissolves into nothing; it simply means that it changes according to its nature and that you are no longer 'a person'. You then let the personality appear and disappear without binding yourself to it.

The second fetter, *sīlabbata-parāmāsa*, is usually translated as 'attachment to rites and rituals', but that is not much of a problem for Westerners. My experience of it, in fact, is that most Westerners would be quite happy to dispense with all the chanting and rites and rituals, so I generally expand that definition to mean attachment to cultural conditioning . The point is, we make assumptions about what is right and what is wrong, how things should be and how things should not be, what a man should be, what a woman should be, what social etiquette and political correctness is, and all the rest. These can be strong attachments that we bind ourselves to — correctness, propriety, the proper way, the way 'we English do things', the way it *should* be done. Now, as with personality belief, it isn't a matter of saying there is anything wrong with cultural conditioning . The point is to observe that which is aware of cultural conditioning and realize that that is not culturally conditioned. Awareness doesn't depend on culture, social positions, political correctness or identity in any personal way. By being aware, one transcends the limitation of conditioning — not by rejecting it but by seeing it for what it is. From my background, from the white middle-class Protestant American conditioning that I experienced, I can see all the assumptions I made in the past. I had certain attitudes which were not consciously recognized but which created suffering for me. I had to see things and hold them in a particular way in order to feel that 'this is right, this is proper, this is what it should be'. But when I went to Thailand, this conditioning was challenged. I couldn't just say, 'Well, you've all got to do it the American way.' For one thing, I didn't know how to say that in Thai, but I also had enough sense to know not to try. Still, there were times when the habit patterns and assumptions of an American conditioning rose up, and I began to notice my tendency to be pulled into them.

The third of the Ten Fetters is doubt. Now, doubt is the result of thinking; and thinking is language, isn't it? You think and you doubt. When you observe the thinking process you see that if you try to resolve conflicts and problems through analysing and thinking about them, you go round in circles, because language itself, or thinking itself, is limited like that. If you use reason, common sense and logic, that is an intelligent way of thinking, but many of our problems are not intelligent, reasonable experiences are they? Emotional experience is not reasonable; it isn't even intelligent; it is feeling, isn't it? We can tell ourselves, 'There's nothing to worry about. Everything is okay. But, you know, something *might* go wrong!' So notice that thinking results in attachment — attachment to cultural conditioning and the personality belief — and this attachment is the real problem. The other things are not problems in themselves; it is our ignorance and attachment that makes something into a problem. Whatever we attach to out of ignorance, we become like that, which is why we experience a feeling of unsatisfactoriness or that something is wrong with us or with the world we live in. Whatever we attach to — no matter how beautiful or idealistic it might be — the result is a feeling of being under threat, or worried, or regret about what we have done or said in the past, or resent what has been done to us. And then the future holds all kinds of possibilities in terms of success, failure, pleasure, pain and so forth.

The reality, however, is now. This is all there is; this is where experience is; this is where consciousness is — right now. 'Tomorrow' is just another perception in this moment, isn't it? I am thinking 'tomorrow' but in the reality of this moment, that is just a concept about the future. It is useable, it works — you can plan what to do tomorrow — but seeing it in terms of dhamma is different from thinking time is your reality, that you are really this person, this separate soul, and that your way of thinking, your cultural conditioning , your attitudes, are either the right ones, or not as good as somebody else's. Now, these attitudes are all acquired after we are born. We are not a personality when we are born; we are not socially or culturally conditioned. Notice, that the first three fetters (personality belief, attachment to conventions, and sceptical doubt) are all man-made artifices. They range from skilful to unskilful and from good to bad. But they are created by us. That is why cultures are different, why we think differently, and why we have values, customs and habits that are not always the same. But that which is aware of these three fetters is not conditioned; it is the dhamma, natural.

Your real refuge is in the dhamma, in awareness, in learning to recognize that it is 'just this', just this present moment; and the thinking process arises from that. Memories come and go, emotions arise and you feel happy or sad, you remember yesterday, ten years ago, maybe forty years ago — but you are aware and see things in terms of dhamma, in terms of all conditions being impermanent. The Buddha in his teachings gets us to recognize this natural state. The unconditioned isn't a created state, it isn't even a state — you can't even call it a state — but it is natural. And consciousness, in terms of this moment, is 'like this'. This is not a matter of concentrating on anything in particular or of doing anything in particular, but of just paying attention.

I have developed over the years this sense of listening, this receptivity — not in order to find anything, get anything, control anything, or do anything — but just as an act of faith and trust. Awareness allows into consciousness whatever arises and ceases in this moment. It is ultimate simplicity. This I would say is right view, right understanding — I call it *'sammādiṭṭhi'* because there are these terms in Pali so you might as well use them! Right view *(sammādiṭṭhi),* then, is 'like this'. Awareness isn't 'me holding a view about Buddhism'; it isn't a viewpoint about Theravada Buddhism; it isn't sectarian or the prerogative of anybody or any religion; it is the recognition that 'this is reality'. And then changing conditions and doubts come: 'Maybe I'm wrong! Maybe I've got it all wrong and I've spent forty years deluded!' But this is thinking again. And the thinking mind is what we might call 'the superego', 'the inner tyrant', the thing up here that is always judging. Now, you have to know this. Most Westerners seem to have tyrannical superegos which hammer away at them and nag them endlessly. And the superego is always 'right'; it is about how you *should* be all the time — 'You shouldn't have said that; you should have said this!' I have watched my superego over many years and now I understand what it is. But it used to throw me into states of doubt because it was always 'right' and I would feel intimidated by what was 'right'! You begin to realize, however, that awareness is not about being right; it is about being present; it is about recognizing — 'just this'.

Conditions come and go, and 'right' and 'wrong' changes. Some are right, some are wrong; and some are right sometimes and wrong sometimes. So in awareness 'right' and 'wrong' do not become absolutely fixed like they do if you are attached to the ideals of righteousness — 'Our way is right and those other oddball Buddhists are wrong!' These things become fixed as 'we're right all the time and they're wrong all the time'. That is the way the thinking mind works. I assume that if I'm right, then you're wrong, and you are *absolutely* wrong, and I am *absolutely* right! With awareness you begin to see this tendency within yourself. But what is it that has to be right? It is the personality belief, the ego, that has to be right. 'I want to be right; I want to belong to the right group. I don't want to join the wrong group; I don't want to spend forty years in the wrong group. You'd have to be crazy to do that! Ours is right!' And you have quotes from the Pali scriptures to prove it. There is plenty of arrogance in Theravada Buddhism, and this is because of personality belief and cultural conditioning ; this is because of not penetrating these fetters.

Awareness, then, is not dualistic. You can recognize the dualism of right and wrong, good and bad, love and hate, and all the rest, but the Buddha was pointing to the third Noble Truth — the realization of cessation, the reality of cessation where conditions cease, the reality of pure awareness where you are not attached out of ignorance to anything. Non-attachment is a natural state; it isn't some refined state that depends on other conditions. If you are caught in delusion, you never recognize or realize non-attachment because your whole momentum and sense of self is created through blind belief and blind attachment. This awareness, on the other hand, is awakened consciousness. The path then is very clear. It is just this here and now. It doesn't have a quality that you can say is absolutely fantastic; it isn't like getting high on drugs or anything like that. It is quite ordinary and nothing that you can get your teeth into. But as you recognize it and value and appreciate it, you begin to see the suffering of wanting to get high, or the suffering of doubting things or doubting yourself. Your superego then gets put in its proper place, and your emotional life is no longer despised or suppressed or takes you over blindly — because you have ways of seeing, of learning from the way you are, from the way your personality is, from the way your emotional habits are and from your desires and fears. From this point here you have perspective on conditions. This is the unconditioned, this awareness; the unconditioned is — 'this'.

Now, notice, I am not saying that the unconditioned is better than the conditioned. We do tend to want to say that the unconditioned is where it's all at and that conditions need to be got rid of. But that is going back into the thinking, discriminating mind again — 'I just want to live in the unconditioned and float about beyond all these worldly things — !' But that is another delusion; it is personality belief again which is very subtle and can take us over very easily. Awareness is aware of obsessions, compulsions and all the habits we have; and once we investigate this, we begin to recognize that 'this is it'. There is nothing complicated about it. Complications come from what we create out of ignorance; and ignorance is resolved by awakening, by mindfulness and investigation. Then we really see for ourselves the suffering of attachment to unsatisfactory conditions. Then the problem is resolved.

To be Right is Not Liberation

'Paying attention', 'here and now', 'awareness' — these are terms which remind us to be alert and attentive. And this is all there really is as experience. There is no past and no future because experience is always now, isn't it? Just reflect on this statement because so much of our lives is lived through the belief in time as reality and planning for the future. The present often gets completely dismissed as unimportant. All the great promises of success and experience lie in the future. Or maybe when you are my age they have all happened in the past! We remember the past, but those memories arise in the present. And the perception of the future is a thought about something that hasn't happened yet, something which has the potential for happiness or suffering. Reflecting in this way is like investigating the way it is, becoming aware of the things that we take for granted — attitudes, prejudices, biases, views — no matter how intelligent or reasonable they might be. This conscious awakenedness is to be recognized because it is, in itself, liberation from suffering.

As I have said many times, I have for years explored and taught what I call 'the sound of silence'. I am the only Theravadan monk, I think, to do this and have therefore taken the risk of stepping outside what is considered orthodox. But I am simply sharing my experience, because as far as I am concerned it works. Whether it is an intrinsic part of Theravadan doctrine or not isn't the point, is it? The point is to use what works, what helps, what assists, what can be used in experience here and now in this moment where we can see clearly — see our own attachments in perspective, see our own thoughts, thinking processes, assumptions and things that aren't all that clear to us.

What has really motivated me in my practice has, of course, been the orthodox teachings of the Theravadan scriptures. I have always used the Four Noble Truths, Dependent Origination and all the essential teachings as my way of practice. And as you begin to recognize what intuitive awareness is, you see that it is emptiness; you realize there is no self in it. Awareness is consciousness and discernment; it is intelligence, but there is no sense of a separate self or anything else within it. You are not holding to a doctrinal position or an attitude of any sort; even 'Buddhism' disappears. Everything resolves itself. This is what is often called *'anattā'*, *'suññatā'*, or *'nibbāna'* (non-self, emptiness, the unborn or unconditioned).

Many years ago I began to experience moments where there was no attachment. There was instead a sense of emptiness and this 'sound of silence', this kind of resonating background. I have heard this called 'the audible sound-stream' — whatever; it is something natural, something not created or dependent on conditions; and it has a continuity to it, a flowing quality like a flowing stream. Once you begin to notice it, recognize and listen to it, you see that it is not something you absorb into. Since it is natural, since you don't create it, you can rest in it, you can be with it; and it stops the thinking process. You actually stop thinking!

This was quite a discovery for me when I first noticed it because I was a compulsive and obsessive thinker. I used to drive myself mad in my first few years as a monk with a mind that would just rant on; it would go on and on. In the hot season in northeast Thailand daily life is as dreary and boring as I have ever experienced it. The afternoons in particular are extremely hot — an unrelenting heat — and the life is just this constant daily routine, day after day. There you are — nothing to do, you might not feel very well physically, the mind starts ranting, just going on and on and on — and little things become exaggerated. I remember one monastery where one could spend all afternoon ranting on about the head monk because he had a very irritating personality. I tried to stop myself doing that, of course, because my idealistic side didn't want to just criticize and think petty little thoughts about somebody all afternoon — 'After all, you're in a monastery! You're supposed to have altruism and compassion!' The conditions, however, didn't stimulate my more altruistic qualities, so I was stuck with this kind of mean, petty, (what we in the military called 'bitching') complaining mind.

But I had begun to notice this audible sound-stream, this 'sound of silence', and I had also been contemplating a kind of *koan*, a conundrum about impermanence. 'All conditions are impermanent!' — I went through that for many years, just observing impermanence. And I began to wonder, 'Is there anything that isn't impermanent?' I had assumed there wasn't 'because Buddha's right, everything is impermanent!' So when I first noticed this 'sound of silence' I thought, 'Well that too is impermanent.' But then I began to question it. Is it impermanent in terms of experience? My ability to stay with it is impermanent — I can forget it and get carried away — but is it really always present like space? We don't usually notice space because we are so obsessed with the things within it, but it is always here. So I noticed the 'sound of silence'; and then I notice that it is unconditioned — 'There is the unconditioned, and therefore there is an escape from the conditioned.' I saw this 'sound of silence' as the unconditioned because it didn't disrupt any condition. It was like the background for conditions in the same way that space is the background for form. Space doesn't make form disappear; forms appear and disappear within space. So, this perspective puts one in this state of the unconditioned, of awareness, of the 'sound of silence'. Thinking then arises and ceases within that.

You can then be aware of thinking and of emotional habits — especially strong emotional experiences where the energy lingers — and you can stop the process. You can stop anger and stop thinking about it, but there remains a lingering energy. If that goes unrecognized and unaccepted, however, it becomes the cause of further thinking. If somebody says something that makes me angry, my thinking process gets going: 'That person is wrong! He's a bad person and he shouldn't have spoken to me like that. Last year he said something that he shouldn't have, and five years ago he insulted the Buddha, and twenty years ago . . !' And I can remember every single thing he did that he shouldn't have done — when I'm angry — even though he might have lived most of his life as a saint. When you are angry the emotion prevents any pleasant, flattering thoughts about the person you are angry with. By resting in this 'sound of silence', however, I become aware of any lingering energy — the kind of feeling that would start me thinking again with angry thoughts and memories — and by being patient with it, I can recognize the presence of anger as well as its absence. So, I can be consciously aware of the presence of a condition, my attachment to it, then non-attachment and its cessation. And I realize that the absence of anger is 'like this'. This is discerning the way it is. This is the wisdom that develops through awareness when one does not just hold to views.

In Theravada Buddhism there are a lot of people who have strong views about the impermanence of all things. Even though this is a right view, attachment to it will blind us; attachment to any view even a scriptural one will blind us to the reality. You meet people who have these strong views from scriptural authority, and they can get very upset if you challenge them. This is not a disparagement of the scriptures, but of this blind clinging. This is ignorance of dhamma. Desire arises from ignorance, and then there is attachment to the desire and the result is suffering (dukkha) — this is how I investigate experience. So, one can pick up some very strong views even from the Thai Forest tradition that I trained under. It is a tradition that has a strict Vinaya discipline and a strict morality; and a sense of righteousness can arise from that. But that can create a kind of snobbery, a tendency to look down on those who aren't very strict — 'those impure monks!' At least this is how a Western conditioned mind like mine can pick up on an Asian tradition — I am not blaming it on the Thais!

When you go to an Asian country with your Western mind-set, you see things from that conditioned mind. I was brought up as a High Anglican in the States, and that left a strong impression on me. That High Church in Seattle, Washington was the only one of its kind, and its members were very snooty. They thought it was better than all the other Episcopal churches — not to mention all the other Christians! So I was brought up with that very snooty, exclusive High Church Christian thing. When I was a teenager, however, I began to feel repelled by it all. I began to notice the hypocrisy and nastiness that came from being righteous and feeling morally superior to others; and it was not a state of mind I wanted to cultivate. That was how I felt even before I came across Buddhism. Later, when I became a Buddhist monk, I went into the Thai Forest tradition; and this is a tradition which follows the Vinaya very strictly. The teacher, however, happened to be wise, so there was the option of using wisdom with this tradition rather than just clinging to the outward form.

Ajahn Chah's genius was in getting us to see suffering, its causes, and its cessation — the teaching of the Four Noble Truths and Dependent Origination — which are incredibly skilful tools for investigation. These are not doctrinal positions to take — they don't make sense in that way — but are practical ways of helping us to look at things in a way we would not unless coming across teachings like these. The thinking mind is dualistic — its function is just on that level — and it is linear. So when you hold onto thinking, you go from one thought to another. If there is 'good' there is always 'bad'; if there is 'right' there is always 'wrong'. And that creates doubt. Thinking can be a skilful means, but as an end in itself it ends in despair. If you think too much, you can't do anything, and inevitably that resolves itself in feelings of insecurity and doubt — unless you have the kind of willpower that holds to a viewpoint by pushing away anything that disagrees with it. But the result of clinging to 'I'm right and everybody who disagrees with me is wrong' — if you become aware of the reality of that feeling — is not a peaceful mental state. To feel everyone is a big threat unless you can force them to agree with you, is a hellish mental state in itself. Is that the way we want to live our lives? Is that liberation?

The thinking mind is also a hierarchical structure, so a word like 'nibbāna' tends to get placed at the top; it is the supreme, the ultimate state in Buddhist terminology, the *summum bonum*, the apex, the best, the superlative. *Nibbāna* then becomes just a remote possibility, doesn't it? If we put it at the peak — as the ultimate attainment — most of us would feel it was beyond us. We would think, 'Oh, last night I had these dreams! And somebody upset me yesterday! And this morning at breakfast I was thinking mean, nasty thoughts! I'll never get to *nibbāna*.' So *nibbāna* gets turned into some kind of goal to be attained. But the Buddha's emphasis was on awareness, not on attaining anything. And whatever we think awareness is, it isn't that; it isn't the concept we have. This is why the encouragement in Buddhism is to recognize, to be aware rather than to think we *should* be aware all the time. It isn't a matter of trying to *make* ourselves aware, but rather of recognizing that awareness is the attentive state in the present. If we try to force it, we miss it. *Nibbāna* is a reality; it isn't an ideal, and it isn't beyond the average person's capability. On the thinking level, we might put it as the ultimate attainment — 'Have you realized *nibbāna*? Have you reached it?' Nobody dare say they have; and if you are a monk you can be disrobed for saying so — it sounds so egotistical. The point is, *nibbāna* is not a matter of attainment, but of awareness and the cultivation of awareness. Generally, in the Thai Forest tradition, *nibbāna* means 'the reality of non-attachment' or non-self. And this isn't about wiping out the personality because we think we shouldn't have one; it is rather about realizing non-personality. And this is what awareness is; awareness is non-personal, empty, pure, unconditioned; it isn't even an 'it'. This is where you try to be accurate with words, but can't!

The Buddha pointed to liberation from suffering: 'There is
the unconditioned; there is escape from the conditioned.' What
is that, then, in terms of here and now? This is an inquiry; this
is looking into the moment. What is possible here and now that
I can recognize and rest in even within the midst of emotional
turmoil? It is this stillness, this 'sound of silence', this audible
sound-stream which underlies everything, which underlies even
emotional upheaval, even music, even Bach or Beethoven, jazz
or the sound of the chainsaw or the lawnmower at Amaravati.
There is a lot of grass at Amaravati and when you are teaching a
retreat this incredibly loud lawnmower comes in — everybody
looks round! Tuning into the 'sound of silence', however, gives
a base even for seeing one's irritation at the sound of the lawnmower. So, how does one develop this in terms of the unconditioned, uncreated, unborn? Notice how language works. You can
talk about the conditioned, the created, the born, the formed, imagination, images, icons, concepts, thoughts, doctrines, dogmas,
opinions, views and everything. These are formed states, aren't
they? And then the unformed — what is that? Can you think of
the unformed? You have a word, you have the negation of the
word 'formed', but you can't make an image of the unformed,
can you? But you can recognize it! It isn't a matter of finding
something called the 'unformed' or the 'uncreated' or *nibbāna*', but of recognizing that the unformed is — 'this'! Space is
the same. Here we are in this room and someone says, 'There's
space in this room,' and suddenly you are aware of it. You are sitting in it — it's all around you — and yet you might never have
noticed it before. So this kind of practice has given me a stability,
a kind of inner stillness.

We talk about 'the still point', 'the inner stillness', 'the un-
shakeableness'. Now, if we stay with this stillness — if we are
this way — then we have perspective on the things that are
shakeable. I can be aware of my emotional reactions to praise
and blame, success and failure, pain and pleasure, but there is a
sense of liberation. Now, if I trust this, I don't really suffer; there

is no suffering in it. Once I forget it, of course, and go back into the conditioned realm, there is a sense of loneliness. It might not be extreme, but there is a sense of something wrong, something threatening, some kind of doubt. This seems to hang around the thinking process and the formed world; it is *dukkha*, in other words; that is its nature. The same with beauty. It isn't that beauty is not beautiful, but attachment to it puts us into the state of unease, of being bound to a condition no matter how good it is. That is why religious fanatics — those who hold to doctrines and get caught in the divisive tendency of quoting, of being right, of being orthodox and condemning anyone who conflict with them — are not in a peaceful mental state. That is not the way of *nibbāna*; that is not the way of the unconditioned. It might be 'right', but it is not liberating. To be 'right' is not liberation.

Being Awareness Itself

S itting quietly, being receptive, listening with awareness to the sounds of the traffic outside, having a sense of non-discrimination, and allowing everything to be what it is at this moment just like the Bodhisattva Avalokiteśvara who listens to the sounds of the universe. What I am encouraging is an attitude of letting go, of relaxing, of non-attachment, of nothing to do, of nothing to attain, of nothing to become — whilst being alert, awake, attentive, receptive. You can be aware of external things — the sounds, the temperature, what passes in front of your eyes, odours, sensations — and you can be aware of what is happening inside — your reaction to that fire alarm that went off a minute ago, maybe, or the traffic which you find too noisy, or whatever. Being aware like this gives you a space in which to notice the way things impinge on your body and mind, and your emotional reactions to them — the liking, disliking, wanting, not wanting, approving and disapproving. In this, your position is as awareness itself, not trying to control the situation according to what you like, but allowing everything to be the way it is, being this knowing, being this infinity, this pure, conscious, non-personal reality.

I am pointing to infinity; that which is immeasurable. Much of the insight meditation taught these days seems to be a kind of obsession around impermanence. Those who attend *vipassanā* courses are told to contemplate impermanence — which is certainly good instruction — but they become so busy noting impermanence they don't notice the very noting itself, this very awareness itself. This is just my impression, anyway. It is following an instruction which says that all conditions are impermanent, so then we get the idea and begin to notice that thoughts are impermanent, sounds are impermanent, body is impermanent, seasons, times, emotional states and subtle physical feelings are all impermanent. It is that which is aware, however, — the awareness itself — which is the path; it is as simple as that! Awareness, mindfulness, is the gate to the deathless. The deathless has no boundary; it is infinite and not subject to birth and death. So, this belief that everything is impermanent that some people do have in the Theravada school — 'and that's it!' — is a kind of dismissal of experience. This is the result of reading the scriptures in a certain way.

One can grasp impermanence as a doctrine: 'If you're a Buddhist you have to believe everything is impermanent!' But 'everything is impermanent' is not a doctrinal position to take. That isn't the point, is it? There is no value in believing that everything is impermanent. If you are going to believe anything, believe in unconditional love or a benevolent God, or something that is at least beautiful and will bring some happiness, more happiness at least than just believing that everything is impermanent. So, insight meditation is not about believing in impermanence, it is about 'investigating' and 'looking into' — these are the kinds of words used in the Pali Canon — 'reflecting', 'observing', 'noticing'. There is nothing in the Pali Canon about believing in doctrines. There is no stated teaching in Buddhism that you have to accept, hold to, and experience life from. The Buddha pointed to awareness, to waking up; and that isn't a doctrine; it is an immanent act. 'Wake up!' isn't just 'I believe in waking up' (which sounds like a British comedy!) it is an encouragement, a pointing to, a kind of cutting through things.

Now, in the Theravada there are these teachings about 'the immeasurables' (space, consciousness, nothingness, and neither-perception-nor-non-perception); and they can get turned into very high attainments — 'First you get the four *jhānas* (absorptions) and then the four immeasurable *jhānas*.' When I first came across this, it all seemed very difficult to me. I struggled even with the first *jhāna*, just wilfully trying to get the first *jhāna* and reading the *Visuddhimagga (The Path of Purification)*. The point is, I am not a faith person; in fact I have a rather sceptical nature. The villagers in Thailand, on the other hand, have great faith in the teacher; or at least those people around Ajahn Chah's monastery did. They had tremendous faith in what he said, so if Ajahn Chah said 'do this, concentrate on that', they would just do it without question — and then get the *jhānas*! If he said 'do this and do that' to a Western monk, he would respond with, 'Why? What's the point?' But you have to have faith in what you are doing because even if you become very concentrated and go into absorption, once you doubt it, it disappears just like that. Sceptical doubt is one of the destroyers of these states.

Having a kind of sceptical nature myself, I couldn't do these things by just following instructions from the teacher; I tended to think, 'Well, I don't know whether the teacher's right!' Rather than debating the point endlessly with myself, however, I began to develop doubt as a technique. This was, in some ways, the result of reading about the Chan *hua-tou* and the Zen *koan* as the means for dealing with doubt. In these methods you use doubt deliberately; you actually cultivate it, in fact. And you find that doubt stops the thinking mind. You can't figure out a *koan*; you can never come up with the right answer to a *koan*; they don't make sense on that level. 'What is your original face before you were born?' — you could spend a lifetime trying to figure that one out. But any question will stop the wandering mind. What is the answer to 'Who am I?' If you ask yourself something like that, there will be a gap, a space, where you are *not* thinking. So you deliberately ask yourself a question and then consciously note the absence of thought. I found this a very useful method because of my sceptical nature; I used the sceptical tendency within myself as a skilful means — and began to recognize infinite space.

Space is around us all the time, just visually. But observe how you have to withdraw your attention from the things *in* the space in order to become aware of it. This was a discovery to me. I would think, 'Of course there's space!' but never really allow myself to be fully spacious; I just took it for granted. Then I asked myself, 'What if I get rid of everything? What if I get rid of the people in the room, then the room itself, then the house, the trees, the world, and . . ? But that is annihilation! Or is space that which allows everything to be?' The space in this room is an important thing, isn't it? We wouldn't be able to use it if there were no space in it. One also begins to realize that by withdrawing one's fascination for people and objects, space has no boundary. Where does space end in terms of now? And consciousness — where does that end?

Consciousness is a big subject these days, and there are a lot of theories about it, but few people in the Western world seem to quite know what it is. We are, of course, all conscious at this moment; it is a natural state, not an artificial one, so we don't create it. It isn't male or female or anything other than consciousness. And it doesn't have any boundaries to it. We do, however, create things *in* consciousness, like thoughts, and we attach to those thoughts and those emotions and create ourselves into 'I am Ajahn Sumedho!' That is a condition I create. Consciousness combined with 'Ajahn Sumedho' then results in the interpretation of experience from this person called 'Ajahn Sumedho' — 'my life, my things, my way, my opinions . . .' Now, with awareness we notice that the ego (*sakkāyadiṭṭhi*) depends on thinking and attachment to memory, names, ideas and views, and that if we stop thinking, consciousness is still here and that it is a state of intelligence. Consciousness without thinking is not a dull state; we do not go into a trance when we are aware but not thinking; we do not become zombies when in awareness. Awareness is very bright, in fact; consciousness is light and there is intelligence in it; and it doesn't seem to have any boundary to it. Infinite consciousness, then, is — 'like this', no-thing-ness.

Now, the fourth of the immeasurable *jhānas* is 'neither-perception-nor-non-perception', and that is a mind-boggler, isn't it? What is neither-perception-nor-non-perception? You might think, 'Well, that's for very advanced people, obviously. Probably only the Dalai Lama knows that one!' But actually the 'sound of silence' serves quite well for that. This is looking at practical means rather than merely being fascinated by the intellectual side of things with its terms and speculations about meanings. These teachings apply to reality. The Buddha always pointed to reality rather than to ideas, ideals, or the future. Buddhism isn't about the future, about the next lifetime or some promised state you will reach if you obey all the moral precepts or anything like that; it is about the here and now: 'There is, bhikkhus, the unconditioned, unborn, uncreated, unformed. And because there is the uncreated, unborn, unformed, unconditioned, there is escape from the created, the conditioned, the formed.' I think this is a brilliant metaphysical statement. It is complete in itself, slightly repetitious, but that is what the texts tend to be. 'Because there is the unborn, uncreated, unformed, unconditioned, therefore there is escape from the born, the created, the formed, the conditioned.' Now, that is a statement. The created and formed are the Five Aggregates[35] and the six spheres (āyatana)[36]. We experience consciousness through the senses, through thought, emotion, sight, smell, taste, touch, and hearing. So, to us consciousness is a sensory experience, and then it is interpreted, always, in terms of 'me' — 'I am this person; these are my feelings, my thoughts, my memories.'

When you recognize non-attachment to thought or perception, that is emptiness, that is awareness, consciousness and wisdom together. It isn't that you are not conscious with awareness; and consciousness functions even if you are totally mad or totally deluded and believing in the most absurd things. So consciousness still operates even though you are not awake and aware of how things really are but merely operating from conditioning . Then

---

35 Form, feeling, perception, mental formations, consciousness.

36 Six spheres (āyatana): the five sense-organs and consciousness.

you are a victim of life. You make yourself into a victim because conditioning isn't always going to be good conditioning , is it? We get a lot of rubbish in our cultural conditioning . Lies and deceit and hypocrisy are part of any cultural conditioning with ideals about how things *should* be. An ideal is a thought, isn't it? It is the very best, the superlative, and has no life. It doesn't breathe or feel anything. That is why idealistic people sometimes lack feeling or empathy with suffering. You can be very idealistic and quite cold-hearted. Somebody is suffering, and you say, 'You shouldn't suffer. You're a Buddhist! — so your mother and father have just died and your cat has been kidnapped and the electricity has been cut off in your house, that's just . . . Well, you shouldn't suffer like this — you're a Buddhist!' Sometimes people are very idealistic about Buddhists, aren't they? 'You're a Buddhist! Why are you upset by anything?'

We can idealize Buddhism and see everyone here as Buddha-*rūpas* made out of bronze or marble. But notice that even though a Buddha-*rūpa* is beautiful, it doesn't feel anything. We, on the other hand, are in a state of feeling, of sensitivity, of consciousness. The human body from birth to death is subject to an unrelenting procession of all the things in the universe affecting it, and one has no control over it. We do try to control things and to protect ourselves, of course, because in a way it is all quite frightening. It can be terrifying to think of our position in the universe and all the things that are affecting us at this very moment, so we tend to restrict ourselves to things that we *can* handle such as beliefs, systems, and conventions. The Buddha, however, encouraged us to investigate the way it is — investigating not judging — and simply recognizing that it is 'like this'.

All conditions are impermanent. We therefore begin to notice our feelings, thoughts, and energetic physical and sensory experiences in terms of the characteristic of change rather than in terms of like or dislike. But that which is aware of change — what is that? Can one condition know another condition? If all conditions are impermanent, can *this* condition know *that* condition? What is it that knows the conditioned? Is that a condition? This is an inquiry. I am not expecting an answer. Some people say, 'Everything is conditioned, so that which is aware of change is conditioned just like everything else.' But in terms of this moment here and now, what is that which is aware of, say, this clock? Consciousness is awareness, isn't it? I am not projecting anything onto this clock; I am just aware of it as it is. This awareness receives the clock, but it also receives everything else. I can focus on just this clock or open to everything so that the clock and you and the ceiling and everything is included — because consciousness is not such that you need to concentrate on one thing; you can concentrate on one thing and open to everything. This is *samatha-vipassanā* practice. *Samatha* is the focusing on one thing, and *vipassanā* is mindfulness which is open, non-discriminative, non-judgemental, non-selective, choiceless — and yet is the knower, the observer. Now, this is recognition of the way it is, of dhamma (putting it into Pali terms); it is 'like this'. This space is 'like this'; consciousness is 'this way'. It is a fact; it is reality; it is not believing or disbelieving any theory about consciousness or about space. It is real. Space, consciousness — there is nothing mysterious about them; they are simply recognized.

Over the years I have used what I call 'the sound of silence' which I find easily accessible and for me works. I am aware of it right now while I am talking to you. It is not a matter of having to shut my eyes and close you off in order to contact it. Like space or consciousness, it is behind everything and allows everything to be what it is — because it is non-discriminative, non-judgemental. Whatever I experience through this form at this time — pleasant, painful, beautiful, ugly, right, wrong, intelligent, stupid — it all belongs. Even stupidity belongs if that is what arises in the present. So when you recognize the way it is, then 'all conditions are impermanent', and the deathless *(amatadhamma)*, the deathless realm *(amarāvatī)*, immortality or whatever you want to call it, is 'just this'; it is awareness itself. This is what the

Buddha was pointing to; and this is the opportunity we human beings have. We are not just conditioned creatures hopelessly trapped in conditioning . This opportunity for awakening, this waking up, is the Buddha's compassion, and it is very simple. It isn't a question of having to cultivate refined states and change our conditioning . Maybe we had some pretty bad conditioning as a child, then got rid of it and cultivated some refined, lovely, beautiful conditioning to live with. But not many of us can do that. And the ego gets involved with that as well — 'I'm above it all! I'm beyond the vulgar herd. The world is much too coarse for me and I have to live in a realm of controlled refinements.' We become like one of these Thai orchids that would die in the British winter if we were put outside; we wouldn't cope!

Whatever the conditioning — coarse, vulgar, refined or what-ever — is not the point. The point is that all conditions are im-permanent. It isn't a matter of believing this, of course, but of exploring it, of seeing it for yourself and then inquiring, 'Well, what is permanent? Can one condition know another?' Maybe you will form some idea that consciousness is a condition which is somehow above all other conditions and can know those other conditions as conditions. I have known people play tricks with their intellects like this. They get the idea that consciousness is a special condition. Now, these are just words, and you have to recognize that we are the ones who create words; they are there-fore limited. 'Consciousness' is also a word we have created. None of this has any word, really. It isn't a matter of trying to make consciousness fit into our definition of consciousness; it wouldn't work like that because then you are stuck with specu-lating about the nature of consciousness.

If you trust in awareness, you realize that consciousness is a natural state. When a baby is born it is a consciousness being; it is a human body that is conscious. Consciousness, then, is nat-ural and cannot be culturally perverted by anything. And that which is natural — that which *is* according to the natural law — is what we really mean by 'dhamma'. We are experiencing consciousness through separate forms. We each experience through 'this' body and the *kamma* of 'this being here'. If we recognize pure consciousness, we then have perspective on the limitations and conditions of the physical body and the emotional habits we have, the memories we have, and the 'self'. And we realize that consciousness has no personal quality. We create the personal, and consciousness then combines with the sense of being a person. If we let go of 'the person', there is just pure consciousness which has no boundaries. And this is immeasurable.

Recognize that to us the universe is mysterious. There is so much out there we simply don't know about; we don't even know what is in the middle of this planet. We also feel separate from the universe, and separate in time and space — I am here and you are there — 'So how do we know our *mettā*[37] practice is helping anyone?' I get asked this question all the time. 'We think we're spreading loving-kindness *(mettā)*, but how do we know it's doing any good? We're sitting here in a nice place like this saying "may all beings be free from suffering!" But I don't think it's doing any good, you know . . . sounds pretty weak, actually, a bit wet.' When you begin to see that consciousness is unified, however, that it is one — and you can't think too much about this because it is a bit of a mind-blowing experience — there is a sense of the power of consciousness, of intelligence, of wisdom; you begin to recognize that which is natural, that which is not created by yourself and not created by Buddhism or any other religion. It is just dhamma, just the way it is. This unity, this universe, this oneness, this consciousness and our relationship to it as a separate entity is then seen in terms of dhamma rather than in the conventional sense of 'I am this person sitting here and there are those people over there, and there are those foreigners, those refugees and all those people trying to get into England,' in the way that some people do if they see the world as a threatening place. In meditation we begin to tune into this universal level by letting go, letting go of this blind holding to conditioned

---

37 Meditation on *mettā* (loving-kindness to all beings).

phenomena. Letting go is not a rejection of anything; it is merely relaxing the intensity of fear and ignorance that holds us to conditions without even realizing how painful and miserable it makes us feel. See 'letting go', then, as opening, receiving, as nothing to fear, and begin to recognize space, consciousness and the 'sound of silence'. This is just a recommendation, of course. The point is, we don't create these things — they are here and now — and yet we might never notice them. If we recognize them, however, we get some perspective on conditions. Then, in terms of living in society, we might still want to do good and refrain from doing bad, we might still help society, work for the welfare of others and try to promote harmony between nations and religions. It isn't a matter of being too ethereal to deal with anything practical; it is just that we no longer come from a place of idealism.

I used to be terribly idealistic, but gradually became disillusioned with every idealistic movement I ever belonged to. It didn't take long after joining some peace movement to realize how unpeaceful peace movements can be! — because peace is an ideal, isn't it? Do people really want peace? If life gets too peaceful, it might seem boring to some. Just imagine a news programme that goes: 'Well, today there is peace in Europe, peace in the Middle East, peace in Britain, peace in America, and peace in Africa. The whole world is peaceful.' Then imagine that being said the following day, and day after day. You would stop listening, wouldn't you? As much as people long for peace, they usually want it when they don't feel peaceful — 'I just want some peace!' But do they really want it, or do they just want a life which gives them what they want without too many obstructions to their desires?

If enlightenment means seeing things as they really are, is that what we actually want? As an ideal it might sound great, but what about the reality of it? There are certain things we would like to get rid of, but there are others that we are attached to, some quite nice things. This is where, with insight, we see the nature of clinging rather than just holding to an idea that we shouldn't cling to anything. The point is, if you are going to cling, really cling and observe the result of that. Don't just be caught in the idealism of 'I shouldn't be attached to anything', because that is another attachment, another ideal. The reality of this moment is that if I am feeling mean and nasty, and somebody says, 'A Buddhist monk should be a moral example to us all! You've been a monk for forty years; you should be beyond petty anger and mean-heartedness; I'm completely disillusioned with you!' I think, 'Oh, I've let everybody down. My life has been a waste,' and I start feeling sorry for myself. What I am willing to do now, however, is to study being nasty. With the determination of not letting it out on others, I now really cling to this nasty feeling, just feel it and know it for what it is. Naturally, clinging to such a thing is suffering *(dukkha)*, but feeling guilty about it and wanting to get rid of it is also suffering.

I am an idealistic person so I don't want nasty states. I want to be this impeccable, wonderful monk for everyone all the time — this unrelenting, permanently compassionate and understanding monk. As an ideal I would like to be that for society. The realities of being human, however, are that some days I wake up and can't stand anyone. But I have studied this grumpiness, this negativity and the guilt connected to it — 'I shouldn't feel like this! A good monk shouldn't think like this!' I have deliberately watched myself feeling guilty until I have had insight into the suffering of clinging. And denial or resistance is also clinging, not letting go, not resolving the problem — that is attaching through aversion. I then began to see, really see, that attachment to any condition — fear, guilt, or a sense of oneself as anything good or bad — is *dukkha*. And more and more one then trusts in the awareness, because awareness allows you to see and let go. You can't make yourself into an aware person, of course; that would be another delusion. Awareness as a natural state, like consciousness, is so normal that the thinking mind can't conceive it. That is why it is undefinable — yet it is recognizable. If I were to try to define space, I could maybe give you formulas and refer to various scientific opinions about it — maybe even recommend particular books and give you a bibliography on the subject — yet space is right here! So what is the point of trying to define it? It is 'this'; it is here and now! The same with consciousness. What is consciousness? The more I try to think about it and define it, the more I get caught up in proliferating views and speculations, when actually it is the natural state — it is 'just this'.

So Buddha-dhamma is awakening to the way it is. And from this we have perspective on the conditioned realm, which for us is our real world. We are committed to the conditioned realm and believe in it. Every society is committed to their conventional view of the world. So we can see that the Buddha went against everything, really, because awakening to the way it is is different from grasping conditioned phenomena and becoming conditioned personalities. We are told what is right, wrong, good, bad, who we are, what we should and should not be, what we should believe in and what not to believe in; and we get caught in conditioning . A lot of it is quite good conditioning — nothing wrong with a lot of it — but still conditioning is not understanding, and still it is the cause of *dukkha*, unsatisfactoriness and unhappiness.

Information Never Cracks the Puzzle

A t ease and relaxed but attentive, awake and aware with the attitude of the knower, the observer, just witness the feelings, emotions, thoughts, memories and sensations that come and go; just observe the breathing, the experience of the body sitting, and maybe the 'sound of silence' (the background to the sounds of the traffic). This attitude of being here and now in the present is what we call 'cultivation' *(bhāvanā)*, which is reminding oneself that there is only the present. The body is present now — it is 'like this'; the breathing is now — it is 'like this'; the 'sound of silence' is 'like this'. Be aware of your mental state, your mood — right now. Is it happy, sad, confused, peaceful, anxious or worried? The quality of your mental state is not the issue here because you are not being the judge or owner of what is present but only the witness. Many experiences don't really have a clear-cut quality to them, do they? You might feel confused, uncertain, anxious, a lack of clarity and a general feeling of unease, sadness or loneliness, but reflecting that 'it is like this' or 'this is the way it is' is using the thinking process not to define or judge but to point to — 'My mood at this moment is like this.' By just thinking these words, you become aware of your mental state, while at the same time being aware of the body and the breath. So this is discerning rather than discriminating. It isn't a judgemental process but an observing, a witnessing without judging anything as right, wrong, good or bad.

It takes determination to trust this kind of awareness, however, because one's conditioning tends always to go towards being judgemental and to think in terms of, 'I shouldn't feel like this! I don't know what to do! How should I meditate?' Whatever you are feeling, however, even if you feel confused about everything, just recognize it — 'Confusion is like this'. Be the one that is aware, not the one that is always trying to figure things out and know everything about everything. As a human being in this position I can't know everything about everything — yet I can know 'this'. Know what you can know! Recognize that knowing is 'this'!

We have this sense of 'I am', and I say 'I am Ajahn Sumedho'. But notice that 'I am' is more or less an acknowledgement of being present *before* any specifics are defined; it is merely a practical statement. The 'I am Ajahn Sumedho', however, aligns me with perceptions such as 'I am a male' and 'I am a Theravadan Buddhist'. But 'I am' — just thinking 'I am' — is a statement of being. And if we use universals and say 'I am love' or 'I am truth', that still isn't defined yet in a personal way. But when I go into the personal — 'I am American' — that defines me, that gives me a sense of nationality and implies all the connections with that perception of being American. Just notice the effect of such identities — 'I am a man', 'I am a woman'; now I can say 'I'm an old man'. Notice how identities trigger off emotions. Experiment, and see how powerful words and concepts can be. We can become enraged, offended, jealous, upset and worried just by the tone of someone's voice, just by the way things are said to us and by the words used. All kinds of things can be thrown at us and we can feel insulted or admired, praised or blamed. Awakened attention, awakened consciousness, however, knows this. Our relationship to conditions — words, emotions, praise, blame and all the rest — is then in the perspective of subject to object.

So what is the pure subject? Pure subjectivity at this moment is not 'I am' or 'Ajahn Sumedho'; it is consciousness from this point here. This is a conscious individual form, a human body conscious before I become 'Ajahn Sumedho'. You can be aware before you become your personality or your body or anything else; you can recognize this pure consciousness, this pure subjectivity from this point here. Then all conditions are in relationship to that. So, even the ego, even the thought 'I am' and then 'I am love' (on a grand scale) or 'I am an American', are objects in consciousness. Begin to experiment and find the way it is. It isn't a matter of belief, but of recognition. What is it to be human? Being born in a human body brings a feeling of separation — we are separate physically. But this is a conscious form, and a natural one, so it belongs in nature. The body follows the laws of nature — birth, growth, old age and death — and needs food and water in order to be sustained just like the trees and plants. It is a sensitive form — a sensitive form in a sense realm. So, begin to notice the obvious realities that you live with and might never have noticed before. We can be so bound up in the narrow conceptions of ourselves, we understand nothing other than our own needs, views, and obsessions. But in insight meditation these things are investigated.

This is not just a matter of agreeing with the Buddha — you are not trying to convince yourself Buddha is right — but of using the teachings. John was saying yesterday, for example, that the Abhidhamma can be very helpful for looking at experience, for looking at a particular angle on the here and now. I am not, of course, suggesting that you should just collect more and more information. That is useless. If you just collect information out of some kind of habitual necessity to learn more, you will never crack the puzzle; you will just always be coming from the ego, from ignorance, and will miss the point; all that knowledge will just be a burden rather than a helpful tool — a bit like carrying a toolkit round with you but not knowing how to use the tools.

I have at various stages in my life found particular aspects of the dhamma incredibly important to me. For several years I explored just this pure subjectivity, for example, in contrast to the ego, in contrast to the sense of 'me as a person'. The personality had seemed so real and true to me — this sense of myself as a person — and I couldn't simply tell myself to believe in non-self — that didn't work. 'I'm a self that believes in *anattā* because I'm Theravadan' is a bit like exchanging jeans for brown robes. If that is all you are doing, it won't really make any difference to your life. So I had a kind of persistence which kept me going, like a rat persistently chewing through a wall until it gets to the other side. If you do that, eventually you *really* know it. Then it becomes profound knowledge rather than just the intellectual acquisition of knowledge from books or teachers. The personality is actually seen as an object. You see it in terms of the three fetters — personality belief, sceptical doubt, and attachment to conventions — the fetters that bind us to illusion and ignorance. The point always to understand is how thought works, how it functions. And in order to do that you cannot just think about it; it isn't a matter of thinking about thinking, but of observing thinking. As you observe thinking, you begin to realize that one thought connects to another in a linear way, and that it is a habit. We acquire language and then think in the pattern of language with its range of opposites and the dualism of concepts — the best and the worst, good and bad, right and wrong, day and night, male and female, and all the ideas of what should and should not be.

When I first came to this country as a monk, I assumed the role of head monk, preceptor and teacher. Later I also became the president of the Buddhist Society which was just for four years — as some of you will remember — and the Sangha in Thailand gave me permission to perform ordinations in Britain, so I became the preceptor for the whole world except Thailand! That is what they told me when I asked them, 'Where is my parish? What are my limits?' and they said, 'Well, anywhere but Thailand.' They had it all organized. I would be infringing on other preceptors' rights if I started ordaining monks in Thailand. As it is now I am the preceptor of the rest of the world. So, as well as monasteries in Britain, a monastery in New Zealand was

established and one in Australia; and I started going to those
countries every two years. Another monastery was later established in California, and also others. The point is, all the things
I was doing seemed like good things at the time — and I like to
help — but I began to feel overwhelmed by my own good intentions! So I started trying to figure out how I was going to fit in
all these roles I had taken on. It wasn't that I was doing anything
bad, but I was becoming burned out; I just couldn't sustain it.
And the more I was put into these positions, the greater my sense
of responsibility and duty.

So I started investigating what I was doing in just practical
ways, on just a conventional level, to make clear intellectually
what I could offer within those roles and whether I really wanted
them. I didn't like the idea of being caught in things without using
them or understanding how they affected my conscious experience of life. At one point I began to explore them in terms of the
indriyas, the twenty-two faculties[38]. This is a rather nice chant in
itself, but was a boring nonsensical list to most of us — we didn't
really know what it meant — but I found that chanting this, fixed
certain concepts in my mind and gradually I began to feel I
knew what it meant. Being human had always been something I
had regarded as common sense, something I had never given any
serious attention to, just always assuming I was a human being
and that was that! And actually, to me, there were things more
important than being human — like being an ajahn and teaching
the dhamma. This seemed much more important than just being
human. Anyway, there came a time when I thought I should give
up being president of the Buddhist Society because I wasn't really doing any good there; and as monks and nuns gained seniori-
ty, they started taking on some of the teaching duties and going
to conferences. Gradually, then, all this brought to me a feeling

---

38 The twenty-two *indriya:* eye, ear, nose, tongue, body, mind, femininity,
masculinity, vitality, bodily pleasant feeling, bodily pain, gladness,
sadness, indifference, faith, energy, mindfulness, concentration, wisdom,
the assurance 'I shall know what I did not yet know', the faculty of highest
knowledge, the faculty of one who knows.

of being part of the human race! I began to appreciate the common ground of being human. What I am pointing to is the ability to put our special positions into perspective. If I just see myself as the abbot, the senior monk, the teacher, and the preceptor, I always identify with special positions and relate to the monks and nuns — even the people I see every day — in those terms. You can get incredibly lonely that way. You can feel isolated from the people you are actually living with if your identity is always with the special roles you have.

Thai people, I find, generally have an intuitive acceptance of their basic humanity and seem to be at ease with each other in a way that we are not. The Tibetans, I think, are the same. The Dalai Lama, for example, is very special — perhaps the most special living Buddhist at this time — yet he always seems to be at ease. When he came to Wembley a few years ago, he sat up on the stage with thousands of people surrounding him and was totally relaxed as if to say, 'There's nothing special about me, nothing to be frightened of.' But for myself, being a teacher and preceptor and president of the English Sangha Trust and so forth, brought this sense of responsibility. These are responsible positions, and anyone from a cultural background like mine having been brought up to 'be responsible' meant that to be irresponsible was despicable. One of the worst insults anyone can throw at me is, 'You're irresponsible!' That shatters me. Even if I were to go around taking on all sorts of responsibilities, however, I know that inevitably somebody is going to say 'You're irresponsible!' Really, then, it is a question of dealing with how words affect me.

So I find we can learn a lot by observing just how our emotional reactions are triggered off by the way people say things, by their tone of voice and the words they use. We can discern what intimidates us, what pushes our buttons so that we go over the top and react too strongly. As humans, we are emotional, sensitive, intelligent beings, and anger is part of that human experience, as too is hatred, fear, jealousy and the sexual drive.

These are primal emotions that are basic to mammalian creatures. Dogs and cats have the sexual drive and get angry, greedy, jealous and frightened. The point is to put these primal emotions into the context of 'the way it is' rather than trying to justify them by saying, 'I'm *only* human!' So, we can see it in terms of 'being human is like this'. Then we will appreciate being human; we will begin to empathize and understand humanity in general, and to find the common ground that we all share as members of this species.

Eventually I realized that the special roles I had taken on were ideals — wanting to be this very good monk, this excellent teacher, this very responsible president, or this impeccable bhikkhu. They are beautiful ideals, and one can get a lot of praise for them. People say, 'You're impeccable! You're a great teacher! You're a very wise man!' It makes you feel good to have people say things like that to you. But then of course the opposite also comes — the criticism, the aversion, the anger and rage. I got a letter last week from somebody calling me 'a white bastard'. That is the first time anyone has said that to me. I don't even know who sent it — obviously someone I had offended! Anyway, reflecting on the way it is is a skilful means which stops thinking and the attempt to try to figure it all out. Each one of us is in a separate form 'knowing' from this position, from the position of being incarcerated within this body, the body that we identify with. Putting it into the perspective of recognizing just the way it is, then, I observe that consciousness within this form is 'like this' rather than getting caught up in projections, loves, hates, values, and habits.

The personality belief, sceptical doubt and attachment to conventions are human creations; they are not natural conditions that we are born with. When these are recognized for what they are, that is what we call 'stream-entry'. Stream-entry is seeing beyond the artificial conditions that human beings create. This is when we let go of the illusions we create around the thinking process, around attachment to memories and the illusion of being a personality, those cultural and social identities. What we are then left with are the natural conditions.

So, then there is the once-returner, and the once-returner still has sexual desire and anger because these are natural energies. Notice that most of us identify personally with sexual desire, and have strong cultural views about it — about whether it is good or bad, impure or pure, dirty, pornographic or unmentionable in public. In modern society people are obsessed by sexuality, and there is a great deal of guilt and self-aversion around it, a lot of po-faced disapproval of anything smacking of immorality — which often means sex outside of marriage. That is how I was brought up, anyway. But that is all cultural, isn't it? That is attachment to conventions and personality belief. I remember as a child never speaking the word 'sex' aloud in public (this was back in the forties in America). When we were being cheeky, we would spell it out s-e-x. But nowadays there doesn't seem to be even any censorship on American films they show on aeroplanes. The point to note, of course, is that sexuality is a natural energy. We wouldn't be here if it didn't exist. Anger is also natural — a kind of necessity for self-preservation — as well as fear and jealousy. You see dogs and cats getting jealous. So I am putting these emotions in the context of natural energies rather than judging them to be right or wrong and wondering whether one *should* be jealous or should just have gladness and empathy, never being jealous or angry and always having understanding and compassion for everybody. To put it in terms of how things should be, of course, is an ideal, isn't it? So if you blow up over something and feel things you shouldn't, you also feel guilty and ashamed, and hope nobody knows!

With stream-entry, then, you still have the personal identities, the moral judgements and social attitudes, but they are put into context; you see them rather than just get bound by them. If you don't see them in terms of what they really are and how they relate to you, they become habitual. But if you are capable of being objective and recognizing these natural energies — the mammalian energies of the body and of this planet — your relationship to them changes from judging them on a personal level where they become complicated and neurotic, to recognizing them. Taking a life of celibacy as Buddhist monks, of course, means we do not act on sexual energy, but neither do we suppress it. It is a matter of recognizing sexual energy and learning from it. Then more and more one trusts the knowing rather than getting intimidated by the energies that one experiences through the body, or the conditioning of the mind, or the emotional results *(vipāka-kamma)* from identities of the past. What I am saying is suppression implies aversion, resistance and getting rid of. But by observing what is happening, you recognize and then find a skilful way of not perpetuating it, not increasing it or reinforcing habit-tendencies around it. With anger or aversion — which are also strong emotions — people can become very afraid. There is a lot of anxiety, worry and fear around one's ability to become angry, and also how to deal with other people's anger. These things can be very threatening. For myself, by developing awareness of the 'sound of silence', I have at least been able to stop the proliferating tendencies around these emotions; just by interrupting anger, the tendency to resist it, suppress it, or follow it, has faded away.

I spent some time once on a tea estate in Darjeeling, and the owners took me to the market one day and bought me a Tibetan *mala.* It was a most unusual one made out of yak bone and inlaid with coral and turquoise, and instead of round beads it had these flat discs. I used it by tuning into the 'sound of silence' and moving these discs across one at a time very slowly, at the same time sustaining my attention on the silence. I would do five of these, maybe, just as a way of training myself to recognize the 'sound of silence' and be completely concentrated. This stopped the proliferating tendency of thought. Then recently somebody gave me a DVD called 'What the Bleep?' Part of it is in cartoon-form about how nerve-endings connect. The point they were making is that if you can separate these nerve-endings for just a few seconds, you can disengage some habit; they were talking about treating addiction. If there is no interruption, then the addiction is just reinforced. Now, that resonated with me — with my use of the 'sound of silence' — because by building up these gaps between things, just by having these spaces between anger, say — which is a pretty strong emotion — and then going into the silence for five counts like I did with the *mala* beads, somehow the anger is reduced. And sometimes after five counts, I couldn't even remember what I was angry about! It was like resting in this space, in this silence.

Now, if this method is compulsive, you are attaching to the idea again — 'I've got to do the sound of silence!' — and you miss the point. What I am suggesting is just doing it and seeing what happens. Then you have the ability to witness. The empty mind, non-attachment, is — 'this'. You know what attachment is and what non-attachment is, what grasping desire is and what non-grasping of desire is. That doesn't mean you never have desire, but that you study it, become an expert on it, and *know* it. The point to remember is that this is a desire realm; it is about the senses, about beauty and the things that attract. The things that are ugly and hideous, we don't want. So desire is a natural condition. This desire realm, this sense realm, this human realm, this sexual realm, is the way it is, and our relationship to it is knowing it, studying it, understanding it.

This, of course, is not what we are. We are not these changing conditions. Change is about death, everything taking us to death. Sexuality is about death — birth and death, beginning and ending. If that is all we are, then we are bound to die, and death is all we can hope for or expect. But awareness brings us home to the reality of deathlessness. Deathbound conditions arise and cease, come and go and change according to conditions. Instead of endlessly fumbling around in the vortex of changing conditions, therefore, have more confidence in the reality, in the deathless. With the attitude of letting go, of non-attachment and awareness, just trust in being the knowing itself without trying to become anyone who knows anything.

Test it Out!

This is the last day of the 2006 Leicester Summer School and our minds are moving towards going home, to the duties and responsibilities waiting for us. The conditioned realm is the reality of conditions changing, so we find ourselves moving according to necessities, programmes and plans. There is that which is stable and trustworthy in all this change, however, and that is the awareness. This is called the 'unshakeable deliverance of the heart'. And awareness is what 'refuge' means once we recognize it. When we take refuge in the Buddha — *Buddhaṁ saraṇaṁ gacchāmi* (I take refuge in the Buddha) — this to me implies awareness.

Now, a refuge is a safe place to be. At this moment we might think Digby Hall is a safe place, but maybe there is a suicide bomber hiding in this room! And lightning struck Beaumont Hall across the road the other day! Besides, we all have to leave today, so it can't be a refuge. The refuge, then, is — what? This is for reflection. I am not trying to tell you anything, but just bring your attention to the here and now. What is the reality? What is *nibbāna*? What is liberation? What is freedom? What is the deathless? If we just think about these things and try to figure them out, we shall get caught in doubt; it isn't a matter of trying to find answers through analysis or holding to ideas, but of trusting ourselves, learning to trust not our thinking mind but this awareness, and then resting in it so that we are actually abiding in and *being* awareness. It isn't a matter of trying to become 'somebody who is aware' any more.

The idea that we are not aware and need to develop awareness, is in itself another creation; 'I'm this person and my awareness is not very good' is a thought. It might seem on one level that we are like this, but by being aware of that very doubt makes us realize that awareness is also aware of doubt and uncertainty and insecurity. Awareness is aware of doubts about our ability to meditate, about being aware. Awareness is aware of wondering what stage we are at or what we have attained, or whether we are just hopeless cases. But wondering whether we are enlightened or just as unenlightened as ever are just ideas, just thoughts in the mind. It is not a matter of seeing ideas as right or wrong, but simply that thoughts are thoughts — they arise and cease. That is why I encourage the investigation of thinking — not by thinking about thinking, but by seeing that thoughts come and go. We can't sustain a thought. Mantra practice is about the best we can do in that direction, and even with that — even if we repeat a mantra over and over again — the experience is still something that comes and goes.

Awareness, then, is what I encourage you to acknowledge and recognize. This is the refuge. Refuge is this simple, this direct. It is a reality. The refuge isn't creating the illusion of a refuge, or some idealized refuge. Recognizing and trusting awareness is what it is about. Test it out! Put it to the test in your own life just with the irritating, frustrating problems of living as a human being in human society. If you trust this refuge and determine to use it, you can practise as life hits you, as you experience life and as your character reacts to it.

This morning at breakfast somebody was talking about meditation techniques. As we all know in the Buddhist world there are a million opinions and views about that, but I prefer to talk from my own experience. Obviously, I have used the Theravadan tradition, but I am not saying that because I have used this convention you should also use it — at least I hope it doesn't sound as though I am. How to use convention is what I am pointing to rather than suggesting you should use the conventions I use. To do that would be misleading, wouldn't it? It would imply that I have attained something through using this convention and am now somehow the authority on Buddhism so you should do what I do and believe in me! That would be reinforcing your delusions, because that is not the way it is; that is not dhamma. The point is to see through this idea that 'I am this person, this Theravadan Buddhist monk, somebody who has found the real dhamma through this practice, and this is definitely the pure, pristine Buddhist teaching!' Then somebody says, 'What about Mahayana?' And I say, 'It's *all* rubbish!' — I have heard monks talk like that, actually. But that is an opinion, isn't it? We can be very attached to opinions. Some opinions can be good — people aren't usually attached to bad ones — but being attached to a good opinion out of ignorance is still suffering. And opinions can be very convincing. Do you ever get intimidated by very confident people who are attached to good opinions? My personality is such that I easily get intimidated. Somebody says, 'I know!' and they can quote scripture too! Then I start thinking about it.

Even though my insight into awareness has been strong, I have had a resistance, a fear even, of trusting it, 'Well, I might be wrong, misguided! Maybe I'm overestimating myself.' My personality is such that I don't want to be the authority and proclaim myself as the enlightened master of the century. Megalomania has never been a particular problem of mine. I tend to move more towards self-disparagement, lack of trust, self-doubt, and a kind of cowardice — I don't dare! I don't want to stick my neck out or put myself into embarrassing positions. The fact is, once you start proclaiming yourself as something, you know, there are forces that are always going to knock you down. So you recognize the danger of proclaiming yourself as some unique, special case. But awareness is not personal. To me this is what all these teachings in the Pali Canon and so forth are pointing to. My personality is never going to be enlightened; it is never going to become anything other than a personality that arises and ceases. When I am operating from a personal level, I think in terms of, 'Well, I'm not enlightened,' — because my personality certainly isn't! My personality hasn't changed much over the years, actually. I still get tired and bored and frustrated and all the rest, personally, emotionally. The development or cultivation of awareness, however, is beyond the personal. It is seeing and recognizing that the personality is something that we create. 'I am this person, and I am this Buddhist monk' is a creation that depends on thinking and language.

That which is aware of thinking, however, is not a thought and is not a person, but it is certainly real and intelligent. In Buddhist terms that is dhamma, that is recognizing the *amatadhamma* or deathless reality, the unconditioned. By recognizing the unconditioned, you have a refuge. No matter how carried away you might become or how deluded at various times in your life, once you establish and trust in this refuge, it is always available to you. You can become totally lost in the craziest mind states, but there will be a point where you suddenly realize — ! And that is the door, that is the gate to reality again.

I used to make vows about not getting angry. This was in the early days when I was still very naïve! I would make a vow, and as soon as you do that, of course, all the forces of Māra[39] descend on you. This is why after a while I stopped making vows! I began to get the point that I was setting myself up for something to happen to make me really angry. Then I would say something terrible, blow up, feel guilty, 'Oh, I've broken my vow! I can't do it! What am I to do about all this anger? I'm not a good monk . . .' and I would just wallow in self-disparagement and guilt. I then began to realize that even if I blow it, even if I say terrible things and make an absolute fool of myself — at that point of going into 'I shouldn't have said that, I'm terrible, I broke my vow, I'm not a good monk' — that that too can be the gate. There is no need to wallow in guilt, remorse and despair every time we fail,

---

39 *Māra:* often called 'the Evil One' appears in the texts both as a real person (i.e. as a deity) and as a personification of evil and the passions, of the totality of worldly existence and of death.

because we can still trust 'this', this point of awakenedness. So this is what I recommend you do. At the point where you suddenly know that you have blown it, gone over the top and made a fool of yourself, at that point, just see 'it is like this'! And really treasure that moment, that awakenedness. That is where to put your attention and trust. Then more and more you will find the tendency to break the cyclical habit of getting angry, blowing up, feeling remorseful and guilty, making the vow again, and then going through the same thing again and again. Every time you break that cycle through awareness — and you can do it at any point — the strength of those habits are lessened. Even if you completely blow up and say terrible things, there is a point at which you can suddenly recognize it. Value that! Trust that!

Now, there are certain roles we get drawn into. Everybody here has been practising for years, but still there can be this assumption of 'I am the teacher and you are the student', that I know more than you do, that I am the authority. And if neither you nor I question this, it becomes the underlying influence, the conventional roles that we find ourselves thrown into. So I am encouraging you to observe this kind of thing, to see how easily you can get pulled into these roles. I found the same thing with my parents, even when I was fifty-five years old and the abbot of Amaravati monastery! My mother became very ill and I rushed back to California to see her, and then I lived in my parents little bungalow for about a month. After we got through the first formalities — 'Hello! Glad to see you!' — the situation sank back into the role of 'you're my mummy and daddy, and I'm your little boy' — at fifty-five! Now, that was interesting because none of us was doing it intentionally; it just seemed to happen; the old attitudes were just triggered off because we were living together again. The same applies in terms of the roles we take on, like 'I am the teacher, I am the expert and you are the student'. So I encourage you to look into these things, and to investigate on that level of personal expectation.

We might have this assumption that we are unenlightened, that our practice is nowhere and we can't meditate. Most people take that for granted; nobody as yet has announced to me that they *are* enlightened; or even if they think it they don't usually go round telling people — except maybe if they live in Totnes! So, what do you do with the assumption 'I am unenlightened and need to practise meditation in order to become enlightened in the future?' To begin with, just become aware of the 'I am'. It isn't a matter of believing or disbelieving it but of just recognizing this 'I am an unenlightened person', say. There is then the awareness of thinking it; so you are beginning to explore the awareness as well as the thoughts. The thoughts come and go, don't they? They are conditioned. The sense of 'I am' and this word 'unenlightened' is the English language (or whatever language you use); and it is something you create. You create this 'I am unenlightened'. But recognize that awareness is not thought. Awareness has no sense of 'I' about it; it isn't 'I' or 'enlightened' or 'unenlightened' or anything; it is just 'this'.

Awareness, then, is pure — pure consciousness and intelligence — which is so bound up with conditions that most of us don't know the difference between them. We experience life through our feelings, prejudices, reactions and emotions. We are convinced that the thinking process is reality, and that the sense of 'I' is an obvious reality, but when we start investigating it, deliberately thinking 'I am unenlightened', for example, we realize that awareness is one thing and language is another. Language arises and ceases in awareness. So awareness *is* before the thought 'I', then there is awareness of each word — 'I-am-unenlightened' — and after that the awareness remains; it is sustained throughout the movement of thought. So, there is awareness of thought, the feelings that the thought might bring, and any emotional reaction to that. But test this out for yourself.

I reached a point in my life when I began to ask myself whether I wanted to be this person full of doubts? Did I want to be this critical personality? And did I want to always have this sense of

'Oh, poor me!' or go on and on about one thing after another? As you get older, you know, you can become increasingly fed up with your own emotions; they've been going on for such a long time! Just by investigating awareness, then, by noticing it intentionally — not just holding to a theory about awareness any more, but by really recognizing and trusting it — it became clear to me that 'this' was my real home. I began to see that the 'I am unenlightened and I have to practise harder in order to become enlightened in the future' is personality belief, sceptical doubt and conventional reality; and I put it into the context of a mental object that comes and goes according to conditions. Now, as you affirm this sense of awareness, you are cultivating it; and the fourth Noble Truth is all about cultivating *(bhāvanā)* the awareness of whatever is happening to you wherever you are. Whether you are here or at home, driving your car, travelling on a train or whatever, it is always here and now. And as you recognize this reality, you develop that recognition. Then worldly conditions will continue to make demands on you, and you will continue to have reactions to them in the way you always have, but you will no longer be totally lost in those habit patterns or be a helpless victim of the conditioning process. It is always here and now whatever state you are in or wherever you are. The point is to see this.

When it comes to sitting meditation, just notice how you feel about the method you are using. It isn't a question of saying how you *should* feel about it, but of recognizing thoughts like, 'I've got to use this method,' or 'This method is the right one and if I practise it and am really sincere and determined, I will get a good result from it.' It might all be very good stuff, but methods are still just conditioning , aren't they? So there might be an unquestioned identity and attachment to it, or the feeling that 'because the teacher gave me this method I should use it'. How many of us have felt that we ought to meditate more than we do? 'Ajahn Sumedho says you should meditate at least one hour in the morning and one hour in the evening.' At the end of a ten-day retreat people say, 'I'm going to do that, Ajahn Sumedho; I'm really going to practise like you said,' and then you never see them again! The point is 'shoulds' are based on 'I should do this because it's good for me; all the wise people tell me so, and the Buddha said so, so I should do it; I should practise more than I do; I should go on more retreats; I shouldn't go to the pub. I'm going to give up going to the pub and those lesser things in order to devote myself to the holy life!' This is good advice, but if one is attached to ideas, what does it do? It reinforces the ego, doesn't it? Then, if you don't do what you *should* do, you feel guilty, you feel you are not a very good meditator, not a real Buddhist. Maybe you think, 'I don't dare visit Ajahn Sumedho now because he told me what I should do and I haven't done it! He's going to think I'm not very good and not worthy of his attention.' But this is all built on delusion, isn't it? It is all personality belief. So I want to stress that there is no method I am encouraging you to do except awareness of the here and now. And that is available all the time, so it is a matter of learning to trust it rather than holding to ideas about yourself and operating from the self-view. Whether that is 'a good self' or 'not a good self' is not the point; it is still delusion. What you *can* trust at every moment here and now is this awareness.

Now in life-threatening situations, you find that something happens to make you very mindful; it is automatic, spontaneous. When a tiger is chasing you, your personality isn't of any importance! Something takes over, a kind of universal intelligence, an instinct for self-preservation, and the ego isn't a problem. Notice how much neurosis there is in a country like this where there is basically the illusion of being in a safe, secure environment. Here, we can afford to be totally screwed up, can't we? We can just ride along in a society like this because there doesn't seem to be any impending danger, no worries of tigers and bears at least. Whereas out there in the jungle, in the wild, a sense of alertness develops. People also experience this in athletics and games. The self drops away and one is completely in the moment. Life in

Britain is such that one can get away with being crazy, heedless, or self-obsessed. I really appreciate this society because it is a stable one. We are not living on the edge of danger or survival here and can take a lot for granted. But even in the midst of comfort, safety, luxury, and seemingly routine ordinary British life, there is danger at every moment — the danger of falling back into delusion. People commit suicide in societies like this because of the way they think. We can carry despair, self-hatred and resentment around with us to where it fulminates and affects our daily lives, makes us chronically depressed, angry and totally miserable all the time. We can create illusions over and over again. Even so, sometimes we do see through them.

I see myself now not as a teacher but as someone who encourages people to trust themselves. If I were to say, 'Now, let me to tell you how you should practise,' that would reinforce the delusion of 'I am the teacher and you are the student; I know and you don't,' but that isn't the way it is; that isn't dhamma; that is just reinforcing your sense of acquiring knowledge from somebody else. You might acquire good and interesting knowledge — which is fine — but it is not going to be liberating; you will not be liberated through that. Liberation is now! It is this immanent reality of awareness wherever you are — on the train, in the supermarket, on a meditation retreat — and with or without a method. Have you become conditioned into believing that you have to use a particular method in order to practise? Have you got used to a method so that it has become a habit like any other? Begin to observe whether any methods you use are really just compulsive. Even the best things can become habits so that we react at the push of a button — push one button and you do *this*, push another button and you do *that*. This is the conditioning process. Awakenedness, on the other hand, is the unconditioned and can never become a habit in the way that things do when we grasp them. Yet it is real. It is enlightenment itself. We are conscious beings and this light is natural to our state. Even when we are asleep there is consciousness. We are not dead when we are asleep. Consciousness, then, is continuous. It is natural and it is light even in the dark.

I remember once being in a place that was so dark I couldn't see my hand in front of my face. My emotional reaction was, 'I can't see anything! I don't know what is there!' But then I thought, 'What is it, then, that sees darkness? I am looking at darkness; my eyes are functioning and seeing darkness.' Then suddenly it became obvious to me that consciousness is light, that even in the dark there is light if you rest in conscious awareness. What your eyes see is darkness, but that is still seeing, isn't it? We usually think of light as coming from outside — from the sun or an electric light bulb — but consciousness is light, isn't it? But this is a light that is coming from within. In terms of experience right now as an individual, awareness is light. It is seeing, knowing, dhamma; it is the way it is.

If I convince you that you are not enlightened, I am saying you are your personality, you are someone; you are this person who is unenlightened and has a lot of defilements, problems, personal difficulties and delusions. I am also saying you have to get rid of those defilements and become a person without any of them. In other words, I am saying you are not good enough the way you are and should practise hard in order to get rid of your anger, greed, neurotic habits and so forth, and that I can teach you how to do that. What would I be doing in that case? I would be reinforcing the whole delusion, wouldn't I? I would be saying that you are somebody, and that the way you are is not good enough, that there is something wrong with you, and that you have to do something in order to improve yourself, in order to make yourself better. The point is this is the world of conditioned phenomena *(saṁsāra)*; this is how it tends to work. We affect each other through approval, disapproval, reward and punishment. The way to get out of the delusion of *saṁsāra*, however, is through awareness; it isn't through going around reinforcing the sense of having to do something or having to change yourself. I encourage you therefore to trust yourself more, and to awaken.

Now, when I say 'trust yourself', people sometimes say, 'Well, you can't expect me to trust myself. I've got a lot of anger, you know, and all sorts of things. Trust myself? I wouldn't dare!' Or they think trusting themselves means trusting their views, opinions and thoughts. But that isn't it, is it? What I am talking about is a subtle recognition, an intuitive sense, a sense which is not created from memory or holding to views about yourself as a person, but is here and now, available all the time, never impossible — unless you believe it to be. If you are committed to your delusions, then the complexity you create makes enlightenment seem like an impossibility for you. But recognize, enlightenment is natural to each one of us; it is nature, not conditioned, not to be claimed as a unique gift that 'I have because I am a special kind of human being'. If you start operating in that way, you will be operating from delusion, won't you? But see that everybody is this; recognize it in everybody. When we recognize it in each other, that helps, because most of society doesn't know it, so there is this endless reinforcement of each other's delusions. We play the game, in other words; we play the games of society and go along with it; we learn how to get by and somehow survive — though we don't always!

Understanding, of course, is outside the game and outside conventions. But that isn't the annihilation of conventions; it doesn't make us say, 'Well, I'm beyond society now,' and have contempt for it. That would be the self again. As soon as you think you understand dhamma better than anyone else, you immediately fall back; you create yourself as somebody who has 'got it' as opposed to the rest of us who don't. That is back with the same personality belief. The point is, it isn't a matter of 'getting it' and then feeling proud of yourself; it is more of a humbling experience because awakenedness doesn't seem like anything at all. That is why it is so easy to overlook and doubt. In terms of worldly values, personal ambition and so forth, this awareness, this liberation, is not what one is expecting!

Glossary

[Note: The canonical texts of the Theravada school are composed in Pali and therefore Pali terms have been used throughout this work. Various Buddhist words have, however, been integrated into the English language in recent years, and these are in the Sanskrit form (of the Mahayana school), terms such as *dharma (dhamma), karma (kamma)* and *nirvana (nibbāna)*, to name the most common. The meanings, however, are more or less the same.]

ajahn (Thai) from the Pali *ācariya*: teacher (in the Amaravati community a monk or nun who has completed ten rains retreats *(vassa)*
akāliko: timeless
akuppa: unshakeable
akuppa-cetovimutti: unshakeable deliverance of the heart
amatadhamma: the deathless or the unborn
amarāvatī: the deathless realm
ānāpānasati: mindfulness of the breath
anattā: not self, no self, non-self
anicca: impermanence
arahant: the accomplished one, the liberated one, liberation of the mind, liberation through wisdom which is free from the fetters and which one has understood and realized.
ariyasacca (Four Noble Truths: (i) the truth of suffering *(dukkha)*; (ii) that all suffering is the result of craving or desire *(taṇhā)*; (iii) that the end of desire or craving results in the end of suffering *(nirodha)*; (iv) the path *(magga)* which is the means to the end of suffering is eightfold (see Eightfold Path).
āsava: taint
attā: self, ego, personality
atthangika-magga (Eightfold Path): right view *(sammādiṭṭhi)*, right thought *(sammāsankappa)*, right speech *(sammāvācā)*, right action *(sammākammanta)*, right livelihood *(sammāājīva)*; right effort *(sammāvāyāma)*, right mindfulness *(sammāsati)*, right concentration *(sammāsamādhi)*.

Avalokiteśvara *(Skt)*: the *bodhisattva* who listens to the sounds of the universe

avīci: one of the most frightful hells

avijjā: ignorance, unknowing, synonymous with delusion

āyatana: six spheres (the five physical sense-organs and sense-consciousness)

bhāvanā: mental development

bhavataṇhā: the desire to become; craving for existence

bhikkhu-sangha: community of monks

bodhisattva (Skt), bodhisatta (Pali): enlightenment being; a future Buddha

brahmacariya: pure, chaste, living the holy life

brahmavihāra: sublime or divine abode (see the four *brahmavihāras*)

Buddha-dhamma: the enlightened reality, the Buddha's teaching

Buddha-Dhamma-Sangha *(ti-ratana):* the three jewels, or the triple gem, which comprises the Enlightened One, the Buddha's teaching or reality, and the community or Buddhist monastic order.

Buddhaṁ saraṇaṁ gacchāmi; Dhammaṁ saraṇaṁ gacchāmi; Sanghaṁ saraṇaṁ gacchāmi (I take my refuge in the Buddha, in the Dhamma, and in the Sangha); the Three Refuges.

Buddha-*rūpa:* Buddha-form, Buddha-statue

cetovimutti: deliverance of the heart/mind

citta: consciousness, heart, mind

dāna: generosity

Dependent Origination: (see *paṭiccasamuppāda*)

devadūta: divine messenger; old age, sickness and death are referred to as the heavenly messengers.

devatā: heavenly being

dhamma: the nature of things; the law, doctrine, phenomena, the Buddha's teaching, manifestation of reality.

dharmakāya (Skt): truth body; the true nature of the Buddha

dhutanga bhikkhus: monks who practice special observances

dukkha: unsatisfactoriness, suffering, not getting what one wants.

ehipassiko: Come and see right now! Wake up! It's here! See for yourself! encouraging investigation.

Eightfold Path *(aṭṭhangika-magga):* right view *(sammādiṭṭhi),* right thought *(sammāsankappa),* right speech *(sammāvācā),* right action *(sammākammanta),* right livelihood *(sammāājīva),* right effort *(sammāvāyāma),* right mindfulness *(sammāsati),* right concentration *(sammāsamādhi).*

ekaggatā: unification (of mind), one-pointedness

Five Aggregates *(khandha):* rūpa, vedanā, saññā, sankhāra, viññāṇa (form, feeling, perception, mental formations, and consciousness.

Five Precepts: see *pañcasīla*

Four Noble Truths *(ariyasacca)*: (i) the truth of suffering *(dukkha)*; (ii) that all suffering is the result of craving or desire *(taṇhā)*; (iii) that the end of desire or craving results in the end of suffering *(nirodha)*; (iv) the path *(magga)* which is the means to the end of suffering is eightfold (see Eightfold Path).

Four *brahmavihāras* (sublime or divine abodes): loving-kindness *(mettā)*, compassion *(karuṇā)*, sympathetic joy *(muditā)*, equanimity *(upekkhā)*.

Four Stages of the Path: stream-enterer *(sotāpanna)*, once-returner *(sakadāgāmin)*, non-returner *(anāgāmin)*, accomplished or liberated one *(arahant)*.

Four Foundations of Mindfulness *(satipaṭṭhāna)*: contemplation of body, feeling, mind and mind-objects.

idappaccayatā: the law of conditionality: when *this* arises then *this* happens; when the conditions arise, this is the result.

indriya: faculty, (see also twenty-two *indriya*)

jhāna: meditative absorption; refers chiefly to the four meditative absorptions

kalāpa: group

kamma (Skt. karma): action (does not signify the result of actions: see *vipāka*)

karuṇā: compassion

khandha: aggregate, mass (see Five Aggregates)

kilesa: defilement, unwholesome quality, impurity

luang por (Thai): (literally 'revered father'), title of respect for an elder monk

magga: path

māna: conceit, pride; one of the Ten Fetters

ñāṇadassana: profound knowledge

mantra: a word or sound repeated to aid concentration in meditation.

mettā: loving-kindness

muditā: sympathetic joy

ñāṇa: knowledge, comprehension, intelligence, insight

nibbāna: (literally 'extinction'), freedom from suffering; the unborn or the unconditioned

nimitta: mental image, sign, mark

nirodha: cessation, extinction

opanayiko: leading onwards

paccattaṃ veditabbo viññūhi: to be experienced individually

paccaya: condition

paccuppanna: existing, present, now

pañcasīla (five moral precepts): abstaining from killing any living being, from stealing, from sexual misconduct, from lying, and from the use of intoxicants and recreational drugs.

paññā: wisdom, understanding, insight

paññāvimutti: liberation through wisdom

paṭiccasamuppāda (Dependent Origination): through ignorance are conditioned the *kamma*-formations; through the *kamma*-formations is conditioned consciousness; through consciousness are conditioned mental and physical phenomena; through mental and physical phenomena are conditioned the six bases (five physical sense-organs and consciousness); through the six bases is conditioned the impression; through the impression is conditioned feeling; through feeling is conditioned craving; through craving is conditioned clinging; through clinging is conditioned becoming; through becoming is conditioned rebirth; through rebirth are conditioned old age and death. Thus arises this whole mass of suffering again in the future.

paṭipadā: way, practice, the road, the path

pīti: rapture

pūjā: devotional observances

puthujjana: ordinary person; someone still possessed of the ten fetters

saddhā: faith

sakadāgāmin: once-returner

sakkāyadiṭṭhi: personality belief; the first of the Ten Fetters *(saṁyojana)*

samādhi: concentration; fixing the mind on a single object; one-pointedness of mind.

sāmaṇera: novice monk

samatha: tranquillity, serenity

saṁsāra: (literally 'perpetual wandering'), round of births, the continuous process of again and again being born, growing old, suffering and dying.

samudaya: origin, arising

saṁyojana: fetter (see Ten Fetters)

sandiṭṭhiko: apparent here and now

sankhāra: formation; the act of forming; having been formed

sangha: community

saññā: perception

sati: mindfulness

satipaññā: mindfulness and wisdom, awareness

satipaṭṭhāna: application of mindfulness

satisampajañña: mindfulness and clarity of consciousness or full awareness.

sīla: morality

sīladharā: ten-precept nun

sīlabbata-parāmāsa: attachment to mere rules and ritual, and conventions.

Six Realms of Existence: the heavenly realm *(devaloka)*, the jealous gods *(asura)*, the animal world, the hell state *(avīci* hell), the hungry ghosts *(petas)*, and the human realm.

sotāpanna: stream-enterer
sukha: pleasure, bliss, joy
suññatā: emptiness, voidness, non-self (see *anattā*)
taṇhā: craving
tathatā: suchness
Ten Fetters *(saṁyojana):* personality belief, sceptical doubt, clinging
    to mere rules and ritual or conventions, craving, ill will, craving for
    fine-material existence, craving for immaterial existence, conceit,
    restlessness, ignorance.
Theravada Buddhism (literally 'doctrine of the elders'), also known as the
    Southern School of Buddhism, is practised mainly in Thailand, Burma,
    Sri Lanka, Cambodia and Laos (as distinct from the Mahayana or the
    Northern School of Buddhism practised mainly in Korea, Japan, Tibet,
    and with the beginnings of a revival in China). The Theravada tradition
    is grounded in the discourses recorded in the Pali Canon.
Three Characteristics of Existence *(ti-lakkhaṇa):* impermanence,
    unsatisfactoriness, and not self *(anicca, dukkha, anattā).*
Three Refuges: *Buddhaṁ saraṇaṁ gacchāmi; Dhammaṁ saraṇaṁ
    gacchāmi; Sanghaṁ saraṇaṁ gacchāmi* (I take my refuge in the Buddha,
    in the Dhamma, and in the Sangha).
Twenty-two *indriya:* eye, ear, nose, tongue, body, mind, femininity,
    masculinity, vitality, bodily pleasant feeling, body pain, gladness,
    sadness, indifference, faith, energy, mindfulness, concentration, wisdom,
    the assurance 'I shall know what I did not yet know', the faculty of
    highest knowledge, the faculty of one who knows.
upādāna: attachment, clinging
upajjhāya: spiritual teacher or preceptor; one who ordains monks and nuns
upasampadā: full admission into the *bhikkhu-sangha*
upāya: skill in means
upekkhā: equanimity
vassa: rainy season; a way of measuring the number of years spent as a
    monk or nun
vibhavataṇhā: craving for non-existence
vicāra: sustained thought, discursive thinking
vicikicchā: sceptical doubt
vijjā: true knowledge
Vinaya: rules of the monastic order
viññāṇa: consciousness
vipāka: result of action, *kamma*-result
vipassanā: insight
vipassanūpakkilesas: imperfections of insight
vitakka: thought, applied thought, thought-conception

Ajahn Sumedho

R obert Jackman (born in Seattle, Washington in 1934) served
in the US navy as a paramedic from the age of eighteen.
Four years later he attended the University of California, obtain-
ing a BA in Far Eastern Studies and an MA in South Asian Studies. The following year he worked as a Red Cross social worker,
and from 1964 to 1966 served with the Peace Corps in Borneo
teaching English. Later that same year he travelled to Thailand
and began the practise of meditation at Wat Mahathat in Bangkok. He subsequently became a novice monk *(sāmaṇera)* at Wat
Sri Saket in Nong Khai, northeast Thailand. Then in May 1967
he received full ordination and became Sumedho Bhikkhu. After spending time in solitary meditation, he eventually found his
way to Wat Pah Pong a forest monastery which was to become
his 'home in the dhamma' for the next nine years under the wing
of Ajahn Chah, the man he learned to admire and trust and who
became his most revered teacher.

Ajahn Chah had set up this monastery in Ubon province in the
1950s at the request of the local people. He taught monks, nuns
and lay people, and his reputation spread. Not only did Ajahn
Sumedho hear of him but many Westerners during the 1960s and
1970s, and some gravitated to this remote monastery in northeast Thailand. In 1975 with Ajahn Sumedho's assistance — having by this time learned the Thai language — Ajahn Chah established an International Monastery called Wat Pah Nanachat, and
this was specifically for his non-Thai disciples. Ajahn Sumedho
was commissioned to be its head monk.

During that same year, 1975, it so happened that the American
forces withdrew from Vietnam, Laos and Cambodia, these areas
falling to the Communists. This led Ajahn Sumedho to consider
what might happen to the twenty or so Western monks at Wat

Pah Nanachat if Thailand too should fall into Communist hands. That was the catalyst that started him thinking of the possibility of establishing a monastery outside of Thailand, an idea he had never before entertained. Shortly after that his mother became very ill and it was thought she might die. He therefore went to stay in his parents' home in Southern California and remained there until she seemed to be getting better. During this time he again considered the possibility of setting up a monastery, wondering whether anyone in the United States might be interested in such a project. Making his way to New York[40], he took the opportunity of visiting Buddhist groups in Massachusetts — including the recently opened Insight Meditation Society[41] — but it became clear that none of these places was for monastics and basically there did not seem to be much interest in the States at that time in regard to starting a monastery.

Ajahn Sumedho's journey back to Thailand took him via London, and there he met the Chairman of the English Sangha Trust, George Sharp, who invited him to stay at the Trust's vihara in Hampstead. The Hampstead Vihara had been established some twenty years earlier in 1956 with the specific aim of accommodating Buddhist monks who came to live in England. After a series of disappointments and failures at the Vihara, however, the Trust seriously considered using the place for lay teachers instead, but the Chairman wanted to stick to its original purpose and was encouraged by two monks[42] to do nothing but wait to see what would happened in time. So the Vihara was closed up 'until the right opportunity showed itself'. This was a couple of years prior to Ajahn Sumedho's visit.

George Sharp went to see Ajahn Sumedho every day during his short stay and finally asked him whether he might consider

40 With Venerable Varapanyo (Paul Breiter) to stay with his parents.

41 Set up by Jack Kornfield and Joseph Goldstein.

42 The highly esteemed Thai monk Ajahn Maha Boowa, and the English monk Ajahn Paññavaddho who had in the past been a resident of the Hampstead Vihara.

living in England. Ajahn Sumedho's response was that he, George Sharp, would need to go to Thailand to speak to Ajahn Chah about such a possibility. So George Sharp went to Thailand and repeated his request. This led to Ajahn Sumedho arriving in England in May 1977 accompanied by Ajahn Chah (to check out the situation). Their arrival was preceded by a fellow monk[43] and followed by two others[44] who were on their way back to Thailand. Ajahn Sumedho suggested that these two should also stay in London, and Ajahn Chah agreed. So they became a Sangha of four. After being in Britain for a month, Ajahn Chah's visit came to an end, and on his departure asked Ajahn Sumedho to promise not to return to Thailand for at least five years. So this was the beginning of a new life for these four Western Buddhist monks. Unaware of the problems he was moving into, Ajahn Sumedho later admitted how naïve he had been.

The monks tried to live according to the Thai Forest tradition as best they could in this conventional British environment, carrying bowls for the morning alms round and venturing onto the streets of Hampstead in their yellow robes. People duly responded — mostly Thais at first — by offering food. The curiosity of the local people and passers-by was also of course aroused, and a year later in 1978, one chance meeting resulted in a gift they could never have imagined — a wooded area of land in West Sussex! This gift of Hammer Wood was in one sense providential because it coincided with George Sharp's idea of selling Hampstead Vihara in order to buy a property more suitable for Forest monks. And in 1979 a derelict mansion came up for sale less than a mile from this piece of land — a perfect place with outbuildings and twenty-two acres of land. The Hampstead Vihara was therefore sold and Chithurst House — later to become the Cittaviveka Forest Monastery — was purchased.

---

43 An Englishman, Venerable Khemadhammo, who some time later set up the Forest Hermitage in Warwickshire.

44 Venerable Anando and Venerable Viradhammo en route to Thailand after visiting their families in America.

Within weeks of moving into Chithurst House, another significant event took place. Four Western women came forward asking if they could join the community. This, Ajahn Sumedho agreed to and the four women duly shaved their heads, donned the white robe of the renunciate and took on the eight-precept training. Within a couple of years, however, the nuns began questioning the inequality of their lifestyle compared to the monks', the nuns being engaged much more in community service. Since the original bhikkhuni (nuns) order had died out in the Theravadan tradition centuries earlier, Ajahn Sumedho sought the aid of one of his monks[45] to see what could be done. Eventually a new model was formulated, and in 1983 Ajahn Sumedho obtained permission from the Thai Sangha for this unprecedented arrangement — and so the Sīladharā order of nuns was formed.

For the next few years renovating the house and grounds at Chithurst became the predominant activity of the Sangha. Also in 1981 a sīmā[46] precinct was laid within the grounds and Ajahn Sumedho was granted ordination authority. The Sangha therefore grew, and so did the interest of lay people who were keen to attend ceremonial days, dhamma talks and retreats. Before long it became clear that, though Chithurst worked very well as a monastery, it was inadequate for the growing numbers of people that, for various reasons, wanted to attend. Additional premises were therefore needed, and in 1984 the English Sangha Trust purchased a former school in Hertfordshire. This became

---

45 The Venerable Sucitto (who later became the abbot of this very monastery) consulted the senior Sri Lankan Sangha in Britain and visiting Thai monks, gradually arriving at a consensus regarding conventions which was to increase the number of precepts from eight to ten so that the nuns became alms mendicants like the monks, aligning them to the bhikkhu-vinaya (rules of the order), designating them 'Sīladharā' (ten-precept) nuns, and changing the colour of their robes from white to dark brown.

46 A consecrated boundary of stones marking out the territory within which the Sangha performs its formal ceremonies including the ordination of new monks and nuns.

the now well known Amaravati Buddhist Monastery. At that time it consisted of a series of wooden buildings and extensive grounds. So, once again the Sangha was engaged in renovation work — and this continued for many years. A magnificent Thai style temple was later added, and Amaravati is now the focal point for many Theravadan Buddhists in Britain. This has been a massive project of renovation and transformation, and in most of its twenty-six year life Ajahn Sumedho has been its abbot. Associated monasteries have also developed in the ensuring years, not only in Britain, but in Europe, the United States, and other parts of the world.

There is no doubt that Ajahn Sumedho has fulfilled the early dreams of the English Sangha Trust, and more than adequately fulfilled his promise to Ajahn Chah not to return to Thailand within five years. But it has not always been an easy road. Trying to merge modern Western values with an ancient Eastern culture — especially in terms of the role of women in the monastic sangha — has been problematic over the years and not less so in recent times. Now in his seventy-sixth year Ajahn Sumedho has decided to retire from the role of abbot of Amaravati and to take his leave — hopefully not entirely from the Western scene — but returning to his dhamma roots in Thailand. And so his journey continues . . .

Bibliography

Buddhist Dictionary, Nyanatiloka, The Corporate Body of the Buddha Educational Foundation, Taiwan, 1970.

The Middle Length Discourses of the Buddha: A New Translation of the Majjhima Nikāya translated by Bhikkhu Ñāṇamoli and Bhikkhu Bhodi, Wisdom Publications, 1995.

Rider Encyclopedia of Eastern Philosophy and Religion, Rider, 1989.

The Sound of Silence, Ajahn Sumedho, Wisdom, 2007.

Index

Other BPG Publications

Buddhism Now an online Buddhist
magazine, can be found at:
www.buddhismnow.com

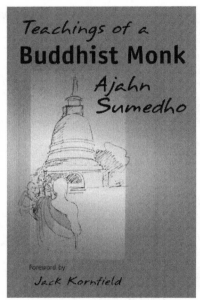

Teachings of A Buddhist Monk
Ajahn Sumedho,
ISBN 0-946672-23-7
Modern practical teachings from
an American monk living within
one of the oldest Buddhist
traditions.

'When we do not create
anything in it, the mind
becomes clear. The mind
itself, the original mind, the
unconditioned, is clear, bright
and peaceful, and can contain
anything. We can allow all
the rubbish in the universe to pass through this original mind
and no harm will come to it. Nothing can soil or damage the
original mind.'

Foreword by Jack Kornfield

Zen teaching of instantaneous awakening

A complete translation of the teachings of Ch'an Master Hui Hai.

Translated by John Blofeld
Foreword by Charles Luk

ISBN 978-0-946672-03-5

Hui Hai, one of the great Ch'an (Zen) Masters, was a contemporary of Ma Tsu and Huang Po, the early masters who followed on from Hui Neng, the Sixth Patriarch. Hui Hai's teachings point to this moment of truth and awakening. The message of this classic eighth-century text is timeless.

'Once a man who practised Ch'an asked Hui Hai, "It is said that mind is identical with the Buddha, but which of these is really the Buddha?"

Hui Hai: "What do you suppose is not the Buddha? Point it out to me!"

As there was no answer, the Master added, "If you comprehend (the mind), the Buddha is omnipresent to you; but, if you do not awaken to it, you will remain astray and distant from him for ever."'

John Blofeld, a noted Buddhist writer and translator, was one of the few Englishmen to have experienced life in Chinese Buddhist temples and monasteries prior to the Communist revolution. His love of China and knowledge of Buddhism enabled him to translate the texts with feeling and insight.

www.buddhistpublishing.com

Perfect Wisdom

The Short Prajnaparamita Texts
Translated by Edward Conze

A collection of the ancient Mahayana Wisdom texts, including *The Heart Sutra, The Diamond Sutra, The Perfection of Wisdom in 500 Lines,* and *The Perfection of Wisdom in 700 Lines.*

ISBN 0-946672-28-8

'[Enlightenment] is the understanding of all dharmas, but that understanding is non-obstruction. And why? For nothing is here understood or penetrated, since enlightenment is the sameness of penetration and understanding and one speaks of enlightenment because all dharmas are understood. And what is the understanding of all dharmas? There is here no enlightenment (*bodhi*) nor understanding (*anubodha*). And why? If one could apprehend enlightenment, then enlightenment could be seized in enlightenment; but there exists no enlightenment in enlightenment; it is thus that this enlightenment should be fully known.'

Experience Beyond Thinking

A Practical Guide to Buddhist Meditation

Diana St Ruth

A simple guide on how to begin meditating, how to practise, and how to become aware of what lies beyond the methods and the thinking mind.

ISBN 978-0-946672-26-4

'There will come a time in meditation when any subject of concentration, the rise and fall of the abdomen, or whatever it may be, will become more of a hindrance than a help in staying with the reality of the moment. How long will this take? That is impossible to say. It will be when the mind doesn't need anything to persuade it to stay open and awake any more; it will be when any use of persuasion, which in essence is what concentration is, will feel heavy and wrong. At such a time, there will be no desire to run into the past or the future, or anywhere beyond what is here and now.'

www.buddhistpublishing.com

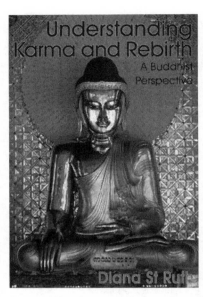

Understanding Karma and Rebirth: A Buddhist Perspective

Diana St Ruth

ISBN 978-0-946672-30-1

A look into the effects of karma, with meditations and exercises to help us go beyond the concepts of birth and death and to live from the unborn moment.

Rebirth and reincarnation are generally accepted realities in the East and have been since ancient times. What the next life will be is usually the question rather than whether it will be. In the West, on the other hand, we have our own religious and secular beliefs which usually do not include living another life, or at least not in this world or in this way. A common idea amongst Westerners is that annihilation is an unavoidable fact: 'When you're dead you're dead!' But unless one wakes up to the truth of it—East or West—one is caught in cultural conditioning and personal beliefs.

Buddhism is about becoming aware of what life actually is rather than being blinded by beliefs and conditioning . The Buddha spoke of a direct 'seeing' into the nature of existence beyond words, beyond the intellect. Understanding the cause and effect process—the nature of karma and rebirth—and what lies behind it is the underlying message of this book.

The Old Zen Master

Inspirations for Awakening

Trevor Leggett

ISBN 978-0-946672-29-5

Stories, parables, and examples in Zen and other traditions.

Trevor Leggett (1914-2000) had the knack of pointing to the spiritual implications in practical events. He lived for a considerable time in Japan and was fluent in Japanese. He was head of the BBC Japanese World Service for twenty-four years, the first foreigner to obtain the Sixth Dan (senior teachers degree) in judo from Kodokan, and has written several books on the subject. Among his many works on Zen are *A First Zen Reader, The Warrior Koans, Zen and the Ways, Yoga and Zen*, and *Fingers and Moons*.

Stories, parables, and examples have been a favoured way of conveying spiritual insights and truths since time immemorial, and Trevor Leggett was a master at it. He had the knack of pointing out the spiritual implications of practical events which people can relate to.

www.buddhistpublishing.com

Fingers and Moons

Trevor Leggett

ISBN 978-0946672073,

With many varied analogies, stories and incidents, Trevor Leggett points to the truth beyond words, beyond explanations and methods. Indeed, the book itself is like 'a finger pointing at the moon'. Fingers and Moons by Trevor Leggett

Buddhism Now is **an online magazine**, giving advice on how to practise Buddhism. buddhismnow.com

Facebook:	Buddhism Now
Google+:	Buddhism now
Instagram:	Buddhism_now
Pinterest:	BuddhismNow
Tumblr:	BuddhismNow
Twitter:	@Buddhism_Now

Robert
Wright

Evit. Bis

Why Buddha
is True.